# STATE AND MINORITIES IN COMMUNIST EAST GERMANY

# Monographs in German History

# STATE AND MINORITIES IN COMMUNIST EAST GERMANY

### Mike Dennis and Norman LaPorte

**Berghahn Books**
New York • Oxford

Published in 2011 by
*Berghahn Books*
www.berghahnbooks.com

©2011 Mike Dennis and Norman LaPorte

**Library of Congress Cataloging-in-Publication Data**

Dennis, Mike, 1940-
  State and minorities in communist East Germany / Mike Dennis and Norman
LaPorte.
    p. cm. -- (Monographs in German history ; v. 33)
  Includes bibliographical references and index.
  ISBN 978-0-85745-195-8 (hbk. : acid-free paper) -- ISBN 978-0-85745-196-5
(e-book)
  1. Minorities--Germany (East)--Social conditions. 2. Minorities--Government
policy--Germany (East)--History. 3. Germany (East)--Social conditions.
4. Germany (East)--Ethnic relations. 5. Honecker, Erich. 6. Germany (East)--
Politics and government. 7. Germany (East)--Social policy. 8. Communism--Social
aspects--Germany (East)--History. 9. Authority--Social aspects--Germany (East)-
-History. 10. Political culture--Germany (East)--History. I. LaPorte, Norman. II.
Title.
  DD281.D46 2011  305.800943'109045--dc23                    2011018002

**British Library Cataloguing in Publication Data**
A catalogue record for this book is available from the British Library
Printed in the United States on acid-free paper

ISBN: 978-0-85745-195-8 (hardback)
E-ISBN: 978-0-8575-196-5

For Kathleen, Nicola and Karen, and Fiona

# CONTENTS

# LIST OF TABLES

# LIST OF ABBREVIATIONS

| | |
|---|---|
| ABV | *Abschnittsbevollmächtigter* (Local Police Commissioner) |
| AKG | *Auswertungs- und Kontrollgruppe* (Assessment and Information Group |
| ANC | African National Congress |
| ARD | *Arbeitsgemeinschaft der öffentlich-rechtlichen Rundfunkanstalten der Bundesrepublik* (Consortium of Public-Law Broadcasting Institutions of the FRG) |
| AWG | *Arbeiter-Wohnungsbau-Genossenschaft* (Workers' Housing Cooperative) |
| BA[rchiv] | *Bundesarchiv* (Federal Archive) |
| BdL | *Büro der Leitung* (Management Office) |
| BDVPLp | *Bezirksbehörde der Deutschen Volkspolizei* Leipzig (Regional Office of the German People's Police Leipzig) |
| BFC | *Berliner Fußballclub Dynam*o (Berlin Football Club Dynamo) |
| BSG | *Betriebssportgemeinschaft* (Enterprise Sports Community/Club) |
| BStU | *Bundesbeauftragte für die Unterlagen des Staatssicherheitsdienstes der ehemaligen Deutschen Demokratischen Republik* (Federal Commissioner for the Records of the State Security Service of the Former German Democratic Republic) |
| BT/RdBLp | *Bezirkstag und Rat des Bezirkes Leipzig* (Regional Assembly and Council of the Leipzig Administrative Region) |
| BRD | *Bundesrepublik Deutschland* (Federal Republic of Germany) |
| BT | *Betriebsteil* (Enterprise Unit) |
| BV | *Bezirksverwaltung* (Regional Administration of the MfS) |
| CC | Central Committee of the SED |
| CDU | *Christlich-Demokratische Union* (Christian Democratic Union) |
| Comecon | Council for Mutual Economic Assistance |
| CSSR | Czechoslovak Socialist Republic |
| CV | *Christliche Verantwortung* (Christian Responsibility) |
| DBD | *Demokratische Bauernpartei Deutschlands* (Democratic Farmers' Party of Germany) |
| DM | *Deutsche Mark* (West German currency) |
| DT-64 | *Deutschlandtreffen-64* (Germany Meeting-64 Radio Station) |

| | |
|---|---|
| DFV | *Deutscher Fußballverband* (German Football Association of the GDR) |
| DTSB | *Deutscher Turn- und Sportbund der Deutschen Demokratischen Republik* (German Gymnastics and Sports Federation of the GDR) |
| DVP | *Deutsche Volkspolizei* (German People's Police) |
| DVU | *Deutsche Volksunion* (German People's Party) |
| EV | *Ermittlungsverfahren* (Preliminary Criminal Proceeding) |
| FDGB | *Freier Deutscher Gewerkschaftsbund* (Confederation of Free German Trade Unions) |
| FDJ | *Freie Deutsche Jugend* (Free German Youth Organisation) |
| FIFA | International Federation of Association Football |
| FRG | Federal Republic of Germany |
| GDR | German Democratic Republic |
| GI | *Geheimer Informator* (Secret Informer) |
| GMS | *Gesellschaftlicher Mitarbeiter für Sicherheit* (Societal Collaborator for Security) |
| GST | *Gesellschaft für Sport und Technik* (Society for Sport and Technology) |
| GZ [gesis-zuma] | German Social Science Infrastructure Services, Centre for Surveys, Methodology and Analysis |
| HA | *Hauptabteilung* (Main Department of the Ministry of State Security) |
| HFC | *Hallescher Fußball Club Chemie* (Halle Football Club Chemicals) |
| IM | *Inoffizieller Mitarbeiter* (Unofficial Collaborator/Coworker) |
| IMB | *Inoffizieller Mitarbeiter zur unmittelbaren Bearbeitung im Verdacht der Feindtätigkeit stehender Personen* (Unofficial Collaborator for Dealing with Persons under Suspicion of Hostile Activity) |
| IMK | *Inoffizieller Mitarbeiter zur Sicherung der Konspiration und des Verbindungswesens* (Unofficial Collaborator for Aiding Conspiracy and Securing Communications) |
| IMS | *Inoffizieller Mitarbeiter zur politisch-operativen Durchdringung und Sicherung des Verantwortungsbereiches* (Unofficial Collaborator for Political-Operational Investigation and Securing of an Area of Responsibility) |
| JHS | *Juristische Hochschule* (Juridical College of the Ministry of State Security, Potsdam) |
| KD | *Kreisdienststelle* (District Service Unit of the MfS) |
| KMSt | Karl-Marx-Stadt |
| KPD | *Kommunistische Partei Deutschlands* (Communist Party of Germany) |
| KuSch | *Kader und Schulung* (Cadres and Training) |
| LDPD | Liberal-Demokratische Partei Deutschlands (Liberal Democratic Party of Germany) |
| LHASA, MER | *Landeshauptarchiv Sachsen-Anhalt, Merseburg* |

| | |
|---|---|
| MDA | *Matthias-Domaschk-Archiv* |
| MFN | Most Favoured Nation |
| MfS | *Ministerium für Staatssicherheit* (Ministry of State Security, also Stasi) |
| NDPD | *Nationaldemokratische Partei Deutschlands* (National Democratic Party of Germany) |
| NES | New Economic System of Planning and Management |
| NKVD | People's Commissariat of State Affairs |
| NSDAP | *Nationalsozialistische Deutsche Arbeiterpartei* (National Socialist Party of Germany) |
| NVA | *Nationale Volksarmee* (National People's Army) |
| OibE | *Offizier im besonderen Einsatz* (Officer on Special Assignment) |
| OPK | *Operative Personenkontrolle* (Operational Personal Check) |
| OV | *Operativer Vorgang* (Operational Case) |
| PDS | Party of Democratic Socialism |
| PLO | Palestine Liberation Organisation |
| RdB | *Rat des Bezirkes* (Regional Council) |
| RENAMO | Mozambican National Resistance Organisation |
| RIAS | Radio in the American Sector (West Berlin) |
| SAL | *Staatssekretariat für Arbeit und Löhne* (State Secretariat for Labour and Wages) |
| SAPMO-BArchiv | *Stiftung Archiv der Parteien und Massenorganisationen der DDR im Bundesarchiv, Berlin* (Berlin Branch of the Federal Archive of the Foundation for the Parties and Mass Organisations of the GDR) |
| SC | *Sportclub* (Sports Club) |
| SED | *Sozialistische Einheitspartei Deutschlands* (Socialist Unity Party of Germany) |
| SG | *Sportgemeinschaft* (Sports Community/Club) |
| SPD | *Sozialdemokratische Partei Deutschlands* (Social Democratic Party of Germany) |
| StAL | *Sächsisches Staatsarchiv Leipzig* (Saxon State Archive Leipzig) |
| SV | *Sportverein* (Sports Club) |
| SWAPO | South West Africa People's Organisation |
| UN | United Nations |
| WTS | Watchtower Bible and Tract Society (also Watchtower Society) |
| ZA | *Zentralarchiv* (Central Archive) |
| ZAIG | *Zentrale Auswertungs- und Informationsgruppe* (Central Assessment and Information Group) |
| ZDF | *Zweites Deutsches Fernsehen* (Second German TV Station) |
| ZIJ | *Zentralinstitut für Jugendforschung* Leipzig (Central Institute for Youth Research Leipzig) |
| ZOS | *Zentraler Operativstab* (Central Operation Staff) |
| ZOV | *Zentraler Operativer Vorgang* (Central Operation Case) |

# PREFACE

The pulling down of the Berlin Wall in November 1989 and the rapid unification of the two German states a mere eleven months later sealed the fate of the German Democratic Republic as a separate socio-political entity.[1] But rather than consigning the German Democratic Republic (GDR) to a mere footnote to the divided German past, these dramatic events opened up a significant and controversial chapter in Germany's history. Debate is often fraught not only on account of methodological problems intrinsic to any historical study and to the construction of typologies of political systems, but also because the unveiling of a relatively recent past touches on the raw nerves of personal memory and experience under a dictatorship. Memory, moreover, is frequently distorted or clouded, as is apparent in a study of the historical awareness of over 2,300 Berlin pupils fifteen years after German unification: every tenth in the western part and every sixth in the east believed, erroneously, that the West German Chancellor Helmut Kohl governed the GDR before 1989. A significant minority – one in ten – thought that the GDR leader, Erich Honecker, held the reins in the Federal Republic.[2] For some EEast Germans, notably those subjected to constant surveillance, like Jehovah's Witnesses, would-be émigrés and many human rights' activists, the GDR was synonymous with repression. Others have less negative recollections. As Jana Hensel, who was thirteen-years old when the Berlin Wall fell, recalls: 'After the Wall, we soon forgot what everyday life in the GDR was like, with all its unheroic moments and ordinary days' (Hensel 2004: 25).

The animated contest over the past has been exacerbated since 1990 by allegations of a western dismantling of the assets of the old GDR and of east Germans' alleged lack of appreciation of western assistance in rebuilding the five *New Länder*.[3] The justified grievances of east Germans with escalating unemployment and many other negative features of the socio-economic transformation of their former country should not, however, be allowed to impede or obfuscate the historical reworking of the GDR's past. Among the main issues in the historical discourse of the old and new Germanies which underpin this book through studies of several minority groups are: the radical reconstruction of the political and socio-economic system in the Stalinist era; the long period of social and political stability after the erection of the Berlin Wall in August 1961; opportunities for living a 'normal' everyday life; opposition to, and popular accommodation with, the regime; the covert power of the weak; the design and concerted application of 'softer' methods of repression by the state security organs from the mid 1960s onwards; the extent to which the Socialist Unity Party (SED) and its myriad instruments controlled and infiltrated society; and the pertinence of theoretical models for interpreting the history of the GDR. These models, which will be examined in detail in chapter one, range from variants of totalitarianism to lower level constructs such as authority as social practice. This book will seek to combine the latter perspective with the notion of the GDR as a post-totalitarian dictatorship.

By focusing on diverse minority groups – Jehovah's Witnesses, the small official Jewish Communities or *Gemeinden*, punks, skinheads, football fans and foreign 'guest' workers – we intend to explore the nature of the interactions between state and populace and the party-state's policy towards minorities and outsiders. A universally recognised definition of the term 'minority' is difficult to devise but certain criteria are applicable. While a particular social and political group might in simple numerical terms be designated a minority, the key criteria are its subordinate socio-economic and political position and its adherence to certain characteristics that set it apart from the dominant group. How minorities with various ethnic, linguistic, religious, gender, generational and other backgrounds are treated and acknowledged, and how they themselves seek to shape their own lives, are pivotal for understanding any social and political system. This observation is especially relevant for the GDR as the SED regime sought to underpin its claim to legitimacy by frequent declarations of commitment to anti-fascism, freedom of expression, social progress, and friendship and solidarity with liberated peoples across the globe. The six groups in this study, ranging from the Jehovah's Witnesses with a pronounced religious and collective identity to the less cohesive youth sub-cultures, have been selected with these aspects in mind.

Some minority groups enjoyed a high level of state support, notably the 60,000 or so Sorbs concentrated in the Lusatia area. Not only were they recognised as an independent minority with their own cultural organisation and 'transmission belt' for the SED, the Domowina, but their cultural activities and language were heavily subsidised by the GDR government (Barker 2000: 20–21, 199–203). In other areas, the gap between rhetoric and reality was palpable, in particular with regard to the small religious minority of Jehovah's Witnesses and the remnants of German Jewry; both of these groups were subjected to discrimination and persecution following a short period of toleration after 1945. While matters improved for the small Jewish Communities with the termination of the regime's anti-semitic campaigns in the early to mid 1950s, they were nevertheless infiltrated by the Stasi and their position was adversely affected by the SED's hostility towards Israel. Not until the mid 1980s, underpinned by the SED's attempt to improve its international image and relations with the U.S.A., did the Jewish Communities experience a boost to their status and to hopes for reversing the numerical decline of an ageing congregation of little more than 350 members. Jehovah's Witnesses, who numbered about 22,000 in 1988, endured consistently high levels of repression throughout the history of the GDR. After surviving state attempts to destroy their organisation in the 1950s and 1960s, they managed to lead a precarious existence in the niches of family and religious congregation and stubbornly persisted in their vital mission work by means of door-to-door activity.

Foreign workers, mostly from fraternal socialist states and countries recently liberated from colonial domination, were employed in the GDR on various types of contracts. They may be regarded as economic migrants who were distinctive in terms of language, social status and often in appearance; some were seasonal commuters from Poland, others were on fixed labour contracts of four to five years. The two largest groups of contract workers during the 1980s were the Vietnamese and the Mozambicans, numbering 52,130 and 15,300 respectively in mid 1989. While these groups were not subjected to the intensity of surveillance and harassment experienced by Jehovah's Witnesses and Jews, neither the GDR nor the sending countries wished to integrate them into GDR society. Furthermore, there are clear signs of a growing hostility during the 1980s on the part of the local population in those areas where a high concentration of foreign workers was regarded as a threat to consumer supplies.

Exclusion, rather than inclusion, tended to be the official operating principle, not only as regards foreigners but also towards the skinhead and several other youth sub-cultures of the 1980s. Their emergence coincided, too, with the spread of a youthful hooligan element in football, the most popular sport in the GDR. The unexpected appearance of small exotic groups of punks and goths, as well as of militant, shaven-headed skinheads, all of whom were scornful of the aridity of the official youth movement, was interpreted by the SED authorities as directly related to the allegedly subversive activities of their imperialist enemies in the West, an interpretation that underlines the centrality of culture for the ideological and political struggle in the Cold War between communism and capitalism. This struggle, a form of proxy for military combat, also extended to the Jewish and Jehovah's Witness communities who were regarded as potential or even actual instruments of imperialism.

In examining the experiences of minority groups and the contours of official policy, historians are no longer encumbered by many of the obstacles once strewn across the path of researchers by the SED. Access to contemporary witnesses and the archival holdings of former opposition groups, as well as of the ruling party – the SED – and other official organisations – above all those of the Ministry of State Security – have set in motion a vast historiographical enterprise. Countless research projects, scholarly monographs, memoirs, exhibitions, novels, films, plays and media reports have all shed new light on old questions such as the degree of popular support for the GDR and the varying efficacy of the mechanisms of political and social control.[4] With the exception of East Germany's Jews, the minorities which form the basis of this book have, until relatively recently, not received the same degree of attention as the Protestant and Catholic

Churches and the small unofficial counter-culture concerned with peace, human rights, gender and the environment. This was also the case before the fall of the Berlin Wall, even though the situation of foreign workers was increasingly being addressed in Church and samizdat publications. Since the end of SED rule, and in particular since the turn of the century, considerable advances have been made with the publication, mainly in German, of well-researched monographs, articles and published interviews on Jehovah's Witnesses (Dirksen 2001a; Hirch 2003b), skinheads (Ross 2000; Bugiel 2002; Fenemore 2007), punks (Galenza and Havemeister 1999; Furian and Becker 2000; Boehke and Gericke 2007), the Jewish Communities (Offenberg 1998; Mertens 1997; Meining 2002), football fans (Braun and Teichler 2003; Willmann 2007) and foreign workers (Behrends, Lindenberger and Poutrus 2003; Weiss and Dennis 2005). In those areas not covered in this book, selective reference should be made to works on the Sorbs (Barker 2000; Granata 2009), homosexuals (Setz 2006; Sillge 1991), and members of the Soviet forces (Kowalczuk and Wolle 2001; Müller 2005). Other than the early works by Krüger-Potratz (1991), albeit with an emphasis on foreign workers, and Voigt and Mertens (1992), little has appeared which combines historical and theoretical context with the detailed case studies to be found in this book.

In conducting their research on minorities and the GDR state, we have drawn extensively on the central and regional archives of the Office of the Federal Commissioner for the Records of the State Security Service of the Former German Democratic Republic (BStU, called the *Gauck-* and then the *Birthler-Behörde* or Authority after its first two commissioners), the Federal Archive in Berlin, regional archives in Leipzig and Merseburg, and the *Deutsches Rundfunkarchiv* in Babelsberg. The investigations of the Leipzig-based Central Institute for Youth Research, set up in 1966, provide an indispensable collection of social-science data on young people's actions and attitudes. Its surveys, though subject to political pressure, produced findings which often made uncomfortable reading for the SED leadership. These can now be accessed on the internet.[5] Also of great value and help were memoirs, interview materials, printed documents, novels, diaries, exhibition catalogues, and the findings of projects in which the authors were partners.

A grant from the Arts and Humanities Research Council funded a two-year project on the history of Vietnamese and Mozambican contract workers in East Germany, and a one-year scholarship from the Leverhulme Foundation enabled Karin Weiss, now the Integration Commissioner of the Land Brandenburg, to participate in the programme. The findings of the project have fed into two exhibitions on migration, one in Cologne (see Kölnischer Kunstverein 2005: 702–9) and the other, in 2009, at the *Brandenburgische Landeszentrale für politische Bildung*, Potsdam. A comparative project was conducted on Jehovah's Witnesses in the Third Reich and the GDR with independent researchers and members of the History Archive of the Jehovah's Witnesses at Selters, Germany. The British Academy supported a study of skinheads and right-wing extremism, as well as an investigation into sport in the GDR. The four projects were based in part on a series of interviews which help us not only to understand the personal situation of the individual without consciously superimposing one's own ideas and perceptions, but also serve as a critical check on the materials compiled by the police, the Stasi, local authorities and the SED. Finally, we wish to acknowledge our debt to the numerous colleagues, but above all to Frau Jaensch of the BStU, who have assisted us in the course of writing this book.

# Notes

1. German Democratic Republic (GDR) denotes the state which emerged from the Soviet Zone of Occupation in 1949 and was incorporated into the Federal Republic of Germany (FRG) in 1990. 'GDR' and 'East Germany' are used interchangeably, but 'east Germany' refers to the geographical unit both before 1949 and after 1990; 'east German' applies to a citizen of unified Germany in the latter area.
2. *Berliner Zeitung*, 10–11 November 2007, p.21. The survey was carried out in 2005 and 2006 by researchers at the Forschungsverbund SED-Staat (Research Association SED-State) among pupils aged fourteen to seventeeni at comprehensive and grammar schools. Considerable differences existed between pupils in the eastern and western parts of Germany as regards perceptions of and knowledge about the GDR. In general, the former had a more positive picture of the GDR than their western counterparts. Kohl was West German Chancellor between 1982 and 1990 and of reunified Germany until 1998. Honecker was SED First/General Secretary from 1971 to 1989 and Chairman of the Council of State from 1976 to 1989.
3. The *New Länder* are the five states – Brandenburg, Mecklenburg-Hither Pomerania, Saxony, Saxony-Anhalt and Thuringia – that, in addition to East Berlin, constituted the former GDR and acceded to the FRG in October 1990.
4. A data bank search revealed that research on the GDR had produced about 7,700 titles between 1989 and the beginning of the new millennium (Kocka 2003: 764).
5. Many of the Central Institute for Youth Research (ZIJ) surveys are to be found on the website of the German Social Science Infrastructure Services (GESIS: Leibniz-Institut für Sozialwissenschaften): www.gesis.org.

# Chapter 1

# STATE, SOCIETY AND MINORITY GROUPS IN THE GDR

## From Upheaval to Stability

While the turbulence of socialist construction is by no means neglected, this book concentrates on the second half of the GDR's history, that is, from the consolidation of SED rule in the mid 1960s to its unexpectedly rapid disintegration a few weeks after the fall of the Berlin Wall in November 1989. The overall aim of this chapter is to provide the historical context for the study of relations between state and minorities and, secondly, to place this development within broad theoretical constructs such as post-totalitarianism. Our argument is that a flexible version of the latter concept, one which encompasses the policies of a repressive state and myriad personal experiences, can be applied to the GDR in the Honecker era to provide an insight into the complex and shifting interactions between state and individuals in society.

The final two decades of the GDR, or at least until the mid 1980s, are usually regarded as a time when, with the socialist revolution in both society and the economy completed and with the Berlin Wall providing indispensable security for the regime, the GDR shifted from a totalitarian to an authoritarian form of dictatorship. The SED leader, Erich Honecker, an experienced communist apparatchik, kept a tight rein on party-political power after he became First Secretary of the SED in 1971. The Berlin Wall had stemmed a demographic haemorrhage, new opportunities for social advancement were created by the reforms associated with the New Economic System (NES) introduced in 1963, and the SED exerted firm control over the other major political institutions. The period of high

Stalinism, between 1945 and 1953, had involved the concentration of power in the hands of a small political-bureaucratic elite assisted by privileged cadres, the enshrinement of Marxism-Leninism as the source of official values and organisation, widespread purges, show trials and the centrality of the security forces and the police. With the elimination of a competitive multi-party system, the East German Christian Democratic Union (CDU) and the other three bloc parties lost their independence, and the mass organisations, such as the Confederation of Free German Trade Unions (FDGB) and the Free German Youth Organisation (FDJ), complied unreservedly with the SED's leadership role. Stability was also based on the continuation of relatively cheap raw materials imports from the Soviet Union and the presence of its armed forces on East German territory.

The onset of détente between the USSR and the U.S.A. was a further stabilising factor as it encompassed the Western powers' diplomatic recognition of the GDR in the early 1970s, notably in the Basic Treaty between the GDR and the FRG in December 1972. This development was capped by the entry of the two German states into full membership of the United Nations in September 1973. The improvement in relations was also followed by a sharp increase in a wide range of transfer payments from the FRG into East German coffers. The hard currency obtained from inter-German transfers in the 1970s and 1980s, fluctuating between DM 1 billion and DM 2 billion per annum, bolstered détente as well as the GDR economy, but it also had the drawback for the SED of gradually increasing East German dependency on the FRG.

As détente came to frame relations between East and West, many old conflicts abated both at home and abroad. Typical of this development was the informal concordat reached in 1978 when Honecker met the executive of the League of Protestant Churches. In the GDR, as in many other states of Eastern Europe, Christian churches had proved to be what Carl J. Friedrich referred to as 'a real bulwark against the claim to total power of the totalitarian dictatorship' (Friedrich and Brzezinski 1965: 314). At the meeting, the culmination of a gradual improvement in relations since the fierce state-church struggle of the 1950s, Honecker offered numerous concessions to the League in return for its willingness to observe the statement of its chairman, Bishop Albrecht Schönherr, that it would act as a 'Church within socialism', albeit neither for nor against the state. A similar pattern was followed in relations between the GDR government and the Jewish Communities (*Gemeinden*) after the wave of anti-semitism and purges of Jewish citizens in the 1950s had subsided.

Perhaps the key determinant of stability, once the border to West Berlin had been closed and the chances of unification seriously diminished, was the perceptible improvement in living standards since the early 1960s, often referred to as 'goulash communism'. Some quantitative indicators of growing material well-being are the rise in the ownership of TV sets and washing machines per household from 16.7 per cent to 88.1 per cent and from 6.2 per cent to 80.4 per cent respectively between 1960 and 1980 (Statistisches Amt der DDR 1990: 325). After Honecker came to power in May 1971, the SED also sought to woo the East German population by granting them permission in 1974 to use the Intershops, where Western goods could be bought for hard currency. Honecker calculated that society could be 'pacified' by promises of further and substantial improvements in living standards, a new housing programme, heavy subsidies for rents and public transport, and extensive social welfare provision. These policy goals were to be achieved by sustained economic growth, supposedly driven by the application of modern scientific and technical advances. Dressed in ideological garb as the 'unity of economic and social policy', it became the leitmotif or totem of Honecker's 'reign' and was perceived as a kind of socio-economic trade-off for tolerance of, or acquiescence in, SED rule

What did East Germans think of these various developments and how did they perceive the GDR? These questions remain difficult to answer due to the lack of independent social science institutions in the GDR and tight restrictions on the publication of survey data. Indeed, as Werner Müller has observed, only on two occasions, in 1946 and 1990, is it possible to assess with accuracy the overall response – on balance a negative one – of East Germans to the key question as to how far the SED and the Soviet Zone and later the GDR could count on their support (Müller 2003: 263). In 1946, the SED, which was not then openly Stalinist, failed to secure a majority of the votes in the provincial elections, and in the March 1990 election to the GDR parliament or *Volkskammer*, the PDS, the reformed version of the SED, came a distant third behind the CDU-led Alliance for Germany. The vote was a strong, though not unqualified, popular endorsement of the latter's programme for rapid monetary union and political unification with the Federal Republic. In effect, the people had dissolved the GDR.

Other indicators of contemporary opinion can also be found in the materials of the Central and Regional Evaluation and Information Groups of the Ministry of State Security and, especially from the mid 1960s onwards, in the investigations of three GDR research groups: the Leipzig-based Central Institute for Youth Research, the SED Central Committee's Academy of Science, and the same body's Institute of Public Opinion Research. While the findings of the three academic groups, unlike those of the Stasi, aspired to meet social scientific criteria, it should be stressed that the representative nature of the surveys they conducted is difficult to assess retrospectively and that tight political constraints were in operation (Dennis 2000a: 121–23; Dennis 2003: 219–22; Friedrich 2002: 14–17). Despite the methodological shortcomings, the data assembled by the Institute of Public Opinion and the other two bodies suggest that, for about two decades from the mid 1960s onwards, increasing numbers of East Germans were supportive of the paternalistic social welfare system of their country, thereby bolstering the stability of SED rule and feelings of identity within the GDR (Friedrich 2002: 15; see also Meier 1994: 276–86). A similar conclusion was reached in the early 1970s by the West German political scientist Gerhard Schweigler. On the basis of interviews conducted by FRG public opinion institutes with West German visitors to the GDR, journalistic accounts and individual experts on East

Germany, he argued that a consciousness of the GDR as a distinct political entity was growing among East Germans without, however, extending to an identification with the GDR as a separate nation (Schweigler 1975: 126–30).

Numerous surveys conducted after the fall of the SED also give good reason for believing that the party's social policy had enjoyed considerable popular support, especially for key aspects such as full employment, greater job opportunities for women and cheap rents (Dennis 2000b: 90–92). It should be noted, however, that the positive evaluation of these elements was given added weight for many middle-aged and older east Germans by the dramatic social upheavals, widespread job losses and deep economic depression in the five *New Länder* after unification. Since 1990, some historians, notably Konrad Jarausch, have been persuaded by the outcomes of the SED's social policy to liken the GDR to a *Fürsorgediktatur*, or 'welfare dictatorship' (Jarausch 1997: 44), while others have drawn an analogy with Bismarck's instrumentalisation of the new social security system for pacifying the working class (Sabrow 2008: 128). Jarausch's view has an antecedent in the interpretation, current in the 1970s, of the Soviet Union as a form of 'welfare-state authoritarianism' (Breslauer 1978: 4–5). With the average age of membership of the SED politburo reaching 67 years in 1989, perhaps its members would have been grateful for such a system, lending substance to Norbert Kapferer's dismissive characterisation of the GDR, as 'an extremely authoritarian old people's home' rather than a prison cell (Kapferer 2000: 35).

Honecker's pragmatic social policy and the modest levels of consumerism epitomised a strategy pursued with varying success and commitment by other communist regimes in the Soviet Union and Eastern Europe to establish an informal 'societal contract' with their populations. This marked a significant shift from the terror and radical socio-economic upheaval of high Stalinism typical of Eastern European regimes during the lifetime of the Soviet dictator and of their aspiration for totalistic domination of the key components of society and politics. For Honecker in the GDR, Gierek in Poland or Brezhnev in the USSR, the major concern revolved around system maintenance, the bureaucratisation of rule and the retention of the communist party's monopoly of power rather than the realisation of totalistic aspirations and the communist utopia.

## Modes of Control: Overt and Silent Repression

Despite improvements in living standards, recognition by the West and a marked degree of congruence between the needs of the population and interests of the regime, the social consensus, while not disintegrating until the later 1980s, remained fragile throughout the Honecker era. Among the main reasons for the brittleness are: the unresolved national question; the slowing down of social mobility and the tendency towards self-reproduction by the intelligentsia in the 1970s and 1980s (Bauerkämper 2005: 87–89); the undemocratic polity and the abuse of human rights, as symbolised by the Berlin Wall; strict censorship of the media; and the palpably higher prosperity enjoyed by the GDR's Western sibling. The former chair of the State Planning Commission, Gerhard Schürer, conceded after the demise of the GDR that East Germans had measured their standard of living against that of West Germany, not against the lower level of socialist countries in Eastern Europe (Schürer 1994: 162).

The lack of democracy was exposed by widespread popular sympathy in the GDR for the Prague Spring of 1968, East Germans' enthusiastic support for Gorbachev's economic and political reforms in the late 1980s, and by opposition to the tight restrictions on travel abroad. As the 1970s drew to a close, the perennial problem of freedom of travel came to form a combustible mix with the broader social and political dissent as articulated in the loosely-structured counter-culture of small peace, ecological, women's, gay and human rights groups. SED concessions on visits to the West, notably a flexible interpretation of the term 'urgent family business', failed to lift popular pressure for emigration which would, by the end of the 1980s, help bring down the Berlin Wall and, belatedly, an end to fatalities on the German–German border. It is difficult to assess how many people were killed at the Wall and on the GDR border with its socialist and capitalist neighbours: some died as a result of drowning and other accidents, while others were victims of shooting by border guards and mines deliberately planted to prevent flight. As a result, estimates of deaths vary from 420 to the much higher figure of 1,135 arrived at by the Arbeitsgemeinschaft 13. August based on all categories of fatality.[1] Whatever the actual number, these statistics bear out what Norman Naimark wrote in 1979: 'Contemporary scholars can no more examine the mechanisms of coercion than criminologists can study prison populations and ignore the fact that prisoners are incarcerated by force' (Naimark 1979: 576).

Not the least of the SED's legitimation problems was its failure to devise a satisfactory solution to the issue of the GDR's separate identity in a divided Germany. In the early postwar years, the party professed support for a united country with a socialist orientation. But as the two German republics drew further apart, and with division literally cemented by the Berlin Wall, new responses were required. In 1969, the West German Chancellor, Willy Brandt, advanced the theory of two states in one German nation; the SED countered with the thesis of a separate socialist nation in the GDR. First propagated in the early 1970s, the thesis posited that the GDR had become a socialist German nation in contrast to the capitalist nation in the FRG. So allergic was the SED to feelings and symbols of a common nationhood that it embarked on a policy of demarcation (*Abgrenzung*), which included the renaming of many institutions containing the term 'German'. Thus the name of the German Gymnastics and Sports Federation (DTSB) was changed to the DTSB of the GDR. This was not a satisfactory solution as the new title contained two references to the term 'German'! Popular memory or personal contacts were also problematic: when East German football fans attended matches involving West German teams, either in the GDR or in other socialist countries, functionaries feared outbursts of sympathy for sporting representatives of the imperialist foe. Popular opposition to the SED's new approach to the national question led to its modification towards the end of the decade and, to widespread surprise, a broadening of the GDR's historical heritage to encompass previously negative figures such as Frederick the Great and Bismarck. Revisionism of this nature, however, ran the risk of reminding East Germans of a common heritage with West Germans in the FRG, a fundamental reason why the SED could not abandon its insistence on the GDR's anti-fascist and socialist essence, even though this raised awkward questions, such as the party's attitude towards, and treatment of, East German Jewry.

Determined to uphold the party's monopoly of power but highly sensitive to the frailty of the GDR's national legitimacy and its vulnerable security on the border between the two rival power blocks, the SED elites were resistant to a fundamental overhaul of the system of domination created between the late 1940s and the mid 1950s. The system remained both hierarchical and comprehensive, encompassing, for example, the SED's unflagging assertion of its leading role in society, Marxism-Leninism as the language of official discourse, and a highly pervasive system of coercion. There had, however, been some notable shifts over the decades. Ideology had lost some of its binding power, with a perceptible and growing discrepancy between SED rhetoric and reality. The scale of repression had slackened, too. In the 1950s, at the height of the Cold War, the targets of the Stasi and the Central Party Control Commission, the SED's organ of inquisition, ranged from Ulbricht's internal party opponents to the small group of Jehovah's Witnesses. The latter's leaders were arrested and imprisoned as part of a concerted campaign to destroy the organisation. Nor were members of the Jewish Communities spared. But, from about the mid 1960s, the more brutal and open forms of repression were scaled down as the SED came to pay greater attention to domestic and foreign opinion. This change was reinforced by the onset of détente in the early 1970s, including the signing of the Final Act of the 1975 Helsinki Conference on Security and Cooperation, and, driven by Honecker out of *raison d'état*, by closer economic and political contacts between the GDR and the FRG.

Some members of the GDR's political elite were highly perturbed by the thaw in East–West German relations and the subsequent rapid increase in personal and official contacts across the German–German border. Erich Mielke, the Minister of State Security and a leading figure on the ultra-conservative wing of the SED, called for heightened vigilance. In his opinion, closer relations with West Germany and the GDR's adherence to the Helsinki accords constituted a Trojan horse, a means whereby the West could exploit the issue of human rights to undermine the socialist system from within. For Mielke and his officers, 'imperialism' was an implacable and ubiquitous enemy which must be thwarted not only internally but also in the West itself, or what the ministry called the 'Operation Area'. The 'enemy', according to the dictionary of political terms issued by the Stasi for the benefit of its staff, consisted of 'persons who in groups or as individuals intentionally develop political-ideological attitudes and views that are alien to socialism and who strive to implement these attitudes and views in practice' (Suckut 1996: 121). While 'foreigners', especially from the 'imperialist' West, automatically came under suspicion, so too did East German groups or individuals with religious, political or cultural links to the West, whether Jehovah's Witnesses or young people susceptible to what the Stasi and SED ideologues referred to as 'political-ideological subversion' by means of Western pop-music and football culture. Culture in this sense was part of the struggle between East and West, in the absence of military engagement, for ideological, moral and political ascendancy.

## The Stasi and Operational Subversion

But how to counter Western influence and control 'hostile' and 'negative' individuals at the same time as the GDR was enjoying substantial economic benefits from the relationship with their Western counterparts, with whom government officials were in frequent contact? While overt coercion was not abandoned, the response was to give greater weight to insidious modes of control by the Ministry of State Security and the prioritisation of what Hubertus Knabe has dubbed a system of 'silent repression' (Knabe 2000) and Jürgen Fuchs a 'soft form' of terror against real or alleged opponents (Fuchs 1994). Honecker's 'unity of economic and social policy' was the public face of this political *modus operandi*, which also found expression in the complex and widespread bargaining for 'softer' budget constraints between the planning bureaucracy and enterprises in the state-run economy (Kornai 1992: 140–45).

The Ministry of State Security (MfS), popularly known as the Stasi, embodied the legacy of what Jens Gieseke has dubbed 'militarised socialism' (Gieseke 2003b: 1010–20), that is, the long-standing militaristic traditions and attitudes within the SED and the culture of violence embedded in its forerunner, the KPD (Communist Party of Germany). The KPD had engaged in street battles with the National Socialists in the later years of the Weimar Republic and endured persecution during the Third Reich. In 1937, Honecker was sentenced to ten years' imprisonment in the Brandenburg-Görden jail for his underground activities. Other KPD leaders such as Mielke, Zaisser, Markus Wolf and Ulbricht had been caught up in the brutal and murderous purges of the party in Stalin's Moscow in the 1930s. Founded in 1950, the Stasi soon became an essential prop of the party-state dictatorship and the security risks associated with East–West détente were adroitly used by Mielke to expand his empire and to undertake a wide-ranging surveillance of society. The number of officers rose rapidly from 32,912 in 1967 to 81,495 in 1982 and its spies, the euphemistically termed unofficial co-workers (*Inoffizielle Mitarbeiter*, or IMs), grew from approximately 106,900 in 1968 to a peak of perhaps 203,000 in 1977 before declining to 173,081 in 1988 (Müller-Enbergs with Muhle 2008: 35). The combined strength of officers and spies across the MfS's numerous central and local service units meant that the GDR, in relation to the size of its population and territory, probably had the most comprehensive surveillance system in history (Müller 2003: 248). This did not, it should be stressed, mean that the Stasi observed and penetrated each sub-system with equal thoroughness throughout the history of the GDR. During the 1950s, it was far too small an organisation to realise such a goal, and even in later decades it simply lacked the resources to do so. It thus aimed for a high concentration of IMs in politically sensitive areas, such as the National People's Army, the border guards, the German People's Police, the tiny political opposition groups and the economy (Gieseke 2001: 136–48).[2]

From about the mid 1960s the MfS came to attach greater weight to repression by stealth, or to what it called *Operative Zersetzung*. This can be translated as operational subversion or, in medical terms, decomposition, to capture the gradual and covert undermining and breaking down of targets behind a façade of societal normality. It soon proved to be integral to the systematic implementation of 'silent repression', which aimed at the prevention rather than the retrospective prosecution of 'offences'. 'Targets' encompassed a broad spectrum of society from the SED's political opponents to non-conformist youth and the tiny and ageing Jewish Communities. Open forms of repression, especially if they came to the attention of the Western media, ran the danger, it was reasoned, of turning high profile individuals into martyrs. The main elements and aims of operational decomposition, which will be referred to throughout this book, were set out in two authoritative ministerial documents: the 1981 guidelines on operational person checks (*Operative Personenkontrollen*, OPKs) and the 1976 ministerial guidelines on operational cases (*Operative Vorgänge*, OVs). The former was usually the prelude to an OV, the most highly organised and comprehensive form of covert surveillance and repression (Schmeidel 2008: 41–45). Both sets of guidelines urged action against 'hostile negative forces', that is, those who planned or attempted to carry out 'crimes against the state'. Jehovah's Witnesses and other such groups were to be 'paralysed, disorganised and isolated' and their activities 'prevented, significantly reduced or completely terminated'. Among the pernicious methods used by the Stasi were the systematic compromising and isolation of a target by means of disinformation and rumour concerning immorality, drunkenness and spying for the West, the interception of mail, the sending of threatening anonymous letters and other means of psychological coercion, and the fabrication of professional, political and personal failure in order to undermine an individual's self-esteem.

IMs – unofficial co-workers or collaborators – were defined in the 1979 ministerial guidelines as the Stasi's main weapon in the everyday struggle against the 'enemy' and constituted an elaborate interlocking of society and state, the private and the public. Originally called 'secret informer' (*Geheimer Informator*), the generic term was changed in 1968 to 'unofficial co-worker' with its connotations of dedication to the cause of socialism. The Stasi was determined to avoid the term *Spitzel* or 'spy' as this was tainted by association with the Gestapo. It was, however, used in popular parlance. As indicated earlier, the number of IMs rose to about 203,000 in 1977, falling by about 30,000 eleven years later. If an annual turnover of about 10 per cent is taken as the benchmark, then an estimated 500,000 IMs collaborated with the Stasi during this period. IM classification underwent frequent changes as esoteric sub-categories proliferated in line with the wide range of tasks performed by the MfS (ibid.: 30–36). IMBs (*Inoffizielle Mitarbeiter zur unmittelbaren Bearbeitung im Verdacht der Feindtätigkeit stehender Personen*) formed an elite group for the subversion of 'enemies' of the state in contrast to the more mundane IMKs (*Inoffizielle Mitarbeiter zur Sicherung der Konspiration und des Verbindungswesens*) who put their flat, telephone or address at the disposal of controllers for clandestine contacts with fully-fledged informers. In general, while the Stasi preferred to recruit agents who were 'true believers' in the expectation that these would be the most reliable and productive sources, it also used, as is detailed in later chapters, various forms of coercion – whether blackmail, bribery or fear.[3]

In addition to its many informers, the MfS could also draw on an array of voluntary helpers such as 'contact persons', SED functionaries, cadre managers and employees' superiors. Other categories included several hundred prison cell informers, the spies of Markus Wolf's foreign intelligence agency (*Hauptverwaltung Aufklärung*), and over 15,000 informers attached to *Arbeitsgebiet* 1 or K1 of the criminal police. It is estimated that over 250,000 GDR citizens, or about one in 48 East German adults, were working for the Stasi, either as an informer or officer in any given year during the 1980s. These figures indicate that the unique feature of the MfS was not so much its techniques as the sheer scale of its surveillance and infiltration of the institutions of state and society and the lives of individuals, even including the esoteric Crow Chief and several hundred other GDR devotees of North American Indians (Borries and Fischer 2008: 127–40, 178–86). This was in keeping with Mielke's guiding principle, as outlined to fellow officers in 1968, 'to control every pulse beat, every stirring and every movement which does not contribute to the strengthening and consolidation of our socialist republic' (cited in Vollnhals 2002: 113). Not only was this aim unrealistic, contradictory and often counterproductive but the ministry also proved to be an inadequate shield against the undesired consequences of détente, the escalating emigration movement, the robustness of informal social networks, the deep religious faith of Jehovah's Witnesses, the dynamic of youth sub-cultures and the resistance of East Germans whether as individuals or in groups.

## The Ruling Party and its Affiliates

Although the Stasi was at the heart of internal control and security, its political clout should not be exaggerated. It was not an independent actor but, as the 'sword and shield' of the ruling party, it had to coordinate its mission with that of the SED as part of a formidable bastion of power. While the Stasi undoubtedly came to exert considerable influence over the carrying out of policy, especially after Mielke had turned the MfS into an institutional colossus, the SED remained the key steering and policy-making instrument, which the Stasi served, in the final analysis, as its monitoring, control and 'compensatory' agency.[4] The SED possessed its own vast network of organs for carrying out its self-proclaimed role as the leading force in society; these ranged from a bedrock of basic organisations (*Grundorganisationen*) in factories, institutions and residential areas to the two main steering mechanisms, the Central Committee Secretariat and the 'Council of the Gods', the politburo. However, while the top level of the party has been relatively well researched, much remains unexplored as to how party bodies were embedded in society and how they interacted with the organs of state in helping to achieve the regime's core aims. These aims, as indicated above, had shifted from the revolutionary construction of state socialism in the 1950s, with a high concentration of economic and political power in the SED oligarchy and the destruction of many traditional social structures, to the more pragmatic system maintenance of the 1970s and 1980s with an attendant loss of political and ideological dynamic.

The membership count of the major organisations in the late Honecker era gives some idea of the reach of the SED and its governmental props. In the late 1980s, there were about 2 million functionaries, and SED membership alone totalled 2.3 million. Some 300,000 to 400,000 *nomenklatura* cadres occupied the key leadership positions in society, and membership of the two main mass organisations, the FDJ and the FDGB, numbered 2.3 million and 9.3 million respectively. The four allied parties – the CDU, LDPD, DBD and NDPD – basically tame adjuncts of the SED, had a combined membership of about 470,000 (Dennis 2000a: 188, 197, 201–2; Fulbrook 2004: 123). There was, of course, considerable overlap between membership of the mass organisations and political parties. If the many other bodies, such as the Association of Allotment Gardeners, Settlers and Breeders of Livestock, the Society for Sport and Technology, the German Gymnastic and Sports Association and the GDR's numerous representative organs from the People's Chamber (*Volkskammer*) downwards, are also taken into account, then only a small minority of GDR citizens did not belong to an officially recognised group or organisation.

Impressive though they might seem, such figures do not, however, tell us why individuals and groups joined a party or an organisation and how much influence these bodies enjoyed. The main mass organisations, it is sometimes contended, were not just pliant transmission belts of the SED but enjoyed considerable scope for the articulation of their members' interests and possessed important consultative functions within the decision-making process, especially at local level. The FDGB, for example, was active in administering the social insurance programme, in providing package holidays for workers, and in the allocation of wages and the setting of work norms. While these functions may be cited in support of the argument that the mass organisations were means by which the SED ruled through and not just over society (Ross 2002: 63), trade union influence was circumscribed in many significant ways. Workers were denied the right to strike, independent trade unions were banned and the SED controlled the appointment of key personnel. At factory level, the 1970s witnessed a marked decline in the influence of the many thousands of voluntary shop stewards (Hürtgen 2001: 143–44, 150–58 ).

The German People's Police (*Deutsche Volkspolizei*, DVP) was pivotal for upholding law and order and for assisting its 'big brother', the Stasi, in carrying out its societal mission and day-to-day tasks and minor misdemeanours such as public disorder at football grounds. Like the Stasi, the DVP was organised along military lines with a pronounced friend–foe mindset. Very much the junior partner, it was kept under close watch by the Stasi's Main Department VII. The informers of the criminal investigation police (*Inoffizielle Kriminalpolizeiliche Mitarbeiter*) were expected to work closely with MfS units and to form a pool from which the ministry recruited some of its own IMs. From the late 1950s onwards, the police force numbered about 60,000 per annum, a figure which included over 8,000 criminal investigation police and about 6,200 local police commissioners (*Abschnittsbevollmächtigte*, ABVs), but not the many transport and riot police. The DVP could also call on thousands of voluntary helpers, ranging from 127,451 in 1965 to about 150,000 by the end of the 1980s.[5]

## A Thoroughly Dominated Society?

The vast coercive power of the party-state and security machine and its seeping into all levels of society give substance to Jürgen Kocka's thesis that the GDR was a *durchherrschte Gesellschaft*, a thoroughly dominated or ruled society (Kocka 1994). However, as will be shown in our examination of the experiences of the Jehovah's Witnesses and other minority groups, many obstacles impeded the efficacy of the regime's controls. Among the main hurdles were: the determination of 'targets' not to succumb to arbitrary actions; an individual's sense of their own interests; the strength of a group's collective values; the existence of informal practices and networks such as the black market; the many contradictions in, and fluctuations of, official policy; and the GDR's limited economic and material resource base. Not least of the SED's problems was the attraction for East Germans of a wealthier and culturally more diversified capitalist neighbour and the state's susceptibility to Western and Soviet political, economic and cultural penetration. Nor, despite the dense organisational network and its messianic Marxist-Leninist ideology, was the party-state apparatus a uniform monolith, as is apparent from the internal party rebellions of the 1950s against Ulbricht's autocratic rule as well as from Honecker's overthrow of the veteran SED leader in 1971. After Honecker came to power, disagreements were triggered among the party elites by his determination to allocate a disproportionately high level of resources for the subvention of social policy and by his desire, in the early 1980s, to continue the controversial rapprochement with West Germany despite the breakdown in relations between the USA. and the USSR. Internal disputes also flared up over lesser matters, as will be discussed below regarding the contest between central and regional party and sport functionaries over the running of football and in relation to the carrot-and-stick approach to non-conformist youth.

## Totalitarianism

Despite a variety of checks on the power of the regime, the GDR was undoubtedly a dictatorship in which the SED was the pivotal player. The concept of 'dictatorship' is so broad, however, that it fails to capture appreciable differences between twentieth-century dictatorial regimes and those of other eras. While the term 'totalitarian dictatorship' was coined as an attempt to meet the first objection, the lessening of physical terror and economic modernisation in the Soviet Union and its East European empire after Stalin's death undermined its relevance. Many Western commentators were persuaded that it was time to pension off the totalitarian paradigm, especially the standard version elaborated by Friedrich and Brzezinski in the mid 1950s. This embraced six intertwining traits – the syndrome – of a single party led by a dictator, a totalistic ideology, a system of terror, a virtual monopoly of mass communications and weapons, and a centrally controlled and bureaucratically administered economy (Friedrich 1969: 134–5, 151). Although the flourishing of the 'totalitarianism' concept is associated with the Cold War and its instrumentalisation by many Western politicians from Harry Truman onwards, its origins can be traced back to the 1920s and 1930s in the U.S.A. and Western Europe as part of a broad liberal and socialist critique of fascism. The term, albeit not the critique, had even been appropriated by Mussolini in his praise for the Italian fascist 'totalitarian state' (Ziemer 2006: 159; Wippermann 2009: 14–17). An early postwar variant appeared in Hannah Arendt's influential historical-philosophical text on the origins of totalitarianism (Arendt 1951), which emphasised all-pervasive terror as a means for imposing total control over the atomised masses available for mobilisation in Stalin's Russia and Hitler's Germany.

Even before the attack on Friedrich's work gathered momentum in the 1960s, the 'syndrome' had already come under fire on both empirical and epistemological grounds. One of the main centres of criticism was the Department (*Abteilung*) for the Study of the Soviet Zone of Occupation at the Institute of Political Science at West Berlin's Free University. Ernst Richert, who had fled East Germany in 1949, was the head of the department between 1950 and 1956 and one of West Germany's foremost experts on the GDR. While acknowledging the value of Friedrich's model for the Stalin era, Richert, Max Lange and other colleagues were dissatisfied with what they regarded as its exaggeration of similarities between totalitarian dictatorships, whether of a fascist or communist persuasion. Furthermore, they insisted that Friedrich overlooked the significance of the complex political and economic changes occurring in the Soviet Union and the Eastern European states after 1953 and that he underestimated the relative failure of the GDR and similar states to realise their goals in everyday life. The desideratum of an informed understanding of the social practice of dictatorship only became feasible, however, after the collapse of communism and the release of hitherto inaccessible sources (see Lange 1961: 187–89; Richert 1961: 26; Richert 1968: 144–48; Hüttmann 2007: 673, 675–76; Thomas 2009: 147–48).

## Authoritarianism

One of the main revisionists in West Germany from the late 1960s onwards, the social scientist Peter Christian Ludz, was dismissive of 'totalitarianism' as an 'empty' normative concept (Ludz 1970: 2). He concluded from his examination of the social profiles of the SED's Central Committee and politburo that fundamental tensions and disagreements had existed since the early 1960s between what he defined as a more dogmatically oriented strategic elite of older party functionaries and an institutionalised counter-elite of younger specialists. The latter – technocrats, economists, engineers – were motivated by notions of rational economic efficiency and technological modernisation in a dynamic, differentiated social and industrial order. The New Economic System in the 1960s boosted the role of such experts who, in Ludz's view, sought to promote reforms from within – not of – the system and served to promote a gradual evolution in the non-democratic GDR towards a form of consultative authoritarianism (ibid.: 12, 45–48, 53, 79). While Ludz had undoubtedly exposed conflicts among party, management and scientific-technical elites, his critics contended that these were exaggerated and that he failed to do justice to the negative aspects of single-party hegemony and to the experiences of the ruled.

Consultative authoritarianism was one of the four categories of authoritarianism identified by Ludz that possessed the potential for developing into a participatory form of authoritarianism. His interpretation reflected the growing influence of the social sciences in comparative communist and Soviet studies and a sharper focus on the role of organised interest and political groups. Researchers in this field, such as the North American political scientists Gordon Skilling and Alfred Meyer, traced competition and conflicts of interest between an array of groups and individuals: party leadership factions, apparatchiks, ministries, enterprises, regions, intellectuals such as writers, economists and scientists, workers, farmers and the churches. In so doing, they were able to identify numerous patron–client networks and a degree of dependence by the political leadership on lower organs for the implementation of policies (Mueller 1998: 70–71). Skilling stressed the diversity of communist systems, ranging from the severe limitations on the independence of action of political groups in the quasi-totalitarianism of Stalin's Russia to their enjoyment of a substantial degree of institutionalisation and influence in the democratising and pluralistic authoritarianism of Yugoslavia after 1966 and Czechoslovakia in 1968 (Skilling 1970: 222–29).[6]

Studies of the interplay of, and the rivalries between, political and interest groups fed into the broader framework of 'institutional pluralism', which drew attention to active societal participation by citizens in the form of written petitions to the authorities and the lobbying of local elites. The approach's many advocates, notably the American political scientist Jerry Hough, anticipated greater autonomy for institutions, such as the courts and government bodies, and therefore significant constraints on the regimes (Hough 1977: 5–6, 9–14, 22–28, 47–48). While they succeeded in shattering the picture of a monolithic system and in identifying cleavages, conflicts and contradictions in society and politics, they tended to overplay the notion of the relative autonomy of institutions. Pluralism had different connotations in the communist system with its rejection of the legitimacy of a Western-style interplay of group competition and the erection of numerous hurdles to the development of a civil society.

## Modernising Societies

While institutional pluralism constituted one major challenge to the dominance of totalitarianism, modernisation theory provided another. Ralf Dahrendorf had already, in his classic study of democracy and society in Germany, defined the GDR as 'the first modern society on German soil', albeit with 'totalitarian substance' (Dahrendorf 1967: 424, 431). Modernisation as a tool of analysis drew heavily on the industrial-society approach of Clark Kerr, Walt Rostow and Talcott Parsons, with some Western scholars predicting a gradual convergence between capitalist and communist societies. Scientific-technological development and bureaucratic rationalisation, it was argued, created the preconditions for the formation of similar, though not identical, political systems. In a kind of double convergence, capitalism and Soviet-type socialism would draw together, possibly culminating in some form of democratic socialism. Others were less convinced: they anticipated that, given its greater adaptive capacity, Western society, in particular the United States, was the model towards which all contemporary societies were moving and that the Western pattern of modernisation would eventually lead to the development in the Soviet bloc of political pluralism and freedom of thought. Many Western analysts were uncomfortable with this positive trajectory of development: the German political scientist Richard Löwenthal, for example, while envisaging a long-term trend in favour of modernisation over utopianism, foresaw the transformation of the communist movement into an essentially conservative bureaucracy (Löwenthal 1970: 54, 110). In summarising the above discussion, modernisation theory, together with institutional pluralism and bureaucratic models of Soviet-type systems, did much to undermine the idea of 'abnormality' inherent in the totalitarianism concept and to encourage notions of the normalisation of communist societies (McNeill 1998: 60; Shlapentokh 1999: 4–5).

Many analysts remained unconvinced, however: not only was the modernisation concept – like its totalitarianism rival – handicapped by confused classification criteria, but it was also encumbered by the sharp dichotomy between phases of tradition and modernity, by a Western-centricity and, at least initially, by an over-optimistic teleology of progress. These objections would lead to a fading of the modernisation approach in the course of the 1980s, especially with the Soviet Union and Eastern Europe showing clear signs of economic stagnation and scientific-technological lag. Needless to say, GDR social scientists poured scorn on convergence in its various shades on account of its 'anti-socialist projection of decline' (Rose 1971: 16).

The collapse of the GDR helped revive the faltering modernisation perspective. Jürgen Kocka, professor of history at the Free University Berlin, in a thought-provoking combination of modernisation theory with notions of the GDR and other East European communist states as post-totalitarian formations during the 1970s and 1980s, depicted the GDR as a 'modern dictatorship' (Kocka 1999). Under the thinly veiled rule of a single party, the GDR resorted to a systematic violation of human rights while exhibiting 'modernity' in technological innovation, industrial and urban expansion, land reform, social welfare and anti-traditionalist elements in everyday life. The latter ranged from family planning and competitive sport to new forms of partnership between men and women. However, the prominence of the destructive elements of GDR modernisation led, in Kocka's opinion, to a modernisation deficit vis-à-vis the FRG. Among the obstacles to modernisation were the persecution and disempowerment of functional elites, especially from the middle class, the crushing of civil society, the lack of autonomous, independent sub-systems and the stifling of creativity and individualisation (ibid.: 18–22, 24). This is pertinent to our discussion of the struggle for expression by youth sub-cultures from the 1950s onwards. Other scholars have also made significant contributions to the debate on the ambiguities of socialist modernity. The east German sociologist Detlef Pollack opted for the term 'semi-modern mixed society' to connote, on the one hand, the SED's attempts at modernisation of the economy in the pursuit of compensatory legitimisation through economic success and, on the other, the party's blockage of the very autonomy in those sub-systems like the economy, law and science essential to a society's modernisation (Pollack 1999: 30–31, 35–36).

## The Rediscovery of Totalitarianism in the East and its Revival in the West

One of the principal objections to the application of modernisation theory to the GDR in the 1970s and 1980s was the neglect of the country's poor human-rights record. This was central to the critique of Norman Naimark, a historian and specialist in Russian and East European studies, who homed in on those American and West German studies of the GDR which underplayed the 'most deadly border in the history of the modern world', the 'trade in humans' and the activities of the Ministry of State Security (Naimark 1979: 553, 569). The coercive base of the GDR was explored in pioneering work by Karl Wilhelm Fricke on the politicisation of justice and the Stasi, though even he, like his father a victim of the secret police, underestimated the extent of the Stasi's infiltration of society (Fricke 1979, 1984). With uncompetitive elections, democratic centralism and other fundamental Stalinist structures remaining in place in the GDR (and elsewhere in the Soviet Union's Eastern European empire), it is not surprising that the totalitarian label was not abandoned but was vigorously defended by, for example, Siegfried Mampel, Jens Hacker and other West German academics attached to the politically conservative Gesellschaft für Deutschlandforschung, or Society for Research on Germany (Ross and Grix 2002: 56–57).

The brutal suppression of the Prague Spring by the forces of the Warsaw Pact in 1968 convinced many independent thinkers and dissidents in Eastern Europe, like the Hungarian political theorists Fehér, Heller and Márkus, the Pole Adam Michnik and the Czechs Zdeněk Mlynář and Václav Havel, of what Jacques Rupnik has called the stubborn survival of a 'permanent "totalitarian" core at the heart of the Communist system'.[7] They reappropriated totalitarianism, though not the Friedrich referent, and employed it as a cultural and political tool for the liberation of society from the post-terrorist phase of 'totalitarian normality' and for the recovery of historical memory or, to use Václav Havel's term, 'living in truth' (Havel 1989). In Havel's case, this led to a searching analysis of the structures of what he called post-totalitarianism and its fundamental difference from classical dictatorships. Such a system, according to Havel, was highly adaptable to 'living the lie' and sweeping individuals along by the self-perpetuating operation of a dehumanised power structure with an 'all-embracing' ideology which, though no longer believed in by the regime or the people, served to justify the perpetuation of party rule (ibid.: 40, 43–46, 50). Havel's fellow Czech, the writer Milan Kundera, was dismissive of the euphemistically termed normalisation in Czechoslovakia after the crushing of the Prague Spring. In an interview with Philip Roth, Kundera attacked totalitarianism for depriving people of memory and thereby retooling them into a nation of children. Kundera developed this theme in his novel *The Book of Laughter and Forgetting*, in which he stressed that mastery of the future was predicated on the erasure of the past. Husák, the communist leader of Czechoslovakia, was derided as the 'president of forgetting' (Kundera 1983: 14, 22, 158–59, 187, 235).[8]

While the concept of totalitarianism had been reactivated in Eastern Europe and had never disappeared as an analytic tool in social-science circles in the U.S.A. and Western Europe, it took the collapse of the communist regimes and, in Germany, the uncovering of the extent of the mass surveillance and repression carried out by the Stasi to trigger a major comeback of the concept, or of what has been referred to as totalitarianism's 'silent victory' (Wippermann 2009: 45). One of its main champions, Klaus Schroeder, the combative director of the Forschungsverbund SED-Staat (Research Association SED-State) at the Free University Berlin, interpreted the GDR as shifting in the age of détente from a totalitarian to a late-totalitarian welfare and surveillance state in which the party leadership had the capacity to carry out its policies and claim control over all movements in the web of party, state and society (Schroeder 1993: 643–48). A semi-official blessing for totalitarianism arrived in 1994 when the German parliament's first Enquete-Commission endorsed the validity of totalitarianism as an appropriate framework for classifying the Third Reich and the GDR. This accorded with the Commission's mission to underpin the 'anti-totalitarian consensus' of the Federal Republic (Deutscher Bundestag 1995, i: 745).

Victims of communist rule who had long insisted on the intrinsically repressive nature of the GDR felt vindicated and erstwhile critics of the totalitarian concept, such as the political scientist Klaus von Beyme of the University of Heidelberg, once an advocate of the GDR as a form of consultative authoritarianism, now acknowledged the value of totalitarianism as a sub-type of dictatorial rule in the post-Stalin era (Beyme 1998: 43, 52–53). Other political scientists, for example, Giovanni Sartori, Juan Linz and Alfred Stepan, all well-versed in the typologies of systems of rule, took advantage of the new findings and insights to develop and refine their classifications of totalitarian and authoritarian dictatorships. Sartori had long been a trenchant defender of totalitarianism as an appropriate typology for comparing the two paramount referents, National Socialism and Stalinism, as well as East European communist dictatorships. To compare, he emphasises, is not simply to equate but also involves differentiation, and he dismisses the polemics surrounding totalitarianism as insufficient reason for its rejection as other concepts, whether democracy or feudalism, have survived in spite of similar controversies (Sartori 1987: 195–96, 199, 202–3; Sartori 1993: 7–9, 12). As part of his search for structural differentiation, he devised seven sets of characteristics to distinguish the authoritarian, totalitarian and simple types of species of the genus 'dictatorship' and to assess variance over periods of time. Among the characteristics were the independence of sub-groups, policies towards fringe groups, and the central role of the party. For example, coercion, mobilisation and arbitrariness are high and unlimited in totalitarian systems but average and within calculable parameters in authoritarian dictatorships (Sartori 1993:15). Similar to the work of Martin Draht and Peter Graf Kielmansegg in earlier decades (see Ross 2002: 21), Sartori distinguishes between defining or necessary and central or contingent characteristics. Thus, whereas terror was once regarded as a defining feature of totalitarianism, the routinisation of totalitarian control makes terror superfluous and renders it an accompanying or contingent characteristic (Sartori 1993: 16–19).

## Post-totalitarianism

Linz and Stepan (1996) built on Sartori's ideas to produce a more elaborate typology that integrated the GDR into a five-fold classification of democratic, authoritarian, sultanistic, post-totalitarian and totalitarian systems.[9] They identify four key dimensions for classification purposes: pluralism, ideology, leadership and mobilisation. Authoritarian regimes, like that of Franco's Spain, tolerate a limited political pluralism, do not impose a central and exclusive ideology, and lack a political mass party. In post-totalitarianism, the GDR being one example of this distinctive regime type, while a measure of institutional pluralism exists – encompassing the party, army, secret services, state-controlled economic units and mass organisations – this should not be confused with political pluralism, which was virtually non-existent by virtue of the party's monopoly of power. Turning to the differences between totalitarianism, as in Stalin's Russia and Hitler's Germany, and the post-totalitarianism of much of communist Eastern Europe, the latter form is held to embody a varying degree of space for a second economy and a parallel culture, which is absent in a totalitarian regime. The non-official second culture, with an active underground samizdat literature, is not possible in totalitarianism and is denied legitimacy and responsibility in post-totalitarianism.

As for ideology, the belief in utopia is much weaker and a shift occurs from ideology to pragmatic consensus. However, while technical competence becomes more significant, access to political office is still determined by political criteria, the highest level of leadership tends to be more state-technocratic than charismatic, and ideology often obstructs bureaucratic rationality. Finally, the extensive mobilisation of the population by an array of societal organisations with an emphasis on activism gives way to a routine mobilisation of the population within mass organisations to achieve a minimum of conformity and compliance. With regard to repression, post-totalitarian regimes do away with the worst aspects but maintain most mechanisms of control. Moreover, as in the case of the East German Stasi, while the security services are less bloody, they may become more pervasive. As Mark Thompson writes: 'Even though widespread killing and torture are eliminated, Big Brother often watches closer than ever' (Thompson 1998: 314). The pertinence of this observation is apparent in our study of Stasi surveillance of religious and other minority groups.

One of the undoubted merits of Linz and Stepan's typology is their identification of three main sub-categories along a continuum of 'early', 'frozen' and 'mature' post-totalitarianism. The first is deemed to be the closest in time and characteristics to its totalitarian predecessor with the important exception of some restrictions on the leader and the cult of personality. In the 'frozen' form, typified by Honecker's GDR and a 'normalised' Czechoslovakia after the crushing of the Prague Spring, almost all the control mechanisms of the party-state remain in place, despite a tolerance of some civil-society critics. In the third sub-category, significant change occurs in all dimensions of the regime. For example, it is less ideological and less repressive than the 'frozen' variant; however, the leading role of the official party remains sacrosanct, as in Hungary from 1982 to 1988. Even though in the mature sub-category leaders of the second culture might be imprisoned, they can nevertheless create enduring oppositional organisations in civil society (Linz and Stepan 1996: 38–43, 47; Meuschel 2000a: 54, 61; Meuschel 2000b: 93; Thompson 2002: 87–88, 91–93). It should be stressed, however, that SED tolerance of autonomous peace and ecological groups and autonomous subcultures was highly conditional, with groups dedicated to human rights enduring a particularly precarious existence.

While the categories devised by Linz and Stepan cannot be as clear cut as many investigators might wish, and will certainly not satisfy those critics who see their work as totalitarianism in a new garb, their typology has the merit of a conceptual map for placing the GDR along a winding path from the period of high Stalinism to the less overtly repressive and more paternalistic system that existed from the late 1960s. Furthermore, the elements of differentiation in the model help counter the criticism (Wippermann 2009: 120–22) that comparison leads to an equation between National Socialist Germany and GDR state socialism, and thereby relativises the crimes of the former dictatorship while demonising the latter. A more flexible analytic tool, and more sensitive to change than the standard variant of totalitarianism, the Linz 'frozen' variant has been adopted as the conceptual framework for the study of the six minority groups that constitute the empirical basis of our book.

## Authority as Social Practice

Juan Linz has insisted that typologies, whether of totalitarianism or post-totalitarianism, should take full account of the multiplicity and diversity of the exchanges between regime and subjects and should explore the rhythms of everyday life under dictatorship. Many of the actions and attitudes of ordinary people, he argues, 'put a limit to the view that coercion and state terror (always latently present) were always overt and omnipresent'; in their ordinary lives people tended not to think of how their society was being ruled unless they were targets of regime hostility. To assert otherwise, he concludes, is to hold a 'simplistic' and misleading view of totalitarianism (Linz 2000: 28). On the other hand, his work, like that of Sartori, does not attempt the kind of nuanced interpretation and depiction of daily experiences in a dictatorship provided, for example, for the GDR by Lindenberger, Lüdtke and other proponents of 'authority as social practice' (*Herrschaft als soziale Praxis*). This orientation, which helps realise Ernst Richert's plea in the 1960s for uncovering the SED's impact on society, posits that even a system like state socialism cannot operate simply on the basis of orders, rules, guidelines and plans issued from above. It must involve some elements of bargaining, compromise, congruence of interest, arrangements and interdependence between purportedly 'active' rulers and the 'passive' ruled. While conceding that the power relationship was asymmetrical and that conflicts existed between rulers and ruled, the advocates of this approach emphasise, justifiably, that ordinary people were not only essential in myriad ways for the implementation of policies in many micro-areas but also influenced those very policies (Lindenberger 1996: 315–16; Lindenberger 1999a: 17, 22, 41; Lindenberger 1999b: 125–26; Lüdtke 1998: 12–13; Ross 2002: 50–51, 62–63). The concept of authority as social practice is not, of course, restricted to the GDR but has been applied to other dictatorships, including National Socialist Germany, which in the case of the latter enjoyed a higher level of support than the SED regime. Studies of the interaction between state and populace which detail the engagement of a growing circle of Germans in the National Socialist regime's persecution of Jews help counter one of the most frequent criticisms of the history of daily life, namely that it plays down the dictatorial character of rule (Bajohr 2008: 17–19; Wippermann 2009: 57–58, 79).

Investigations into everyday life home in on those who have tended to be largely anonymous in history and on the small units, whether in work or non-work (Lüdtke 1995: 3–4, 15). The exploration of the microcosm of society not only uncovers the 'normal' but also the 'abnormal' as well as the mundane and the dramatic in everyday life. While these polarities (and their intertwining) were extreme in the racist and genocidal Third Reich, they existed in the GDR, too, revolving around matters such as conformity, complicity and collaboration, on the one hand, and resistance and opposition on the other. The whole issue of what constitutes a 'normal', 'perfectly ordinary' and 'unexceptional' sphere of a diverse 'everydayness' under a dictatorship – that is, with minimal political intrusion – is highly problematic, depending in part on place, time period, gender, age, social and political position as well as on the accuracy of memory of those who were, or were not, victims of the regime. While a worm's-eye view of an everyday life in which many just wanted to get on with their own business is essential for the reconstruction of GDR history,[10] what was 'normal' might vary from the life of a party functionary or Stasi informer to the mundane tasks of an ancillary worker on a factory assembly line. For others it was highly problematic: Jehovah's Witnesses, Jewish Community members and foreign workers who, when trying to normalise or, rather, to cope with their private and public affairs and maintain their individual and collective values, frequently endured arbitrary interventions in their lives by representatives of the police, the SED and the Stasi.

Questions surrounding normality and continuity in daily life have been explored not only in memoirs, films and novels but also by historians who have drawn on the methodologies of social history and the history of mentalities. Recent histories in this vein have been influenced by the 'historicisation' of the Third Reich, an approach developed by Martin Broszat at the Institute for Contemporary History in Munich with an emphasis on critical reconstruction without prior prejudice. Individualisation, self-determination (*Selbstbehauptung*) and *Eigen-Sinn* – roughly 'a sense of themselves' or 'a sense of one's own self and worth' – are three of the key concepts utilised by historians to try and capture the variety and complexity of patterns of living in the GDR and how East Germans sought to create meaning in their immediate social environment. Individualisation, it is presupposed, is more likely to be found among certain groups and milieux such as the churches and intellectual circles although, according to the findings of the Leipzig Central Institute for Youth Research (ZIJ), a cultural revolution was in progress in the GDR from the late 1970s onwards, characterised by young people's keener awareness of their own worth and a more pronounced desire to conduct and enjoy life free from the shackles of the SED and the FDJ. This individualisation found expression in greater involvement in informal cliques and unofficial peace groups as well as in changing attitudes towards traditional patterns of marriage and family relationships (Friedrich 1990: 34–36; Madarársz 2006: 12–15, 174). The emergence of goths, punks and other non-conformist youth sub-cultural groups, influenced by Western tastes and styles, was also part of this radical shift. *Eigen-Sinn*, which is partly related to individualisation, covers a broader and somewhat eclectic spectrum of attitudes and actions, among them ardent idealism, an opportunistic cooperation with the agents of state and party, outwardly loyal but inwardly distant behaviour, recalcitrance, non-conformity, open dissent and resistance. One major advantage of the concept, as delineated here, is that it shifts the focus from the small minority who actively opposed the SED to the majority of East Germans, who were for the most part 'reluctantly loyal' to, or passively tolerant of, the state (Lindenberger 2007: 32–33, 36).

*Eigen-Sinn* and self-determination underpin several investigations into areas of life which, though by no means islands of political seclusion, enjoyed a limited degree of autonomy from the all-encompassing institutions and mechanisms of SED domination. Located at the base of society, the work collective, the religious congregation, the family, personal networks, the sports club, the football fan club, the 'beat' music group and so forth were spheres which indicate that society had not withered away and that 'normalcy' was not just a façade. Leisure activities were mainly pursued independently in the company of friends and relatives. The family, though fundamentally affected by the state's extensive mobilisation of women for work and by intrusions into private relationships by the police and the Stasi, retained some of its functions as a relatively autonomous agent of socialisation and reproduction. The decline in the GDR birth rate since 1965, despite the pro-natalist measures of the SED, was in part the conscious reaction of women who refused to be 'rolled over' by the disproportionately heavy burdens of parenthood, employment and housework arising from the state's social and labour policies (Harsch 2007: 307, 310–19).

The economy is another crucial area where the diversity of interaction with the authorities is being unravelled by historians and social scientists. The work collective, though conceived from above as a transmission belt, sometimes served as a social buffer between the individual and the state, helping to counter management pressures for improvements in labour productivity (Engler 1999: 283, 289). A substantial parallel or grey economy existed in which goods and services in short supply could be obtained in personal networks outside the official channels, sometimes without the exchange of money. Alena Ledeneva has dubbed this, with reference to the Soviet Union, an 'economy of favours' (Ledeneva 1998: 1–4). Foreign workers, like the Vietnamese and Poles, were embedded in this kind of system. Applying this mode of analysis, the social reconstruction of the past becomes not simply a history from the bottom up but the study of kaleidoscopic and shifting interactions between 'lowly' social actors and the various organisations of the authoritative state. Furthermore, the exploration of the lives of 'ordinary people', whether East Germans or foreign nationals, and their subjective experiences provides a fuller picture and a more sensitive understanding of GDR history from which 'little people' can emerge as agents, however minor, and not simply as objects of the dictatorship (see Eckert 2008: 116).

One frequent criticism of depictions of daily life is that they can drift into a nostalgic and romanticised view of a GDR in which citizens could lead lives virtually untouched by the instruments of dictatorship, thereby trivialising or underestimating repression and, by their inaction, help indirectly to perpetuate the regime. There is, of course, good reason for an undogmatic exploration of everyday life in the GDR, one that does not suppress the diverse memories and self-image of east Germans nor focus simply on opposition and domination. After all, as the former dissident Gerd Poppe has pointed out, East Germans were 'not a people of oppositionalists, but even less one of denunciators' (Deutscher Bundestag 1995, I: 53). The Leipzig-based social scientist Thomas Ahbe has stressed the importance of combating the prejudices and the gaps in what he sees as the dominant and primarily west German-shaped debate that, by focusing on negative aspects of the GDR, presents life in the GDR as essentially a story of repression. Open discussion should not, he contends, be confused with nostalgia and a desire for a return of the GDR, but rather be seen as a crucial element in an integration strategy which provides east Germans with opportunities for articulating the experiences, memories and values which diverge from those of the west German majority (Ahbe 2005: 277–79).

Ahbe's strictures notwithstanding, east Germans have vigorously engaged in the historiography of their former state, often, not surprisingly, disagreeing among themselves. For example, the PDS interpretation of the GDR's historical legacy as presented to the cross-party Enquete-Commission of the German Bundestag in 1994, which combined an acknowledgement of the system as a dictatorship of the SED leadership with elements of democracy, was rejected by many east Germans, especially former dissidents (Dennis 2004: 18–27; Kocka 2003: 768–69). A balanced assessment was offered by the east German theologian Richard Schröder of Humboldt University in Berlin: GDR citizens' awareness of the system's positive features can be encapsulated in the statement that 'Much was bad in the GDR, BUT we had no unemployed, no drug problems'. He stresses, however, that the advantages which stand after the 'BUT' are much smaller in number than those which appear in front (Schröder 1993: 21). While the authors of this book incline towards the latter, it will become apparent that the line was not so sharply drawn.

## Subjects and Objects of the Study

The following chapters will take up the themes and issues discussed above regarding the structure of power and social interactions, and will address one of Sartori's criteria for identifying the nature of dictatorship; that is, policies and attitudes towards fringe groups, in particular towards the value structures of the Jewish Communities, Jehovah's Witnesses, foreign workers and youth sub-cultures and, on the other hand, the groups' responses to, and 'negotiations' with, the authorities. These groups can be defined as minorities and also, for the most part, as outside, whether consciously or not, the frequently ill-defined boundaries set by official norms and policies. The groups have been selected partly, as indicated earlier, because they are relatively under-researched, but also because they represent milestones in the unfolding history of the GDR and its meanings. Thus, the treatment of the Jewish Communities and the Jehovah's Witnesses should have embodied a break with the genocidal National Socialist past and symbolised an enlightened, socialist future. The presence of foreign workers in the 1980s, too, especially those from fraternal states such as Vietnam and Mozambique, was hailed by officialdom as testament to the GDR's commitment to international socialism and assistance for victims of exploitative imperialism and colonialism. The generation born after the construction and consolidation of the GDR is the final focus of the book, and here we look at those groups – notably punks, goths, skinheads and football fans – who in many ways broke with the socialisation of GDR youth as all-round socialist personalities and sought to subvert the cultural hegemony of the SED state.

We can now sum up the key questions: in the case of the Jehovah's Witnesses, why did the SED seek – and fail – to destroy the movement in the 1950s and 1960s? What kind of impact did persecution have on the family life of Jehovah's Witnesses in the Honecker era? Why did the authorities' treatment of, and attitudes to, Jehovah's Witnesses differ so appreciably from their treatment of members of the Jewish congregations? How did both the East German Jehovah's Witnesses and Jews assert their own values and sense of worth? Was SED policy influenced by anti-semitism, and why, in the 1980s, did the party seek better relations with the Jewish Communities and Israel? As for punks, skinheads and football fans, were these part of a generational shift which crossed East–West political and cultural barriers? What were official perceptions of, and policies towards, youth sub-cultures in the final decade of SED rule and to what extent did they differ from those of earlier periods? How did such groups respond to surveillance and repression? And, finally, how did foreign workers, especially the Mozambicans and Vietnamese, perceive the GDR and how did they shape their lives at work and in the niches of their hostels? The sum of the answers to these questions will, it is intended, serve as a critical barometer of the state's respect for human rights and freedom of expression and provide a differentiated depiction of the GDR as a post-totalitarian state in which authority was both coercive and socially dependent.

## Sources

The primary sources held by the State Security Service (BStU) and the Federal Archive in Berlin (BA) form the main storehouse of the materials on which this book is based. While copious files were consulted from the Central Archive (ZA) and the archives of the regional branches (*Außenstellen*) of the BStU, they represent only the lower slopes of the Himalayan mountain of its overall holdings. The BStU, which was created by legislation promulgated by the Bundestag in December 1991, is the Office of the Federal Commissioner for the Records of the State Security Service of the Former German Democratic Republic. In 2009, it was responsible for over 260 kilometres of written documents if extended end to end. These include Stasi Central Departmental analyses of a particular situation or issue, ministerial instructions and guidelines, speeches by officers, interim and final reports on major operations, officers' dissertations and transcripts of meetings between IMs and their controllers. Other sources include copies of materials from the DVP and other official bodies, many of which are also held in the Federal Archive; these may be sub-divided into the documentation of the organs of state such as the Council of Ministers, the State Secretariat for Church Affairs and the police and, second, into those emanating from the SED and the mass organisations. Where we have consulted and cited from the latter type in the Federal Archive in Berlin, they are designated SAPMO-BA. In addition, local government and factory records have been drawn upon from the Merseburg branch of the Landeshauptarchiv Sachsen-Anhalt (LSA), which, like many of the files of the DVP, tend to focus more sharply on the microcosm of daily activities than is often the case in Stasi and SED Central Committee Secretariat documentation but, when combined with the latter group, provide an essential basis for a socio-political history of the GDR.

While posing significant methodological difficulties, Stasi materials are invaluable not just for the reconstruction of the ministry's penetration of society and its role as the main instrument of repression but also for assembling a mosaic of life under the SED dictatorship. Stasi materials for the latter purpose become more plentiful from the late 1960s onwards, when the rapidly expanding ministry extended the operations normally associated with a secret police and a powerful controller-general to the role of a general factotum for combating inefficiencies in the economy and even reporting on the details of the football fan scene and fringe sub-cultures such as the punks and heavy-metal fans of the 1980s. Together with SED, factory management and FDGB reports, central and local Stasi units' assessment of economic performance and of popular views on consumer shortages and foreign workers are important correctives to the ideological distortions to be found in many other official materials.

Primary sources are also crucial for rectifying distortions of the East German past. The two-volume survey of the history and role of the MfS compiled by former officers is part of a concerted revisionist effort on their part to legitimise the activities and functions of the ministry, even claiming that operational decomposition was in the interest of the 'targets' to prevent them from transgressing the law (Grimmer and Irmler 2002: 295, 302). This conveniently overlooks the fact that many of the measures implemented by the Stasi were both arbitrary and illegal under GDR law. While this kind of exculpatory literature can be subjected to critical judgement by means of primary evidence, the latter nevertheless presents significant methodological problems. Taking the Stasi records as an example, the growing professionalism of the ministry since the 1960s found expression in numerous efforts to devise appropriate norms and quality checks to ensure that its sources of information – especially the IMs – were reliable, accurate and of political and operational relevance (Engelmann 1995: 246–53). Yet ludicrous errors crept in. When one IM informed his controlling officer that a person called Voltaire had been mentioned at a meeting of artists, this triggered a search for a Voltaire in the Stasi's data base (Hecht 2001: 423). On another occasion, punks in Dresden outwitted the Stasi by spreading false information about a forthcoming party for over 200 punks; the police on alert at the main station were left to idle away the time (Stadtmuseum Dresden 2007: 16).

When drawing on the records of state and party institutions, it should be borne in mind that they are infused with official Marxist-Leninist ideology and that their highly formalised bureaucratic language contrasts sharply with that used in everyday life. Great care is therefore required in using the written record, as it is necessary to disaggregate and deconstruct terms with heavy ideological baggage, such as 'negative decadent' groups and 'hostile negative' forces. The former refers to a wide range of behaviour, which includes youthful non-conformity, and was interpreted by Stasi officers as the result of the ubiquitous imperialist foe's political-ideological subversion of misguided youth. Similarly, the official record associated Jehovah's Witnesses with 'hostile negative' characteristics and portrayed them as instruments of the nefarious class enemy. While this kind of language and ideological rigidity, which is to be found in both public statements and top-secret internal documents, helped produce a cohesive security apparatus, by externalising the determinants of 'undesirable' social and political behaviour, it overlooked GDR-specific conditions and so acted as a barrier to an understanding of the 'problems' (Engelmann 1995: 256–67). Furthermore, given that the security forces' primary mission was to identify and prevent threats to the system, the historian and other users of Stasi materials run the risk of seeing the GDR through the distorted lens of the Ministry of State Security and the DVP. The GDR was not simply Stasi and police.

Other methodological issues surround the status and reliability of the records of the interrogations of alleged 'enemies' of the state, such as the Jehovah's Witnesses, especially in the 1950s and 1960s; these were compiled by interrogators who frequently used psychological and even physical pressure to force their victims to sign them (see Chapter 2). With regard to a controller's written report on a meeting (*Treff*) with an IM, this tended to be a distillation of what the former regarded as operationally significant from the written or oral account by the informer. The latter would be influenced by what had been remembered and by their motives (ibid.: 255–56). This could lead to factual errors and to the meetings being used by informers to achieve personal and political goals which did not necessarily conform to those of the Stasi. While the Stasi controlling officer usually held the upper hand, the following chapters provide instances of attempts by IMs, such as the Jewish writer and historian Helmut Eschwege, to instrumentalise their contacts with the MfS.

In summary, the chapters in this book are designed to show that the GDR was not a uniform monolith and, despite the high level of political organisation and mobilisation, society was not, as Sigrid Meuschel has argued, shut down and absorbed by the state and nor did it wither away (Meuschel 1992: 10-17). On the contrary, society was differentiated along status, gender, ethnicity, age and other lines and was characterised by myriad informal networks. As with the totalitarian syndrome of Friedrich, the alleged dying away of society runs the risk of overlooking what Pollack refers to as 'tendencies that went against the clear distribution of power distribution, and of underestimating conflicts, forms of resistance, individual possibilities for action, cultural contradictions, communication niches, forms of protest and pretended collaboration' (Pollack 1999: 27). Moreover, while from about the mid 1960s the GDR may, if one wishes to apply an overarching concept, be defined as a post-totalitarian dictatorship, this does not necessarily imply a rigid division between ruled and rulers. Allowance can – and should – be made for the complex and contradictory realities that can be found in a thoroughly organised and penetrated society, ones which can be fruitfully explored by means of lower-level concepts and approaches linked to the history of daily life under changing forms of dictatorial rule throughout the history of the GDR. This, hopefully, avoids model and ideal-type mania and the multiplicity of interpretations which, as Walter Laqueur asserts, may well result in the generation of light in inverse proportion to the heat engendered (Laqueur 1994: 89) or, as Torsten Diedrich and Hans Ehlert state, with tongue in cheek, lead to the definition of the GDR as a 'modern socialist welfare dictatorship of a Stalinist-Soviet character' (Diedrich and Ehlert 1998: 25).

## Notes

1. Hertle and Sälter (2006: 674–76). The authors stress that deaths at the Wall and border were the tip of an iceberg of violence and repression, which included among its victims tens of thousands who were arrested and imprisoned for trying to leave the GDR, as well as would-be émigrés who suffered discrimination and criminalisation.
2. On Main Department I's surveillance of the NVA and the border guards, see Wenzke (2005: 321–24). In 1987, 7.5 per cent of all members of the army were IMs.
3. See Kerz-Rühling and Plänkers (2004: 15–17, 124–43, 231–37) for an analysis of motives based on interviews with twenty former IMs.
4. See Dennis with Laporte (2003: 41–46) for a brief survey of SED–Stasi relations, an area which is still under-researched.
5. BStU, 'Das Arbeitsgebiet 1 der Kriminalpolizei. Aufgaben, Struktur und Verhältnis zum Ministerium für Staatssicherheit', 1994, pp.14–20; see also Lindenberger (1998: 132–33), Dennis with Laporte (2003: 92) and Gieseke (2003a: 96–99, 112).

6. Helpful overviews of the debates on appropriate models and concepts for what Skilling has called 'imperfect monism' can be found in Brown (1983: 61–75, 91–95) and Almond and Roselle (1993: 27–66).

7. See Rupnik (1988: 224, 228–48) for an impressive assessment of the various ways – market economy, civil society and liberal traditions – for exiting totalitarianism developed by Hungarian, Czech, Polish and Russian intellectuals after 1968. Fehér and his two colleagues, members of the Budapest School, argued that while the Soviet Union ceased to be a terroristic totalitarian state after Stalin's death, it remained totalitarian (Fehér, Heller and Márkus 1983: 146).

8. Husák (1919–1991) succeeded Dubček as First Secretary of the Czechoslovak Communist Party in 1969 and became President of the country in 1975. His complex political biography is noted primarily for his tightening of state and party repression after 1968, in what has been called the 'normalisation' process.

9. The overview in this and the following paragraph is based on Linz and Stepan (1996: 42–50); see also Thompson (2002: 83–85).

10. See 'Empfehlungen der Expertenkommission zur Schaffung eines Geschichtsverbundes "Aufarbeitung der SED-Diktatur"' (2006), p.15. Retrieved 20 June 2007 from: http://www.stiftung-aufarbeitung.de/downloads/pdf/sabrow-bericht.pdf.

# Chapter 2

# BETWEEN TORAH AND SICKLE: JEWS IN EAST GERMANY, 1945–1990

## After the Holocaust

$A$t the end of the Second World War, the Jewish presence in the Soviet Zone of Occupation had been reduced to a mere shadow of its former vitality and strength. The Jewish Communities (*Gemeinden*)[1] had been dismantled, their synagogues ruined and their property seized by the National Socialists. When they emerged from the concentration camps, from hiding or from displaced persons' camps, those survivors with a choice faced the agonising dilemma of whether or not to live in a Germany whose rulers had been responsible for the extermination of several million Jews. If they opted to stay, they sometimes encountered fierce opposition from Jews elsewhere for remaining in a land where so many 'ordinary' Germans had been collaborators or bystanders.

The scale of the unprecedented disaster which struck German Jewry can be seen in the bare statistics.[2] Almost 190,000 had been murdered, about 260,000 had emigrated and little more than 30,000 remained in the country. Before 1939, 150,000 had belonged to the Jewish Communities in the region that became the GDR; seven years later, a mere 2,094 survivors remained in the Soviet Zone and 2,535 in the Soviet sector of Berlin. Dresden only had twelve Jews of faith whereas it had boasted 11,000 before Hitler came to power. For these survivors, the destruction of the Third Reich could only be a radical improvement and a reason for hope. One who had survived, thanks to his marriage to an 'Aryan', was Victor Klemperer, a professor of literature and also well-known for the diaries he kept during the periods of the Third Reich and the GDR. The son of a rabbi but an assimilated Jew who had converted to Protestantism, the 63-year-old Klemperer wrote in his diary on 17 July 1945: 'I have to tell myself a little too often: you are in Paradise now, compared to the previous situation' (Klemperer 2004: 24).

Why paradise would be so elusive in the GDR, a self-styled democratic anti-fascist state, is the central theme of this chapter and will be examined in relation to interactions between the state and East German Jews with particular regard to several key issues: the treatment of the Jewish community as an indicator of the credentials of the GDR as representing a clear break with the fascist and capitalist past; the wave of anti-semitism in the early 1950s; hierarchies of Jewish and communist victimhood; the dilemma of a complete assimilation into socialism over a commitment to the Jewish faith and Jewish culture; East German Jews' criticism of their government's anti-Zionism and hostility towards Israel; and their otherwise habitual acquiescence regarding state policy. Special attention will be paid to the last quinquennium of SED rule when the party leadership around General Secretary Erich Honecker sought to reinvigorate the miniscule Jewish Communities in a vain attempt to boost the GDR's domestic and international legitimacy. These diverse strands of East German Jewish history will be explored through subjective experiences as recorded in published memoirs and interviews (e.g., Ostow 1989, 1996; Eschwege 1991; Axen 1996; Borneman and Peck 1995) but above all on the basis of archival materials of the Socialist Unity Party (SED), the Ministry of State Security (MfS) and the State Secretariat for Church Affairs. An impressive series of monographs (e.g., Keßler 1995; Herf 1997; Hartewig 2000; Mertens 1997) has drawn on newly available primary sources to plug many of the gaps in the historiography of Jews in East Germany. There are, however, considerable differences of interpretation and emphasis, particularly regarding the prevalence of anti-semitism in the GDR and the degree of collaboration by prominent East German Jews with the SED and Stasi. Whereas Michael Wolffsohn (1998) typically offers the most critical and sometimes polemical assessment of the actions of the Jewish Communities and individual Jews, Mertens and Hartewig are more insightful regarding the travails and complexities of life under a dictatorship, including those Jewish communists who were assimilated into both party and socialist society. This observation is also true of the power structures of the GDR in that, while differences of approach within the SED itself and between party and governmental bodies over policy towards Israel and the Jewish Communities emerge clearly from the research conducted by Hartewig and Herf, the studies by Wolffsohn and Keßler incline towards a representation of a uniform party-state monolith.

## The Jewish Communities

In a narrow sense, a Jew is a person who belongs to a Jewish Community, that is, a Jew by faith with at least a Jewish mother. This definition does not, however, embrace the much broader but often less easily identifiable – and more numerous – group of those of Jewish descent who remained outside the Community framework for a number of reasons, such as political creed and a rejection of religious orthodoxy. The Jewish Communities were the most visible expression of Jewish identity and existence in the GDR. However, as the National Socialists had disbanded all the Communities by 1943, revival was both slow and difficult.[3] A few shoots began to appear soon after the end of the war when tiny groups were formed in Leipzig, Magdeburg, Dresden, Chemnitz, Erfurt and Halle. The largest and most significant Community, that of Greater Berlin, took shape in the course of 1945. Despite the many problems posed by the destruction of war, the divergent interests of the occupying powers and the flow through the city of Jewish refugees from Eastern Europe, a Community administrative headquarters was set up in the Oranienburger Strasse in the Soviet sector.

The focus of Community work was on essential tasks such as education, social welfare, the revival of Jewish religious practice, and the restoration of places of worship and burial. The Communities were permitted the use of a small proportion of their former property, notably cemeteries and synagogues, and were given modest assistance for their upkeep. A representative organisation of all the newly formed Communities, excepting that of Greater Berlin, was founded in November 1946. After considerable delay and with a discernible lack of enthusiasm, the Soviet authorities authorised it as a legal body in spring 1947 with the title of the State Association of Jewish Communities in the Soviet Zone of Occupation (*Landesverband der Jüdischen Gemeinden in der Sowjetischen Besatzungszone*). Julius Meyer, a survivor of Auschwitz, whose wife and child had been murdered there, was appointed its first president after serving as acting chair.

In addition to the emergence of a rudimentary Community structure, East German Jews had other reasons for hope. Memories among many communists and Jews of their suffering in National Socialist concentration camps lay behind the efforts of prominent SED politicians such as Paul Merker and Leo Zuckermann to obtain restitution and compensation for Jewish victims of the Holocaust. Furthermore, with the Communist Party (KPD) and then the SED anxious to establish the credentials of the Soviet Zone and the GDR as an anti-fascist polity, Jews were officially recognised in 1945 as 'victims of fascism' and prosecutions were instigated against former National Socialists. The official de-nazification programme in the Soviet Zone led to about 450,000 of the 1.5 million former National Socialist Party (NSDAP) members either being dismissed or not reinstated (Dennis 2000aa: 18). As 'victims of fascism', Jews were entitled to a pension which was higher than the average but lower than that of a person defined as a 'fighter against fascism'. Communists were the main beneficiaries of the latter category, which deliberately excluded Jews who had been active resistance fighters.

## Being Jewish in East Germany

Whether or not to live in Germany depended, where an alternative existed, on a range of factors from the pull of family and home to economic necessity.[4] Of those Jews who opted to remain in, or return from exile to, the Soviet Zone and the later GDR, among them about 3,500 returnees (Stern 1996: 58), many were communists and left-wing socialists who came to occupy positions of influence in politics, the economy and the arts and were committed to building a socialist society. A long list includes the SED politburo members Albert Norden and Hermann Axen, the State Secretary for Religious Affairs Klaus Gysi and the Minister of Culture Alexander Abusch. The playwright and physician Friedrich Wolf, the actress Helene Weigel, and the writers Stephan Hermlin and Anna Seghers were among the luminaries of the cultural sphere. Wolf's two sons, Konrad and Markus, would become a film director and the head of Stasi foreign intelligence respectively. Advancement in the elite strata, especially for communist political functionaries such as Axen and Norden, was premised on the abandonment of their Jewish identity and 'red assimilation' (Hartewig 2000: 613). This precondition was largely derived from the view of the prewar KPD that the complete emancipation of German Jews and the end of discrimination could be achieved only through the communist movement and integration into socialist society, not in a liberal or social-democratic order. Assimilation of this kind entailed a high level of political and cultural conformity and the virtual abandonment of a party member's Jewish identity. To do otherwise, especially in the early days of the GDR, was to risk the charge of Zionism and, at best, political disfavour (Groehler 1993: 52; 1995: 6).

Hermann Axen, born in Leipzig in 1916 to a Jewish family, typified the process of 'red assimilation'. Joining the Communist youth organisation in 1932, he was sentenced in 1935 to four years in prison for planning high treason. In 1940 he was interned in the concentration camp at Le Vernet in France and was later deported to Auschwitz and Buchenwald. His elder brother, Rudolf, a KPD official, was murdered by the Gestapo in 1933 and their parents were probably executed in occupied Poland in the early months of the Second World War (Axen 1996: 29, 68). Joining the SED in 1946, Axen served as a top functionary of the party's youth organisation (FDJ) for several years before his appointment as head of the party's Department of Agitation. He became a member of the SED's two leading bodies, the Central Committee Secretariat and the politburo in 1950 and 1963 respectively. In 1980, Axen, by now the SED's main foreign affairs spokesperson, revealed to several British journalists that he regarded Judaism as simply a religion which he had long ago abandoned, just like those Anglicans who withdrew from the Church of England (Meining 2002: 524). Axen had left the Israelite Jewish Community in Leipzig soon after he had been confirmed as a thirteen-year-old (Axen 1996: 26). Yet conformity to the party did not bring immunity from discrimination for, as Thomas Fox has argued: 'East Germans of Jewish descent could look, dress, talk, and act like other East Germans. They could join the Party and eschew Zionism. But many remained somehow outsiders, both in their own eyes and in those of their fellow citizens' (Fox 1999: 3). The temporary eclipse of dedicated communists like Norden and Axen in 1953, when anti-semitic persecution was at its height, is indicative of the suspicion attached to Jewish origins. Axen was demoted from his post as a Central Committee Secretary and Norden as head of the Press Department (Timm 1997a: 120).

Another eminent politician whose career suffered a setback during the anti-semitic wave was Klaus Gysi, the State Secretary for Church Affairs between 1979 and 1988. Born in Berlin in 1912 to a Jewish mother and a non-Jewish doctor, he joined the KPD in 1931. During the Third Reich he spent several years in exile in England and France. Escaping from internment in France, he returned to Germany in 1940 to carry out underground political activity. His career and his aspiration to build a more just society suffered a blow when, in 1951, his Jewish origins cost him his post at the League of Culture. This proved to be a temporary setback: he became Minister of Culture from 1966 to 1973 and, after a period as ambassador to Italy, State Secretary for Church Affairs in 1979. By the mid 1980s, the arrival of a reform-minded leader in Moscow, Mikhail Gorbachev, and the SED's efforts to revive the GDR's Jewish Communities created a more favourable climate for the expression of Jewish identity. Gysi began to refer to his Jewish background in private and, as State Secretary for Church Affairs, to play an active role in the reinvigoration of Jewish life and culture (Kaufman 1997: 206, 209–13; Hartewig 2000: 179–80).

Gysi's career was full of paradox. His original vision of a new and just socialist society was compromised by power politics and career considerations. When he became head of the Aufbau publishing house in 1957, he replaced the purged Walter Janka, a fate which had befallen Gysi several years earlier in the League of Culture. While Gysi tried to convince himself that he would follow the path of reform charted by Janka, not only had he opted to cooperate with a dictatorial regime and its secret service but also helped them destroy intellectual revisionism. His years as an informer (known as 'Kurt') from 1956 to 1964 covered most of his time in charge of Aufbau, during which he contributed to the exposure and imprisonment of members of the so-called 'counter-revolutionary group' around Janka and Wolfgang Harich (Vollnhals 1996: 96; Hartewig 2000: 176–77).

## Subordination, Persecution and Flight: 1948 to 1953

The hopes of East German Jews, whether communist or not, for a just society remained alive in the immediate postwar years. The KPD programme of June 1945 called for the establishment in Germany of 'an anti-fascist, democratic government, a parliamentary, democratic republic with all democratic rights and freedoms for the people' (cited in Dennis 2000aa: 20). It also referred to the shared guilt of those Germans who failed to resist while Hitler destroyed all democratic organisations and murdered the best Germans. The KPD was not the only political party to be licensed by the Soviet military administration in 1945. The authorisation of the Social Democratic Party (SPD), the Liberal Democratic

Party (LDP) and the Christian Democratic Union (CDU), ranging from the left to the right of the political spectrum, held out promise of a plurality of political views and representation.

The suffering of Jews and Jehovah's Witnesses was recognised by the granting of the status of 'victims of fascism' and they were able to resume worship in their congregations. With Paul Merker and Leo Zimmermann among the main advocates, serious consideration was given to the restitution of Jewish property, and several *Land* administrations granted Jewish Communities financial compensation. However, the ideal of a democratic polity without religious discrimination was dealt a fatal blow by the gradual imposition of a Stalinist-type model on the Soviet Zone and GDR between 1948/49 and 1953. While the founding of the SED as a forced merger between the SPD and KPD in 1946 was a crucial step towards Stalinisation, the Soviet dictator and his East German allies were constrained by domestic and external considerations from introducing a fully-fledged Soviet administrative command system in their part of Germany. Stalin in particular was reluctant to abandon his twin-track policy of enforcing Soviet control in his zone while clinging on to the prospect of an all-German option favourable to Soviet interests.

However, once flagging hopes for the restoration of a united Germany had been dashed by the Berlin crisis of 1948/49, the Soviets and the SED leadership around Walter Ulbricht had less need for circumspection in their dealings with other political parties and institutions in their zone. At its first party conference in January 1949, the SED took the crucial step of adopting the Bolshevik model of a party based on hierarchical centralism and a uniform Marxist-Leninist ideology. Three years later, with East and West Germany more deeply embedded in their respective power blocs, Ulbricht, by now General Secretary of the SED, announced, with Stalin's approval, the start of the construction of socialism in the GDR. This entailed the collectivisation of agriculture, the elimination of private business and discrimination against the churches. The proclamation of the SED as a Marxist-Leninist party was accompanied between 1949 and 1953 by sweeping purges of the membership in order to create a disciplined and ideologically pure party more in tune with the Bolshevik model than the original KPD–SPD hybrid. Such purges typified the Stalinist terror inflicted on other Eastern European countries between 1948 and 1953. The targets of the main investigative body, the SED Central Party Control Commission, included not only former social democrats but also non-conformist communists and all those suspected of links with the 'enemy in the West'. In an atmosphere bordering on the paranoia so typical of the early Cold War, the array of suspects comprised 'Trotskyists', 'Western agents', 'cosmopolitans' and 'Zionist agents'. In 1952 and 1953, cases against agents, saboteurs and economic criminals rose sharply and the number of prison inmates mushroomed. Repression and fear precipitated flight from the republic: 182,393 left in 1952 and 331,390 in the following year (Dennis 2000a: 63).

Stalinist terror had profound implications not only for the evangelical churches and the Catholic Church but also for the small religious communities such as the Jehovah's Witnesses and the Jewish congregations. A high level of autonomy over their internal affairs and their religious faith were incompatible with the SED's political aspirations and well-entrenched hostility to religion as the opiate of the masses. Repression was particularly intense against the evangelical churches in 1952 and 1953: they were forbidden to conduct religious education in schools, politically active ministers were imprisoned and church officials dismissed. Jews, both within and outside the Communities, were affected not only by the political purges but also by the wave of virulent anti-Semitism inaugurated by Stalin towards the end of his life. A press campaign initiated in Moscow in 1947 against 'cosmopolitanism', a coded term for Jews, eventually developed into a full-scale attack on Zionism and Jews in the Soviet Union and much of Eastern Europe, culminating in the Slánský trial in Czechoslovakia in 1952 and the 'discovery' of the so-called 'Doctors' Plot' in Moscow in January 1953.

The anti-semitic campaigns in the GDR from 1950 onwards were probably orchestrated from behind the scenes by the Soviets, whose People's Commissariat of State Affairs (NKVD) and the East German Ministry of State Security kept the Jewish Communities under constant surveillance for signs of anti-communist tendencies and contacts with the West (Groehler 1995: 16; Keßler 1995: 41–42). In the first wave of persecution, leading SED functionaries such as Paul Merker, Lex Ende and Leo Bauer were removed from the party in 1950. Leo Zuckermann, who resigned from his post as head of President Wilhelm Pieck's chancellery, fled to West Berlin on 14 December 1952. Zuckermann, born in Lublin in 1908, had joined the KPD in 1927, escaped from Germany in 1933 and spent much of the Second World War in exile in Mexico City. His mother was deported to Łódź and his father to Auschwitz (Hartewig 2000: 359). All but Merker, the highest profile political victim, were of Jewish origin. Entangled in the internecine political struggles, Merker was ejected from the SED politburo in 1950 and imprisoned in December 1952. Mocked by his Stasi interrogators as 'king of the Jews', he was accused of links to an alleged American spy, the enigmatic Noel Field, and of helping American finance capital through his vigorous support for Jewish compensation and restitution claims for Jews in Germany. He was sentenced to eight years' imprisonment at a secret trial held in 1955, only to be released in the following year without having recanted (Herf 1997: 145–46, 150–51, 154–55). While Merker's fall served as a warning to those who sympathised with Jewish suffering, the fact that a non-Jew had been the chief target for prosecution, unlike in Hungary and Czechoslovakia, indicated that, with memories of the Holocaust still fresh, the SED was not insensitive to charges of overt anti-semitism.

Stalinist terror and anti-semitism drove hundreds of Jews to flee a state whose ruling party was hostile to religion and suspicious of individuals with links to Israel and American 'imperialism'. The overall fall in numbers was dramatic: from 3,800 in 1948/49 to 1,900 in 1956. The toll was heaviest between 1952 and 1953: 200 Jews left for the West in December 1952, including Leo Zuckermann, 450 by the end of January 1953, and 527 until the beginning of April 1953 (Groehler 1995: 17, 19, 23; Keßler 1995: 149; Timm 1997a: 174; Gay 2002: 222–23). With the exception of Willy Bendit, six out of the seven leaders of the Jewish Communities fled. Among them was Leo Löwenkopf, the chair of the Dresden Jewish Community, a survivor of Auschwitz and the Warsaw ghetto. Julius Meyer, the head of the GDR State Association of Jewish Communities, left after his interrogation in early January 1953 by Günter Tennert, the deputy chair of the Central Party Control Commission. He stood accused of links to Slánský and Zionists (Groehler 1995: 17, 18; Geller 2005: 173). Heinz Galinski, Meyer's co-chairman of the Jewish Community in Greater Berlin, fled to West Berlin in January 1953. Unlike his wife and mother, he had survived the Auschwitz death camp.

Why were so many Jews victims of persecution so soon after the defeat of the Third Reich and in a state ostensibly committed to anti-fascism? The answer does not lie in a visceral, biological racism, as espoused by National Socialists, but in a nexus of factors ranging from traditional socio-economic prejudice to Cold War antagonisms. The initial trigger was the importing into the GDR of Stalin's own anti-semitism and paranoia, a reflection of the overwhelming influence of the Soviet leader on his East German satellite. Stalin's prejudice, however, reinforced a widespread social bias among members of the GDR's ruling party, such as Jenny Matern and Fritz Reuter (Groehler 1995: 22–23; Herf 1997: 83; Geller 2005: 99). In October 1945, the former, a KPD member, protested against financial aid for Jews on the grounds that they were interested only in money. Reuter, the East Berlin SED cadre chief, alleged that Jews came mainly from petty-bourgeois strata and were not allied to the working class. SED antipathy sprang from another source: the purported linkage between Jews and the GDR's main Cold War adversaries, American and West German imperialism, Israel, and capitalism in general. This negativity, reinforced by the febrile security climate, found expression in a resurgence of charges of an international Jewish conspiracy (Herf 1997: 127, 158).

One way in which prejudice and phobia intertwined can be seen in the use of the term 'cosmopolitanism', which, according to an authoritative article in the SED theoretical journal *Einheit* in 1949, represented the ideal of the 'money man' and 'the most complete image of capitalist exploitation'. Its global centre was the U.S.A. (ibid.: 111–12). The word 'cosmopolitanism' reared its head again in the infamous SED document, 'Lessons from the Trial against the Slánský Conspiracy', compiled in 1952 by Hermann Matern, the head of the SED Central Party Control Commission. He attacked 'the criminal activity of Zionist organisations' allegedly working with 'American agents' to destroy the people's democracies of Eastern Europe and he accused Slánský and his co-defendants in Czechoslovakia of using 'the poison of chauvinism and cosmopolitanism ... to contaminate the workers with the most reactionary bourgeois ideology" (quoted in ibid.: 126–27).

Matern's tirades were integral to the consolidation of an anti-fascist myth that relegated the genocide of the Jews to a secondary place behind communist resistance in the hierarchy of victimhood. The issue of the victims of National Socialism had generated a lively debate in the immediate postwar period in bodies such as the Association of Victims of the Nazi Regime. Paul Merker's views on victimhood and restitution had been shaped by his war-time exile in Mexico City, where his links with Zuckermann represented a symbol of solidarity between German communists and Jews. Although a politically orthodox functionary, Merker was convinced of the justice of Jewish claims to restitution and regarded racial anti-semitism as integral to National Socialism rather than as a by-product of the class struggle.

Merker's line of argument, also supported by East German Jews such as Julius Meyer in East Berlin and Leo Löwenkopf in Dresden, was pitted against the view of communists incarcerated in concentration camps and prisons and involved in the resistance movement against the Third Reich. These communists claimed a privileged position as the main victims of National Socialist persecution and as 'fighters against fascism' in contrast, or so it was alleged, to the Jews who, while suffering grievously, had not fought against National Socialist terror. Any equivalence between political and racial or religious victims was therefore rejected (Groehler 1995: 8, 10–11). Although Ulbricht would purge some members of this group, he and other key figures in the SED, such as Hermann Matern, were in accord with the concentration camp victims' version of the fight against fascism and they saw the Holocaust and Jewish issues in terms of the class struggle and National Socialist anti-semitism as secondary to its anti-communism. Furthermore, in accordance with Marxist-Leninist tenets, the SED clung to the position of its KPD predecessor that National Socialist anti-semitism targeted the Jewish proletariat, whereas Jewish business and capitalists were suspected of a willingness to aid the NSDAP in order to secure their economic position (ibid.: 6–7, 9–10). While the bravery and sacrifices of many communists cannot be denied, the stubborn adherence of the SED and the Soviet Union to the Comintern's 1935 interpretation of fascism as a class problem endemic to capitalist society was a major obstacle to an appreciation of the Holocaust in terms of its ethnic and religious dimension. Construct socialism and establish a classless society, so it was concluded, and the vital preconditions would be created for the disappearance of anti-semitism and religion. The history of the GDR would refute this axiom.

The anti-fascist myth and its assertion of the primacy of communist suffering and resistance would persist virtually unchanged throughout the remainder of the history of the GDR, finding expression in the minor role accorded the Holocaust at the official National Warning and Memorial Sites of the GDR, such as the Buchenwald, Ravensbrück and Sachsenhausen concentration camps, as well as in history textbooks (Nimtz 1975: 206; Fox 1999: 35–36; Agethen 2002: 131–36). The myth also acted as a protective political and ideological shield against critical enquiry into the so-called 'grey areas' of history. Among the main taboos were the 10,000 SED members who, in 1954, had belonged to the NSDAP before May 1945 (Bergdorf 2009: 118), the secret protocol in the 1939 Nazi–Soviet pact, the collaboration between communist Kapos and the SS in Buchenwald, the attitudes of East Germans towards Jews during the Third Reich, and the anti-semitic phase in the formative years of the GDR. By drawing a historiographical veil over popular reactions during the Third Reich, by denying that the GDR was the legal successor to the Third Reich and by emphasising its close ties to the Soviet Union, the GDR would come to represent itself as a 'virtual' victor in the fight against National Socialist Germany. Furthermore, by locating fascism in the capitalist system, guilt and responsibility for restitution were conveniently exter-nalised, that is, transferred to the capitalist Federal Republic, which was attacked by SED propagandists as a haven for fascism and anti-semitism.

## Exhibits in a Socialist Museum?

Already decimated by the Holocaust, the remnants of East German Jewry reeled from the shock of the SED's anti-semitic campaigns. Not only did the Jewish Communities suffer a severe haemorrhaging of numbers, but they also lost expe-rienced and skilful persons and, in the case of Zuckermann, Galinski and Meyer, individuals with political influence. The overarching body, the State Association of Jewish Communities, had to be almost completely restructured as only three officials remained in the country, among them the new chair, Hermann Baden from Halle (Offenberg 1998: 108). Although the Association did not immedi-ately sever its ties with the All-German Central Council of Jews, retaining its of-ficial membership until 1963, it had been grievously wounded as a representative organ. Deprived of several able leaders, under close surveillance and heavily de-pendent on the state for material and financial aid, the Association would prove, especially after the death of Baden in 1960, to be compliant in most political and cultural areas, an observation which is also applicable to the individual Commu-nities (ibid.: 164–65).

With the exception of Chemnitz, whose board remained intact, all other re-gional Communities had to find new board members. The East Berlin Jewish Community was hit hard, losing board representatives, ordinary members and staff who had worked in its old people's and children's homes. The depletion in numbers had the incidental effect of increasing the proportion of SED members among officials. Willy Bendit, a former forced labourer, became the Community's general secretary, a position he held until 1958. A member of the SED, he was enlisted as a Stasi informer in October 1959 after several unsuccessful attempts at recruitment (Hartewig 2000: 391–92). Under Bendit, the East Berlin section of the Jewish Community of Greater Berlin separated from that in the western part of the city; however, a series of internal disputes over respective spheres of interest and authority delayed its entry into the GDR State Association until 1961.

The survival of the Jewish Communities was closely linked to the shift in So-viet and SED policy in response to the June 1953 Uprising in the GDR. Shaken by the revolt, the SED leadership was obliged to defer to the new Soviet rulers' preference for a more conciliatory attitude towards the East German population and a slowing down of the pace of revolution. With the fierce Church–state struggle abating and the regime once more anxious to display its anti-fascist credentials, the Jewish Communities came to enjoy a greater, but conditional, tolerance. Exploited by the state and performing what Bodemann has called 'ideological labor' (Bodemann 1996: 212), the emasculated Communities seemed to be little more than exhibits in a socialist museum. Membership would continue to fall and the average age to increase over the next three decades. In 1976, the Stasi's Main Department XX/4 reported that only one Jewish marriage had taken place since 1945 and the last Jewish baptism in 1968.[5] By the end of 1987, the Communities had around 350 registered members, about half of whom resided in East Berlin. The chair of the Community in Mecklenburg, Friedrich Bodo, was in his late 80s.[6] After the death of the 'red rabbi', Martin Riesenberger, in 1965, the Communities were reliant on the help of rabbis from the state socialist countries and occasionally from the West for funerals and the celebration of Jewish high holy days.

The desolate state of the Jewish cemeteries was of the utmost significance as cemeteries are a historical record of German Jewry, including the graves of many victims of the Holocaust, as well as resting places of the dead, who are to be guaranteed the eternal inviolability of their graves. With so few staff to help maintain over 130 cemeteries, the Communities were heavily dependent on financial support from the state, especially for the cemeteries in East Berlin's Schönhauser Allee and Weißensee district. The latter, opened in 1880, is one of Europe's largest Jewish cemeteries, and had as many as 115,000 graves in 1988. In 1974, Peter Kirchner, the chair of East Berlin's Jewish Community, reckoned that only about two percent of its graves could be properly maintained.[7] Desecration was a perennial problem. Among the many incidents were the desecration of forty-two graves in East Berlin in August 1969, thirty-five in Mühlhausen in May 1988 and eighteen in Potsdam two months later (Mertens 1997: 262, 264–65). Not only were the state authorities determined to suppress information about such incidents but they were also often indifferent to the significance of Jewish cemeteries. In 1986, plans were hatched to construct a new Stasi district office as well as a road bordering on wasteland in the Weißensee cemetery of the former Adass Yisroel Community. The road was intended to relieve heavy traffic congestion expected from a major housing construction programme in the Hohenschönhausen district of the capital.[8] A similar idea had been abandoned three years earlier due to a campaign organised by Johannes Hildebrandt, the minister to the evangelical congregation of the Sophienkirche (Ostmeyer 2002: 151–57). With Hildebrandt once again to the fore, aided by opposition groups around Bärbel Bohley, prominent individuals such as Stefan Heym and Western supporters, the SED and state authorities were forced to drop their plans for the road and the Stasi office.

Despite occasional internal disagreements over Jewish cultural sites and SED policy towards Israel, the eight Communities were usually acquiescent towards governmental representatives. Typical of official perceptions were the remarks, in

May 1988, of the Stasi office responsible for religious bodies: 'the overwhelming majority of the members of the Jewish Communities actively support the policy of our state and, where possible, participate in societal life ... [and they] show their positive political attitude in official declarations at major political events'.[9] The compliance of the Communities' leaders was based on a number of factors: the tenuous existence of a dwindling and senescent membership; surveillance by the Stasi, often with the cooperation of a small number of Jewish officials; a high representation of SED members; and, as Peter Kirchner freely acknowledged, various forms of financial aid from the state.[10] In the late 1980s, the latter amounted to 670,000 GDR Marks per annum for the maintenance of community life and the restoration and care of buildings and cemeteries. An additional 150,000 GDR Marks went to the Weißensee cemetery.[11]

The internal affairs of the Communities were occasionally disturbed by petty rivalries, disagreements over appointments and the observance of ritual. A serious controversy erupted in 1984/85 when three leading members, Peter Kirchner, Eugen Gollomb and Helmut Eschwege, protested against the continuation in office of Karin Mylius, the chair of the Jewish Community in Halle since 1968. She was an active member of the SED and a converted Jew. Eschwege, in a letter to Helmut Aris, President of the Association of Jewish Communities, belittled her as an 'actress'.[12] Although it had been known since the early 1980s that her father had served as a police officer during the Third Reich, Aris had tried to suppress the fact. However, under pressure from his colleagues, reinforced by the threat of a public scandal, he authorised her dismissal in September 1986.[13]

## Relations with Israel and the Question of Restitution

SED policy towards Israel, together with the related issues of victimhood and restitution, constituted the major source of tension between the party and the Jewish Communities. As the distinguished East German writer Stephan Hermlin, a Jew by origin, remarked in March 1990: 'Israel is not a state like any other. It is a state that emerged from the longest and most merciless persecution of a small people ... a phoenix arising from the blood and ashes of the most terrible massacre in history. And there is a German shadow over this state' (quoted in Timm 1997b: 166). The attitudes of individual East German Jews towards this phoenix were mixed. A considerable number of Jewish communists were animated by anti-Zionism in their opposition to Israel. As the national embodiment of Zionism, Israel was perceived as a challenge to the notion that discrimination could only be ended by the complete assimilation of Jews into socialist society (Hartewig 2000: 563). Members of the Jewish Communities were torn between their political loyalty to the state and empathy with Israel for religious, private and family reasons. This is apparent from an interview conducted with Herbert Ringer by the American writer John Dornberg at the end of the 1960s. Ringer, a member of the SED, vice-president of the Association of the Jewish Communities in the GDR and chair of the Thuringia Jewish Community, told Dornberg: 'Of course, our government's relationship with Israel is somewhat painful for us. Most of us have many relatives and friends there'. He then turned to an orthodox political position:

> But we also have many relatives and friends in the United States and the relationship of the U.S. toward the GDR is just as painful for us. After all, this is a socialist state here and Israel is still capitalist. This makes a harmonious relationship difficult. We must be realistic and support the policies of our government. At least it is not as hypocritical as West Germany's which supplied military equipment to Israel. (Dornberg 1969: 302)

Except for two short periods, at the beginning and towards the end of SED rule, relations between the party and Israel were characterised by mutual suspicion and hostility. The initial honeymoon was determined largely by Moscow's interest in extending its influence in the Middle East through the establishment of a 'progressive' Jewish state in Palestine. A subordinate SED fell into line behind the Soviet Union, backing the decision of the United Nations (UN) in November 1947 to divide Palestine between an Arab and a Jewish state and publishing favourable comments by Wilhelm Pieck and Andrej Gromyko on the creation of the latter.[14] Relations between the two new states, Israel and the GDR, soon deteriorated under the impact of the anti-semitic campaigns of the early 1950s, finally collapsing in the wake of the joint Israeli, British and French attack on Egypt in 1956. With the replication in the Middle East of Cold War divisions in Europe, the GDR, which was fiercely critical of Israel as an outpost of aggressive imperialism, drew closer to Egypt and other Arab countries. East Germany also supplied foodstuffs as well as military and economic assistance to the Palestinian Liberation Organisation (PLO) in its resistance to partition, especially after Yasser Arafat became chair of the movement in 1969. However, not until then did the GDR manage to secure the important breakthrough of diplomatic recognition from Egypt, Iraq, Syria, the Sudan and South Yemen, thereby reducing its international isolation among non-socialist states (Timm 1997a: 271, 275, 278–79).

East German hostility towards Israel as a Trojan horse of imperialism in the Middle East culminated in a resurgence of anti-Zionism and one-sided criticism of Israel for its actions in the Six Day War in June 1967, the Yom Kippur War in 1973 and the invasion of Lebanon nine years later. As part of the overall campaign against Israel in 1967, the SED politburo attempted to mobilise the Jews of East Germany behind the 'Declaration of GDR Citizens of Jewish Faith' that condemned the 'aggression of Israel' and likened the creation of Israel to 'a breach of promise and annexation' (Timm 1997b: 61). Although the resolution was drafted by the politburo member Albert Norden, neither he nor Axen, both Jews, signed the document. Of the ten Jewish signatories, among them Lea Grundig and Franz Loeser, none belonged to a Jewish Community. Moreover, the Declaration pushed the normally compliant Community leaders, such as Aris and Ringer, into criticism of the GDR's failure to acknowledge the Arab threat to Israel's security and they warned of the danger of provoking popular anti-semitism by the negative portrayal of Israel and Jews in the East German press (Offenberg 1998: 202–3). A line had been drawn under the limits to which the Communities were prepared, at least in private, to be instrumentalised.

In the run-up to the outbreak of the Yom Kippur War in October 1973, the SED sought once more to obtain an unequivocal denunciation of Israel. At a crucial meeting at the end of January 1973 between officials of the State Secretariat for Church Affairs and the heads of the Jewish Communities, the combative chair of the Leipzig Israelite Community, Eugen Gollomb, insisted that Israel was entitled to secure its citizens against provocation.[15] The ultra-loyalist Karin Mylius was the only chairperson to toe the party line on the situation in the Middle East, maintaining that the class question took precedence over that of the nation and that socialist states should help Arab countries against the Israeli imperialists.[16] In her summary of the discussion, Barbara Janott of the State Secretariat for Church Affairs concluded that most Community chairs regarded themselves first and foremost as Jews and only secondly as GDR citizens. Israel was viewed primarily as a Jewish state, which provided refuge for, and represented the interests of, co-religionists and relatives.[17]

The Jewish Communities also clashed with the SED interpretation of Zionism when, after the outbreak of the Six Day War, the Soviet Union, with the GDR in full support, revived the odious anti-Zionism of the early 1950s. The SED notion of Zionism was summed up in an internal document compiled by the State Secretariat for Church Affairs in 1972 as a 'reactionary-nationalist ideology of the Jewish Big Bourgeosie' and as an ally of imperialism in the struggle against communism (quoted in Timm 1997a: 248). Three years later, the GDR voted in favour of the UN resolution condemning Zionism as 'a form of racism and racial discrimination' (ibid.: 251–52). This interpretation was propagated by the East German media, with the teachers' organ, the *Deutsche Lehrerzeitung*, asserting that: 'There is a common ideological platform between Zionism and fascism. It is racism' (ibid.: 253). When the UN resolution was discussed at a private meeting between the State Secretary for Church Affairs, Hans Seigewasser, and the chairs of the Jewish Communities in March 1976, Eugen Gollomb was, as usual, outspoken in his criticism. Denouncing the resolution as shameful, he reminded his audience that Gromyko had stated before the UN in 1947 and 1948 that the Jewish people had suffered more in the Second World War than any other people and thus enjoyed a special relationship with Palestine. To the discomfort of state officials, Gollomb averred: 'No Zionist could have formulated this better'.[18]

The GDR's official hostility towards Israel continued well into the 1980s. The Israeli invasion of Lebanon in 1982 was denounced by the government as Israel's fifth war against the Arab states. This was bolstered by the National People's Army magazine, *Volksarmee*, which published a lengthy article in August 1982 likening Israeli aggression against the Palestinian and Lebanese people to the crimes of German fascism in the Second World War and those of American imperialism against Vietnam. Protests were lodged in private by Aris, Kirchner and other members of the Jewish Communities against the equivalence of Israeli actions in Lebanon and 'the imperialist aggression of fascist Germany' (ibid.: 284, 287). One obnoxious cartoon, which appeared in the *Berliner Zeitung* on 10 December 1985, was sharply criticised by Kirchner in a letter to Karschack, the newspaper's editor-in-chief, for depicting an Israeli officer with the kind of nose found in cartoons in Gauleiter Julius Streicher's semi-official National Socialist broadsheet *Der Stürmer*.[19]

SED relations with East German Jews and Israel were also bedevilled by the highly complex legal, political and moral issue of restitution and compensation for Jewish victims of the Holocaust. Some modest progress had been made towards a solution in the immediate postwar years. As indicated earlier, Paul Merker and Leo Zuckermann emerged as powerful advocates of restitution and Saxony-Anhalt and several other *Land* administrations in the Soviet Zone provided Jewish Communities with some financial compensation. Without regaining full possession in law, Communities were also given use of some former communal property, mainly cemeteries, synagogues and offices. Berlin, under the occupation of the four Allied powers, proved to be an intractable problem (see Meng 2005: 618–20). Plans for a comprehensive restitution were terminated by the division of the city in the wake of the Berlin blockade and by the anti-Zionism of the early 1950s. With the SED adopting a hard line on restitution, an unsatisfactory compromise was reached in 1958. The East Berlin municipal authority (*Magistrat*) allowed some Jewish property, mainly that of individuals, to be returned to those currently holding legal rights to it. Although the *Magistrat* was anxious to divest itself of the financial burden of administering the holdings, it retained control over the East Berlin Jewish Community's property with the exception of the cemetery in Weißensee and four other objects, which the Community was permitted to use as if it were the owner.

While the Jewish Communities had little option but to acquiesce in these arrangements, the SED came under considerable external pressure from Israel and Jewish agencies such as the Conference on Jewish Material Claims. The latter, an umbrella organisation for Holocaust survivors outside Israel, included the World Jewish Congress and the American Jewish Committee. Dealings between the GDR and Israel were normally conducted through intermediaries as the two states did not formally recognise each other. In 1952, the Luxemburg Agreement between Israel and the FRG put added pressure on the SED. The Agreement committed the West German government to pay DM 3 billion to Israel for the social integration of about 500,000 Jews living in Palestine and Israel and DM 450 million to the Conference on Jewish Material Claims outside Israel. The GDR, however, refused to make a contribution, contending that the Agreement boosted capitalist profit and the expansion of the Israeli army. The GDR felt obliged to modify its rigid stance after the establishment of diplomatic relations with Western powers in the early 1970s, most notably the offer in 1976 of a one-off grant of $1 million for American Jews who were victims of National Socialism. The Claims Conference returned the cheque: not only was the sum deemed inadequate but the Conference also suspected, correctly, that the GDR was hoping to use the offer to terminate the whole claims issue (Timms 1997b: 109–11).

The SED case against a comprehensive restitution package rested on a series of arguments that changed little over four decades. The GDR, so it was asserted, had fulfilled its liabilities for the damage wrought by National Socialism as it had paid reparations to the USSR and Poland in accordance with the Potsdam Agreement. In fact, as the SED well knew, the issue of restitution and compensation had not been resolved at Potsdam. Other specious arguments were advanced. As Israel was located in the imperialist camp and therefore belonged to the 'Western reparations circle', it should, according to the Potsdam Agreement, be paid from what had been the three Western zones of occupation. It was even contended that as Israel had not been at war with National Socialist Germany, it had no right to reparations and to represent Holocaust survivors. Furthermore, SED propagandists repeatedly asserted that compensation for Jewish citizens, some of whom were capitalists, would undermine the public ownership of the means of production, and thereby put at risk the foundations of the socialist system which had destroyed the preconditions for fascism and racism. Finally, the SED repeatedly asserted that all victims of fascism in the GDR, including Jews, were guaranteed a secure livelihood and above-average pensions (Timm 1997a: 131; Timm 1997b: 72, 85, 91–92). This social paternalism struck a responsive chord among many East German Jews. For example, Siegmund Rotstein, the President of the Association of Jewish Communities, stated before a specially invited audience in November 1988 that people of Jewish faith in the GDR, 'are respected, enjoy material security and [the] care of our society' (Association of Jewish Communities 1988: 37).

Not until the late 1980s did some progress take place on the restitution issue. The GDR's pragmatic desire to improve its international image as a means of securing trade benefits from the U.S.A. was linked to negotiations with American and Jewish agencies on the settlement of Jewish claims in a so-called package deal. In June 1988, Honecker gave Galinski, the President of the Central Council of Jews in Germany, to understand that the GDR would consider compensation ranging from $10 million to $100 million. Galinski, who had fled the GDR in 1953, regarded this as an indication of a 'fundamental willingness' to make concessions on Jewish compensation claims. His optimism was not shared by the Executive Director of the Claims Conference, Saul Kagan, who, together with a colleague, Rabbi Israel Miller, had led discussions with the GDR (Mertens 1997: 283; Timm 1997b, 133, 148). The visit to the United States by Hermann Axen in May 1988 justified Kagan's scepticism. Not only did Axen stress that the GDR was unwilling to meet the Conference on Jewish Material Claims ''s demand for the minimum payment of $100 million but his address to the American Institute for Contemporary German Affairs resonated with the traditional commitment to 'red assimilation' of a veteran Jewish communist. He made it clear that, as the sole survivor of the Holocaust from his immediate family, he prioritised the building of an anti-fascist, socialist state. With the GDR unwilling to make major concessions on compensation and human rights, negotiations on the package deal collapsed in September 1988 (Timm 1997b: 137–43; Meining 2002: 453). Besides ideological and political factors, the SED was reluctant to open up the complex of compensation issues for legal and financial reasons. This is apparent from a report compiled in 1988 by the Office of Legal Protection (*Amt für Rechtsschutz*), which anticipated that Israel would probably seek a lump sum for the possessions of murdered German Jews. Other likely demands were compensation for the assets of former German Jews living in Israel as well as Jewish property seized by the National Socialists and later transferred into state or private ownership in the GDR (Meining 2002: 353).

## Collaborating with the Stasi

Despite the relaxation of persecution after 1953 and their general compliance, the Jewish Communities became the focus of what Karin Hartewig has called 'preventive investigation' by the SED (Hartewig 2000: 390). This reflected the aim of the SED and Stasi to control by stealth and pre-emptive action those religious groups such as the Jewish Communities and evangelical churches to which they had an aversion on account of a certain degree of organisational autonomy and a set of values which did not accord with the political faith of Marxism-Leninism. In addition, the Jewish Communities were perceived as a security risk on account of their links with Western 'imperialism' and personal contacts with Israel. Such links, it was suspected, might serve as conduits to undermine socialist society by what the MfS called 'political-ideological subversion'. As a result, the affairs of the Communities were subject to interference and steering by the State Secretariat for Church Affairs, the SED Central Committee's Working Group for Church Affairs and the Stasi. As with the Protestant churches and Jehovah's Witnesses, Main Department XX/4 was the Stasi unit primarily responsible for the control and surveillance of the Jewish Communities.[20] Other groups were also involved. Main Department II, for example, kept watch over Western visitors to the Jewish Communities.

As was its practice with the evangelical churches and other religious groups, the Stasi recruited unofficial informers (IMs) from among members of the Jewish Communities to try and influence decisions and provide a wide range of information on internal affairs. Although it is impossible to determine the exact number of IMs among the Jewish Communities, most were run by the Stasi's regional and district offices. Helmut Aris (Dresden) in 1954, Hans Levy (Magdeburg) in 1956, Heinz Schenk (East Berlin) in 1960 and Willy Bendit (Association of Jewish Communities) in 1959 were some of the senior figures recruited by the Stasi. Among other informers were Dr Peter Fischer, who became the secretary of the Association of Jewish Communities in the GDR in April 1989, Dr Peter Kirchner, the chair of the capital's Community since 1971, and two members of its board of directors, Dr Werner Zarrach and Dr Irene Runge. The latter, a co-founder of the 'We for Ourselves' group (*Wir für uns*), collaborated with the

Stasi between 1962 and 1966 and again, between 1971 and 1985, after she had come under observation as part of a Stasi operation.[21] Her main area of work for the MfS concerned the non-conformist cultural scene, journalists and foreign contacts rather than simply Jewish matters (Offenberg 1998: 161).

As the Stasi was central to the repressive nature of the SED dictatorship, some commentators, above all Michael Wolffsohn, incline to a blanket condemnation of the GDR. Collaboration is judged as a pact with a system blighted by anti-semitism, a testament to its endemic corruption, and the expression of an individual's political or career opportunism (Wolffsohn 1995; 1998: 117–64). As is discussed below, this exaggerates the political reach of the Stasi and it oversimpli-fies both the complexity of the political situation and the personal biographies of members of the Jewish Communities. The motives and functions of Stasi agents varied considerably not only between individuals but also, not infrequently, over the course of a collaboration. In terms of function, some agents simply put their apartment or telephone at the disposal of the Stasi, whereas others were employed to subvert and destroy their targets. Although individual motives are difficult to reconstruct from the Stasi files and post-unification interviews, material and ca-reer advantages as well as psychological pressure were among the most common reasons for collaboration. For some, including Jewish Community officials, the Stasi was seen as an extension of the state and a means of achieving group goals.

Helmut Aris became a secret informer (known as 'Launus') in 1954, when he was a member of the board of the Jewish Community of Dresden. Although Aris's file indicates that he was recruited out of political conviction, the Stasi ended the contact after only two years as he frequently failed to keep appoint-ments and provide operationally relevant information (Wolffsohn 1995: 88; Of-fenberg 1998: 162–63). One of the Stasi's main collaborators in the Honecker era was Dr Peter Kirchner. A neurologist and psychiatrist, Kirchner was born in Berlin in 1935 to a Jewish mother and a Christian father. He was originally attracted to the GDR by its democratic and anti-fascist potential, which, as he admitted after German unification, proved to be an illusion (Eckhardt and Na-chama 2003: 155–56). Kirchner, known as 'Burg', was registered as an IM in 1977, and then as a higher-category agent (IMB) in December 1980; he was still cooperating with the Stasi as late as autumn 1989. As head of East Berlin's Jewish Community, Kirchner was an invaluable source, supplying the Stasi with details of the international contacts and internal affairs of the most important Jewish group in the GDR (Wolffsohn 1995: 96–98; Wolffsohn 1998: 152–53; Offen-berg 1998: 159–60). Although the state authorities regarded him as a 'reliable' official,[22] he was kept under observation in connection with his travels abroad as a representative of the Community. Another reason for surveillance was that his views sometimes strayed from the party line, especially on Israel. One example concerns the refusal of party officials to allow him to present a paper to a meet-ing of the Peace Council of the Foreign Information Department held in the GDR in 1978. It was known that he intended to raise Israel's need for security on account of the past persecution of Jews (Illichmann 1997: 235). As with so many IMs, Kirchner's precise motivation is difficult to determine. His remarks in an interview with Robin Ostow in January 1991 perhaps offer a clue. It was necessary, he argued, for Jewish Community officials to reach some form of arrangement with the state in order to ensure its survival (Ostow 1996: 22). While cooperation with the State Secretariat for Church Affairs was both legitimate and essential, after the end of SED rule Kirchner regrettably failed to address directly and openly the issue of his collaboration with the MfS.

Dr Peter Fischer cooperated, though not unproblematically, for many years as an IM. He became secretary of the Association of Jewish Communities in the GDR in 1989 and leader of the Berlin branch of the Central Council of Jews in Germany one year later. Fischer was born in London in 1944 to a Jewish mother, who was the only member of her family to survive the Holocaust. His father, a KPD functionary during the Weimar Republic, was imprisoned by the Nazis in the Lichtenberg concentration camp in Berlin (Wroblewsky 2001: 67–68). Although Fischer claimed that the Stasi left him alone after his refusal in 1973 to inform on Wolf Biermann, a dissident artist and son of a Jewish communist father (ibid.: 70), he worked for Main Department II as an IM, known as 'René', from 1969 to 1974. Despite numerous problems over issues such as East German policy towards Israel and the surveillance of Biermann, he resumed his collaboration with the ministry, as an IMS known as 'Frank', between August 1987 and December 1989 (Offenberg 1998: 163; Wolffsohn 1998: 156–59).

The career of Helmut Eschwege (1913–1992) and his cooperation with the Stasi also sheds light on some of the intricacies of collaboration: he was both an agent and a target of the MfS and was motivated by personal advantage as well as altruism. Born to Jewish parents in Hanover, Eschwege emigrated to Palestine in 1937, became a civilian worker in the British army, and returned to Germany – to the Soviet Zone of Occupation – as a committed communist in 1946 (Eschwege 1991: 46, 53–54). A self-confessed *enfant terrible*, he was thrown out of the SED in 1953 for his criticism of anti-semitism in Czechoslovakia and the GDR. Although the ejection was commuted to an official reprimand in 1954, this was not the end of his problems. Put under observation by the Stasi in 1953, his mail was intercepted and his views and movements tracked by secret agents (Meining 2002: 207–8). Undeterred, he was active in the Dresden Jewish Community and, though denied an academic post, conducted research from the mid 1950s onwards into the persecution and history of the Jews in Germany. One of his most notable publications consisted of documents, pictures and reports of National Socialist crimes against Germany's Jews (Eschwege 1966). Its publication owed much to his determination to overcome countless political and bureaucratic obstacles (Eschwege 1991: 184–211). Subsequently, he bombarded the authorities with requests for access to archival materials on topics such as Jewish cemeteries and synagogues, but was unable to find a publisher in the GDR for a major study of Jewish resistance during the Third Reich as this broke an ideological taboo. The book finally appeared in the West in 1984 (Eschwege 1984 ; see also Maser 2003: 21).

Eschwege was an active member of several autonomous Christian–Jewish groups founded in Dresden, Leipzig, East Berlin and elsewhere in the 1970s and 1980s. The Stasi, suspicious of this dialogue, his many contacts in the West and his criticism of SED policy towards Israel, launched an operational case against him in 1982 (OV 'Zionist'). Organised by the Dresden Regional Administration, Eschwege's mail was intercepted, his room searched and unofficial collaborators, such as IMB 'Meißner', informed on him. While the MfS was convinced that Eschwege was an anti-communist and 'enemy' of the GDR, it failed to uncover evidence of criminal activity and closed the case in 1984.[23] However, though Eschwege was happy to refer in his 1991 autobiography to his clashes with the SED and his frequent conversations with what he described as his long-standing Stasi 'minder', his death in 1992 spared him from having to confront in public his work as an informer and so blemish the high reputation he otherwise deservedly enjoyed in the West for his research on Jewish history and engagement in dialogue with the evangelical churches.[24] He collaborated with the Stasi as GI 'Bock' between 1956 and 1958, and then again, as IMS 'Ferdinand', from November 1985 to mid November 1989. In November 1967, his unsolicited offer to serve as an agent was rejected by the MfS. During his first period as an informer, he produced reports on leading Jewish officials, including contacts made during a visit to Israel in 1957. The MfS also hoped he would be able to induce his close friend Leo Löwenkopf to return to the GDR. Löwenkopf, the former chair of Dresden's Jewish Community and president of Saxony's central bank, had fled to West Germany in 1953. The failure to achieve this aim was one of the reasons for the Stasi's termination of its work with Eschwege. Other factors included Eschwege's neglect of his other tasks and, to the annoyance of the local party, his open criticism of the SED.

When the Stasi's Dresden Regional Administration recruited Eschwege once more, in the mid 1980s, IMS 'Ferdinand' was required to provide information about colleagues in the Jewish Communities, the 'Encounter with Judaism' circle and his personal contacts in Israel and the U.S.A. The ministry, distrustful as ever, used agents such as IMS 'Sylvia Lüders' to provide feedback on his views (Meining 2002: 235). In his regular and full reports, Eschwege was not sparing in his criticism of certain colleagues, especially the party-loyalist Karin Mylius, the chair of the Halle Jewish Community since 1968, Helmut Aris, the President of the Association of Jewish Communities in the GDR, and the latter's successor, Siegmund Rotstein. It should be mentioned that he was not averse to criticising these three in Jewish circles too. He regarded Rotstein as unsuitable for the position as, in his opinion, he had a poor knowledge of religious matters.[25] Eschwege was still working for the Stasi on the eve of the collapse of SED rule. At his last meeting with his controlling officer, on 15 November 1989, he handed over the statute of the embryonic Social Democratic Party, while making no secret of his intention to join the party.

Assessments of Eschwege's collaboration with the Stasi tend to differ on one crucial point. While acknowledging Eschwege's harsh criticism of colleagues and the regularity of his detailed reports on the Communities' internal affairs, Joachim Käppner's reading of the Stasi records of Eschwege's meetings with his controllers persuade him that the informer's comments were not seriously damaging to others (Käppner 1999: 270–71). This perhaps errs on the side of generosity for, as Stefan Meining observes, Eschwege spied unscrupulously on his associates and failed after the collapse of the GDR to admit to his collaboration (Meining 2002: 238). Yet, as with Aris, whom Eschwege accused in his memoir of fostering a personality cult (Eschwege 1991: 10), collaboration between informer and controller did not always run smoothly and like adroit individuals such as Manfred Stolpe, the top lay official of the evangelical churches, he tried to use the ministry for his own purpose. Karin Hartewig suggests that Eschwege might have used his Stasi links to shield himself against the consequences of his criticism of the GDR and the SED and, secondly, as a lever in his persistent struggle against a fossilised party and state bureaucracy in the hope that the GDR might become a springboard for a democratic socialism (Hartewig 2000: 193–94). Furthermore, and perhaps above all, as an academic outsider and an indefatigable researcher, his Stasi connections were potentially useful in helping him gain access to materials in GDR archives as part of his study of Jewish history, in particular the Holocaust (Käppner 1999: 263–71). This aspiration is yet one more illustration of a cat-and-mouse game involving Eschwege, the SED and the Stasi. But, as with other informers, the MfS usually held most of the trump cards, keeping Eschwege under constant observation.

## Reinvigorating the Jewish Communities in the 1980s

The Stasi interest in Eschwege in the 1980s was partly related to his efforts to reinvigorate Jewish culture in the GDR at a time when the microscopic Jewish Communities were in danger of extinction. Their parlous condition was highlighted in a speech given in March 1982 by the State Secretary for Church Affairs. According to Gysi, the Communities had a mere 465 members, with only six under twenty-five years of age.[26] Whereas the SED leadership had seemed intent in the early 1950s on the destruction of East German Jewry, over thirty years later it embarked on a philo-semitic course, with Gysi as its main advocate and helmsman. Political and economic pragmatism motivated Honecker and other senior party figures. Eager to instrumentalise the Communities to boost the GDR's legitimacy as an anti-fascist state and to improve relations with the U.S.A. and Israel, they could ill afford to allow the Jewish organisations to wither away.

Action followed soon after the presentation of a paper by the State Secretariat for Church Affairs to politburo member Werner Jarowinsky in August 1986. Jarowinsky was Central Committee Secretary for Trade, Consumer Supplies and Church Affairs. The Communities, it was proposed, should be given greater financial and material support and Jewish history incorporated into the broad cultural heritage and traditions of the GDR.[27] New ideas on the latter had been gathering pace since the late 1970s as part of a general reassessment of the historical legitimation of the GDR and the simplistic dichotomy between the GDR and the FRG. Whereas the GDR had been associated with the progressive traditions of Müntzer, Marx and Thälmann, the FRG had been depicted as the embodiment of the reactionary traditions of Luther, Bismarck and Hitler in German history. Party historians were now encouraged to devise a less selective picture of the past and to place the GDR within the broad sweep of German history without severing the umbilical cord to its traditional socialist precursors. The most striking development was the embellishment of Luther's image and a more differentiated interpretation of Prussian history. Rather than being a pivotal link in Germany's 'chain of misery', historians unveiled new 'progressive' elements in Hohenzollern Prussia, for instance, Frederick II's contribution to social progress (Dennis 1988: 3–7).

There were significant implications, too, for the history of Germany's Jews-. On the eve of the fall of the Berlin Wall, one of the main contributors to the heritage debate, Professor Walter Schmidt, Director of the Academy of Sciences' Central Institute of History, identified some of the deficiencies in previous GDR histories of German Jewry: the lack of work on German Jews' contribution to science and culture; the failure to do justice to the suffering of millions of Jews during the fascist era; and the disproportionate attention paid to the anti-fascist struggle of the 'revolutionary working class movement'. Schmidt also broached another sensitive issue: the failure of most Germans to assist the Jews and their disastrous passivity and culpabilility during the National Socialist era (Schmidt 1989). Such lacunae had, as Schmidt admitted, tended to characterise the work of GDR social scientists and historians; in contrast, film, art and literature had been more active in exploring and raising public awareness of the persecution and annihilation of the Jews (ibid.: 696). Jurek Becker, Stefan Heym, Günter Kunert, Stephan Hermlin and Johannes Bobrowksi were among writers who had done so, without, as Thomas Fox has pointed out, dismantling the standard anti-fascist myth (Fox 1999: 138–40).

The reappraisal of the history of Germany's Jews and plans for a revival of the Jewish Communities were primarily a consequence of the growing enfeeblement of the SED state and the palpable artificiality of Honecker's attempt to generate a popular consciousness of the GDR as a socialist nation separate from that of the capitalist nation of the FRG. Faltering economic performance and a rising hard currency deficit caused alarm bells to ring in the politburo and the State Planning Commission, prompting the SED to explore ways of attaining Most Favoured Nation (MFN) trading status with the U.S.A. While trade between the U.S.A. and the GDR remained modest throughout the 1980s, recognition of MFN status would at least help relieve some pressure on the GDR trade deficit with capitalist countries as it would lead to the lifting of the 30 to 40 per cent customs duties on imports into the U.S.A. However, by late 1988 hopes for the granting of MFN status and an invitation for Honecker to visit Washington, following on from those issued to the West German and French capitals, were dashed by American disapproval of the GDR's human rights record, the SED's obstructive approach to compensation for Jewish victims of National Socialism and the party's antagonism towards Israel.

In the meantime, with the backing of Honecker, Gysi's office had assembled the basic components of the new policy towards the Jewish Communities and Jewish culture: the establishment of a Centrum Judaicum and the restoration of parts of the New Synagogue in East Berlin; additional state funding for Jewish sites; the appointment of a rabbi from the U.S.A.; a cautious reappraisal of Jewish restitution claims and ownership of property administered by the Communities; the lifting of some restrictions on access to Jewish archival materials held by the state; the revival of the synagogue community Adass Yisroel; and the elaborate state-managed commemoration of the fiftieth anniversary of Crystal Night. State and party bodies had different levels of interest in this policy shift (Hartewig 2000: 380, 603–7, 610; Dennis 2003 with LaPorte: 150–51). While Honecker was primarily motivated by foreign policy and economic considerations, Gysi was more committed to the revitalisation of Jewish culture and institutions. As the servant of the ruling party, the MfS had to adjust to the new line, even though it continued to regard East German Jews as conduits of Western subversion. Not only did the continued use of terms such as 'Zionism' and 'World Jewry' underscore the ministry's ideological conservatism, they also testified to the persistence of a latent prejudice against the few Jews in its employment (Brehmer 1991: 25, 27).

Not all initiatives to revive Jewish life and culture took place within the orbit of party and state. There was also a modest popular basis. The 1970s and 1980s witnessed efforts by Action for Atonement (*Aktion Sühnezeichen*) and the Work Group Church and Judaism to build on an earlier tentative Christian–Jewish dialogue (Maser 1989: 162; Ostmeyer 2002: 214–21, 230–33, 296; Meng 2005: 628–29). Among the leading figures in Leipzig were pastor Siegfried Theodor Arndt, who became chair of the Work Group Church and Judaism in 1972, and Eugen Gollomb of the Leipzig Israelite Religious Community. Helmut Eschwege from Dresden was also active in the group's programme, which included the co-ordination of Jewish–Christian work in the GDR, lectures on Jewish themes and protests against negative reports about Israel in the official GDR press. During the 1980s, the annual meetings in Leipzig attracted an increasing number of visitors from abroad and groups were also established in East Berlin, Magdeburg and Rostock. An East Berlin group was founded in December 1975, partly to protest against the UN resolution on Zionism. The minister of the small congregation of the Sophienkirche, Johannes Hildebrandt, the group's pivotal figure, cooperated closely with the chair of the Jewish Community, Peter Kirchner. Numbers increased steadily from about 400 registered participants in 1985 to about 500 three years later.

Dresden was another important location for Christian–Jewish understanding. On the suggestion of Helmut Eschwege, the Encounter with Judaism circle was founded there in 1982. Open to all interested individuals, it emphasised encounter rather than just dialogue. On average, about 300, mainly young, people attended the bi-monthly events. These encounters and the dialogue between Christians and Jews were underpinned by the evangelical churches' willingness to take a more critical look at their role in the Holocaust and by their support for the efforts of Action for Atonement to preserve some Jewish sites. Founded at the 1958 synod of the Evangelical Churches in Germany as a joint East–West organisation, the group aimed to atone for the sins of the National Socialists. In addition to organising summer camps and arranging voluntary help for the upkeep of Jewish cemeteries in the GDR, it sought to fill in some of the gaps in knowledge about Germany's Jews by providing information about Crystal Night, Jewish culture and related themes.

The establishment of links between the East Berlin Jewish Community and the 'We for Ourselves' group (*Wir für uns*) held out further promise for the reinvigoration of Jewish life. Formed in 1984, the group's main appeal was to children of communist parents, including the daughter of Hermann Axen, with a keen interest in exploring Jewish culture and traditions and their own Jewish origins and identity. Partly to broaden its base, East Berlin's Jewish Community sought to cater for this interest by organising a meeting in May 1986 for non-members with a Jewish background. Subsequent events regarding Jewish history and culture attracted between sixty and one hundred members of 'We for Ourselves' (Ostow 1989: 52; Mertens 1997: 204–5; Offenberg 1998: 217–18). State and party bodies welcomed this development as it fitted into the goal of resuscitating the Communities.[28] However, few participants in 'We for Ourselves' desired to join the East Berlin Jewish Community on account of the strict religious criteria for membership. These included the Halacha requirements of a Jewish mother and circumcision for males. Tensions arose, according to one of its members, Vincent von Wroblewsky, because of the perceived threat posed to the conservative and ageing membership by a younger and more dynamic element (Wroblewsky 2001: 157).

## An American in Berlin

Differences between orthodoxy and reform would undermine the work of a new rabbi in East Berlin, Isaac Neuman. When he was inaugurated in 1987, he became the first rabbi for more than twenty years to occupy the post permanently. His appointment was the outcome of an improvement in relations between the GDR and the U.S.A. and Gysi's plans for nurturing Jewish culture. The American Jewish Committee, which had undertaken the responsibility for the recruitment of a rabbi, found only one candidate, Neuman, the recently retired rabbi of a Reform Synagogue in Champaign, Illinois. The sexagenarian, a Pole by birth and a German speaker, had lost both parents and seven brothers and sisters in the Holocaust. A survivor of Auschwitz and Mauthausen, he emigrated to the U.S.A. in 1950. Neither the MfS nor the Central Committee Working Group for

Church Affairs had been keen on a rabbi from the U.S.A. or West Berlin, regarding such a move as politically questionable.[29] Gysi, on the other hand, anxious to set the seal on an agreement, assured Honecker in June 1986 that an appointment would provide the GDR with a lobby in the U.S.A. (Mertens 1997: 174; Offenberg 1998: 214; Meining 2002: 438–39).

Neuman assumed his duties three months after his inauguration as the rabbi of the Jewish Community of East Berlin in September 1987. His approach fitted in with the overall goal of reinvigoration. He was eager to instruct children as well as adults in Hebrew and Judaism and to reach out to non-members. However, in seeking to implement radical changes, such as equality between women and men in religious services, he ran into opposition from Kirchner, Simon and other Community officials as well as the elderly members.[30] An already difficult relationship was exacerbated by disputes over Neuman's official responsibilities, his alleged neglect of pastoral duties, personal animosity with Kirchner, and his unconventional behaviour, as encapsulated in his nickname the 'Hollywood rabbi'.[31] His brief stay in the GDR ended in open and mutual recriminations, including the charge by Neuman of anti-semitic traits in GDR policy towards Israel and the demonisation of Jews in newspapers.[32] After submitting his formal resignation in May 1988, he returned to the United States engaged to Eva Grünberg, the divorced daughter of a former Deputy Minister of the Interior, Herbert Grünstein. For both father and daughter, their Jewish descent was of no practical or emotional significance.[33] The lack of a suitable successor and the fiasco of Neuman's tenure meant that he was not replaced, even though the State Secretariat for Church Affairs and the Association of Jewish Communities in the GDR were willing to try again.

## The Israelite Synagogue Community Adass Yisroel

One of the most curious offshoots of the shift in SED policy was the re-emergence of the Orthodox Israelite synagogue community Adass Yisroel. Founded in Berlin in 1869 as a counter to the dominant Liberal movement, its property was seized and the organisation dissolved by the National Socialists in 1939. After the end of the Second World War, the decimated Community, although continuing to exist *de jure*, was unable to resume its activities. Its property, including the cemetery in the Wittlicher Straße, passed into state hands and was cared for by the East Berlin Jewish Community. After the retirement of its caretaker in 1974, the cemetery became a target for vandals (Illichmann 1997: 273; Mertens 1997: 345; Gay 2002: 239, 241). Little changed until the mid 1980s when, in June 1986, the site was officially recognised as a cultural monument; two years later, it was reopened as a cemetery. This development owed much to the tenacity and skill of Mario Offenberg who, together with his father Ari, aspired to revive the former Adass Yisroel Community. The younger Offenberg had grown up in Israel before moving to West Berlin, where he joined the city's left-wing intellectual milieu and embraced anti-Zionism. By the mid 1980s he had returned to the religious traditions of his family and devoted himself to the creation of a viable Adass Yisroel in the East German capital. From his base in West Berlin, he inundated Honecker and GDR officials with demands and complaints. He had chosen his moment well. Honecker was eager to improve the GDR's international reputation, a goal that Gysi believed could be advanced through links with Adass Yisroel which, though tiny, was believed to enjoy considerable influence in the U.S.A. and Israel.[34]

Once the issue of the reopening of the cemetery had been settled, a tug of war developed over Offenberg's more ambitious plans, unveiled in February 1988: the formal recognition and reconstitution of Adass Yisroel in the GDR and the return of the Community's rights and power of disposition over the property confiscated by the National Socialists. In order to help him realise these aims, Offenberg drew on the Society for the Advancement of Adass Yisroel. Located in West Berlin, it had been set up, on Offenberg's initiative, by congregationalists during their visit to the cemetery in East Berlin in 1986. Although they authorised Offenberg to negotiate on their behalf, neither the West Berlin Senate nor the Jewish Community in the West accepted the Society as a legitimate representative of the old Community (Gay 2002: 245). On balance, the State Secretariat for Church Affairs under Klaus Gysi was more sympathetic to the reconstitution of Adass Yisroel and the return of some property than Bellmann's SED Central Committee Working Group for Church Affairs. Gysi envisaged that such a move would benefit the GDR internationally and put a stop to what he described as Offenberg's 'hysterical telegrams'. He hoped, too, that it would forestall accusations of a second expropriation – by communists.[35] Honecker was also well disposed, informing Offenberg in writing on 27 June 1988 that he had instructed Gysi to devise a feasible solution. The SED leader repeated this assurance on 8 November, at a time when the SED was anxious to create a favourable impression in connection with the commemoration of Crystal Night. Before invited guests from home and abroad, he personally told a delegation of Adass Yisroel in Berlin and the chief rabbi from Jerusalem that the Community would recover all its rights.[36]

Honecker's assurances notwithstanding, many obstacles remained, in particular what Gysi called the 'small time bomb' of the restitution of Jewish Community property in East Berlin. First, as Gysi informed Honecker in January 1988, while the GDR denied that it was the legal successor to National Socialist Germany as regards Jewish property seized in East Berlin, 'we invoke *de facto* this legal succession'.[37] Comparison between the Jewish Communities in East and West Berlin would also be highly embarrassing: whereas all of the latter's freehold had been restored, it had become state owned in the GDR capital. The cemeteries, the synagogue in the Rykestraße and the administrative offices in the Oranienburger Straße continued to be administered by the Department of Public Property (*Volkseigentum*) of the East Berlin *Magistrat*.[38] Thus the specific claims of Adass Yisroel raised the wider issue of the ownership and restitution of property, not only of East Germany's Jewish Communities but also of other Jews in the GDR and abroad. Any public debate, Gysi admitted, would be both 'embarrassing' and 'detrimental', especially in light of the forthcoming Crystal Night commemoration. In consequence, he favoured the return of the cemetery to Adass Yisroel and the discreet and rapid return of the property of the Jewish Community of East Berlin.[39]

Kurt Löffler, who succeeded Gysi as State Secretary for Church Affairs in July 1988, was also anxious lest concessions to Offenberg encourage citizens of other states to seek compensation for their mistreatment as forced labour on what was now the territory of the GDR.[40] His concerns were shared by the *Magistrat* and the SED Central Committee Working Group for Church Affairs, who feared that accepting all Offenberg's demands would have 'unforeseeable consequences'.[41] The Central Committee officials were anxious that once Honecker's promise had been fulfilled, Offenberg would submit new demands and, looking ahead, they wondered what would happen if another 'Offenberg' and additional Jewish Communities appeared in East Berlin.[42] Furthermore, the notion of a group based in West Berlin succeeding to property on the territory of the GDR was anathema to the party-state authorities, who also contested the legitimacy of Offenberg's Society for the Advancement of Adass Yisroel to be the legal successor to the 'old' Adass Yisroel. They were also unhappy about the reconstitution of the Community in the GDR capital as it would create 'a kind of extra-territorial organisation' which would be able to operate without reference to GDR law. Although a *Magistrat* decree in June 1988 had entered in the land registry the Israelite Synagogue Community Adass Yisroel as owner of both the cemetery in the Wittlicher Straße and the former Community Centre in the Tucholskystraße, the right of ownership could not, according to Kraußer of the Central Committee Working Group for Church Affairs, be then transferred to Offenberg's 'foreign' society as this was not identical to the original Adass Yisroel Community.[43] This did not, however, necessarily debar Offenberg's group from using the facilities.

The subsequent labyrinthine story is one of procrastination by the SED and the gradual abandonment of Honecker's undertakings. An exasperated Offenberg authorised his solicitor, Lothar de Mazière,[44] to submit a formal demand in December 1988 for a governmental declaration on the restoration of the Community to all its rights and official recognition of its autonomy. Only after Honecker was overthrown did matters improve: in December 1989, Modrow's government accepted the demands made by de Maizière and the Community was able to embark on activities in East Berlin with generous financial aid from the state (Mertens 19897: 349; Broder 1993: 96–98; Illichmann 1997: 285–86). It also received a crucial source of new members: Russian immigrant Jews. Unification brought new problems as the full restoration of Adass Yisroel's rights was not endorsed by the Berlin Senate and was contested by the Unified Jewish Community of Berlin, which was also disconcerted by the emergence of a potential rival. Not until 1997, after the matter was sent to the Federal Supreme Administrative Court for resolution, was Yisroel Israel finally recognised as a public corporation

(Broder 1993: 101–5; Illichmann 1997: 287; Mertens 1997: 349–50; Offenberg 1998: 263–65; Gay 2002: 248).

## Centrum Judaicum

When a Centrum Judaicum was set up in 1988, it was the culmination of a series of suggestions about an appropriate forum for the study of Jewish culture in the GDR. A proposal put forward in 1975 by Salomea Genin, a journalist and member of East Berlin's Jewish Community, envisaged a museum in the ruins of the synagogue in the Oranienburger Straße for the promotion of the history of Germany's Jews from a 'class-oriented position'. Administered by East Berlin's Jewish Community, she wanted the museum to attract those SED members of Jewish origin who did not wish to commit themselves to the Jewish faith.[45] Practical difficulties and the SED's desire to control the museum concept led to the abandonment of the idea. Ten years later, party and state stepped into the vacuum. In May 1986, the State Secretariat for Church Affairs and the Jewish Communities agreed on the creation of a Centrum Judaicum Foundation with a wide remit: to conduct research into, and organise exhibitions on, the entire history of Jews in Germany, provide a place for prayer and worship, establish a museum and, in general, foster and preserve Jewish traditions and culture. However, when the Council of Ministers decree on the Foundation was finally issued in May 1988, the definition of its functions showed that the communist past bore heavily on the present. While the Foundation was enjoined to commemorate Jewish victims of German fascism, it also had to ensure that due regard be paid to the communist resistance.

The New Synagogue in East Berlin's Oranienburger Straße was selected as the site of the Centrum Judaicum. Inaugurated in 1866, the building had suffered some damage under the National Socialists during Crystal Night, but more severely from Allied bombing attacks in November 1943. When the remnants of the main hall were pulled down in 1958, only the façade survived. The board of the Centrum Judaicum was set up on 5 July 1988, with Dr Hermann Simon as its director. The foundation stone of the building project was laid on the fiftieth anniversary of Crystal Night and an International Curatorium was established on 9 November 1988. Siegmund Rotstein, the President of the Association of Jewish Communities in the GDR, was installed as president of the Curatorium. Progress was slow. The Curatorium did not meet until six months after its launch, donations from external sources proved to be a disappointment and the reconstruction of the façade and the administrative offices of the New Synagogue were not completed until the rededication ceremony in May 1995, in the presence of the President of the Federal Republic, Roman Herzog (Illichmann 1997: 266; Rebiger 2005: 28–29).

## The Fiftieth Anniversary of Crystal Night, 1988

The start of work on the New Synagogue and the creation of the Centrum Judai-cum were planned to coincide with an SED-inspired extravaganza, the commem-oration of the fiftieth anniversary of Crystal Night. The significance attached by the SED to the event is evident from the central role played by the politburo in its design and organisation.[46] While numerous memorial ceremonies across the GDR signalled a shift in SED policy, a completely new political leaf had not been turned. Party and state officials such as Jarowinsky and Löffler insisted that the event should not be a Jewish matter alone and that primacy be given to the com-munist opposition to racism and fascism.[47] The close linkage of the commemo-ration of Crystal Night and the persecution of the Jews to the anti-fascist myth of the GDR was articulated by Honecker in his keynote speech in the Council of State building on 8 November.[48] 'With the pogroms still raging', Honecker told his audience, 'the KPD and its central organ, *Die Rote Fahne*, took an im-passioned and resolute stand against that outrage and called on all the people to stop the murderous ways of Nazi hangmen'. And he quoted from an article in the special issue of *Die Rote Fahne* in November 1938 that: 'The struggle against the anti-Jewish pogrom is an inseparable component of the German struggle to achieve freedom and peace and overthrow the Nazi dictatorship' (Association of Jewish Communities 1988: 11).

The official reception by Honecker of the Presidium of the Association of Jewish Communities was flanked by an academic conference and commemora-tion ceremonies at Jewish cemeteries and synagogues and at Ravensbrück and other national memorial sites (ibid.: 98–104). The 'commemoration epidemic' (Mertens 1997: 182) left a favourable impression on the more than one hundred foreign guests, a welcome outcome for the SED and its assertion that the GDR had assumed responsibility for the past by the emancipation of Jews (Illichmann 1997: 272–73). Others were not so impressed. Younger members of Dresden's Jewish Community felt that the dearth of information in the past about Jewish culture and religion could not suddenly be rectified by the outburst of activity in 1988.[49] Many non-Jews, too, were concerned about the implications of official support for Jewish projects. Data collected by the Stasi Zwickau District Service Unit drew attention to considerable popular dissatisfaction with reports of an alleged SED offer of a restitution payment of $100 million to the World Jewish Congress. Such a large sum, so some locals objected, should have been invested in the state economy or in imports to ease consumer shortages in the GDR.[50] In East Berlin, telecommunications staff were anxious about the impact of the visit of Miles Bronfman, the President of the World Jewish Congress, to the GDR in October 1988. With a cordial relationship having been struck between Honecker and Bronfman, workers feared the visit would damage the GDR's relations with Arab countries and the PLO and enable the 'Zionist lobby' to exploit the GDR at a time when the SED was unable to satisfy the needs of its own people.[51] The visit also stirred traditional forms of prejudice among Stasi officers in Main Department XX. Closer relations with the GDR would, it was asserted, enable the World Jewish Congress to strengthen its influence on Jewish Communities and further the imperialist policy of destabilising the GDR.[52]

These reactions to the SED's revision of its Jewish policy show that anti-Jewish prejudice did not lurk far beneath the surface in a state that claimed to have eliminated the essential preconditions of anti-semitism. As discussed earlier, this claim was contested by Rabbi Neuman as well as by leading members of the Jewish Communities such as Aris, Gollomb and Kirchner. They were openly critical of the stereotyping of Jews in the GDR media at the time of Israel's conflict with its Arab neighbours in 1967 and protested at the desecration of graves in Jewish cemeteries. The anxiety of the authorities to keep such unwelcome incidents out of the public domain led to a severe rebuke for the chair of East Berlin's Jewish Community. Kirchner had complained openly to guests at a film preview in February 1979 about the inadequacy of the way in which the persecution of the Jews was taught in schools. He also divulged the Jewish Community's dissatisfaction with the authorities' decision not to continue proceedings against offenders who had damaged over 200 graves.[53] Summoned to the office of the State Secretary for Church Affairs, Kirchner was warned to take greater care over where he expressed views that might be misused by the Western media.[54] News of the desecration of graves and the growing problem of skinhead militancy in the late 1980s could not be kept out of West German newspapers, however. In May 1988, the *Süddeutsche Zeitung* published Kirchner's criticism of the official explanation of right-wing radicalism among skinhead groups in the GDR as exclusively the result of the influence of Western media. This was, he stated, only a partial explanation; other causes were to be found in the frustration of young people with the failings of the education system and society, and in the authorities' unwillingness to confront right-wing radicalism which, among skinhead groups, exhibited fascistic and anarchist tendencies.[55]

## After the Revolution

The disintegration of communist hegemony produced an improvement in the situation of Jews in East Germany. After taking over the government in November 1989, the SED-PDS Minister President Hans Modrow sought to establish diplomatic relations with Israel. After he was ousted in the elections of March 1990, the East German parliament asked Jews everywhere for forgiveness and Israel to forgive it for the hypocrisy and hostility of official GDR policy towards it. Parliament also pleaded for forgiveness for the persecution and degradation suffered by the Jews of East Germany since 1945 (Mertens 1997: 343–44). However, while German unification took place before diplomatic relations were established between Israel and the GDR, and before any agreement could be reached on compensation, the Jewish Communities experienced a religious and cultural boost. A Jewish cultural association was formed as a successor to the 'We for

Ourselves' group, and Adass Yisroel was officially recognised in December 1989. In addition, Adass Yisroel sought, like the larger East Berlin Community, to help the many Jewish immigrants arriving in the GDR from the Soviet Union. The de Mazière government had initiated a shift in policy when in early 1990, in response to a surge in racism in the Soviet Union, it authorised 2,000 Jews to reside in the GDR. With immigration continuing after the demise of the GDR, the Jewish Communities were able to reverse their numerical decline.

Yet the disappearance of the SED and the unification of the two Germanies brought new problems. Most of the Jewish immigrants did not speak German and lacked a basic familiarity with Jewish culture and traditions. Some members of the Jewish Community of East Berlin resented the way in which the organisation was disbanded in 1991 and absorbed into its much larger Western equivalent without due consideration for their interests (Ostow 1996: 20–22). Feelings of dislocation were reinforced by an escalation of anti-semitic agitation, which involved stabbings in towns such as Rostock and Brandenburg in 1991. Anti-semitic attitudes, which surveys from the early 1990s indicate was initially more widespread among west Germans, began to rise in the *New Länder*, especially among younger cohorts (Friedrich 2002: 75–78). The collapse of the GDR and state socialism had repercussions, too, for the multi-layered identity of many East German Jews, such as those who had adhered to the SED. The GDR, for all its warts, had been, for some, preferable to the Federal Republic and had represented the basis of their 'socialist' identity.

## Notes

1. The term 'Community' is capitalised when reference is made to an institution.
2. See Mertens (1997: 20, 27–28) and BStU, MfS, ZA, HA XX/4, no.2943, 'Zur Lage der Jüdischen Gemeinden in der DDR', 12 May 1988, p.1.
3. The revival of the Communities can be followed in Timm (1997b: 19–22), Offenberg (1998: 16–30, 35–39), Gay (2002: 151–66) and Geller (2005: 90–96).
4. See the interviews in Ostow (1989, 1996), Bornemann and Peck (1995), Wroblewsky (2001) and Eckhardt and Nachama (2003).
5. BStU, MfS, ZA, HA XX/4, no.2213, 'Verband Jüdischer Gemeinden in der DDR', 11 July 1978, p. 3.
6. BStU, MfS, ZA, HA XX/4, no.2043, 'Zur Lage der Jüdischen Gemeinden in der DDR', 12 May 1988, p. 1.
7. BA, DO 4/1369, 'Entwurf. Stellungnahme zur Situation auf den jüdischen Friedhöfen in der Hauptstadt der DDR–Berlin', 10 December 1974, p.564. The document was signed by Kirchner.
8. BA, DO 4/1351, 'Vorlage für das Sekretariat der Bezirksleitung Berlin der SED. Betrff: Information über die Schaffung einer durchgängigen Verbindungsstraße im Abschnitt zwischen Indira-Gandhi-Straße und Michelangelostraße zwischen den jüdischen Friedhöfen', [1986], p.346. This was signed by East Berlin *Oberbürgermeister* Erhard Krack.

9. BStU, MfS, ZA, HA XX/4, no.2043, 'Zur Lage der Jüdischen Gemeinden in der DDR', 12 May 1988, p.2.
10. Transcript by the Staatliches Komitee für Rundfunk, Redaktion Monitor of the programme 'Jüdisches Leben in Berlin', transmitted by SFB II on 31 May 1987: BA, DO 4/1340, p.169.
11. BStU, MfS, ZA, HA XX/4, no.2043, 'Zur Lage der Jüdischen Gemeinden in der DDR', 12 May 1988, p.2.
12. BA, DO 4/1344, Eschwege to Aris, Dresden, 15 November 1984, p.1581.
13. See Mertens (1997: 138–42) and Offenberg (1998: 123–25). Mertens believes that members of the Association of the Jewish Communities, such as Aris, Gollomb, König and Ringer, may have been aware of the affair since 1969 but that no action was taken until it resurfaced in the 1980s (Mertens 1997: 139). Among the many documents, see the letters of Eschwege and Kirchner in BStU, MfS, ZA, HA XX/4, no.612, pp.106, 111–14 and the report by HA XX/4, ibid., 'Information zur Vorsitzenden der Jüdischen Gemeinde Halle, Karin Mylius', 7 January 1985, pp.123–24.
14. Gromyko, later Foreign Minister, was then the Soviet Union's delegate to the United Nations.
15. SAPMO-BA, DO 30/IV B2/14/174, 'Information über das Gespräch mit den Vorsitzenden der Jüdischen Gemeinden in der DDR am 30.1.1973', 1973, p.2.
16. Ibid., p.6. Rotstein rejected Israel's demands for reparations, arguing that the GDR had done more for East German Jews than was understood by the term reparations.
17. Ibid., pp.6–7. See also Illichmann (1997: 229) and Timm (1997a: 259).
18. SAPMO-BA, DY 30/IV B2/14/174, 'Bericht über das Gespräch des Staatssekretärs mit den Vorsitzenden der Jüdischen Gemeinden in der DDR am 22.3.1976', 23 March 1976, p.2.
19. BA, DO 4/1342, Kirchner to Karschack, 11 December 1985, p.1033. See also Mertens (1997: 331).
20. As a result of a restructuring in 1964, Main Department V/4 was renamed Main Department XX/4. The former had been founded ten years earlier.
21. Runge was born in New York in 1942, emigrated with her parents to the GDR in 1949, and eventually became a lecturer at the Humboldt University in East Berlin.
22. This was the view of the State Secretariat for Church Affairs and the Ministry of State Security according to a note from the former body: SAPMO-BA, DY 30/IV B2/14/174, 'Information für den Genossen Paul Verner – Mitglied des Politbüros', 3 November 1978, p.1.
23. BStU, MfS, ZA, HA XX/4, no.605, 'Abschlußbericht zum OV "Zionist", Reg.-Nr.: XII 1463/82', 23 July 1984, pp.154, 159.
24. On his activities as an agent, see Eschwege (1991: 92, 107–111), Offenberg (1998: 162), Wolffsohn (1998: 155), Käppner (1999: 263–71), Hartewig (2000: 189–94), Meining (2002: 208–10, 234–39) and Maser (2003: 22–23).
25. BStU, MfS, ZA, HA XX/4, no.605, 'MÜNDLICHER BERICHT des IMS "Ferdinand" zur Situation im Verband der Jüdischen Gemeinden', 23 May 1986, p.212. See also Käppner (1999: 269).
26. BStU, MfS, Außenstelle Neubrandenburg, BV Nbg, Abteilung XX, no.196, 'Genosse Klaus Gysi, Staatssekretär für Kirchenfragen: "Die Politik der SED und des Staates gegenüber den Kirchen und Religionsgemeinschaften"', 5 March 1982, p.99.
27. SAPMO-BA, DY 30/9051, 'Information zu Problemen der Jüdischen Gemeinden in der DDR', 21 August 1986, pp.1–3. See also Offenberg (1998: 211–12).
28. BStU, MfS, ZA, HA XX/4, no.2185, 'Konzeption zur Vorbereitung des 50. Jahrestages "Kristallnacht" und zur Lösung weiterer Probleme der jüdischen Gemeinden in der DDR', 1 September 1987, p.4.
29. SAPMO-BA, DY 30/9051, 'Stellungnahme zur Konzeption des Staatssekretärs für Kirchenfragen "Zum Wiederaufbau der 'Neuen Synagoge' in Berlin, Hauptstadt der DDR" vom 1.12.1986', p.4.

30. The latter point was made by Kirchner to the head of the office for Church Affairs of the East Berlin *Magistrat*: ibid., 'Aktenvermerk über ein Gespräch mit dem Vorsitzenden der Jüdischen Gemeinde Dr. Kirchner am 11.11.1987', [November 1987], p.1. This was sent by Schabowski to Jarowinsky on 13 November 1987.
31. See BArch, DO 4/1342, Kirchner to Community members', 4 May 1988, p.1067. See also Mertens (1997: 176–79) and Offenberg (1998: 219–20).
32. BArch, DO 4/1342, Kirchner to Community members', 4 May 1988, p.1071. See also Mertens (1997: 179) and Offenberg (1998: 220–21).
33. See Ulrike Baureithel's article, 'Jüdischer Luna-Park?' *Freitag*, 7 July 2000. Retrieved 10 August 2001 from: http://www.freitag.de/2000/28/00281101.htm.
34. SAPMO-BA, DY 30/9051, Gysi to Honecker, 15 January 1988, p.3. See also Mertens (1997: 346–47).
35. SAPMO-BA, DY 30/9052, 'Information', 20 July 1988, pp.5–6; this was sent to Krenz on 22 July 1988.
36. For details on the assurances given to Offenberg, see his letter to Honecker: SAPMO-BA, DY 30/9053, 12 February 1989, pp.1–2. See also Broder (1993: 92), Illichmann (1997: 279–80) and Offenberg (1998: 252–54).
37. SAPMO-BA, DY 30/9051, Gysi to Honecker, 15 January 1988, p.2.
38. Ibid., pp.1–2.
39. Ibid., pp.2-4. See also Hartewig (2000: 591–92).
40. SAPMO-BA, DY 30/9053, Löffler to Honecker, 8 April 1989, p.6.
41. SAPMO-BA, DY 30/8946, 'Beratung bei Genossen Jarowinsky am 13.3.1989', p.1.
42. SAPMO-BA, DY 30/9053, Krußer to Jarowinsky, 24 January 1989, pp.1–3.
43. Ibid., Krußer to Jarowinsky, 24 February 1989, p. 3; SAPMO-BA, DY 30/9052, Krußer to Krenz, 20 July 1988, pp.1, 3. See also Broder (1993: 94).
44. Lothar de Mazière, who acted as Offenberg's lawyer, was the Deputy Chair of the Council of Ministers and in charge of Church Affairs in the Modrow government between November 1989 and March 1990. He was Minister President of the GDR from April to October 1990.
45. SAPMO-BA, DY 30/IV B2/14/174, 'Vorschlag für den Aufbau eines Jüdischen Musuems in Berlin, Hauptstadt der DDR', April 1975, pp.1–2.
46. See SAPMO-BA, DY 30/9051,'Maßnahmen zum 50. Jahrestag der faschistischen Pogromnacht (Beschluß des Politbüros)', 30 March 1988.
47. SAPMO-BA, DY 30/8946, 'Beratung bei Genossen Jarowinsky am 26.10.1988', pp.1–2.
48. SAPMO-BA, DO 30/9051, 'Empfehlungen für ein Gespräch des Generalsekretärs des ZK der SED und Vorsitzenden des Staatsrates der DDR, Genossen Erich Honecker, mit dem Präsidium des Verbandes der Jüdischen Gemeinden in der DDR', 31 May 1988, pp.1–8.
49. BStU, MfS, Außenstelle Dresden, AKG, PI, no.252/88, 'Information über die gegenwärtige Situation in der Jüdischen Gemeinde Dresden (Bitte des Gen. Modrow)', 9 November 1988, pp.5–6.
50. BStU, MfS, Außenstelle Chemnitz, AKG, no.586, vol.1, 'die Stimmung und Reaktion unter der Bevölkerung', 11 November 1988, p.173; ibid., 'die Stimmung und Reaktion unter der Bevölkerung', 3 November 1988, p.191.
51. BStU, MfS, ZA, HA XX/4, no.2182, 'Information zu ersten Reaktionen zum Aufenthalt/ Ergebnissen des Präsidenten des Jüdischen Weltkongresses, Edgar Miles Bronfmann, in der DDR', 21 October 1988, p.79.
52. Ibid., p.76.
53. SAPMO-BA, DY 30/IV B2/14/174, SED Hausmitteilung, Abteilung Agitation to Bellmann, 16 February 1979, p.1.
54. Ibid., 'Aktenvermerk über ein Gespräch mit Dr. Peter Kirchner, Vorsitzender der Jüdischen Gemeinde von Berlin, beim Staatssekretär am 9.4.1979', 11 April 1979, p.1.
55. A photocopy of the short report, published on 16 May 1988, is to be found in BStU, MfS, ZA, MfS Rechtsstelle, no.510, p.267.

# Chapter 3

# JEHOVAH'S WITNESSES:
# FROM PERSECUTION TO SURVIVAL

## Victims of Communism

*E*xcept for the short and fragile period of tolerance immediately after the end of the Second World War when, like East German Jews, they were officially recognised as 'victims of fascism', Jehovah's Witnesses were severely persecuted throughout the history of the GDR. The SED and its instruments of repression, notably the Stasi, were determined to destroy the organisation and faith of the approximately 20,000 brethren of the Jehovah's Witnesses who lived in the country. As is discussed in other chapters, the modalities of repression changed over time, ranging from brutal repression in the early 1950s to a greater emphasis on the more subtle, albeit nefarious, policy of subversion from the mid 1960s onwards. The shift was determined by domestic and international circumstances as well as by the realisation that a quick knockout had not been achieved by the banning of the organisation in 1950 and the subsequent show trials. Consequently, the authorities' goal was amended to the gradual dissolution of the Witness organisation and its *Gleichschaltung* or 'incorporation' as a compliant religious group into the SED-dominated political and social system. Why the SED and the security forces were so determined to destroy the Witness organisation, how they sought to realise this goal in the final two decades of the GDR, how the Jehovah's Witnesses responded to persecution, and how they pursued their vital mission work are the major issues examined in this chapter, which is based on the voluminous archival record, oral testimonies and recent work by German scholars, notably Hans-Hermann and Annegret Dirksen.[1]

---

Notes for this section begin on page 83.

## Jehovah's Witnesses: Faith and Mission

To contextualise the fate of Jehovah's Witnesses in the GDR, a brief survey of the development of the Witness movement since the late nineteenth century follows. Under the leadership of their founder, Charles Taze Russell (1852–1916), the Jehovah's Witnesses emerged from a series of movements which, mainly located in the nineteenth-century United States, adhered to a millenarian belief and the return to earth of Christ. Building on earlier initiatives, Russell founded the Zion's Watchtower and Tract Society in 1881, which was renamed as the Watchtower Bible and Tract Society four years later. Russell's successors as president, notably Joseph Franklin Rutherford (1869–1942) and Nathan Knorr (1905–1977), streamlined the organisation, further developed its doctrine and turned it into a world-wide movement of over two million members by the time of Knorr's death. In 1931, the movement's followers changed their name from Bible Students to Jehovah's Witnesses. As far as developments in Germany were concerned, the Bible Students became officially active in 1896 and shortly before the outbreak of the First World War numbered between 3,000 and 4,000. Boosted by the organisation's registration in 1921 as a foreign corporation with legal status, the number of members rose rapidly from 5,445 in 1919 to 22,535 in 1926. This was the largest national following outside the United States (Garbe 1994: 56–58; Hirch 2003b: 28–30).

Although Witness doctrine has often been in a state of flux, there are several key concepts constituting the basis of a faith for which brethren have been prepared to suffer imprisonment and death. Their faith is founded on the belief that the entire Bible is God's inspired Word and that all the books of the Bible are consistent with each other. One of the key and most controversial of Witness doctrines relates to the second, and invisible, coming of Christ, who, it is claimed, originally sacrificed his life as a ransom for sinful humanity. The second coming is the time when Christ 'takes Kingdom power toward this earth' and begins to rule as king of God's heavenly government (WBTS 1982: 137, 143, 147). Dating the return of Christ has led the Watchtower and Bible Tract Society and its presidents into considerable semantic and eschatological confusion, as have predictions of the Armageddon, or the final showdown between the forces of good and evil. In 1966, the Society indicated that the battle would begin before the 1,000 year period (millennium) starting in 1975. After this battle, God's Kingdom would be the only government ruling over the earth in perfect conditions without war, disease and unemployment. However, the survivors of Armageddon, no matter what the anticipated date, would have no guarantee of eternal life as Christ and his 144,000 associate kings would then have to judge mankind; that is, both the righteous and the unrighteous resurrected dead.[2] This so-called Judgement Day lasts for 1,000 years, during which those who wish to serve Jehovah under paradise conditions will receive everlasting life and the 'wicked ones' will be destroyed. However, one ultimate challenge lies ahead: once Christ has handed over the Kingdom to God at the end of Judgement Day, Satan and his demons will be released from the abyss where they have dwelled for 1,000 years and will test the perfect humans to see if they turn away from God, as did Adam and Eve (ibid.: 164, 175–78, 180–81).

While the confusion surrounding the date of the commencement of Armageddon led to the defection of brethren after 1975, East German Witnesses regarded this issue as of secondary importance compared to the reassuring message that the Kingdom of God will ultimately arrive and that those willing to obey God's laws will have the opportunity to live forever in a paradise earth. One striking feature of Jehovah's Witnesses is that, like Christ, they do not isolate themselves from society but as God's ambassadors are bound to preach to as many people as possible and to make disciples, a vital task which determines who will be saved and who will be damned eternally. This activity requires brethren to make great personal sacrifices, for as a Watchtower publication states, 'Satan and his world are sure to try to stop you, even as they tried to stop Christ's earlier followers from preaching' (ibid.: 253). Anxious that all should hear the good news of God's Kingdom, Witnesses engage in intensive mission work, in particular calling on people in their own homes and selling Witness literature such as the magazines *The Watchtower* and *Awake!* This active door-to-door work, known as 'preaching' or 'publishing', has frequently aroused the suspicion and hostility of secular authorities worldwide and led to the harassment and imprisonment of Witnesses.

Other central aspects of life as a Jehovah's Witness include 'righteous conduct', celebrating the annual Memorial and maintaining what the Society regards as a politically neutral stance. Righteous conduct entails monogamy, a rejection of homosexuality, moderation in drinking, and striking a balance between the roles of men and women. While the man acts as head of the house, the wife should focus on caring for the family and is not expected to play a significant role in congregations. The Lord's Supper, or the Memorial meal, is the most important event in the year and commemorates Jesus's sacrifice of his life. It attracts both ordinary members as well as individuals with an interest in Witness teachings. In 1986, the Memorial was celebrated by over eight million across the globe.

Two especially contentious issues in relations with secular governments have been the Witnesses' conscientious objection to military service and their notion of political neutrality. While the Watchtower Bible and Tract Society insists that Jehovah's Witnesses pay their taxes and obey the laws of the country in which they live, these laws must not conflict with those of God, to whom they owe their primary loyalty. Seeing themselves as soldiers in God's army, not of the secular state, and committed to the sacredness of life, not only do Jehovah's Witnesses come into conflict with governments for refusing to perform military service and war-related work but so too, especially in authoritarian states like the GDR, does their rejection of membership of political parties and participation in a number of societal activities. All secular states, whether democratic or authoritarian, were seen as part of the world of Satan.

Jehovah's Witnesses in twentieth-century Germany were part of an elaborate worldwide organisational structure that, despite many changes under the leadership of Rutherford and Knorr, helped to sustain the demanding proselytising mission and to reinforce the faith of brethren. Local congregations, comprising ordinary members or 'publishers' and officials, above all the elders, formed the basis of a pyramid which led up via the districts, circuits and national branches to the central Governing Body of the Watchtower Tract and Bible Society in Brooklyn. The Governing Body, which was established formally in 1971, became the supreme ruling council of the Society in 1975, when it consisted of eighteen members. The original administrative branch of the Society in Germany was based in Magdeburg, a city which found itself situated in the GDR after the division of Germany in 1949. Pioneers are among the most active of congregation members: some are full-time and salaried, whereas others are unpaid and are expected to respond flexibly to the Society's assignments. From the early 1970s onwards, the elders, under the supervision of the circuit overseers, constituted the key officials at the base of society and carried out a series of functions ranging from the supervision of congregational meetings to keeping watch over the use of money and property. A central feature of life in the congregations is the study of Society publications such as the monthly *Our Kingdom Ministry* and *The Watchtower* magazine, which, together with training for mission work, occupies a more important role than the prayer or ritual associated with Christian worship and acquaints brethren with the doctrine of the Governing Body in Brooklyn. As Jehovah's Witnesses in the GDR were so severely persecuted, and their organisation banned from the 1950s onwards, the administrative structure and the rhythm of activities deviated in several fundamental respects from this pattern.

Witnesses had already experienced various forms of persecution in Germany before 1945. Some were incarcerated during the First World War for refusing to serve in the armed forces and subsequently, during the Weimar Republic, Witnesses were persecuted and sometimes imprisoned for their attitude towards military service and for their mission activities. Some 1,169 Bible Students, as they were then called, were arrested in 1927; however, most were acquitted (Hirch 2003b: 29–32). By 1933, there were about 25,000 Jehovah's Witnesses in Germany. Persecution by the National Socialist regime was partly based on traditional prejudices rooted in the Witnesses' perception of their obligations to the secular state and to God, their conflicts with the established churches, and their rejection of blood transfusions and various products with a blood content. The government of the Third Reich compounded this antipathy by its visceral hostility towards international organisations and those suspected of aiding the communist revolution. Not only was the Society banned but thousands of brethren were imprisoned and many others lost their lives for constituting, in the vocabulary of National Socialism, 'elements harmful to the German people' and a 'menace to the state'. According to Johannes Wrobel, about 10,700 Witnesses suffered in various tragic ways during the Third Reich – the loss of employment, imprisonment, the seizure of their children and execution. Some 8,800 were arrested and a further 2,800 sent to concentration camps, where they were assigned a badge with a purple triangle to distinguish them from other prisoners. Most of the 950 who lost their lives in the camps were executed for conscientious objection; some were murdered as part of the euthanasia programme (Wrobel 2006a: 90).

At least 500 Witnesses were double victims of the National Socialist and SED dictatorships, with 325 being imprisoned by the two regimes (Dirksen 2006: 191). Ernst Seliger was one of these victims. Incarcerated by the National Socialists in the Sachsenhausen concentration camp and by the East German communists in the Waldheim penal institution, he spent over forty years in prison. Meanwhile, his younger brother Martin was executed in Brandenburg prison in 1943 for refusing to serve in the military. Despite his great personal suffering, Seliger remained firm in his faith: 'But, with the apostle Paul, we can say that "in prison ... in blows to an excess, in near-deaths often ... in labor and toil", we are determined to be steadfast as "ministers of Christ"' (Seliger 1975: 426). His experiences and the statistics of repression bear witness to the hostility of both the Third Reich and the SED towards the active missionaries of an organisation with its headquarters in Brooklyn, allegedly the centre of a plot, whether by Bolsheviks or by Western imperialists, to subvert the National Socialist People's Community and the socialist system respectively. The antagonism culminated in the banning of the Witness organisation as well as the persecution of individual Witnesses in both the Third Reich and the GDR. But, unlike the Third Reich, repression in the GDR did not escalate into an attempted eradication of every Jehovah's Witness but, especially from the early 1960s, into a combination of less draconian forms of coercion and the covert subversion of the Society's activities and its clandestine organisation (Hacke 2003: 323–36).

## The Ministry of State Security and its Perception of the Witness 'Threat'

Although numerous agencies were deployed against the Witnesses, among them the Ministry of Justice and the German People's Police, the main agent of control, surveillance and persecution was the Stasi. Ministry of State Security (MfS) officers perceived an interlocking internal and external threat in the form of close organisational links between the congregations in the GDR on the one hand, and the Watchtower Bible and Tract Society's Brooklyn headquarters and its West German branch office in Wiesbaden on the other. The latter's special Eastern Bureau, which was located in West Berlin until 1961, directed the affairs of the Jehovah's Witness organisation in the GDR, appointed the leading servants and was responsible for the courier system which enabled Witness literature to be smuggled into East Germany (Hirch 2003b: 112, 120–22, 139). Nevertheless, given the Stasi's plethora of tasks, why did an overburdened apparatus invest substantial resources in the repression of a relatively small number of Jehovah's Witnesses? After all, had not Witnesses, like so many communists, suffered imprisonment and death in the camps of the Third Reich? And did not the Stasi's informers and officers frequently acknowledge that Witnesses were noted for their industriousness, modesty and politeness?

An answer should first be sought in the intrinsic and seemingly irreconcilable antagonism between the doctrines and practices of the Jehovah's Witnesses and those of dictatorial systems, whether of a fascist or a communist persuasion. While Witnesses also come into conflict with governments of pluralist polities, the level of tolerance is normally far higher there than in a dictatorship like that of the SED with the characteristics of an exclusive political religion and with an abhorrence of autonomous sub-systems. In an atmosphere of mutual fear and suspicion, especially in the early years of the Cold War, when the SED was constructing a system which demanded adherence to Marxist-Leninist doctrine, loyalty to the state and full engagement in societal activities, the Witnesses' conscientious objection to military service and their notion of political neutrality prompted the SED to regard the brethren as political and social 'outsiders' and as agents of the implacable imperialist foe.

Whereas several established religious groups, such as the Mormons, the Jewish Communities and the New Apostolic Church, managed to survive the ruthless persecution of the 1950s and came to enjoy legal recognition and a restricted space for practising their faith, Jehovah's Witnesses were subjected to a ban on their organisation in 1950, the closing down of the branch office in Magdeburg, a series of show trials and the imprisonment of leading servants in 1950/51. A second wave of arrests occurred in 1965, followed one year later by the imposition of lengthy prison sentences. The official 'case' for the banning of the Witness organisation was set out in August 1950 by Karl Steinhoff, the GDR's Minister of the Interior, who argued that the Witnesses:

> have pursued systematic agitation against the existing democratic order and its laws under the cloak of religious meetings. Further, they have continually imported and distributed illegal publications, whose contents violate the Constitution of the German Democratic Republic as well as efforts to maintain peace. At the same time, it has been established that 'Jehovah's Witnesses' have served as spies for an imperialistic power. (cited in Dirksen 2001b: 216)

The authorities knew that the latter allegation was without foundation, as is apparent from declassified police and Stasi files: in August 1950 the criminal police openly admitted in a top-secret memorandum that no evidence existed of espionage by Jehovah's Witnesses (Hacke 2003: 319, n. 48).

Although the accusations levelled against the Witnesses by Steinhoff and the charge of warmongering in the show trials were palpably untrue, a mountain of confidential reports and other materials compiled by Stasi officers point to the conclusion that the authorities' actions were neither a matter of political convenience nor a temporary phenomenon but the expression of a deep-rooted hostility. Among these materials, which are held in the central and regional archives of the Federal Commissioner for the Records of the State Security Service of the Former German Democratic Republic (BStU), are eleven dissertations and one lengthy in-house thesis which, written between 1975 and 1985, were concerned solely with Jehovah's Witnesses in the GDR.[3] The writing of a dissertation formed an important element of an officer's training on full- and part-time courses run by the Stasi's Potsdam-based College of Legal Studies (*Juristische Hochschule*) whose aim was to enhance the professionalism of staff and further their practical skills in security and intelligence work.

As the dissertations were intended for internal consumption only and were composed by officers in the field, they represent an invaluable insight into the MfS's perception of the Jehovah's Witnesses and its officers' modus operandi at a time when the focus had shifted from open coercion to operational subversion. The image of the 'Witness enemy' portrayed in the dissertations is consistent with previous pronouncements by the Stasi, in particular the notion that the Watchtower Society, with its headquarters in Brooklyn, was a tool of the reactionary wing of American business, government and intelligence services and that it formed an integral element in the psychological warfare waged by imperialists in the international class struggle against socialism. What this entailed, according to Lieutenant Bartnik of Department XX of the Suhl Regional Administration, was the spread of anti-communist, nationalist, racist and clerical ideas (Bartnik 1977: 4). Virulent anti-communism against the Soviet Union in particular, but also against the GDR, was regarded by the Stasi as a fundamental component of the Watchtower Society's political-ideological subversion.[4] Among the main means of transmission were 'ostensibly' religious magazines such as *Awake!* and *The Watchtower*.[5] While the anti-communist stance of the Witnesses is hardly surprising in view of their persecution in the Soviet Union and Eastern Europe, the officers' charge that they were the lackeys of imperialism conveniently overlooked the discrimination suffered by Jehovah's Witnesses in countries such as the U.S.A. and Canada, and it failed to take account of the Watchtower Society's criticism of the capitalist system. Similarly, the designation of the Witness community as an underground political organisation ignored the palpable fact that it was the 1950 ban which had driven it underground in the first place.[6]

A comparison between statements in authoritative documents issued by the Stasi's regional and central organs with those in the trainee officers' dissertations shows that staff views were firmly embedded in ministry thinking. An information bulletin, which was circulated to police officers in 1984, catalogued the Jehovah's Witnesses' alleged 'societal-hostile' traits: obstructing the development of a socialist consciousness; refusing to perform military service; declining to take part in elections and other forms of 'democratic' decision-making; fostering superstition and hostility towards science; discouraging young Witnesses from entering post-compulsory education; putting children's lives at risk by denying them the opportunity for blood transfusion; and associating socialism with the kind of fear and uncertainty endemic in bourgeois-capitalist society.[7] Major Engelhardt of the Karl-Marx-Stadt Regional Administration expounded on this last point in a circular to district service units. According to Engelhardt, Jehovah's Witnesses instrumentalised their end-of-the-world 'propaganda' to denigrate socialism by linking it to the contradictions and crises which were intrinsic to capitalism – such as wars, hunger and unemployment. In his view, this deliberately ignored socialism's many social achievements – for example, job security and a comprehensive vocational training programme for young people.[8] He chose, however, to ignore the many hurdles erected by the state against young Witnesses who wished to embark on an apprenticeship. The threat to peace supposedly posed by Jehovah's Witnesses led the

Stasi into the realms of political fantasy. For example, a report issued by the Stasi Greifswald District Service Unit in 1983 accused the Society of welcoming a future global atomic war as a desirable and feasible preliminary stage to Armageddon.[9]

Such unfounded and exaggerated accusations against the Jehovah's Witnesses were not confined to confidential internal reports and dissertations but were propagated in a book which was incorporated into the Stasi's overall strategy to disrupt and undermine the Witness organisation (see Gebhard 1971). First published in the GDR in 1970, the book appeared in West Germany in the following year. Although Manfred Gebhard was named as editor, the actual author was a former Witness, Dieter Pape, who had been recruited as a Stasi agent while serving a prison sentence. Recent research has shown not only that he cooperated actively with the Stasi but also that the real driving force behind the production of the book was Main Department XX/4, and in particular Oskar Herbrich. Herbrich, who rose to the rank of major, had been engaged in directing operations against the Witnesses since 1958/59 (Hirch 2000: 55–58, 65; Dirksen 2001a: 34). The book was used as an instrument for discrediting the Society as an agent of American business and as a government manual for training Stasi officers in the arts of subversion against the Witnesses (Besier 2003: 141–44; Hirch 2003a: 305–12). Typical of the book's smear tactics were the accusation of collaboration between Witness leaders and the Gestapo and the falsehood that the Witnesses had actively sought to engineer the collapse of the GDR during the June 1953 Uprising (Gebhard 1971: 153, 158–70, 275–77). Moreover, it made no reference to the victimisation and sufferings of Witnesses during the Third Reich.

Despite their hostility to the Jehovah's Witnesses, certain 'ideal' characteristics frequently attracted officers' grudging admiration. Among these was the Society's mobilisation and control of the brethren by what Majors Wenzlawski and Kleinow referred to as the highly centralised, authoritarian and tightly organised structure of the Society from the leadership down to the lowest level, a structure which served to ensure unconditional obedience to the Governing Body and Society doctrines (Wenzlawski and Kleinow 1975: 6–10). This hierarchical organisation, together with the Witnesses' clandestine practices, had another merit in that, according to Second Lieutenant Prescher, it impeded the Stasi's penetration of the Society's security screen (Prescher 1980: 5, 7). It is necessary, however, to add a caveat. As the Witness organisation in the GDR had to operate under cover in the face of persecution, Stasi officers realised that local congregations and elders in regions such as Schwerin and Karl-Marx-Stadt sometimes had to act on their own initiative.[10]

## The Persecution of the Witnesses from 1965 to 1989: Operational Decomposition

'Operational decomposition' measures had been implemented against the Jehovah's Witnesses in the early years of SED rule, for example in 1956/57, when the party had staged a carefully calculated bout of de-Stalinisation. The rationale for decomposition was put forward in a Stasi report to the SED Central Committee in 1956: arrests should be kept to a minimum as they had failed to achieve a significant weakening of the Witness organisation and to elicit a favourable reaction among the East German population, who regarded Jehovah's Witnesses as 'honourable, simple' people (Hirch 2003a: 122; Schmidt 2003b: 88–89). A greater measure of coordination was introduced from the early 1960s onwards when Stasi campaigns against the Witnesses were integrated into the Central Operational Case 'Swamp' (*Zentraler Operativer Vorgang 'Sumpf'*). Six regional sub-operations (*Teilvorgänge*) and Operational Case 'Tower' (*Operativer Vorgang 'Thurm'*) were integrated into the central operational case (ZOV).[11] When the latter was launched in 1963, its main goal was the destruction of the leadership groups, which had been reconstituted after the building of the Berlin Wall. The new organisational framework of the Witnesses consisted of the 'three brothers committee', or executive body, headed by Werner Liebig, five *Bezirke* or districts, each under a servant, and a further sub-division into seventeen *Kreise* or circuits guided by circuit servants. The latter maintained contact with the rungs immediately below them – that is, the territories, the congregations and the Bible study groups, each with their own Bible study servant. About four to six people attended home Bible studies. For reasons of security, the executive, which was given the cover name 'Emmeberg', was expected to meet only with the district servants, and the latter with circuit servants (Dirksen 2001a: 678–82; Hirch 2003b: 140–41).

Central Operational Case 'Swamp', whose aims also included the severing of Witness links with the West, culminated in the arrest of seventeen leaders in November 1965 and the imposition of heavy prison sentences of between five and twelve years in 1966 (Dirksen 2001a: 682–713). Main Department XX/4 hailed these measures as 'a great success' for, in its opinion, not only had the central and local leadership structures been liquidated but the remaining groups had been forced to concentrate on religious matters only.[12] This view was not, however, shared by Department XX of the Karl-Marx-Stadt Regional Administration since it was aware that the arrest of two leading Jehovah's Witnesses, Rink and Dietzsch, had failed to curtail the 'illegal activity of the organisation' in its area of responsibility.[13]

When ZOV 'Swamp' was revised in March 1966, the new work directive followed the Karl-Marx-Stadt line of thinking. The directive's acknowledgment that the ministry was caught up in a protracted struggle against the Society[14] was soon borne out by an increase in the number of brethren and the thorough overhaul of the Witness organisation between 1965 and 1969 (Hirch 2003b: 150). The latter was accomplished with the assistance of the Wiesbaden branch office and through the efforts in the GDR of Helmut Martin and newly appointed district servants such as Wolfgang Meise and Rolf Hintermeyer (Dirksen 2001a: 716). Among the Society's other countermeasures was the issuing in 1967 of a document entitled *Hirten schützt Jehovas Herde* ('Shepherds protect Jehovah's flock'). Despatched to all district and circuit servants, it provided detailed and practical advice on how to deal with the Stasi's machinations. Congregation members were to avoid visits to leading servants in their apartments; concerted efforts were made to prevent the Stasi from bugging conversations in cars and houses; brethren were advised not to use family names; and elders were to be identified by a number, not their name.[15]

The outcome of the Stasi's reappraisal of its aims and tactics can be followed in the ZOV 'Swamp' work directive. The key aims were: the prevention of a revival of the Witness organisation; the severance of its contacts with Wiesbaden; the suppression of the courier system; and the liquidation of the 'hostile' activities of the remaining officials. To achieve these aims, greater support was to be given to what the Stasi referred to as the Witness 'opposition movement' which the MfS had formed around the *Christliche Verantwortung* (Christian Responsibility) association. In addition, more unofficial collaborators (IMs) were to be recruited from among leading Witnesses and an improvement was planned for the coordination of campaigns. Stasi regional administrations and the subordinate district service units were allotted responsibility for carrying out sub-operations (*Teilvorgänge*) and OVs. Main Department XX/4 remained in overall charge of ZOV 'Swamp' and monitored its progress by means of biannual assessments.[16]

The year 1966 marked the transition to a new stage in persecution: from this point onwards, priority was given to the gradual and systematic subversion or 'decomposition' of the Witness organisation rather than to the swift liquidation of the leadership. Not only had the removal of existing leaders proved equivalent to cutting off the head of the Hydra but overt persecution had also created a feeling of martyrdom, tightened bonds between publishers and leading servants, and reinforced rather than weakened the faith of brethren (Bergner 1976: 26; Kownatzki 1979: 11). External opinion was another crucial factor in the deployment of 'softer' forms of control as openly terrorist methods threatened to damage the reputation of the GDR both before and after it secured diplomatic recognition by the West in the early 1970s. It should not be overlooked, however, that while 'hard' measures against the Witnesses declined in frequency, coercion, arbitrary imprisonment and injustice remained endemic.

## The Apparatus of Repression

As is discussed in other parts of this book, Stasi officers were expected to integrate various decomposition measures into concerted campaigns against 'targets'. Despite all that is now known about the damage done to the health, reputation and personal relationships of victims, former Stasi officers have asserted that operational decomposition was for the benefit of the targets who were deterred from committing a crime and engaging in subversive activities (Grimmer and Irmler 2002: 303). The 'benefits' were not appreciated by Witnesses caught up in the net of surveillance, control, denunciation and prison, however. Gisbert Scholze was jailed for eight years after the show trials in May 1951. After his release from the traumatic experience of prison, he recalls that he was subjected to regular surveillance and intimidation and could no longer trust his neighbours and work colleagues.[17] Many other Witnesses had a similar experience. While appreciative of the help provided by brethren in their locality, some nevertheless felt threatened by a sense of being watched, whether by spies, the police or neighbours, especially at the time of the Memorial and home Bible studies.[18]

As part of its relentless pursuit of Jehovah's Witnesses, and to further the process of decomposition of the Society, the Stasi placed great emphasis on the recruitment of IMs. The ministry was particularly keen to attract informers from among the ranks of couriers and leading officials, notably the district, circuit and territory servants, so that it would be able to infiltrate the innermost council of the Witness organisation, to identify pivotal figures, to uncover the organisation of the courier system and evangelising, and to obtain 'insider' information about the impact of decomposition measures. These proved to be elusive goals, partly because the Society frequently changed the ranks of servants in the congregations and study groups (Kleinow and Wenzlawski 1977: 28) and partly because it took pre-emptive action against the MfS. For example, the so-called 'fire-wall regulations' debarred from office any Witness who had once belonged to the SED, restrictions were placed on discussions between district, circuit and local congregation officials, and checks were carried out on the slightest suspicion of contact between a Witness and the Stasi (Baenz 1976: 10; Kleinow and Wenzlawski 1977: 43).

The major obstacles to the recruitment of informers were not of an organisational and tactical nature, but the deep religious faith of the Witnesses and the Society's singular concept of the secular world. According to Kleinow and Wenzlawski, Witnesses regarded Stasi officers as the 'tools of Satan' and they were imbued with a clear image of their enemy (Kleinow and Wenzlawski 1977: 45). The latter phrase was typical Marxist-Leninist jargon. Given the zeal of the Jehovah's Witnesses and the barriers to infiltration by the Stasi that the Society created, brethren who collaborated with the ministry tended to do so for only a short time and were more likely to be found on the periphery than at the heart of the Witness organisation (ibid.: 28; Hirch 2003a: 124, 126), a situation which caused Herbrich of Main Department XX/4 to complain about the inadequacies of the Stasi's work with IMs.[19] Although the total number of IMs deployed against the Jehovah's Witnesses is as yet unknown, one survey of informers run by Department XX/4 of the Karl-Marx-Stadt Region, located in one of the main areas of Witness activity, provides some idea of relative weightings. Out of a total of sixty-seven IMs, only five were used against the Jehovah's Witnesses, as opposed to forty-two against the evangelical Lutheran churches.[20] Two of the region's informers were IM 'Günther' and IM 'Quermann'. The former was an elder and the latter had returned to the Witness organisation after having been cast out in the mid 1950s.[21]

The Stasi provided recruiting officers with a template for identifying the personality traits of the 'model' IM. With regard to Jehovah's Witnesses, the Stasi favoured the recruitment of young, single men as this would help avoid the conflicts of conscience and other problems arising from married life; furthermore, women tended to be located on the edge of Witness organisational structures (Baenz 1976: 7, 17–18). Recognising, however, that the Society encouraged young single males to marry, officers Kleinow and Wenzlawski advocated the recruitment of single or divorced middle-aged men who were unlikely to remarry in the near future and urged that consideration also be given to childless couples or couples whose children had become independent. The drawback to the latter course, a last resort in the opinion of Kleinow and Wenzlawksi, was the serious difficulty of adjusting to life as a Witness and, on account of their age, the decreased opportunity for attaining a leadership position (Kleinow and Wenzlawski 1977: 51–52). Other personality traits which were regarded as compatible with a 'model' Jehovah's Witness were a high level of intelligence, reliability, an unassuming nature, faithfulness in marriage and abstemious behaviour. These criteria were so exacting that the Stasi had to lower its sights and recruit candidates who met only some of the prerequisites. Careful training and preparation by controllers would, it was hoped, enable IMs to carry out their duties conscientiously and efficiently (ibid.: 54, 91, 93–94).

As 'true believers' were expected to be the most productive and the most committed agents, the Stasi was particularly keen to recruit individuals who were well disposed to the GDR's brand of socialism and not primarily motivated by financial payments. A contact of the Stasi Ilmenau District Service Unit felt a sense of guilt, describing the DM 50 received for informing on fellow Witnesses as a 'Judas payment'.[22] However, as Jehovah's Witnesses were unlikely to meet the Stasi's political and ideological requirements, other levers had to be used or, as Herbrich told fellow officers, 'use all chances, all possibilities'.[23] Officers' dissertations show that recruiters and controllers were certainly not squeamish about using blackmail and other nefarious methods (Bartnik 1977: 29; Kleinow and Wenzlawski 1977: 39; Kownatzski 1979: 19–22). Infidelity, a prior penal offence, an interest in pornography, drunkenness, profligacy, the desire for an apartment were all used as levers to enlist Witnesses or interested persons as agents. In 1955, a female Jehovah's Witness (GI 'Mark'), was mobilised by the Ilmenau District Office to try and recruit a fellow Witness as an informer after he had attempted to seduce her.[24] Young Jehovah's Witnesses were regarded as especially vulnerable if they could be detached from the influence of experienced members of their congregation for a lengthy period – for example, while in prison or at a holiday camp. Those who were serving a prison sentence for refusing to do military service should, it was recommended, be approached by IMs among the other prisoners and by the prison's cultural and education department (Bartnik 1977: 30–31).

As Jehovah's Witnesses proved so resistant to the blandishments of the Stasi, the MfS was forced to seek recruits from outside the Society. This posed many problems for controllers as their charges would be obliged to adapt to a completely different lifestyle and to the Witness belief system. They were expected to withdraw from politics, retreat into the intimate world of the congregations, possibly forego watching TV and raise their children according to Society doctrines. An alternative course was to entice former Witnesses; however, if an IM returned reluctantly to the Witness fold, controllers feared that they were likely to sever their links once more with the Society (Kleinow and Wenzlawski 1977: 39, 42).

## Stasi Operations Against the Witnesses

Countless declassified Stasi sources, among them ZOV 'Swamp' monitoring reports, reveal in detail how the MfS planned and carried out its many dirty tricks as part of the operational decomposition strategy. The targets were not just East German Witnesses but also West Germans, including the head of the Eastern Bureau in Wiesbaden.[25] The plethora of measures included the overt and intimidatory surveillance of places where baptisms, Bible study and other activities were held and the encouragement of rumours that certain Witnesses were Stasi informers. Other methods included sending anonymous or pseudonymous complaints to the Eastern Bureau in Wiesbaden and seeking to destroy the reputation of leaders by allegations of immorality, criminal behaviour, homosexuality and links to National Socialism (Bergner 1976: 31–32, 34; Kleinow and Wenzlawski 1977: 91, 93–95).[26] Stasi units were urged to be 'innovative': tried and tested measures should be combined with new ones as part of what Lieutenant Kownatzki called 'their creative application' in order to catch Witnesses off guard (Kownatzki 1979: 15–16).

The depths to which the Stasi plunged are apparent from Lieutenant Bergner's account of a 'successful operation' against a Witness functionary in 1965. After an IM reported that the official had allegedly touched a young girl's genitals while she was out walking with him and her mother, a letter campaign resulted in the official's dismissal from his post (Bergner 1976: 31–32). There was, it should be stressed, no proof that an offence had been committed. Bergner's dissertation received the rating 'very good' from the Stasi assessor, who commended it for its 'scientific' approach and for its contribution to practical work (ibid.: 49–50). In 1983, Bergner became head of Department XX/4 of the Gera Regional Administration despite extorting about 30,000 GDR Marks from an IM in 1976, ironically the same year in which he had submitted his highly-rated dissertation.[27]

Stasi central and regional agencies were determined to integrate individual decomposition measures into operational cases (OVs). Despite, and sometimes because of, the attention to the minutiae of an operation, OVs were often not concluded as quickly as was desired. Herbrich acknowledged this at a meeting of Stasi regional administrations in 1972 when he urged officers not to allow OVs against Jehovah's Witnesses to drift.[28] OV 'Diener' ('Servant'), which was launched in June 1978 against a Witness who lived in Salmünde, can be taken as one example among many as to how a clandestine operation functioned. The Stasi's Saalkreis District Service Unit in the Halle Regional Administration was responsible for the campaign and for the submission of regular progress reports. The main target of the operation was a territory servant whose local congregation was active in the recruitment of new brethren, the organisation of Bible study groups and the cultivation of contacts with the West and Potsdam. The aims of the OV were to uncover the target person's 'subversive' activities, the elimination of courier links with Wiesbaden and, in general, to liquidate the activities of members of the 'sect' by means of focused decomposition measures. 'Focused' was a favourite term of the Stasi as it implied efficiency and accurate targeting. In conjunction with the police and the public prosecutor, houses were searched, Witnesses were interrogated and the Stasi seized *The Watchtower* and other literature. Although in their final report the Stasi officers congratulated themselves on the fulfilment of the operation's aims, their grudging admission that decomposition had only been a temporary success demonstrates just how difficult it was for the MfS to deliver a decisive blow. Publishers and servants, it emerges from the report, continued with their preaching and other activities in even greater secrecy and some, like the chief target of OV 'Diener', moved to another area.[29]

OV 'Diener' is indicative of the wide range of Witness activities and individuals that the Stasi sought to suppress by means of this type of operation. Leading servants, the courier system, Bible study, baptism, house-to-house calls, the annual Memorial and external contacts all came under the MfS's microscope. The Memorial, a key event in the Society's calendar, was attended by thousands of ordinary believers and interested persons, and every effort was made to keep the location of the ceremony secret. A cat-and-mouse game took place in which the Stasi and the police, as well as factory management, sought to uncover the location of and dissuade Witnesses from attending the service, especially if it was not held in the privacy of their own home. 'Preventive talks' with believers and 'disciplinary talks' with the so-called 'hard core' were the Stasi's preferred method of intimidation.

Although Stasi regional administrations devoted considerable time to the disruption of the Memorial, head office in East Berlin was often dissatisfied with the outcome. For example, in 1985, of the fifteen regional administrations only two, Neubrandenburg and Potsdam, had managed to obstruct the celebrations in their area of responsibility.[30] Four years later, the fifteen disciplinary and preventive talks conducted by the Leipzig Regional Administration with Witness leaders and active publishers had discouraged some brethren from attending the Memorial, but others had seized the opportunity for communication with Stasi personnel to press for a lifting of the ban on their organisation or to glean information about the security organs.[31] A crude overall cost–benefit analysis of the Stasi's campaigns against the Memorial shows how resources were dissipated, as in the two-day IM surveillance in 1988 of Helmut Jahn, a circuit overseer from Schwerin. The case file runs to eleven pages and abounds with trivia, such as when the family left the house and the time spent by IMs on surveillance. The IMs took up their observation post at 07.00 hours on the day of the Memorial; they had nothing meaningful to report until 18.40 hours (Hirch 2003b: 188).

As explained above, the Jehovah's Witness courier and communication system was the lifeline of the Watchtower Society. It kept the local congregations in touch with developments in the Society at large, helped strengthen their resolve in the face of persecution and gave them access to 'spiritual food' such as audio cassettes, books and magazines. *The Watchtower* was particularly important for providing direction and guidance in religious matters and for underpinning doctrinal uniformity. Although the building of the Berlin Wall severely disrupted links with the Federal Republic, many were soon restored and further opportunities arose with the easing of East–West relations and the sharp increase in personal contacts from the early 1970s onwards. West German pensioners smuggled literature into the GDR; materials were posted to non-Witness friends for redistribution in the GDR; advantage was taken of Leipzig's international fair; magazines were reproduced on microfilm as well as in reduced format on thin paper; and duplicating facilities were set up in the GDR. A special GDR edition of *Awake!* was launched by the headquarters of the German Watchtower Society located in Selters.[32] In addition, a cover name was devised for each courier and courier link, cover addresses were used for the receipt of literature, and a communication system was developed in the GDR for the secret transfer of materials by couriers using official transit routes and special drop-off points on trains. Links were not confined to the two German republics but extended to the Scandinavian countries and neighbouring Poland and Czechoslovakia.[33]

Stasi operations against these clandestine networks demanded a high level of coordination between Main Department XX/4, individual desks in Department XX of the fifteen regional administrations, Main Departments VI, VIII and IX, and the GDR customs authorities. Main Department XX/4 was expected to uncover and pass on information about the plans of the Eastern Bureau as regards couriers, Main Department VIII to keep the couriers and their contacts under constant supervision, and Main Department IX to advise on the appropriate penal measures (Prescher 1980: 15–16, 20–24). Heavy fines were imposed, especially in the 1980s, on those who were trapped by the customs authorities. When in 1987 a car driver was caught smuggling 150 copies of a magazine into the country, as he had been doing for the last five years, he was fined DM 1,000 (Hirch 2003b: 176).

The Stasi frequently boasted of the success of its operations against the courier system. According to Herbrich, about 70 per cent of material failed to reach Witnesses in the GDR in 1972,[34] and the MfS calculated that sixty-nine courier links had been put out of action between 1976 and 1983.[35] In one of many such operations, a tip-off by an IM revealed that a courier, a former GDR citizen with contacts in the Dölbeln district, had managed to smuggle about 24,000 copies of *The Watchtower* and 3,200 books into the GDR between June 1976 and March 1978 (Prescher 1980: 12–13, 18–19). These operations and Herbrich's claim notwithstanding, problems abounded. Information moved slowly down the line from Main Department XX/4 to local Stasi units, and officers sometimes lacked the requisite knowledge and training (ibid.: 35–36). The Schwerin Regional Administration admitted in 1985 that although evidence existed of an organised courier system in the region, conclusive proof was lacking; furthermore, literature was reaching Witnesses more quickly in 1984 than in the previous year.[36] In its review of the year 1986, Main Department XX acknowledged that the courier system provided Witnesses with a relatively regular supply of Society materials, including about 20,000 copies of the special GDR edition of *The Watchtower* every fortnight, together with thousands of books and pamphlets (Hirch 2003a: 182).

One of the Stasi's favoured forms of decomposition against the Witnesses was the Christian Responsibility group (*Christliche Verantwortung*, CV). Described by Herbrich as 'the main means in the offensive against the Witness organisation',[37] the group was founded as an association in the city of Gera in 1965 and was subsequently run by the Gera Region's Department XX. Willy Müller, the editor of the group's eponymous journal until his retirement on health grounds in 1970, was recruited under duress as an informer while serving a prison sentence in 1959. He had been a leading servant in Thuringia and Gera North (Besier 2003: 145). Other pivotal figures in the association were Dieter Pape (IME 'Wilhelm'), Müller's successor Karl-Heinz Simdorn (alias Wolfgang Daum, IME 'Wolfgang') and the last editor of the journal, Werner Henry Struck (IME 'Rolf') (Hirch 2003b: 291–300, 359). By promoting a critical attitude among readers of the journal, it was hoped to persuade Witnesses to break with the Society and also, with the aid of IMs, to undermine the Witness organisation 'from within'.[38] In order to further its aims, the Stasi also arranged for the journal to be sent to Witnesses both inside and outside the GDR as well as to other religious communities, such as the Protestant and Catholic churches. The circulation was raised to about 6,000 copies in 1984 (ibid.: 360). While Christian Responsibility was well-regarded by some non-Witnesses, the poor quality of the journal's articles and the association's thinly disguised political agenda aroused the suspicions of Witnesses and rendered it ineffective as an instrument of decomposition (Hirch 2003b: 373–79, 398–99; Schmidt 2003b: 268–69).

## Administrative Fines

From early 1967 onwards, the GDR authorities, increasingly sensitive to domestic and international opinion, no longer imprisoned Witnesses on criminal charges for their mission activities. Instead, the security forces sought to intimidate brethren by drawing on their repertoire of 'dirty tricks' and by making extensive use of the possibilities afforded by minor offences legislation, in particular the 1968 revised Ordinance on the Authorisation of Printed Materials, the 1968 Decree on Minor Offences and the 1975 Decree on the Formation of Associations. Fines of 10 to 300 GDR Marks, and on occasions even 1,000 GDR Marks, were imposed for infringements relating to these decrees. Fines were increased if Witnesses reoffended (Wenzlawski and Kleinow 1975: 100; Hacke 2000: 80; Hirch 2003b: 166–72). Administrative offence procedures rose sharply from 96 to 269 between 1983 and 1984. Two years later the number stood at 310, a slight fall from 324 in the previous year (Hirch 2003b: 168–70). In 1987, a fine of up to 100 GDR Marks was imposed in 50 and over 500 GDR Marks in 31 out of the overall total of 317 cases.[39]

Bible study groups, door-to-door visits, the distribution of literature and baptisms, all of which helped to create what Schmidt has called a 'community of solidarity' among Witnesses (Schmidt 2003a: 259), were among the main activities targeted by the Stasi and police for harassment by means of administrative offence procedures. As proselytising by door-to-door visits was of central importance for service as a Jehovah's Witness, many were willing to brave police and Stasi persecution. While they took precautions – for example, varying the time and the order of house visits – other Witnesses, understandably, felt unable to cope with the stress associated with house-to-house calls, opting instead for informal and discreet forms of field service.[40] Financial penalties could be heavy. In 1983 one Witness was fined 300 GDR Marks for calling on citizens in their apartments in Angermünde and another publisher had to pay 50 GDR Marks for approaching people in a cemetery in Hoyerswerda.[41] When a sister from the congregation in Gera, Marianne Büchner, refused to pay a fine of 700 GDR Marks for preaching in a village, 100 GDR Marks were deducted from her monthly wage (Eichler 2001: 74).

Partly because many Jehovah's Witnesses appealed against their fines, often using their constitutional right to submit a petition to state leaders, and formally contested the legal basis of the whole procedure, Herbrich reminded his subordinates at a meeting in 1986 that 'spectacular actions' should be avoided when implementing minor offences legislation.[42] In accordance with this precept, the Stasi's Main Departments XX/4 and IX and the Main Department of the constabulary police had been trying since 1982 to standardise procedures to ensure a smooth coordination between police district offices and the Stasi's district service units.[43] This approach enjoyed only mixed success. In 1986, Department XX in the Leipzig Region admitted that the five administrative offence procedures had not achieved the desired 'decomposition' effect. Offenders had not been identified and the police had devoted insufficient time to the cases.[44] Another problem from the perspective of the Stasi and police is that the offenders were not pursued with equal vigour in all regions. This was the case in the Schwerin, East Berlin and Suhl Regions in 1984,[45] with the consequence that the 'illegal activity' of Jehovah's Witnesses had been on the increase in the capital. One final statistic highlights the limited impact of the police and the Stasi on Witness field service: between June 1984 and July 1985 the time spent by Witnesses on initial house-to-house visits had increased by about 61,000 hours and return visits by about 10,000 hours.[46]

The Stasi was as equally determined to restrict home Bible study as it was to prevent house-to-house evangelising. In the early years, Bible study groups met once per week, and from the mid 1960s twice per week. Attendance hovered around four to six persons, even increasing to between ten and fifteen at the 'mini congresses' of the 1980s (Hirch 2003b: 158–59). Fines, together with IM surveillance and oral warnings, were just some of the weapons used by the police and Stasi against members of Bible study groups. In response, the latter sought to confuse the Stasi and its snoopers by gathering together in small numbers, changing the time of meetings and only addressing each other by their first name. However, as SED rule drew towards a close, Bible study groups benefited from the general improvement in the situation of the Jehovah's Witnesses. Goran

Westphal's study of the congregation in Weimar has shown that from the mid 1980s onwards Witnesses began to sing during meetings. Bettina Brüggemeier and her husband Peter recall that they enjoyed good relations with neighbours and had few problems with the police for not casting their vote in elections. They did acknowledge, however, that the atmosphere was more liberal in Weimar than in a town such as Gera (Westphal 2001: 247).[47]

## Military Service and Imprisonment

Of all the Jehovah's Witnesses' alleged offences, it was their refusal to serve in the military on grounds of conscience which was most severely punished by the East German authorities. Although the SED introduced military conscription in 1962, it became possible two years later to opt for the alternative of service in a construction unit. As the Watchtower Society's doctrine did not require total conscientious objection, an unknown number of Witnesses chose to become construction soldiers. Many others refused to take advantage of this provision, partly because they perceived, correctly, that it was not a genuine civilian alternative to normal military service. As a result, thousands of Witnesses were prosecuted as conscientious objectors in the military courts according to the Military Service Laws of 1962 and 1982 and other discriminatory legislation. Between 1963 and 1987, 2,750 Jehovah's Witnesses were arrested and imprisoned for periods of between eighteen and twenty-four months for refusing to serve in the armed forces. The length of a sentence was normally twenty months (Dirksen 2001a: 866, 868, 875). The suffering of the Witnesses in prison is one of the darkest chapters in the history of the GDR. Johannes Wrobel has estimated that as many as 8,000 were arrested in the period covered by the Soviet Zone of Occupation and the GDR, and that sixty-two died while on remand in custody or in prison between 1945 and 1949 (Wrobel 2006b: 170–71). While the harshness of repression was tempered in the later 1950s and the Witnesses experienced a general improvement in prison conditions following the promulgation of a new penal law in 1977, they still had to endure poor sanitary and medical provision, a monotonous daily routine, poor nutrition and difficulties in obtaining a copy of the Bible (ibid.: 175, 181, 183–84). Not until the mid 1980s did the East German authorities become less ruthless, no longer punishing Jehovah's Witnesses after 1986 for refusing to perform military service. Old habits died hard, however, as the military authorities tried to prevent Witnesses from avoiding conscription.

## Young Jehovah's Witnesses

Before their imprisonment, many Witnesses had already suffered discrimination at school and, even in the less oppressive 1980s, were frequently deprived of an apprenticeship for refusing to take part in various forms of pre-military education at school or in organisations such as the Society for Sport and Technology (GST).[48] As this was also usually combined with their rejection of membership in the Pioneers and the Free German Youth (FDJ), the door was normally closed on studying for the *Abitur* at upper school or entry to a university. As one male Jehovah's Witness, U.H., recalls, since the brethren openly disagreed with aspects of the official curriculum, they were confined to the bottom rungs on the occupational ladder. In his case, 'my whole working life has been restricted to doing menial jobs in a garage' (cited in Dirksen 2006: 202; see also Dirksen and Dirksen 2001: 246–47). Witnesses had to endure another form of pressure: acceptance for an apprenticeship was made conditional on signing a document confirming a willingness to take part in pre-military training. As Witness parents and their children were not prepared to do so, one option, as in the case of a family with three sons at the Käthe-Kollwitz school in Karl-Marx-Stadt, was to find alternative semi-skilled jobs with a private firm.[49] Although young Witnesses tended to perform well at school and to exhibit many of the traits, such as diligence and politeness, which the East German education authorities thought desirable, their grades were often deliberately lowered by the school for their refusal to join the FDJ and the Thälmann Pioneers and to take part in pre-military education (Dirksen and Dirksen 2001: 246–47). The youngsters also had to face the mockery of peers towards 'outsiders' who refused to conform and the pressure applied by teachers to force Witness pupils to salute the East German flag, join in the rendering of the national anthem, participate in the *Jugendweihe* – the state ceremony for fourteen-year-olds – and make the appropriate ritual greetings. The resulting marginalisation and severe forms of discrimination underscore the observation by Annegrete and Hans-Hermann Dirksen of the 'normality' of repression facing all Jehovah's Witnesses in the GDR (ibid.: 273).

The militarisation of school life posed the most serious challenge to young Witnesses, especially with the appreciable increase in military-related topics in the school curriculum from 1971 onwards. Seven years later, this culminated in the highly controversial introduction by the SED of compulsory theoretical and practical pre-military training in schools for pupils aged fourteen to sixteen. This was linked, according to the SED, to the need for members of society to demonstrate their love for and willingness to defend the socialist fatherland. The new measures created an additional personal dilemma and acute stress for Witness families, even though parents were sometimes able to reach a compromise with schools. A general survey by the Stasi in 1983 of reactions to instruction in the use of weapons indicated that some Witnesses allowed their children to participate in this activity, albeit passively. The children did not, for example, become involved in marching and managed to avoid practising with air guns and hand grenades. While some schools devised ad hoc solutions by allowing children to go home early or finding them cleaning jobs,[50] most young Witnesses had to endure social and educational discrimination and various forms of isolation, a situation which served to reinforce the importance of the compensatory support provided by their families, congregations, like-minded peers and their personal faith (Schmidt 2003b: 285–86).

## Surviving Persecution

Data on membership of the Watchtower and Bible Tract Society in the GDR highlight the Stasi's failure to attain its main goal – the liquidation of the Witness organisation – and help explain why the MfS ultimately settled for a policy of containment or, as Main Department XX/4 expressed it, keeping the Witnesses 'as a whole … under control' (Hirch 2003b: 153). According to Hans-Hermann Dirksen's exhaustive investigations, there were about 23,160 publishers in 1950 and only slightly less, about 21,160, forty years later (Dirksen 2001a: 864–67). In the intervening decades, numbers fluctuated, mainly as a result of state persecution. After the imposition of the ban on the organisation, membership dropped sharply only to recover quickly in 1952, reaching 20,292 in the following year. Much to the delight of Stasi officers, the upward trend between 1963 and 1975 was checked by disappointment among publishers at the failure of the Society's prophecy that Armageddon would occur in 1975. Numbers did not begin to rise again until 1980, reaching a peak of 22,821 in 1988. Membership figures do not, it should be stressed, provide a full picture as they do not take account of interested persons and the thousands of non-publishers who celebrated the Memorial each year; about 15,000 attended this in 1973, and a similar number in 1988.

While these figures are indicative of the ultimate failure of Stasi persecution, ministry reports are replete with references to 'successes' in its campaigns against the Jehovah's Witnesses: the creation of a comprehensive data bank on the Witness community; continuous surveillance of the activities of publishers and pioneers; the infiltration of the Eastern Bureau and the disruption of its communications with East Germany; the recruitment of Witnesses as informers; and the nurturing of the Christian Responsibility 'opposition movement'. The list can be extended to include the dissolution of organisational structures; the removal of key leaders; impediments to baptism; and the disruption of the Memorial, home Bible study and congregation meetings. The Stasi also noted the problems experienced by the Witness organisation in the GDR in recruiting and training servants and elders and finding suitable pioneers to strengthen its presence in the north of the GDR.[51] On occasions, notably in 1950/51, the Stasi seemed to be on the verge of liquidating the Society in the GDR. Once this had proved beyond its reach, the emphasis was switched from harsh and open repression to gradual decomposition and the transformation of the Witnesses into a tame religious community. But, as Main Department XX/4 and its units in the regional administrations were forced to recognise, covert measures against the Witnesses, albeit combined with overt punitive actions, such as imprisonment and fines, did not have a lasting impact. The transience of 'negative successes' is apparent in Stasi assessments of its persecution of the Witnesses from the early 1950s to the late

1980s (ibid.: 19). The following remarks in a report issued by Department XX of the Schwerin Regional Administration in 1984 are typical:

> no long-term uncertainty has been achieved by the implementation of the political decomposition measures. Only for a relatively short period of time of up to about ½ [a] year after carrying out these measures did a decline in activities occur and then predominantly only among those members directly affected or in the particular congregation.[52]

Inadequacies in coordinating operations between district service units and the specialist department in overall charge had, it was admitted, enabled Witness leaders to regroup and 'discipline' their members.[53]

This admission underlines the significance of factors which are inherent in the structures and role of the Stasi and which provide part of the explanation for the MfS's limited success. Confronted by determined opponents such as the Jehovah's Witnesses, whose organisational and territorial structures did not correspond with those of the GDR and its security forces, a high level of coordination was required between the forces of the Stasi, the police and SED organs, as well as between the Stasi's own units. Given the legion of tasks which the MfS was increasingly driven to perform, ranging from the intractable problem of stemming emigration and flight from the GDR to patching up the many cracks in the country's ailing economy, the Stasi's local and regional units were often overworked and their resources spread too thinly (Kleinow and Wenzlawski 1977: 106). It is therefore not surprising that the Halle Regional Administration conceded in 1986 that its district service units did not regard the Jehovah's Witnesses as a priority.[54] In the mid 1980s the situation was even more problematic in the Erfurt Region: no operations had taken place against Witnesses on account of other more pressing matters.[55] Even when operations were conducted elsewhere, as against Martin Jahn on the occasion of the 1988 Memorial, resources were dissipated on passive surveillance. And a reading of Stasi reports from the 1980s suggests that many of the control measures which officers and IMs carried out in connection with the annual Memorial were more a matter of routine than a vital element in a crusade against 'hostile' forces (Hirch 2003b: 189–91).

The Stasi's wide-ranging societal remit meant that local units lacked an adequate IM base for penetrating the inner sanctum of the Watchtower Society.[56] Without sufficient 'eyes and ears' and other resources, the MfS frequently failed to uncover the Witnesses' organisational structures and to identify leading servants; this fundamental failing caused much soul-searching at the coordination meetings which Main Department XX/4 held with representatives of regional administrations.[57] Even on those occasions when the Stasi utilised Witnesses as IMs in crucial operations, it was still unable to overcome some of its intrinsic difficulties and found itself outwitted. A comparison between an analysis by the Stasi's Karl-Marx-Stadt Regional Administration and the post-unification recollections of a leading Witness illustrates this point. In 1979 the Karl-Marx-Stadt office congratulated itself on decomposition measures which had led to the break-up and suspension for three years of a Kingdom Ministry School organised in Zwickau for leading preachers and to the release of the instructor, Martin Jahn, from his office for one year. This had been achieved with the aid of two IMs in Zwickau, IM 'Günther' and IMB 'Kreutzer' (as well as IMB 'Quermann'), who were both elders.[58] However, in an article written after the collapse of the GDR, Martin Jahn disclosed that the Stasi had been outmanoeuvred: aware that Stasi agents were probably among them, Jahn had informed local elders of the suspension of the School; in reality, training continued in secret and neither he nor the circuit servant, Horst Kolbe, had stepped down from office (Jahn 2001: 11–14; see also Hirch 2001: 68–73).

Moving from the local to the central level, the Stasi's knowledge gap is also apparent from Main Department XX/4's assessment of ZOV 'Swamp' in 1986/87. Two out of eighteen top officials had not been unmasked and 21 circuit overseers, 73 territory servants and about 1,300 local congregation officials could not be named.[59] A lack of information was by no means the only problem; delusion, too, was a factor, for while Stasi officers hoped to turn the Christian Responsibility association into an effective instrument of subversion, they conceded that Witnesses were fully aware that the group was an organ of the MfS.[60]

Surviving persecution was certainly not just an outcome of the Stasi's own weaknesses and problems; the explanation must be sought above all in the organisational structures and the doctrines of the Society, as well as in the faith of the brethren themselves, a shield that helped Witnesses withstand state interference elsewhere in Eastern Europe and in the Soviet Union. The Witness policy of self-defence was frequently conducted under the direction of the Eastern Bureau in the Federal Republic. Not only did this encompass the regular restructuring of the Witness organisation in the GDR and improvements in the training of leading servants, but it also covered the tightening of internal security according to the fire-wall principle and the rebuilding of courier links.[61] The Society did not, however, confine itself to protecting itself within its own walls: when it was deemed opportune, members were encouraged to protest openly against OVs, administrative fines and other forms of intimidation. But, it was, above all, the Witnesses' faith and their solidarity as a community which enabled them to withstand, often with great stoicism, the decomposition and liquidation measures to which they were subjected perhaps more consistently and over a longer period than any other minority. Brethren were united by a number of shared beliefs and activities: a deep religious conviction underpinned by the prospect of the post-Armageddon Kingdom; the ingenuity required to obtain and distribute Watchtower literature; the intensive study and internalisation of the teachings of the Society; the conversion and baptism of new brethren; and the personal dedication of elders and other servants. Other binding factors included: the widespread belief in the need for discipline in, and obedience to, Watchtower Society instructions and organisational guidelines; expulsion from the Witness community and other measures as sanctions against deviance; the perception of persecution as a test and confirmation of faith and mission work; and the reassurance derived from belonging to a worldwide organisation. The financial and psychological assistance given by congregations to members who were fined and imprisoned also played a crucial role in sustaining Witnesses against persecution (see Schmidt 2003b: 262–76, 283–84, 293–302). Although Stasi officers paid tribute to the organisational resilience of the Watchtower Society and the effectiveness of its 'conspiratorial' measures, they failed to appreciate the vital significance and depth of the Witnesses' faith as their image of the publishers was clouded by the MfS's Marxist-Leninist ideology and the concomitant perception of the Society as a tool of ultra-reactionary imperialism.

Finally, the fate of Jehovah's Witnesses in the GDR, like that of the Jewish Communities, was interwoven with the external environment: not only were they dependent on support from the West German Branch Office and the Eastern Bureau but also on developments in the Soviet Union and its client states, as well as on East–West relations in general. Détente, for example, had a decisive influence on the shaping of the 'silent terror' of decomposition. The repercussions of the general crisis of the communist system in the 1980s were of greater significance, however. The relaxation of persecution against Jehovah's Witnesses in Hungary and Poland in the mid 1980s and the coming of Gorbachev to power in the Soviet Union in 1985 were a source of great encouragement for East German brethren and raised expectations of a lifting of the ban on their organisation. In the GDR itself, the final quinquennium of SED rule was a time in which hope and coercion coexisted (Hacke 2000: 264). On the one hand, Jehovah's Witnesses were no longer imprisoned for refusing to do military service and they were able to conduct religious services more openly. They were not, however, free of intimidation and repression as regards mission work, the celebration of the Memorial, and job and training opportunities. Indeed, it would not be until 14 March 1990, several months after the fall of the Berlin Wall and the disintegration of the SED, that the coalition government of Hans Modrow lifted the ban and the Witness organisation in the GDR finally received legal recognition from the state authorities as a religious community. A lengthy struggle was required, however, before the Berlin state government finally granted Witnesses the status of a public corporation in June 2006.

## Notes

1. See H.-H. Dirksen (2000, 2001a, 2001b), Dirksen and Dirksen (2001) and A. Dirksen (2006).
2. The Society teaches that the 144,000 persons who stood with Jesus Christ on Mount Zion belong, together with Christ, to the final heavenly congregation of God redeemed from Earth.
3. A list of the dissertations, with abbreviated titles, their authors and their archival classification can be found in the bibliography.

4. See, e.g., the thesis by Majors Gerfried Wenzlawski and Hans-Jochen Kleinow (1975: 6–10).
5. Riedel (1980: 5–6, 8). Riedel was a captain in the Stasi's Karl-Marx-Stadt Regional Administration.
6. Riedel's view echoed that of his superior officer in Main Department XX/4, Oskar Herbrich, who, at a meeting with the Karl-Marx-Stadt Regional Administration in 1974, stated that political-ideological subversion by the Jehovah's Witnesses consisted of a blind anti-communism and an end-of-the-world view, whose aim was to undermine the loyalty and socialist consciousness of GDR citizens: BStU, MfS, Außenstelle Chemnitz, no.876, 'Bericht', 19 February 1974, p.158.
7. BStU, MfS, ZA, HA IX, no.51, 'Kurzauskunft "Wachtturm-, Bibel- und Traktat-Gesellschaft" (WTG) – Organisation "Zeugen Jehova"', 21 May 1984, p.71.
8. BStU, MfS, Außenstelle Chemnitz, KD Zwickau, no.20, 'Verbotene Sekte Zeugen Jehovas', 10 May 1977, pp.282, 285, 288–89, 292.
9. BStU, MfS, Außenstelle Rostock, BV Rostock, Abteilung XX, no.552, vol.4, 'Sachstandbericht zum "OV Diener"', 19 January 1983, p.156.
10. BStU, MfS, Außenstelle Schwerin, BV Schwerin, KD Gadebusch, no.11288, 'Einschätzung zur Situation und zu Tendenzen in den Aktivitäten der Funktionäre und Mitglieder der in der DDR verbotenen Organisation "Zeugen Jehova" im Bezirk Schwerin', 5 December, p.29; BStU, MfS, Außenstelle Chemnitz, XX, no.747, 'Information zur Tätigkeit der verbotenen Sekte "Zeugen Jehovas"', 6 May 1975, p.9.
11. The six Stasi Regional Administrations which ran sub-operations were Leipzig, Halle, Magdeburg, Erfurt, Dresden and East Berlin. OV 'Thurm', which had commenced in the Karl-Marx-Stadt Region before the ZOV was launched, was attached to the ZOV as an OV. For details, see Dirksen (2001a: 681–82).
12. BStU, MfS, Außenstelle Chemnitz, XX, no.738, 'Arbeitsdirektive der HA XX/4', 10 August 1966, pp.27–29.
13. Ibid., 'Einschätzung über den Stand der politisch-operativen Bearbeitung der verbotenen Organisation "Zeugen Jehova"', 4 April 1966, p.135.
14. Ibid., 'Arbeitsdirektive der HA XX/4', 10 August 1966, p.34.
15. BStU, MfS, Außenstelle Chemnitz, XX, no.734, 'Operativ-Information', 30 December 1969, pp.5–7. See also Hirch (2003b: 154–55) and Schmidt (2003b: 266–68).
16. BStU, MfS, Außenstelle Chemnitz, XX, no.738, 'Arbeitsdirektive der HA XX/4', 10 August 1966, pp.31–33.
17. See the interview in Schmidt (2003b: 190).
18. See the interviews in ibid. (208–11, 225).
19. BStU, MfS, Außenstelle Leipzig, BVfS Leipzig, Abteilung XX, no.00175/03, 'Protokoll über Ablauf der Koordinierungsberatung auf der Linie illegale Organisation "Zeugen Jehova", am 24.11.87', 1 December 1987, p.48.
20. BStU, MfS, Außenstelle Chemnitz, XX, no.375, 'Analyse über das IM-System des Referates XX/4', 13 April 1970, p.171.
21. BStU, MfS, Außenstelle Chemnitz, XX, no.747, 'Information zur Tätigkeit der verbotenen Sekte "Zeugen Jehovas"', 26 September 1975, p.12.
22. BStU, MfS, Außenstelle Suhl, BV Suhl, Abteilung XX, no.107, 'Treffauswertung über den durchgeführten Treff mit der KP "Fritz" am heutigen Tage', 10 August 1960, p.76.
23. BStU, MfS, Außenstelle Chemnitz, Abteilung XX, no.1890, 'Arbeitsbuch des Mitarbeiters Joachim Riedel, 1978', p.34.
24. BStU, MfS, Außenstelle Suhl, BV Suhl, Abteilung XX, no.107, 'Operativplan zur weiteren Bearbeitung des Gruppenvorgangs Rg. Nr.: 3/55 Deckname "Seuche" angelegt am 11.3.1955, op. Mitarbeiter Koch', 20 May 1955, p.11.
25. HA XX/4's plans to discredit Egon Peter are to be found in: BStU, MfS, Außenstelle Chemnitz, XX, no.738, 'Maßnahmeplan zur gemeinsamen Bearbeitung des Leiters des Ostbüros der Organisation "Zeugen Jehova" in Wiesbaden/BRD', 8 October 1980, pp.290–91.

26. See ibid., 'Einschätzung über den Stand der politisch-operativen Bearbeitung der verbotenen Organisation "Zeugen Jehova"', 4 April 1966, p.133.

27. BStU, MfS, ZA, KuSch, no.420/89(II), pp.30–31, 36, 39–53. Bergner had to repay the money.

28. BStU, MfS, Außenstelle Halle, BV Halle, Abteilung XX, Sachakten, no.776, 'Bericht über die Koordinierungsvereinbarung zwischen den Bezirksverwaltungen Frankfurt/Oder, Cottbus, Potsdam, Magdeburg und Halle auf der Linie XX/4 – "Zeugen Jehovas"', 3 March 1972, p.27.

29. BStU, MfS, ZA, HA XX/AKG, no.5509, 'Eröffnungsbericht zum OV "Diener"', 13 June 1978, pp.2-5; ibid., 'Abschlußbericht zum OV "Diener"', 29 January 1983, pp.9–12.

30. BStU, MfS, ZA, HA XX/4, no.1239, 'Information über die Durchführung operativer Maßnahmen am 4.4.1985 gegen illegale Zusammenkünfte der "Zeugen Jehovas"', 15 April 1985, p.614.

31. BStU, MfS, Außenstelle Leipzig, BVfS Leipzig, Abteilung XX, no.00175/09, 'Politisch-operative Ergebnisse und Wirksamkeit der realisierten Vorbeugungs- und Zersetzungsmaßnahmen gegen die verbotene Organisation "Zeugen Jehova" in Vorbereitung und Durchführung des sogennanten Gedächtnismahls am 22.3.1989 ', 4 April 1989, pp.15–17.

32. BStU, MfS, Außenstelle Leipzig, BVfS Leipzig, Abteilung XX, no.02221, 'Operativ-Information über markante Tendenzen im Zeitraum Juli 1982 bis Juni 1983 bei der Entwicklung der Organisation "Zeugen Jehova" in der DDR', 24 August 1983, p.6.

33. BStU, MfS, Außenstelle Halle, BV Halle, Abteilung XX, Sachakten, no.776, 'Information über die verbotene "Wachtturmgesellschaft (WTG)" im Sicherungsbereich der BV Halle', 16 May 1977, pp.2–4; and Prescher (1980: 5, 7).

34. BStU, MfS, Außenstelle Halle, MfS BV Halle, Abteilung XX, Sachakten, no.776, 'Bericht über die Koordinierungsvereinbarung zwischen den Bezirksverwaltungen Frankfurt/Oder, Cottbus, Potsdam, Magdeburg und Halle auf der Linie XX/4 – "Zeugen Jehovas"', 3 March 1972, p.27.

35. BStU, MfS, Außenstelle Leipzig, BVfS Leipzig, Abteilung XX, no.00175/03, 'Protokoll zur Koordinierungsberatung auf der Linie illegale Sekte "Zeugen Jehova" ZJ-Bezirk 3 am 25.10.1985 in der BV Leipzig', 13 December 1985, p.8.

36. BStU, MfS, Außenstelle Schwerin, MfS-BV Schwerin, KD Gadebusch, no.11288, 'Einschätzung zur Situation und zu Tendenzen in den Aktivitäten der Funktionäre und Mitglieder der in der DDR verbotenen Organisation "Zeugen Jehova" im Bezirk Schwerin', 5 December 1985, pp.29–30.

37. BStU, MfS, ZA, BV Halle, Abt. XX, Sachakten, no.757, 'Einschätzung der Ergebnisse der Koordinierungsberatung der Linie "Zeugen Jehova" am 30.11. und 1.12.1982', 6 December 1982, p.146.

38. BStU, MfS, Außenstelle Dresden, BV Dresden, Abteilung XX, no.9191, 'Gegenwärtige Wirksamkeit der Studiengruppe "Christliche Verantwortung"', 30 October 1985, p.2.

39. BStU, MfS, ZA, HA IX, no.51, 'Information über geahndete Rechtsverletzungen gegenüber Angehörigen der verbotenen Organisation "Zeugen Jehova" im Jahre 1987', 20 December 1988, p.105.

40. See the interview with Sabine D. in Schmidt (2003a: 93).

41. BStU, MfS, ZA, HA IX, no.51, 'Übersicht über den Stand der Bearbeitung von Ordnungsstrafenverfahren gegen ehemalige Mitglieder der verbotenen Organisation "Zeugen Jehovas"', 10 February 1984, p.47.

42. BStU, MfS, Außenstelle Leipzig, BVfS Leipzig, Abteilung XX, no.00175/03, 'Protokoll zur Koordinierungssberatung auf der Linie der Organisation "Zeugen Jehova" – ZJ-Bezirk 3 am 26.11.1986 in der BV Leipzig', 4 December 1986, pp.24–25.

43. BStU, MfS, ZA, HA IX, no.51, 'Einschätzung zur vorliegenden Information des MdI/Hauptabteilung Schutzpolizei vom 14.03.1985 über den Stand und die Entwicklungstendenzen bei der Ahndung rechtswidriger Aktivitäten der verbotenen Organisation "Zeugen Jehovas"', 18 April 1985, p.80; and Dirksen (2001a: 792–802).

44. BStU, MfS, Außenstelle Leipzig, BVfS Leipzig, Abteilung XX, no.02221, 'Lageeinschätzung auf der Linie illegale Sekte "Zeugen Jehova" im Verantwortungsbereich der BV Leipzig/I. Halbjahr 1986', 7 July 1986, p.47.
45. BStU, MfS, ZA, HA IX, no.51, 'Einschätzung zur vorliegenden Information des MdI/Hauptabteilung Schutzpolizei vom 14.03.1985 über den Stand und die Entwicklungstendenzen bei der Ahndung rechtswidrigen Aktivitäten der verbotenen Organisation "Zeugen Jehovas"', 18 April 1985, p.80.
46. BStU, MfS, Außenstelle Leipzig, BVfS, Abteilung XX, no.00175/09, 'Information über Pläne und Absichten der Feindzentrale der Organisation "Zeugen Jehova" gegen die DDR', 14 February 1986, pp.2–3. Stasi operatives acquired the data from Eastern Bureau records.
47. Eichler mentions that in the late 1980s singing took place both at the beginning and at the end of meetings in Gera (Eichler 2001: 77).
48. Before 1982, young Jehovah's Witnesses were usually able to take up an apprenticeship but when pre-military education became a compulsory element of training as an apprentice from the September of that year, the door was completely closed: see Hacke (2000: 265).
49. BStU, MfS, Außenstelle Chemnitz, XX, no, 897, 'Aktenvermerk zum Treff mit dem GMS "Bär"', 24 September 1981, p.65.
50. BStU, MfS, ZA, HA XX/AKG, no.5495, 'Bericht über Reaktionen der "Z.J." zum Wehrkundunterricht', 28 June 1983, pp 55–56.
51. BStU, MfS, Außenstelle Leipzig, BVfS, Leipzig, Abteilung XX, no.00175/03, 'Protokoll über Ablauf der Koordinierungsberatung auf der Linie illegale Organisation "Zeugen Jehova", am 24.11.87', 1 December 1987, p.40; BStU, MfS, Außenstelle Leipzig, BVfS Leipzig, Abteilung XX, no.00175/09, 'Information über Pläne und Absichten der Feindzentrale der Organisation "Zeugen Jehova" gegen die DDR ', 14 February 1986, pp.3–4.
52. BStU, MfS, Außenstelle Schwerin, BV Schwerin, KD Gadebusch, no.11288, 'Analyse über die Aktivitäten der Organisation "ZJ"', 15 March 1984, p.8.
53. Ibid., p.21.
54. BStU, MfS, Außenstelle Leipzig, BVfS Leipzig, Abteilung XX, no.00175/03, 'Protokoll zur Koordinierungsberatung auf der Linie der Organisation "Zeugen Jehova" – ZJ-Bezirk 3 am 28.11.1986 in der BV Leipzig', 4 December 1986, p.28.
55. Ibid., 'Anhang: Diskussionsbeiträge bzw. Lageeinschätzung der beteiligten BV – Linie XX/4', 13 December 1985, p.13.
56. This was the tone of the comments by the regional administrations of Halle, Erfurt, Suhl, Gera and Leipzig: ibid., 'Protokoll zur Koordinierungsberatung auf der Linie der Organisation "Zeugen Jehova" – ZJ-Bezirk 3 am 26.11.1986 in der BV Leipzig', 4 December 1986, pp.28–31.
57. See Herbrich's comments in ibid., 'Protokoll über Ablauf der Koordinierungsberatung auf der Linie illegale Organisation "Zeugen Jehova", am 24.11.87', 1 December 1987, p.43.
58. See Riedel (1980: 14–28), Hirch (2001: 68–73) and Jahn (2001: 12–15).
59. See Hirch (2003b: 152).
60. BStU, MfS, Außenstelle Chemnitz, Abteilung XX, no.190, 'Information', 7 December 1981, p.458.
61. BStU, MfS, Außenstelle Leipzig, BVfS Leipzig, Abteilung XX, no.00175/03, 'Protokoll zur Koordinierungsberatung auf der Linie illegale Sekte "Zeugen Jehova" ZJ-Bezirk 3 am 25.10.1985 in der BV Leipzig', 13 December 1985, pp.7–11.

# Chapter 4

# ASIAN AND AFRICAN WORKERS IN THE NICHES OF SOCIETY

## Foreigners in the GDR

**W**hen the Berlin Wall fell, not the least of the many surprises was the revelation that over 191,000 foreign nationals were living in the GDR. Although foreigners had always formed a relatively small proportion of the population of the GDR (1.2 per cent in December 1989), their background was diverse, ranging from political refugees, schoolchildren and students to apprentices, diplomats and workers. While Poles, Vietnamese, Mozambicans, Hungarians, Bulgarians and Cubans were well represented, Great Britain and the U.S.A. had less than 150 residents in the GDR in late 1989 (Elsner and Elsner 1994: 77–78). In addition to these nationalities, there were also over 360,000 Soviet troops stationed in the country and their 200,000 dependants.

To what extent foreign nationals were incorporated into the work environment, what motivated the sending countries and the East German government, how the foreign labour contingents interacted with each other and the local population, and how they were perceived and treated by the Stasi and police will be the subject of this chapter. Rather than attempt an overall survey of foreigners in the GDR, however, the focus will be on two of the largest groups during the 1980s; that is, the Vietnamese and Mozambicans who were employed on fixed-term labour contracts of four to five years. The study of their experiences will show that, like their Algerian and Hungarian predecessors, they were by no means passive subjects of surveillance and an elaborate state bureaucracy but were able, albeit to a limited extent, to assert some basic demands and to create

Notes for this section begin on page 118.

their own social and ethnic networks in the niches of society.[1] In this respect, they afford a further illustration that society during the SED dictatorship was far from *stillgelegt* ('shut down') and was differentiated according to criteria such as occupation, gender, ethnicity and age.

Although the GDR did not sign the UN Convention on Refugees of 1951, it did provide refuge for many who suffered persecution in their own countries, among them several thousand Greeks, Chileans, Spaniards and members of the Palestinian Liberation Organisation (PLO), the African National Congress (ANC) and the South West African People's Organisation (SWAPO). In addition, the GDR, as one of the most advanced industrial powers among the Council for Mutual Economic Assistance (Comecon), was a major provider of vocational training for several thousand apprentices in colleges and enterprises and students in institutions of higher education. Comecon was the Soviet bloc's overarching economic organisation. The training programmes not only aimed to improve vocational standards among the state socialist countries as part of Comecon's professed goal of social and economic convergence but they also fitted into ideologically and politically driven notions of proletarian internationalism and solidarity with fraternal socialist countries. Links were established, too, with liberation movements and young national states and hailed as part of the GDR's commitment to their release from the yoke of imperialism, and to the promotion of economic growth in what were less developed countries.

As the 1960s progressed, the GDR took a growing interest in recruiting workers on short-term contracts who could help plug the country's inadequate labour supply. Bilateral agreements were signed between the East German government and Hungary (1967), Poland (1971), Algeria (1974), Cuba (1978) and Mozambique (1979). Others were concluded with Vietnam, Mongolia, Angola and China in the 1980s. While all the agreements incorporated arrangements for training programmes to enhance the skills of foreign workers, this aspect declined sharply in significance as the GDR's economic, financial and labour problems mounted during the 1980s. The first bilateral agreement on contract working, with Hungary in 1967, had been preceded one year earlier by the GDR's so-called transit accord with Poland which enabled large numbers of Polish commuters to obtain employment in East German enterprises close to the border with Poland. For most of the 1980s, an estimated 3,000 to 4,100 Polish commuters found work each year in the GDR, most of them women (Röhr 2001: 76–78, 162–68, 262). Commercial contracts represented the third major type of bi-national cooperation. Predominantly affecting Poles, the contracts were negotiated between individual state-controlled enterprises specialising in assembly and construction work. In June 1987, Polish workers numbered 24,000 out of the overall total of 29,800 on commercial contracts.[2]

The most important form of labour activity involving foreigners from the late 1970s onwards was short-term contract work based on intergovernmental agreements. Some idea of its rapid increase and relative weighting can be obtained from the data bank of the State Secretariat for Labour and Wages. Whereas 9,300

Vietnamese and 7,700 Mozambican contract workers were resident in the GDR in 1987, by mid 1989 the figures had soared to 52,130 and 15,300 respectively. At the end of June 1989, of the 150,400 foreign workers in the GDR, about 85,020 were contract workers.[3] They were located in all Administrative Regions (*Bezirke*) of the GDR, with the highest concentrations in East Berlin and the southern industrial conurbations, notably the Karl-Marx-Stadt (Chemnitz), Dresden, Leipzig and Halle regions. Employed predominantly on multi-shift systems and in jobs whose low skill content made them unattractive to East Germans, most of the workers were located in the textile, motor vehicle and chemical industries, large laundries and abattoirs, lignite mining, and the machine-building industry (Elsner and Elsner 1992: 58; Müggenburg 1996: 16).

The social profile of the Vietnamese differed in two ways from the pattern typical of contract workers in that, over the ten-year duration of their government's bilateral agreement, women constituted about 37 per cent and married persons about 60 per cent of Vietnamese employees (FES 1991: 5–9). By contrast, women were significantly under-represented in the Mozambican workforce as young men were believed to be the most productive and flexible form of labour. At the beginning of 1989, the Mozambican group was overwhelmingly male, with about 1,500 women out of a cohort of 15,228.[4] The composition of the Vietnamese contingents changed over the course of the bilateral agreement. In the early years, the emphasis lay on former soldiers, the descendants of resistance fighters and the widows of young soldiers. Towards the end of the 1980s, there was a shift to recruitment across all social strata and to a higher level of qualification and a greater readiness to re-employ workers after the end of their original fixed contract.

The model for all subsequent arrangements for the deployment of contract workers was the intergovernmental agreement concluded between Hungary and the GDR in 1967 and its subsequent modifications. The various bilateral agreements, which were subject to regular review, regulated the length of labour contracts, working conditions, vocational training, wage levels and bonuses, social security rights, the transfer of goods home, travel to and from the GDR, and accommodation (Gruner-Domić 1996: 208). By the mid to late 1970s, however, the GDR was forced to look beyond the socialist states of Eastern Europe for the replenishment of its labour stock as the supply of workers was drying up in Hungary and elsewhere. Algeria and Cuba were the first two non-European countries to send contract workers to the GDR, in 1974 and 1978 respectively. The number of Algerians varied from 3,500 to over 4,000 per annum for much of the ten-year agreement and Cubans up to about 6,500 until an appreciable increase in 1985 (Mac Con Uladh 2005b: 52, 56–57). The Algerian connection would prove to be particularly troublesome: Algerian workers went on strike on various occasions between 1974 and 1984 in pursuit of higher pay and better training opportunities. Conflicts, sometimes violent, took place with the local population, often over the Algerians' relationships with East German women. With the coming to power of Chadli Benjedid in 1978, the Algerian government became so disenchanted that the intergovernmental agreement was terminated in 1984 (Riedel 1994: 6–7, 84–85; Mac Con Uladh 2005b: 56–57). Violence involving Cuban workers in the GDR, as well as in Czechoslovakia, was one of the reasons behind Cuba's threat not to send any workers in 1988. Two years earlier, about 1,000 Cubans had been repatriated.[5]

### The Bilateral Agreements with Mozambique and Vietnam

With the GDR's labour and economic problems escalating, it looked to Africa and Southeast Asia for relief. It already enjoyed diplomatic relations and modest economic exchanges with two countries, Mozambique and Vietnam, and could claim a mutual interest in combating the imperialist enemy. Links had been established in 1963 with the Liberation Front of Mozambique (Frelimo), the spearhead of Mozambique's successful struggle for independence from its Portuguese colonial rulers. Formal diplomatic relations commenced in 1975, shortly after the proclamation of Mozambique's independence. Despite numerous political and ideological ties, the GDR showed little interest in economic cooperation until it decided to embark on an export offensive designed to relieve its pressing foreign trade and hard-currency problems. In 1979, the two countries signed a Treaty of Friendship and Cooperation, a Treaty of Long-term Economic Cooperation, and an agreement on the deployment of Mozambican contract workers in the GDR. Mozambique would benefit from East German supplies of agricultural machinery and lorries, the expansion of the electric power system and coal mining, and vocational training programmes for its labour force. In return, the GDR would receive grain and coal and several thousand contract workers. At the time, Mozambique was one of the poorest countries in the world, with the average wage a mere U.S. $1 per day and a high level of hard currency indebtedness on its foreign trade. The illiteracy rate was 70 per cent and most inhabitants were little more than 20 years old (Döring 1999: 143–47, 159, 161; Rüchel 2001: 7, 9–10). The Mozambican government had been engaged since 1975 in conflict with the anti-communist organisation Renamo, which was supported by South Africa and Rhodesia. One former Mozambican contract worker from Suhl recalled during an interview that when he visited his family in 1984, he had to be escorted by Frelimo troops to his home village; at night, his parents and sister hid in a tree for fear of attacks (Scherzer 2002: 32). The death or disappearance of friends and relatives in Mozambique was a source of great anxiety and sometimes led to serious mental health problems for their compatriots in the GDR (Marburger et al. 1993: 28).

Links between the GDR and Vietnam predated those with Mozambique. In October 1949, the then Democratic Republic in the north of Vietnam entered into diplomatic relations with the newly founded GDR; however, another five years elapsed before ambassadors were exchanged. Both states were treated as political lepers by the Western world and the sense of a common cause was evoked by Horst Sindermann, the chair of the GDR People's Chamber and a member of the SED politburo, when he told a delegation from Vietnam in 1973: 'You have inflicted a defeat on USA imperialism, the same USA imperialism which is just a few kilometres from us' (Huong 1999: 1314). Bordering South Africa and its apartheid regime, Mozambique was in a similar position. Until the final liberation of South Vietnam in 1975, the GDR and other state socialist countries supplied appreciable military, financial and economic aid to the North in the name of solidarity with peoples and states struggling for freedom and national independence from colonial rule and imperialism. One important form of cooperation was the agreement concluded in 1966 which provided training opportunities in the GDR for several thousand Vietnamese apprentices, skilled workers, engineers and students.

After the end of the Vietnam War in 1975 and the formal reunification of North and South Vietnam in the following year, the GDR continued to send solidarity contributions, but it also began to place greater weight on mutual economic benefit. Vietnam itself desperately needed external assistance in its struggle to overcome the ravages of war, to cement the unification of two disparate economic and political systems, and, throughout most of the 1980s, to cope with rampant inflation, a protracted war with Cambodia and a soaring external debt. Large swathes of the country were on the verge of famine and poverty was endemic. With the economic reform (*doi moi*) introduced in 1986 failing to produce immediate benefits, the government was eager for economic and financial cooperation with the GDR. Under these circumstances, individual Vietnamese looked to employment in the GDR, as well as the Soviet Union, Bulgaria and Czechoslovakia, for desperately needed external assistance for themselves and their dependants.

While SED leaders were well informed about the plight of Mozambique and Vietnam, they failed to advise their own population of the situation and to explain why the GDR was recruiting so many guest workers from these and other non-European countries. It was politically more convenient to portray the bilateral agreements as a deepening of fraternal cooperation in order to avoid drawing attention to the GDR's economic plight. While the GDR would be disappointed in its South-east Asian and African partners as a source of raw materials and goods, their contract workers did at least help compensate for the termination of the agreements with Hungary and Algeria and a fall in the number of Polish labourers. Calculations by East German economic planners at the beginning of the 1980s estimated that the Vietnamese would attain an annual average output of 22,000 GDR Marks, the same level as the Algerians and Hungarians but 5,000 lower than that of GDR workers. The Mozambicans would bring up the rear.[6] When the costs for accommodation, inter-continental flights, cultural and social provision, the separation allowance, training, clothing and other items were deducted from these sums, then the net annual value of the output of Vietnamese and Mozambican contract labour was expected to be 15,910 GDR Marks and 7,025 GDR Marks respectively.

Given the relatively high costs associated with the deployment of Vietnamese and other non-Europeans, the SED politburo and the Council of Ministers aimed to dispense with most foreign workers by 1988 through labour rationalisation programmes and a more effective utilisation of existing plant. This aspiration encountered determined resistance from the nationalised enterprises which benefited from heavy government subsidies for foreign labour.[7] Central planning had to be readjusted accordingly. The year 1987 was the turning point as, in the words of East German Foreign Minister Oskar Fischer, 'the workers are needed with the utmost urgency'.[8] His comment was directly linked to the SED politburo's decision on 9 December 1986 to increase markedly the production of children's shoes, anoraks, trousers and coats. Finally, with labour rationalisation schemes failing to hit their target, and with the Cuban connection running into serious difficulties, the East German government reached agreement with its Vietnamese counterpart for the despatch of a further 17,570 Vietnamese workers for employment in light industry by the middle of 1988, of which all but 3,342 were to be sent in 1987.[9]

The number of Mozambicans also increased sharply between 1987 and 1989, from 7,700 to 15,300, as their work was judged indispensable for factories in the textile, chemical, motor vehicle and other industries. Some were also destined for the lignite industry; most of the first contingent of Mozambicans had been located in the Senftenberg, Espenhain and Lauchammer lignite combines.[10] This became an embarrassing matter for the Mozambican government when, in 1988, reports appeared in the South African press about the unhealthy working conditions in the mines. The Mozambican response that its workers were mainly employed in textiles, construction and other spheres was a deliberate misrepresentation of the situation (Marburger et al. 1993: 11).

In addition to alleviating their countries' chronic unemployment problems, the Vietnamese and Mozambican governments derived numerous advantages from their agreements with the GDR. Vietnam did not incur any costs from the arrangements and the East German government made several significant annual financial transfers to the Vietnamese treasury, notably a per capita contribution to pension insurance funds and child allowance. In addition, the workers themselves were obliged to allow the GDR to transfer 12 per cent of their gross monthly wages to the Vietnamese state as a contribution towards 'the construction and defence of the Vietnamese fatherland'. In the later 1980s, according to Huong, Vietnam was receiving from its own citizens over 200 million GDR Marks per year from this and other types of transfers (Huong 1999: 1329).

The Mozambican government, too, was determined to exploit its workers in order to help relieve its economic problems and service its debt with the GDR. This can be seen in its manipulation of wage transfers. Like the Angolans, the Mozambicans were initially permitted to transfer home no more than 25 per cent of their net monthly wages above 350 GDR Marks. This was later increased to 60 per cent for the Mozambicans and the remittances were converted into their own currency. The Mozambicans could also send child benefit payments to their homeland.[11] However, the whole transfer procedure was subject to delay, the levying of heavy charges and a lack of transparency. Earnings were subject to income tax in the GDR before being sent to the Labour Office in Mozambique, where a 10 per cent tax was levied and the workers were unable in principle to draw on their income until they returned home. In fact, remittances were often confiscated without the workers' consent and subsequent reimbursement proved extremely difficult (Marburger et al. 1993: 21; Müggenburg 1996: 22; Döring 1999: 239). The exploitation of the Mozambican contract workers is apparent, too, from the idea first floated in 1987, but not implemented, that an increase in numbers was essential for reducing their country's debt with the GDR. In 1988, the SED politburo proposed, without success, that the Mozambican debt be slashed by over 500 per cent within seven years by means of obligatory wage transfers from a larger cohort of workers (Müggenburg 1996: 10–11, 77–79; Döring 1999: 234–38).

Despite governmental interference and their many personal problems, working in the GDR was an attractive proposition for young Mozambicans and Vietnamese. Homesickness, separation from friends and family, including children, and the fundamentally different landscape, mentalities, diet, language and climate of the GDR were among the main adjustment difficulties. The deep snow in winter came as a shock for new arrivals dressed only in silk trousers and sandals.[12] H., a former contract worker at factory in Glachau, vividly remembered one colleague who had been obliged to leave her eight-month-old child at home in the care of her husband so that she could support the family.[13] Nevertheless, a short-term stay in the GDR held out many advantages, being likened by H. to a form of 'paradise'.[14] Another interviewee, T., a former soldier who had worked at an enterprise in Dresden, stressed the security, mutual help and the feelings of solidarity that characterised his stay in the GDR.[15]

As the GDR authorities were aware, by far the most important motive for entering 'paradise' was to support the extended family of children, partner, parents and grandparents in Mozambique and Vietnam. This was referred to as the workers' 'family mission' and explains why the Vietnamese, for example, were so keen to boost their income by devoting much of their spare time to making garments. The Mozambicans, who were also determined to help alleviate poverty at home, worked long hours in jobs which were unpopular with East Germans. In their eagerness to acquire a contract abroad, many falsely claimed to have reached the minimum age of eighteen years.[16] Other personal, albeit secondary, motives for working in the GDR should not be overlooked (Mehrländer, Ascheberg and Uelzhöffer 1996: 474–86, 493–95). They included improving qualifications through vocational training, and for the Vietnamese, especially after the introduction of *doi moi*, acquiring the means to set up a small independent business on their return home. Furthermore, some younger recruits – like T., who had served in the North Vietnamese army against the Americans – were attracted by a sense of adventure and new experiences.[17]

With employment in the GDR such an eagerly sought prize, potential recruits attempted to turn their Communist Party of Vietnam membership, army service, and educational and vocational attainments to their advantage. Bribery of officials also played a crucial role, with doctors often demanding payment in return for the requisite health certificate. Department XVIII of the Stasi's Erfurt Regional Administration noted another practice. In order to raise the equivalent of an estimated 8,000 GDR Marks to bribe officials to allocate a work contract, villagers rallied round to borrow the money from Chinese 'usurers' at an interest rate of between 60 and 80 per cent over the period of the loan. The loan, it was anticipated, would be repaid within two years, thus leaving three years for a worker to earn money to support themselves and their family.[18]

## The Terms of Intergovernmental Agreements

The basic terms governing employment and residence of Mozambican and Vietnamese contract workers were set out in bilateral agreements and adjusted in subsequent annual protocols. The GDR's agreement with Mozambique was signed in February 1979 and that with Vietnam in April 1980. The implementation of these and other governmental agreements was regulated at local and regional level by state bodies and factory steering groups. Although the workers enjoyed significant rights, such as the transfer home of goods and remittances, the GDR and its Vietnamese partner regarded workers primarily as 'work machines' (Huong 1999: 1332) and as 'pawns' in relations between the two states (Kolinsky 2000: 150). The Mozambicans sometimes referred to themselves as 'wage slaves', which, though exaggerated, does draw attention to a persistent and fundamental socio-economic problem.[19] Despite frequent governmental proclamations of 'friendship between peoples', foreign workers were unable to choose their job and place of residence. Vulnerable to harsh disciplinary procedures, they could be deported by factory managers, the State Secretariat for Labour and Wages and the police for transgression of work discipline and social misdemeanours. Furthermore, the GDR sought to restrict workers' contacts with East Germans to officially prescribed spheres; in the SED's 'agenda of exclusion', ethnic diversity had no established place (ibid.: 149). This is certainly the perception of one Vietnamese, H., who came to realise that contract workers were no more than second-class citizens in a country which lacked democracy and creativity.[20]

Turning to the 1979 and 1980 agreements, only the key points can be mentioned here.[21] Each agreement was valid for five years and modifications were made by both governments at formal annual review meetings. The labour contracts of workers were limited to four years, albeit with the possibility of an extension for Mozambicans. In 1987, Vietnamese were allowed to remain for five years, although earlier protocols had already extended this to seven years for highly qualified workers who were deemed invaluable to the GDR (Müggenburg 1996: 9). Permanent residence was neither intended nor desired by the signatories. Younger workers were the key targets as they were expected to be the most productive group. In the case of the Vietnamese, a ceiling of eighteen to thirty-five years of age was imposed on skilled workers, but up to forty years on cadres with a higher and technical college qualification (ibid.: 84). Like the Chinese and Angolans, Mozambicans were recruited from among younger cohorts, predominantly those aged eighteen to twenty-five years. The Mozambicans' level of qualification was much lower than that of the Vietnamese, the minimum requirement being the completion of the fourth year at primary school.[22] While all contract workers were entitled to practical training and work experience, by the time of the signing of the agreements with Mozambique and Vietnam, the significance of vocational training was in decline and would become a mere adjunct to economic imperatives from 1987 onwards.[23] Obtaining a job in the GDR was determined by the authorities of the sending countries; for example, the Ministry of Labour was responsible for the selection and delegation of workers from all parts of Mozambique (Döring 1999: 232). Close relatives of contract workers were normally debarred from working in the GDR at the same time as each other and even when exceptions were made married partners had no claim on shared accommodation.

The costs of flights between the GDR and Vietnam were covered by East German enterprises, but Mozambique was required to pay for its citizens' return journey. Unlike the Vietnamese, Mozambicans were not entitled to a holiday in their own country (Broszinsky-Schwabe 1990: 23). If workers wished to travel to the state socialist countries of Eastern Europe, they needed the permission of their embassy in the GDR and an entry visa for the country of their destination. Work and social insurance was equivalent to that enjoyed by East Germans and wages were paid in accordance with GDR labour law. The Mozambicans' original right to transfer 25 per cent of monthly net income exceeding 350 Marks was increased to 60 per cent in 1987 (Marburger et al. 1993: 21). Like the Cubans, the Vietnamese had the right to send home remittances amounting to 60 per cent of their net monthly earnings above 350 GDR Marks. However, in view of the high rate of inflation of the Vietnamese dong and the losses incurred from charges on the compulsory exchange of the inconvertible GDR currency, workers preferred instead to ship home items which were in short supply, such as clothing, electronic equipment and household goods. This was done in various ways – for example, by taking advantage of their annual entitlement to send home twelve packages, each worth 100 GDR Marks, and six parcels which were not subject to customs levies or limits on their value. Finally, a worker was entitled to take a large crate as air freight at the end of their labour contract and a smaller crate when returning for a holiday. A significant amendment was made to the system in March 1989 when the GDR, against the wishes of the Vietnamese government, imposed controversial official export quotas on particular goods. No more than two mopeds, five bicycles, two sewing machines, 150 metres of cloth, one camera, eight anoraks, and 100 kilogrammes of sugar could be dispatched to Vietnam.

Contract workers were allocated dormitory-like accommodation in hostels for a maximum monthly rent of 30 GDR Marks, a figure which compared unfavourably to that paid by East Germans. By the time of the agreement with Vietnam, the guidelines required that no more than four people should share a room, with each enjoying an average space of five square metres. Among the other entitlements were one cooking ring per three persons, a clubroom for fifty workers and sanitary facilities. Despite these official norms, standards varied considerably between hostels, as did their distance from the place of employment, which was not supposed to exceed forty minutes travel by public transport. Although foreign workers were free to spend their leisure time as they wished, stipulations regarding access to hostels and visits outside the GDR were designed to restrict their freedom of movement and private contacts with East Germans. Integration was not on an aspiration of the authorities. The enterprises were responsible for the appointment of caretakers to check entry into the hostels. Visits had to be registered and hostel wardens, minders (*Betreuer*), group leaders (*Gruppenleiter*) and interpreters carried out room inspections at night. An infringement of hostel regulations could result in deportation without the right of appeal. All these restrictions, if applied rigorously, could cut the Vietnamese and Mozambicans off from East German society and create a form of ghettoisation.

## Employment and the Control of Contract Workers

Given the SED regime's deep suspicion of 'foreignness' and 'foreigners' and the desire of the GDR, Vietnamese and Mozambican authorities to restrict private contacts between each other's citizens, foreign workers found themselves enmeshed in an elaborate system of administrative and security controls. The main central agency for all matters relating to the employment of the workers was the State Secretariat for Labour and Wages (SAL), which was directly responsible to the Council of Ministers. Immediately below SAL were the ministries which utilised foreign labour and the numerous groups involved in the coordination of programmes at the regional and local level. It was, however, the enterprises which bore the main responsibility for turning plans and regulations into concrete measures regarding wages, occupational training, accommodation, and medical and cultural facilities.

Basic liaison and control functions were carried out by hostel wardens, minders, group leaders and interpreters and, at a higher level, by Regional Commissioners. Minders were GDR citizens who were appointed by enterprises to maintain order, safety and cleanliness in the hostels. One of their main functions was to enable the workers to cope with their environment – for example, by helping them with personal and everyday problems such as visiting the doctor. Each group leader, a foreign national, was responsible for up to fifty workers, which was regarded as the optimum size for the economic deployment of a unit of foreign workers. The foreign group leaders played a key role in organising cultural activities and in ensuring that workers fulfilled their work norms and did not infringe labour discipline. These functions gave them considerable authority over their charges, persuading Huong, who was appointed an adviser to the Office of Foreigners' Commissioners in Berlin after German unification, that the Vietnamese group leaders were petty dictators who had no hesitation in denouncing compatriots to their Vietnamese and East German superiors (Huong 1999: 1333).

Some group leaders took advantage of their position to move out of the hostels and to boost their income. For example, a group leader and an interpreter at a factory in Glachau pocketed the substantial difference between the claim for the hire of ten coaches and the four actually used to transport workers from their hostel to work. In addition, they forced the Vietnamese to hand over the two fur coats to which each worker was entitled, purchased at a discount, and they then sold them on at a profit. The factory specialised in making coats for export to Siberia.[24] Mozambican group leaders were also sometimes criticised for failing to set a good example to their charges. At the Ammendorf wagon construction works one group leader was taken to task for his failure to ensure that hostel regulations were observed regarding the level of noise, unauthorised visits by young women and alcohol consumption.[25]

Regional Commissioners were appointed by the foreign embassies to supervise about 2,000 contract workers each, a figure which was often exceeded. In conjunction with group leaders and the East German factory management, they were responsible for ensuring the ideological and political conformity of their charges. They did not, in East German eyes, always carry out these duties efficiently. For example, the Vietnamese Commissioner for the Halle Region, who was also responsible for the Leipzig area, was deemed by the Halle Office for Labour and Wages to be indecisive, inconsistent, dilatory, 'completely overtaxed' and, with 167 groups under his wing, unable to carry out his leadership function in the enterprises.[26]

Last but by no means least were two central organs of control, the Ministry of State Security and the German People's Police (see Feige 1999: 7–20). Numerous Stasi units were involved in observing and controlling foreigners and a special working group for foreigners, which was set up in 1976, was responsible for the overall coordination of activities. Main Department IX investigated offences involving foreigners, interrogated offenders and cooperated closely with the East German customs administration. Among Main Department XX's many tasks was the political-operational securing of foreign workers and students and Main Department XVIII exercised not only overall responsibility for the 'securing of the national economy' but also coordinated operations relating to foreign workers in the GDR. Finally, Desk 1 of Department X, under its leader Major General Willi Damm, was entrusted with relations with the security forces of other socialist countries, including Vietnam. The 1977 Treaty of Friendship and Cooperation authorised the Stasi and the Vietnamese Ministry of the Interior to carry out surveillance of each other's citizens in such matters as illegal attempts to cross the GDR border and marital plans by East Germans and Vietnamese.

Cooperation was not restricted to the territory of the GDR as the Stasi also conducted investigations on behalf of the Vietnamese security forces in the FRG, for example, collecting information about the East Asia Society in Hamburg (ibid.: 100, 106–7).

In typical Stasi jargon, Main Department XVIII's responsibilities entailed the frustration of 'enemy' plans to use foreign employees for subversive activities and the identification of offences committed by GDR citizens against foreigners.[27] These 'negative' aspects included violent clashes between Algerian workers and East Germans, infringements of labour discipline and, in the case of Vietnamese students and apprentices in the late 1970s, allegedly spreading Maoist ideas.[28] The Vietnamese contract workers were not, however, regarded by the Stasi as 'hostile negative forces'; indeed, they usually emerge from Stasi and factory reports as highly industrious and indifferent to politics and ideology.[29] Although this judgement fits in with the stereotypical picture of outward compliance by the Vietnamese and of their 'drive for harmony' (Huong 1999: 1335), there are clear indications of a greater boldness on the part of the Vietnamese towards the end of the 1980s. In a report compiled in September 1989, Colonel Roigk of Main Department XVIII noted that the Vietnamese in particular were showing 'an ever greater level of self-assertiveness in defence of their interests', which frequently transgressed what he called legal and societal norms.[30] The main concern of Roigk's Department, as well as of the police and factory management, was to ensure that the Vietnamese and other contract workers fulfilled their work norms, did not disrupt the production process and did not clash with the local population. The latter issue was of greater relevance as regards the Mozambicans. Violent conflicts, usually incited by East German youths, at discos and pubs triggered so many protests by East Germans that the Mozambicans were transferred from eastern Saxony to other regions and replaced by Vietnamese workers.[31]

## Hostels as Niches

Hostels were central to migrant workers' stays in the GDR. Not only did the Vietnamese use them for the bulk storage of goods and for doing work in their spare time, but the hostels were also places of social activities and mutual-support structures. Meal times played an important part in reinforcing these links. The food which was cooked in the hostels, often chicken and rice, was done in a manner as close as possible to their normal diet, unlike most of the fare on offer in factory canteens.[32] The Mozambicans, too, prepared their favourite dishes in the kitchens, even though the strong smell of garlic was not to the liking of East Germans who lived in the vicinity of a hostel in Suhl (Scherzer 2002: 92–94).

Earlier studies of the everyday experiences of Vietnamese and other foreign workers tended to depict a continuous and strict enforcement of hostel regulations as well as the exclusion of the workers from East German society and the surrounding environment. While hostel regulations could be very restrictive, as testified by contemporaries,[33] and seem to have been applied relatively effectively as regards the small contingents of Vietnamese who arrived in the early 1980s, recent research has shown that Hungarian, Algerian and other contract workers were able, even in the 1970s, to circumvent many of the restrictions on access to and activities in the hostels (Mac Con Uladh 2005b: 53–54). Workers sometimes managed to leave the hostel to live with East German partners, as did some Mozambicans in 1988 at a hostel in Wittenberg.[34] The position of the Vietnamese appears to have changed markedly from about 1987 onwards, when a surge in numbers, combined with an expansion of Mozambican labour, imposed an even greater strain on local resources. This development posed a major and intractable problem for the local authorities and factories as they were obliged to find suitable hostel accommodation without draining significant investment from funds earmarked for the construction of apartments for East Germans. The heaviest load fell on the administrative regions of Karl-Marx-Stadt, Dresden, East Berlin and Leipzig, which had to find 5,405, 2,625, 1,700 and 1,400 housing units respectively. Several regions were simply unable to meet their target. Potsdam, which was required to find accommodation for 650 Vietnamese, had to appeal to the capital for temporary assistance.[35] Chaos reigned at the Heringsdorf hostel for the ninety-two Vietnamese and eighty-one Mozambicans who were employed in construction work at the North Lubmin nuclear power station in the Rostock Region. There was no clubroom, the kitchens were inadequate, up to three hours were required for travel to and from the enterprise, and the lack of control at reception meant that Vietnamese from other areas lived undetected in the hostel.[36]

The provision of hostel accommodation was often a bone of contention between enterprises, local authorities and the SAL. In 1988, the Merseburg District Council clashed with a Leipzig enterprise over the latter's request for temporary premises for seventy Vietnamese in the historic town of Bad Lauchstädt. The council contended that the concentration of over 3,400 foreign workers in the area made it impossible to fulfil official norms.[37] Police, factory, local authority and Stasi records abound with other instances of breakdowns in communication between official bodies. Under these circumstances, it became increasingly difficult to implement hostel regulations, such as the obligation of residents to return before 22.00 hours, and to curb speculative entrepreneurial dealings and unauthorised overnight stays.[38] Some workers used the crowded conditions to their advantage by hiding illegally in a hostel after the expiry of their work contract. Efforts to implement restrictions on access encountered stubborn resistance, as at the hostel of a knitting enterprise in Lübben, where the Vietnamese received visits from compatriots based in Cottbus and other towns. East Germans, too, frequented the building. An attempt to force visitors to register with the caretaker triggered heated arguments and a refusal by the Vietnamese to hand over their identity cards.[39]

A chaotic situation existed in 1988 at the hostel of a clothing enterprise in Zwickau. The hostel was overcrowded, with up to eleven people herded together in a four-room dormitory and up to seven in a room designed for three. This resulted, according to the local Stasi office, 'in real problems in the control and supervision of the movement of people in the building, which are compounded by a series of organisational deficiencies and errors in the appointment of minders'.[40] The location of the room of the minders and caretakers on the first floor had resulted in the 'uncontrollable stay of unauthorised GDR citizens, children and in part the entire families' of some of the Vietnamese workers.[41] The Stasi regarded most of the female East German minders as unsuitable for their job and, in typically negative terms, denigrated them for what MfS officers regarded as inappropriate political activity and sexual behaviour. One of the minders had applied to leave the GDR and another, it was alleged, had had sex with a number of Vietnamese partners.[42] The Stasi conveniently overlooked the fact that many minders were underpaid and poorly trained. In 1989, Main Department XVIII/4, in what proved to be its final annual review of the overall situation among foreign workers in the GDR, drew attention to a widespread phenomenon which had been identified by numerous governmental officials, police officers and factory staff in the course of hostel inspections:

> According to all reports, the hostels of the Vietnamese workers are veritable warehouses. In addition to industrial consumer goods, foodstuffs are increasingly being stockpiled there. Stripped-down motorbikes, including fuel containers, are to be found in the rooms and on the balconies and staircases. As a result there are serious breaches of the safety, fire, health and hygiene regulations. Unauthorised overnight stays have increased. They are used to carry out speculative activities. Entry checks are sporadic on account of shortages of staff.[43]

## Working in Their Spare Time

Main Department XVIII's reference to 'warehouses' is indicative of the determination of the Vietnamese to devote much of their free time to what the Stasi called 'intensive trading activity'. Department II of the Stasi's Halle Regional Administration estimated in September 1988 that up to 50 per cent of the Vietnamese contract workers in the region were involved in 'untaxed spare-time activities without permission' and 'speculative transactions'.[44] Showing great initiative, the Vietnamese had converted hostels into mini-workshops for making jeans, shirts and other garments, mainly in response to local demand, and were incorporated into a complex series of personal networks and channels of exchange. These activities, which did not explicitly contravene GDR law, were on a scale far beyond anything envisaged by the framers of the 1980 bilateral agreement. By identifying a scarcity and thus a niche in the GDR's economy, the Vietnamese were able to supply at a fair price goods which East Germans found it difficult to acquire in the state retail outlets. Although making trousers and basic garments was the major form of endeavour, some of the more entrepreneurial Vietnamese also managed to exploit the demand for higher quality items. A former contract worker from Karl-Marx-Stadt copied the pattern of an expensive brand-name coat which he had paid for in hard currency at an Intershop. Obtaining a brown dye from a friend who had brought it from Turkey, he cooperated with a colleague to make about eighty coats which were sold for 100 GDR Marks on the marketplace in Plauen. Sales were brisk and the profits high (Kolinsky 2005a: 103).

The experiences of forty-three Vietnamese who had been employed since 1984 at the steel and rolling mill in the town of Gröditz provide a further insight into how the system functioned at the local level. After the lifting of a ban on sewing activities in their free time, the Vietnamese resumed making good quality trousers at reasonable prices, normally within two days. A pair of cords fetched about 180 GDR Marks and a pair of poplins about 110 GDR Marks. According to the Stasi's Riesa District Service Unit, GDR citizens welcomed the speedy service provided by the Vietnamese.[45] East Germans flocked to buy the garments not only from the vicinity but also from Karl-Marx-Stadt, Döbeln and Grimma. At weekends, the number of customers rose to between 150 and 180. In order to capitalise on the demand, one of the Vietnamese used the apartment of an East German woman with whom he was living, without permission, in order to make trousers for East Germans from the Dresden, Cottbus and Leipzig regions.[46] While this kind of practice reveals that these forms of personal contact between East Germans and Vietnamese were much more numerous than hitherto realised, they were predominantly functional and directly related to the vital 'family mission' of the contract workers.

East German reactions to the Vietnamese's entrepreneurial spirit were not uniformly positive. The Stasi's office in Riesa reported that inhabitants of the town of Gröditz and employees at the local steelworks and rolling mill accused the Vietnamese, the 'lazy Fidschis', of pretending to be sick in order to find time to sew trousers throughout the night. Not only did their detractors believe that the Vietnamese were 'taking it easy at work', but also that they were 'making a packet' and avoiding taxation.[47] In April 1986, the enterprise management reacted to this kind of criticism by reimposing a ban on sewing in the hostel. The Vietnamese response was to remove their equipment and materials and resume sewing in the apartment of an East German woman.[48] The affair indicates that this kind of ancillary activity was tolerated by the authorities as long as it was not regarded as detrimental to labour discipline and did not arouse much local opposition. Not until 1989 would the SAL finally seek to impose an outright ban on the use of hostels for storage and production purposes. In the meantime, hostel staff sought to restrict activities by applying the regulations relating to fire risks and unhygienic conditions.

Another example of the extensive nature of part-time work and trading networks can be found in reports compiled by the local police and the Stasi's Schleiz District Service Unit on the 100 Vietnamese contract workers at the Hirschberg leather factory. The Vietnamese, it was claimed, feigned sickness so that they could spend more time on making trousers and shirts in their hostels. Some were sold at the factory, the shirts fetching between 80 and 120 GDR Marks. About 100 mainly second-hand sewing machines had been purchased privately from East Germans; most of the machines were destined for Vietnam, as were bicycles and various spare parts.[49] Nor were the activities of this group of Vietnamese restricted to the making of garments. The local passport office unit was informed by an East German worker that the Vietnamese were selling Western cassettes and car radios which they had obtained in Leipzig and then sold on to East German colleagues for between 800 and 1,000 GDR Marks.[50] Hostels, factories and flea markets were not the only sales outlets. Street vending by Poles and Vietnamese took place in Potsdam's main shopping area, along the Klement-Gottwald-Straße. Some of the Vietnamese were employed at a local factory and about a third of them had taken sick leave. According to information reaching the Stasi, local inhabitants objected to the Vietnamese plying their trade in public. Whereas black marketeering had been necessary after the end of the Second World War, forty years later such practices were considered to be 'unworthy of the dignity' of the GDR.[51]

## Sending Goods Home

The mass dispatch of items to Vietnam, whether by post, air or sea, was often accompanied by the flouting of customs regulations in order, as Department XVIII of the Frankfurt/Oder Region observed, 'to provide maximum assistance for their family' in the form of foodstuffs and industrial consumer goods which were in great demand in Vietnam.[52] Among these goods were mopeds, bicycles, spare parts, new and second-hand sewing machines, cloth, soap and sugar. As the Mozambicans had greater difficulty in acquiring goods and as they had to pay a higher proportion of their earnings to their government than the Vietnamese, they were unable to send as many commodities home as the Vietnamese. Although some restrictions existed on the export of the number of mopeds and certain other goods, not until 1989 did the GDR introduce stricter and more comprehensive controls.

Regular meetings were held between GDR officials and their Vietnamese counterparts to regulate the sending of goods to Vietnam and to prevent smuggling and speculation. One such meeting was held on 26 November 1987 between a top GDR customs official and a commercial councillor attached to the Vietnamese embassy in East Berlin.[53] The East German representative complained about three Vietnamese contract workers in the Frankfurt/Oder Administrative Region who had attempted to send home twenty small motorbikes, 250 kilogrammes of sugar, 5,500 pages of photocopy paper as well as several bicycles and spare parts; the total value exceeded 40,000 GDR Marks. The East German side also objected to the chaos at customs when the Vietnamese flew out of East Berlin's Schönefeld airport. The large crates were so tightly secured that opening them for inspection was a time-consuming process. In addition, the Vietnamese often failed to provide the requisite customs and currency declarations and departees received unauthorised packages from third parties after their luggage had been inspected. In response to the criticism that 'an orderly and cultural customs clearance' had become impossible, it was pointed out that the Vietnamese, who saved between 30,000 and 40,000 GDR Marks during their stay, were not normally interested in luxury goods but, unlike GDR citizens, only in those which were required for everyday use. In other words, the two sides remained far apart. Further, the GDR authorities could expect little assistance from embassy staff in implementing limits on the shipment of goods, especially as the Vietnamese government, which regarded contract labour as 'a strategic element of its foreign trade',[54] had already removed restrictions on imports by returnees and was fully supportive of its citizens' initiatives.

The SED politburo's response, which was influenced by its wish to appease growing popular dissatisfaction among East Germans, was to tighten up the regulations. One of the justifications for this action was that the East German postal service was being overwhelmed by the sheer volume of parcels destined for Vietnam (Müggenburg 1996: 25-26; Kolinsky 2005b: 155). Although opposed by the Vietnamese government, a new set of regulations introduced by the SAL in March 1989 imposed export quotas on the number of bicycles, mopeds, radios, sewing machines, soap, cloth, sugar and other goods (see above). In addition, the Vietnamese were to be informed of these restrictions and warned that they were not to spend income earned from spare-time activities on buying goods for export. Hostels, it was stressed, could no longer be used for production purposes and that 'living areas are not storage rooms for goods'.[55] The restrictions provoked fierce opposition: when customs officials tried to enforce the new guidelines, Vietnamese in the town of Hennigsdorf threatened to go on strike and damage property.[56]

## Smuggling and Speculation

Despite export quotas, restrictions on movement within the GDR and the ban on taking GDR currency out of the country, ample opportunities existed for smuggling and currency speculation by both East Germans and foreign nationals. The different exchange rate between the GDR Mark and hard currencies such as the Deutsche Mark afforded one such opportunity. Other possibilities included making a profit from the sale of video recorders, car radios, quartz watches and other consumer items initially purchased in the GDR's hard-currency Intershops or acquired from embassy staff and other 'privileged' individuals. These goods normally fetched a high price in GDR Marks. Vietnam, too, was an important source of cosmetics, kimonos, jewellery and other goods, usually imported illegally by new arrivals.

Although several Vietnamese contract workers and students had been involved in speculative trading and smuggling for several years, it was not until the late 1980s that serious offences began to spiral, albeit, it should be stressed, by only a tiny minority of those resident in the GDR (Feige 1999: 74–82). By 1988, smuggling and speculative trading had reached such a magnitude in some areas that Department XVIII of the Stasi's Erfurt Regional Administration described organised smuggling as 'mafia-like' in its area of responsibility.[57] Some intricate networks extended beyond the borders of the GDR into neighbouring states, including not only the FRG but also other socialist countries, especially Poland, Hungary, Bulgaria and Czechoslovakia. In 1988, there were about 30,000 Vietnamese in Czechoslovakia, where, according to East German customs officials, the situation was similar to that in the GDR.[58] A range of goods was smuggled into the GDR, among them home electronics, Polish silverware and car parts. One lucrative transaction was smuggling in computers either by foreigners travelling from the West or by Vietnamese living in the 'non-socialist economic area'. Many deals involved members of African embassies in East Berlin, who sold computers to the Vietnamese; the latter then made a profit on a further sale.[59]

Some Mozambicans became embroiled in dubious transactions. In 1988, the East German customs authority reported an increase in their recruitment by the main organisers of illegal activities. Investigations in conjunction with preliminary proceedings against East German citizens revealed that between June and August 1987, thirteen Mozambicans at a factory in Dresden were engaged in the sale of computers and other equipment valued at 2.6 million GDR Marks which had been brought into the GDR. They were, it was recognised, only small cogs in the system and that advantage had been taken of their inexperience and ignorance of the law. Mozambicans at other factories were also involved in similar activities.[60]

Some idea of the overall scale of smuggling and speculation can be obtained from reports compiled on a regular basis by East German customs. For example, in September 1987, its investigative arm concluded that the Vietnamese share of customs and currency penal offences had risen appreciably since the end of 1986. In the first eight months of 1987, the twenty-six criminal proceedings against Vietnamese citizens suspected of serious customs offences and currency speculation represented a doubling of penal offences of this kind in comparison to the whole of the previous year. The customs authority sought prison sentences for thirteen of the accused. The inspectors calculated that goods worth 4.4 million GDR Marks could be categorised as serious smuggling and speculation offences. Enquiries were also being conducted concurrently into a further eighty Vietnamese suspected of customs and speculation misdemeanours. Finally, the combined value of all smuggling and speculation penal offences under investigation was estimated to be at least 15 million GDR Marks.[61] Most customs and penal offences were committed in the southern regions such as Dresden, Erfurt and Leipzig, and falsified passports and identity cards, sometimes issued by foreign embassy staff, enabled workers to carry out activities in West Berlin as well as capitalist and socialist states.[62]

## Working in the State Economy

Basic wages were paid in accordance with East German labour legislation and bonuses were linked to the shift-work system, qualifications and positions of responsibility. One former Vietnamese worker stated, when interviewed, that he earned 900 GDR Marks per month from his job as a group leader and instructor, whereas a skilled worker earned 200 and a semi- or unskilled colleague 500 GDR Marks less (Kolinsky 2005a: 101). He was an exception as contract workers were normally concentrated on the lower rungs of the wage and occupational ladder, the exact position being determined not by negotiation but by intergovernmental agreements and enterprise requirements. It was difficult to ascend the ladder as a prior qualification was sometimes inappropriate for a job in the GDR and contract workers were often unable to complete an apprenticeship or gain the requisite qualification until towards the end of their stay. The Vietnamese, as well as the Mozambicans, were not necessarily averse, however, to employment in lower wage groups if earnings could be supplemented – for example, by bonuses for physically demanding and dirty jobs.[63] In effect, this meant that contract workers were employed in a range of unskilled ancillary jobs, such as vehicle cleaners and assistants to fitters and bricklayers.

Although vocational training was difficult to combine with regular working hours, shift schedules and the limited amount of disposable free time, many foreign workers still managed to obtain some form of qualification. Data compiled by Eva-Marie and Lothar Elsner indicate that, until 1987, about 75 per cent of all foreign workers qualified as skilled workers and a further 15 per cent were semi-skilled (Elsner and Elsner 1994: 53–54), a figure which probably verges on the high side given the poor proficiency in German of most contract workers and the primacy of employment. Clearly, the sudden influx of Vietnamese and Mozambicans in the late 1980s left hard-pressed state enterprises with little alternative but to prioritise employment over training. The qualification pattern of the Vietnamese was varied: not all were unskilled as many arrived in the GDR with a good qualification, partly in response to the GDR's request in 1987 that 50 per cent of workers should hold the equivalent of a skilled-worker certificate. Some of those in the latter category found, however, that they were overqualified for menial jobs in the GDR, while unqualified workers were discouraged by the high level of unemployment in Vietnam from taking an East German craft certificate.

Andrzej Stach has argued convincingly that, once they had settled in, most contract workers fulfilled their production norms and were regarded as reliable colleagues (Stach 1994: 14). Diligence was reinforced by the separation allowance (*Trennungsgeld*) which was paid at the rate of 4 GDR Marks per day but was subject to deductions for unauthorised absence from work and other infringements of labour discipline. Stasi and SAL assessments show that while some national cohorts certainly underperformed, this was rarely the case with the Vietnamese. A typical illustration is the SAL's comments on the first contingent of Vietnamese contract workers. At that time there were 1,534 Vietnamese in 49 factories, of whom 850 had come directly from Vietnam and 684 had already completed a vocational training in the GDR. The SAL observed that the Vietnamese were highly disciplined, committed to their work and, on account of their existing qualifications, attained most of their work norms after a relatively short period of adjustment. There was, however, a disturbing aspect, which would reoccur in the following years: East German workers who had 'a poor attitude to work' resented the industriousness of the Vietnamese.[64] A similar pattern occurred at an enterprise making mopeds in Suhl where, according to Rudi Gradtke, a former East German foreman, East German workers on the assembly line resented their Mozambican colleagues' determination to maximise their earnings but were themselves lazy and drank during working hours (Scherzer 2002: 78–82).

While the Vietnamese rightly enjoyed a reputation for hard work, the devil was sometimes in the detail. Performance varied from one factory to another. For example, in 1988, the Vietnamese at a factory making men's clothes in the town of Helbra achieved only 94 per cent of their work norms, while those at a factory in nearby Eisleben managed to exceed their target by 16 per cent. The factory management and the Office for Labour and Wages of the Eisleben district pinpointed poor work discipline as the cause of the problems at Helbra: some workers failed to turn up for work, others fell asleep at their sewing machines, and a bad example was set by the Vietnamese group leader to his seventy-four colleagues. On occasion, the Vietnamese downed tools on the grounds that their work was too exacting.[65] The quality of work, as opposed to quantitative norms, was an issue which concerned enterprise management, as in the Magdeburg Region. In mid 1988, the Stasi district service offices in Burg, Gardelegen, Halberstadt, Oschersleben and Schönebeck noted that while the Vietnamese were fully integrated into the work process, many of their products had to be refinished or repaired. The Stasi explanation was that in seeking to complete their norms as quickly as possible, the Vietnamese had attempted to circumvent technical and safety standards, and many had arrived at work exhausted by sewing and other activities in their hostels.[66]

As the 1980s drew to a close, the Vietnamese and Mozambicans became more assertive at work as they sought to capitalise on their growing economic leverage based on an enhanced sense of solidarity and on their indispensability to certain branches of the East German economy at a time when the country's economic problems were multiplying and East Germans were reluctant to bear the burdens of multi-shift work in unattractive jobs.[67] In the spring of 1989, strikes and other serious labour problems erupted at several construction sites over Vietnamese dissatisfaction with their rates of pay, their assignment to lower wage groups and their onerous physical work. Although a few so-called 'troublemakers' were deported to Vietnam, the SAL and the Ministry for Construction were obliged to approve the transfer of the workers to a higher wage group and to make allowance for 'their weaker physical constitution' in the allocation of jobs.[68] Sometimes the trigger for unrest was resentment at other nationalities: Mozambican dissatisfaction with the higher earnings of the Vietnamese workers at the ferry port of Mukran on the island of Rügen led to tensions between the two groups and was one reason for a high absence rate from work by seventy-seven Mozambicans in 1988.[69] Another source of conflict was officialdom's attempts to clamp down on the dispatch of goods to Vietnam. In 1989, norm fulfilment fell from 113 per cent to 80 per cent at the Stern radio enterprise in East Berlin when customs officials sought to impose the new export quotas.[70] In June 1988, disputes over their rate of pay and what they regarded as unjustified deductions at a greenhouse complex in Vockerode in the Halle Region triggered protests by about fifty Mozambican female workers and minor scuffles involving the Mozambican group leader and the East German enterprise director. The police had to be called in to restore order.[71] The outcome of these and other industrial actions was that all Mozambican workers benefited from the agreement of the GDR and Mozambican governments in May 1989 to a lowering of the compulsory transfer from 60 to 40 per cent of their net monthly wage above 350 GDR Marks.[72]

## Interaction with East Germans

The SED framed contacts between the indigenous population and foreign workers and students within the broad context of the GDR's solidarity with the foes and victims of imperialism. However, although the contract workers encountered East Germans as work colleagues, occasionally as friends in their free time and as participants in events organised by enterprises and trade unions, close personal contacts and spontaneity were discouraged by the East German government and those of the sending nations. Indeed, in some factories Vietnamese were restricted to their own separate toilets and canteens.[73] Not only was the Vietnamese embassy in East Berlin anxious to isolate its citizens from East German society, but it also threatened them with deportation if they betrayed 'state secrets' and made themselves unduly conspicuous.[74] Although complete isolation was not feasible, regular and meaningful contacts outside the workplace were not customary, partly because most Vietnamese and Mozambicans could not speak German fluently. Language instruction was usually limited to providing the workers with little more than the basic vocabulary necessary to carrying out their jobs (Broszinsky-Schwabe 1990: 33–34). On the other hand, as will be seen, contacts and friendships were established, the attraction for East Germans sometimes being the exotic aura attached to individuals from non-European countries, such as Algeria, Cuba and Mozambique.

The Vietnamese, perhaps more than any other national group in the GDR, tended to focus on their own ethnic community and culture[75] and spent much of their free time on manufacturing clothes, cooking and socialising in the communal hostel environment. This was not simply a consequence of a restrictive official policy but also accorded with the desire of the workers to pursue their leisure activities and interests in the company of their compatriots. The largely separate worlds of East Germans and foreign nationals emerges from a survey conducted in 1990. Some 60 per cent of East Germans stated that they had no personal contact with foreigners and knew little about them; two-thirds of the foreign nationals did not spend their free time in the company of East Germans (Breuer 1990: 59; Müggenburg 1996).

Time spent outside regular working hours was in part the responsibility of the enterprises, which were supposed to provide facilities for what was termed 'purposeful and structured free time'. Not all enterprises, however, had the capacity or inclination to fulfil this obligation. The preference of the enterprises was to provide contract workers with organised activities, such as excursions to the surrounding area, visits to museums and the theatre, and participation in enterprise sports festivals, photography groups and work-brigade events. Some socialising with politically reliable East German families was also fostered. This kind of provision was by no means well-received. East German organisers complained about the workers' reluctance to participate, whereas the latter wanted the enterprises to pay more attention to their particular wishes and preferences and, very much like young East Germans, to have more outlets for spontaneous activities.[76] This might involve going to a pub and disco, playing table tennis, football and badminton, and gossiping with each other. Noise coming from hostels was a frequent cause for complaint by locals. When Mozambicans celebrated birthdays and played music, this was deemed too loud by East German staff at an enterprise in Halle; a suggestion that a 'more meaningful free-time' programme be provided in the form of sewing and cooking circles was not likely to arouse much enthusiasm.[77] Elsewhere, the shortage of books, videos and newspapers in the workers' own language came in for much criticism. With the exception of one half-hour Friday evening radio programme in Vietnamese, the GDR electronic mass media failed to transmit any programmes in the language of foreign nationals (Broszinsky-Schwabe 1990: 30).

Although close contacts and friendships were difficult to establish, one pioneering study carried out in August 1990 found that 74 per cent of the 327 foreigners and 82 per cent of the Vietnamese in the sample rated their East German work colleagues as friendly, understanding and willing to help them before the collapse of SED rule (Grundmann, Müller-Hartmann and Schmidt 1991: 6, 58–59). Personal interviews with Vietnamese who worked in mixed brigades with East Germans often back this up (Kolinsky 2005a: 100–1). One area of positive interaction was initiated by the churches. Vietnamese, Mozambicans and Cubans, many of whom were Christians, were able to take advantage of activities organised by the churches and to meet congregation members (see Krüger-Potratz 1991: 111–13; Mac Con Uladh 2005a: 113–15). They could take part in weekend seminars, bilingual joint prayer services, and sewing and photography courses. The Mozambicans even managed to establish church choirs and their own autonomous ecumenical parishes. A major role in fostering these and other kinds of contacts, as well as providing pastoral help and advice, was played by the Berlin Ecumenical Missionary Centre (set up in 1985) under its director, the pastor Gottfried Berger, and, secondly, from the late 1980s onwards, by the Cabana clubs for foreigners. While Main Department XVIII, like the Vietnamese authorities, tended to view these contacts as a means whereby the churches could exert an undue influence on foreign workers, the MfS was not uniformly hostile. In September 1989, the aforementioned Stasi unit noted that the churches' growing engagement on behalf of foreign workers did have the advantage of helping to stabilise their situation and to curb illegal activities.[78]

Interviews have shown that many contract workers look back on their experiences in the GDR in a favourable light, as living conditions were far better than those at home, employment was guaranteed and many opportunities existed for supplementing their regular earned income. This positive attitude is encapsulated in the view of one former contract worker, referred to earlier in this chapter, that the GDR was a form of paradise. Others were also appreciative of life in the GDR, one interviewee feeling that he had been the equal of his East German colleagues and that the rules and regulations provided a stable and defined environment (Kolinsky 2005a: 100–1). But this was not a view shared by all. Another interviewee, Nguyen Tien Duc, objected to petty restrictions on riding a moped, the length of hair and contacts with East German women.[79] He could have added the paternalism and moralising tone adopted by the authorities towards foreigners who drank in pubs, notwithstanding the fact that alcoholism was a growing problem among the Stasi's own staff in the 1980s.

The numerous administrative barriers to, and the Stasi surveillance of, private relations between East Germans and foreigners, as well as manifestations of racism and sexism towards East German women who befriended male foreigners, constitute one of the darker aspects of the history of contract labour in the GDR. As most foreign workers were male, it was East German women who were most frequently the point of contact and of negative comments. When one East German woman, 'Barbara Babor', had an illegitimate black child by her Mozambican partner, Pedro, she was accused behind her back of having no morals and no sense of decency (Scherzer 2002: 146). Prejudice helps explain why so few binational marriages took place: in September 1989, the Stasi's Main Department XVIII reckoned that whereas 1,000 children had been born out of wedlock from a relationship between Mozambican men and East German women, only three marriages were known to have occurred. Official policy, too, played a crucial role. The annual protocol of 1981 required the repatriation of Mozambican women who became pregnant and marriage was banned by the Mozambican government on the grounds that East German women would be unable to cope with conditions in Mozambique.[80] This accorded with the view expressed by a former East German in charge of a hostel for Mozambican contract workers. In his opinion, many East German citizens had an image of African countries as places where only palm trees, sun, sea, beaches and a holiday paradise existed (ibid.: 127).

Like their Mozambican counterparts, the Vietnamese ran into many difficulties with their government. Marriage was banned between Vietnamese contract workers in the GDR and if a close personal relationship developed with an East German, then the contract worker ran a high risk of being sent home by the Vietnamese authorities. However, should the partners wish to marry, approval was required from both the East German government and the Vietnamese embassy. This was a protracted, highly complicated and stressful process. An application had to be submitted by the East German and full documentation was required from the Vietnamese partner. If an applicant intended to remain in the GDR, they were obliged to 'repay' the costs of their stay. Although marriage to an East German entitled a contract worker to a residency permit in the GDR, marriage did not automatically remove the obligation to leave the country at the end of the contract. Bribing staff at the Vietnamese embassy in East Berlin was one way of circumventing this obligation. In 1988, the rates were 5,000 GDR Marks for an unskilled worker, 10,000 GDR Marks for a skilled worker, and 15,000 GDR Marks for a cadre with a higher-education qualification. Although higher payments are also known to have been required, workers might still have to leave the GDR even if a child was expected or had already been born. Moreover, paternity also had to be proven (Müggenburg 1996: 19; Feige 1999: 118).

A long delay in, or the refusal of, permission to marry usually led to the permanent separation of couples. If an East German citizen wished to reside abroad, they had to declare that no contacts existed with relatives or other persons in the West. While the Stasi's seal of approval was also required, an additional hurdle was the objection of the Vietnamese government to an East German citizen moving to Vietnam on account of what representatives of the Foreign Ministry referred to as 'the complicated conditions in the country' (Feige 1999: 117). Finally, when the whole laborious and painful procedure seemed to be approaching a successful conclusion, permission to marry could be withheld at the last minute. These many obstacles notwithstanding, by the end of the 1980s, 323 marriages had taken place between East Germans and Vietnamese residing in the GDR (Mac Con Uladh 2005b: 65).

Police files contain many poignant narratives of East Germans and Vietnamese who were victims of snooping by the police and the Stasi and whose cases reflect the negative and paternalistic views usually attached by officialdom to binational relationships. In one case, an East German woman and a Vietnamese factory worker desired to set up a household with their young child in the town of Zeulenroda. When police enquiries indicated that the woman did not intend to marry her Vietnamese partner, a police officer added the not untypical gratuitous and censorious comment that she was 'disorderly and careless', had many male friends and associated with 'negative persons'.[81] In 1989, an East German woman from the town of Brandenburg, a divorcee with a young child, appealed to SED General Secretary Erich Honecker to support her wish to marry a Vietnamese who was employed at a railway construction works. The Vietnamese, with whom she enjoyed a stable live-in relationship, had been told that he must leave by the end of May. Returning home would, she feared, mean 'unemployment in Vietnam and not being able to return to our republic'. Even if he was granted permission to go back to the GDR, it would be financially impossible on account of rampant inflation and the shortage of work in Vietnam. There was another reason for urgency in the matter: 'As I am at the moment six weeks overdue, I have the well-founded suspicion that I am expecting a child'.[82] These stories are just another example of the SED's attempt to determine personal relationships and to deny, not always successfully, the individual's right to shape their own life.

All female contract workers, with the exception of Poles, were forbidden to give birth to and live with their child while resident in the GDR, a situation described by the Elsners with considerable understatement as 'an especially bleak chapter' (Elsner and Elsner 1994: 55). Until the regulations were amended in 1987 and 1989, if a contract worker became pregnant she was faced by deportation or a forced abortion. In some cases, the women inflicted bodily harm on themselves in order to induce a miscarriage. A Vietnamese woman with a child born out of wedlock could anticipate many personal difficulties on her return to Vietnam as this brought shame both on the individual and her family. There were also serious financial penalties. In addition to a fine, the mothers were obliged to repay the costs of their stay in the GDR. It is estimated that in each year until 1988, about 1 per cent of Vietnamese women returned prematurely to Vietnam on account of pregnancy.[83] Some were more fortunate, however. The wife of an interviewee, a group leader and interpreter, had been allowed to join him in the GDR in 1989 and was allowed to give birth to their child because both came from families belonging to Vietnam's political elite.[84]

Pregnancy was rare among Vietnamese women in the early stages of the intergovernmental agreement. Although pregnancy was not specified as a reason for repatriation, article one of the bi-national agreement was used to justify such a course of action, as happened to thirty-six Vietnamese women in 1984. The reference in the agreement to employment and vocational training in the GDR was seized upon as the pretext for repatriation as, in the dry bureaucratic language of the SAL: 'The burdens associated with pregnancy and motherhood are incompatible with these requirements'.[85] This kind of statement highlights the official perception of the Vietnamese as, first and foremost, work machines. Factories also pleaded lack of capacity in order to justify discrimination. The East German state authorities adopted a similar line, claiming that hostel accommodation 'provided only limited social and sanitary facilities for the care of small children' and that 'in the interest of the mother and the small child, care is better at home in the extended family'.[86] The latter assertion stood in blatant contradiction to the GDR's official stance on the benefits of public institutions in helping East German families raise their young children.

In 1984, when several Vietnamese women managed to resist or evade premature repatriation to Vietnam, 'discriminatory' measures were implemented by the GDR. It was, however, recognised, albeit off the record, that the Vietnamese entitlement to the labour and social insurance rights enjoyed by GDR workers should have precluded the use of administrative pressure if the Vietnamese women were unwilling to return to Vietnam before their contract expired. It was, or should have been, incumbent on the enterprise, in conjunction with the relevant local government authorities, to provide suitable facilities for a delivery in the GDR as well as for the accommodation of a mother and her child.[87] Giving birth to a child in the GDR was rare, only two cases are known in 1980 and no more than fifty-two as late as 1989, when official constraints had lessened (Mac Con Uladh 2005a: 179).

With contract labour expanding so rapidly from 1987 onwards, the GDR and the Vietnamese governments were anxious to prevent a rise in the number of pregnancies. As a result of an agreement between the SAL and its Vietnamese counterpart in July 1987, contraceptives were to be issued free of charge and if a pregnant woman's 'personal circumstances' justified the birth of the baby in the GDR she would be permitted to return home with her child when she was fit to travel (Huong 1999: 1334). These and other measures failed to achieve their goal as pregnancies increased, in part a sign that the taboo on sexual relations outside marriage was being eroded and in part because of the inadequacy of sex education. Under pressure from the Vietnamese embassy, the GDR agreed in March 1989 that a pregnant woman would no longer be deported against her will and would be allowed to continue working in the GDR. The enterprises and state authorities were obliged to meet the costs of a place in a crèche and the mother was entitled to pregnancy, maternity and child benefits (Marburger et al 1993: 29-30; Müggenburg 1996: 18). The concession did not apply to Mozambican women, and as an abortion was officially forbidden, it was noted by the Erfurt Regional Administration in spring 1989 that the number of Mozambican workers had fallen by over 50 per cent in some factories.[88] Subsequently, Mozambique seems to have adopted a more relaxed attitude, the Halle Regional Council observing in July 1989 that the Mozambican embassy had bowed to the fait accompli of the increase in abortions.[89] However, as the SED regime collapsed only a few months later, the new regulations as regards the Vietnamese made little impact.

## Hostility Towards Foreigners

Despite the relative social isolation of so many Vietnamese, Mozambican and other foreign workers, they sometimes found themselves the targets of popular hostility, a phenomenon which was on the increase by the late 1980s. Negativity was not a new development: archival records testify to sporadic extreme-right activities in the 1960s and 1970s and of animosity and occasional bouts of violence between East German youths, Hungarians, Poles, Algerians and other foreign residents, whether outside pubs and discos or in the vicinity of hostels (Ross 2000: 86–87). The determinants and frequency of incidents varied according to which national group was concerned, with the Vietnamese tending to be less involved in violence and racist incidents than the Mozambicans, partly because the latter were more likely to 'intrude' on the social space of the indigenous population, and partly because of the greater underlying racist antipathy of some East Germans towards 'black' Africans.[90] Although police and Stasi reports need to be treated with care as both organisations were always alert to minor as well as major confrontations and offences, they indicate that foreign workers were more likely to be victims than perpetrators of penal offences such as theft, bodily harm and traffic accidents.[91]

Overt conflicts, usually inflamed by alcohol, tended to occur most frequently in or near pubs and discos as East Germans resented the intrusion on 'their' territory of foreigners who wanted the opportunity to drink and relax in a more congenial atmosphere than in the confines of the hostels. Disagreements and fights also arose over local prejudice against relations between male contract workers and young East German women. It should be mentioned in parenthesis that rivalry over women also triggered clashes between contract workers, for example between Mozambicans and Vietnamese at a hostel in Bitterfeld in 1988. One Vietnamese and three Mozambicans suffered injuries after being thrown out of the windows of the hostel.[92]

An indication of an underlying mix of the sexual chauvinism and racism of some East Germans towards foreign workers can be gleaned from one of the nine interviews conducted in 1982 by Landolf Scherzer with East German and Mozambican workers at a factory making vehicles and hunting weapons (*Fahrzeug- und Jagdwaffenwerk*, Fajas) in Suhl. Klaus Meurer, who was forty-two years of age at the time of the interview and on good terms with some Mozambicans from the nearby hostel, insisted that black and white did not belong together, certainly not East German women and the 'blacks' (Scherzer 2002: 22). A pastor, Eberhard Vater, and his wife, Christina, also interviewed by Scherzer, had carried out missionary work in Africa before settling in a parish about twenty kilometres from Suhl where they had set up a hostel for foreigners, would-be émigrés and others who suffered discrimination. East German women were able to stay there overnight with their Vietnamese, Cuban and Mozambican partners. Not only did some parishioners disapprove of this kind of work but the Vaters also became targets of personal abuse. Even close friends and villagers who came to the meeting place expressed surprise and anxiety that the couple allowed black people to dry their hands on their towels, and Christina, when visiting other places in the district, was sometimes accused of being a 'nigger slut' (ibid.: 43–45, 47).

Among the many violent public incidents involving Mozambican contract workers and young East Germans are those recorded in police and Stasi reports from the late 1980s. In 1987, towns such as Zittau, Niesky and Dresden were scenes of clashes between the two nationalities. One especially serious incident occurred in Dresden when three East Germans, aged between nineteen and twenty-three years, attacked Mozambicans with chains and fists. The motive, according to statements by the East Germans, was the 'dark skin' of the Africans.[93] In May 1988, fighting broke out with East Germans when three Mozambicans were allowed to visit a local youth-club disco in the town of Spremberg. Entry had been denied to a group of thirty East Germans. When the Mozambicans were forced to return to their hostel, they were joined by about thirty of their compatriots who sought to drive off the East Germans. Stones and clubs were used by both sides in a further outbreak of violence.[94] In June of the same year, fighting erupted between Mozambicans and East Germans after a dance in Großenhain in the Dresden Region and, more seriously, in the town of Stollberg in the Karl-Marx-Stadt Region where an East German died during an incident in which knives had been brandished.[95] These and other disturbances were attributable, according to the Stasi, to the drunkenness of both the East Germans and Mozambicans, and to the Africans' sensitivity and aggressive reaction to racist taunts.[96]

The East German authorities were highly concerned about the mounting tension arising from the increase in, and high concentration of, foreign workers in the Halle Administrative Region and other areas of the GDR with serious social and economic problems.[97] In the Halle Region, one factory in the town of Hohenturm, which employed fifty Mozambicans in the production of steam boilers, had great difficulty, together with the local authority, in satisfying the leisure and social demands not only of these and the other 100 foreign workers from Poland and Hungary but also of the 2,300 East Germans in the area. Only two small pubs were available, one of which was the scene of violent clashes in May 1988 between Mozambicans and six East German workers. The Germans hurled racist abuse at the Africans and shouted 'Germany for the Germans'. Although the factory undertook disciplinary and political-ideological countermeasures against the perpetrators, the Mozambicans were nevertheless badly shaken by the East Germans' brutality.[98] The events in Hohenturm fit into a general pattern: Main Department XVIII expressed its anxiety in 1987 over an overall failure to accommodate the foreign workers' free-time interests and the increase in incidents, especially those involving Mozambicans. It proposed that ideological work be stepped up among the indigenous population and that incidents and criminal offences involving foreign workers should be judged 'objectively'. The first signs of racial discrimination and xenophobia were to be combated rigorously and by all possible means.[99]

Various forms of socio-economic chauvinism were at the root of much East German hostility towards foreign workers, especially those from Poland and Vietnam. The chauvinism was not fuelled by competition for jobs, as it would be after the collapse of SED rule, but rather by features specific to the GDR's shortage economy, notably a lack of new apartments, spare parts and some consumer goods. Furthermore, antipathy and resentment would be quickened by the repercussions of the legitimacy crisis of the communist system during the 1980s. The Vietnamese, who were perceived as fierce competitors for commodities in short supply, were accused by East Germans of hoarding and buying up goods and transporting them back home in an allegedly ostentatious manner. In Gera, locals complained that Vietnamese workers were allowed to purchase children's clothes for an hour before the official opening time of the state-owned department store.[100] East Germans were particularly irritated over what they saw as a deterioration in the consumer supply situation, especially in the southern regions. Vietnamese – and Polish – workers were criticised for stripping shops bare and for stepping outside their regulated space into areas which local inhabitants regarded as their own domain. This was the kind of reaction reported in August 1988 by the Stasi District Service Unit in Karl-Marx-Stadt/Land in places such as Limbach-Oberfrohne, Hartmannsdorf and Neukirchen.[101] Elsewhere, in the Plauen-Chrieschwitz residential area, people were aggrieved at the situation in the two local market halls. Not only were they frustrated at wasting so much time in queues because of the inadequate supply of meat, sugar and other items, but they were also angry at the Vietnamese for exacerbating the shortages by their bulk purchasing of rice, pork, soap, sugar and poultry.[102] This kind of criticism typically lacked sensitivity towards the needs of the Vietnamese – rice and chicken, for example, being staples of their cuisine and often unavailable on factory menus.

Envy was also stirred by the provision of hostel accommodation to foreign workers, thereby exacerbating the serious housing problems in the regions concerned and undermining one of the main planks of SED social policy under Honecker, 'the solution to the housing question as a social problem by 1990'. The health service was another bone of contention. Medical staff at the outpatient clinic at the Leuna Works in the Halle Region objected to those Vietnamese who, in their opinion, were exploiting their poor command of German in order to obtain medical certificates. They also felt that the Vietnamese took advantage of the free medical service, visiting the doctor for every little thing and obtaining expensive medicines which were not required for minor illnesses.[103] 'The treatment of the Vietnamese', it was further alleged, 'ties up a considerable number of medical staff – instead of 500 Vietnamese one could treat 5,000 Leuna workers'.[104] An East German interviewee recalls that at the hospital in Stendal, where she worked as a nurse, one of the women doctors felt so nauseous when treating a Vietnamese that she wore gloves, although there was no medical reason to do so.[105]

Other grievances which fostered hostility towards foreigners originated in a belief that foreign workers failed to match the work ethic of East Germans. Had the SED explained to its citizens why it needed to recruit so many foreign workers, this might have helped to combat prejudice or the 'gossip factory' among an East German population unaware of the positive contribution of the Vietnamese towards the East German economy.[106] However, from the point of view of the SED, to open up the latter issue would have meant exposing fundamental deficiencies in the GDR's planned economy and further eroding the fragile legitimacy of the regime. Only as the SED tottered towards collapse did a few reports appear in newspapers in early 1989 concerning the contribution of contract workers to light industry, lignite mining and other branches of the economy (Krüger-Potratz 1991: 64–65). This belated and feeble acknowledgement did little to combat popular misperceptions and rumours: in 1989, production workers at the Chemical Combine Bitterfeld asserted, according to the Stasi's Halle Regional Administration, that the Vietnamese workers were of no benefit to the East German economy on account of their idling. And with regard to foreign workers in general, it was widely believed that they cheated the GDR, would be unable to find work in their own countries, and, rather than doing any regular work, carried out illegal activities in the hostels for their own personal gain.[107]

Yet even when the Vietnamese did commit themselves to their work targets, which was their normal pattern of work behaviour, some East Germans workers still expressed dissatisfaction. Animosity manifested itself against the hard work and discipline of the very first contingent to arrive in the GDR. At the motor vehicle works in Ludwigsfelde, for example, a group of East German workers with a reputation for poor work discipline used threats and even physical violence to try and force the Vietnamese to lower their output. The offenders were sentenced for severe 'rowdyism'. Similar incidents were recorded at factories in East Berlin, Aschersleben and elsewhere.[108] Other work-related complaints can be found in Stasi reports after the SED had instructed the ministry's district service units to track popular attitudes in the Karl-Marx-Stadt Region to the employment of Vietnamese after it had been decided to accelerate production in light industry.[109] Workers at a clothing factory in Gerinswalde complained that the arrival of Vietnamese workers would lead to the introduction of the unpopular multi-shift system and create a shortage of kindergarten and crèche places.[110]

Two major grievances which East Germans harboured against the SED – tight restrictions on travel to the West and access to hard currency – were transferred into accusations against foreign workers, as happened to the Vietnamese at the Bruno-Freitag laundry in the vicinity of Limbach-Oberfrohna. Four rumours, regarded as completely unfounded by the Stasi's local office, indicate the kind of prejudice which confronted the Vietnamese:

- each Vietnamese receives four U.S. dollars pay each day
- they keep chickens in the hostel
- they can travel regularly to the FRG and West Berlin
- two cases of AIDS among them[111]

The foregoing discussion reveals that the antipathy towards foreign workers had been caught up in growing popular dissatisfaction with the GDR's socio-economic system and with its failure to deliver adequate consumer items, accommodation and economic performance. While xenophobia was not so rare as was once believed, much of it was, as the Stasi found in the Erfurt Region, 'hidden' and consisted of 'sporadic incidents'.[112] Hostility towards the Vietnamese remained intermittent and low-key until the rapid escalation of new recruits in the late 1980s, a development which also coincided with a surge in the number of Mozambicans and tensions with Cuban workers. Internal secret police files began to detect 'instances of a growing hostility towards foreigners ... which are no longer to be found just among politically negative young citizens'.[113] In September 1989, Main Department XVIII highlighted what it regarded as 'the starting positions for negative discussions among the GDR population', some of which applied directly to the Vietnamese and Mozambicans. The key factors, according to the Stasi, were: a divergent lifestyle, especially of non-European workers; high-profile incidents in public involving foreign workers; idling and a negative attitude to work; and unwarranted wage demands backed by strike action, the deliberate exploitation of the shortage of domestic labour, and other methods which, supposedly, were known to East German workers only from capitalist countries. The Stasi report also homed in on popular criticism of foreign workers' alleged materialism, especially that of the Vietnamese and Poles, and their speculative activities and buying up of consumer goods. This exemplified, it was asserted, a parasitical lifestyle combined with the glorification of capitalism. The industrial conurbations were identified as the main centres of East German dissatisfaction with contract labour, a mood which not only hardened prejudices against foreign nationals but also reinforced opposition to the East German authorities who were held to bear much of the blame for the deteriorating situation.[114]

The Stasi analysis contains yet one more example of the familiar lament of officialdom that the xenophobia of the indigenous population was aroused by foreigners' attitudes and actions. In 1989, a Stasi assessment of the reasons for problems such as criminal offences, disorderly behaviour and bodily harm focused on the Mozambicans' sensibility, heightened by excessive alcohol, towards 'alleged' racist discrimination, a lack of discipline in relations with East Germans, and ignoring societal norms, especially in the moral sphere. While the responsibility for the troubles was placed on the shoulders of the Mozambicans, and East German racism was not conceded, the report did acknowledge the inadequacy of preparations for the deployment of workers in the regions, notably in the provision of leisure facilities, and that the failure to explain the wage structure in the intergovernmental agreement had triggered labour disputes.[115]

## The Failure of the State and the Resistance of the Weak

The main goal of the SED, the Stasi and other organs of state and party was an efficient and smooth incorporation of contract workers into the labour process. Social integration was not intended, while institutionalised supervision and, at best, semi-isolation was. As Oliver Raendchen has argued, 'integration' was equated with political conformity, the uncritical observance of all regulations and subordination to the authorities (Raendchen 2000: 96). The official line that the Vietnamese and Mozambican presence constituted an act of socialist brotherhood helped to gloss over the primary reason for their residence in the GDR – that is, their value as labour – and precluded a flexible approach by officialdom to their specific needs and aspirations. The SED's stance not only fuelled widespread misunderstanding but also animosity among sections of the population, albeit much of it latent. While the Vietnamese and Mozambicans were frequently turned into scapegoats for deficiencies in the system, they were able nevertheless to turn these flaws to their own advantage. The Vietnamese stepped into the consumer void by providing goods to East German clients, overcame many of the hostel regulations to carry out sewing and other activities, and, in the late 1980s, were increasingly assertive of their rights as workers. Like their East German colleagues, they became adept at using the labour situation to take time off work. All of these actions, as well as smuggling and speculation by a small minority, served the main purpose of their stay in the GDR – to help their extended families at home.

The social behaviour of the Vietnamese and Mozambicans highlights the contrast between the theory and practice of official controls, a gap which became ever wider as SED power began to disintegrate. But once decline had become irreversible and state socialism had collapsed, devastation was wrought on foreigners who found themselves in a social and legal no-man's land (Kolinsky 1999: 196). Hostels were closed, unemployment soared and xenophobic violence erupted in many eastern German towns. High levels of popular antipathy were recorded towards the Vietnamese.[116] The number of Vietnamese in the former GDR fell from about 59,000 at the end of 1989 to about 21,000 twelve months later, and Mozambicans from about 15,100 to 2,800 (Weiss 2005: 80). The new existential uncertainties and dislocations persuaded many that 'paradise' had been lost. As one former Vietnamese group leader and minder stated: 'a structure existed in the GDR. After the *Wende*, this structure no longer existed. Suddenly, every person is responsible and one must decide whether to return or to remain here'.[117] These problems notwithstanding, the many contract workers, above all Vietnamese, who decided to stay in eastern Germany after unification would become integral to aspirations to develop a democratic political culture and to form a civil society which included, for the first time in the former GDR, the inclusion of non-Germans regardless of cultural orientation or ethnic origin (Kolinsky 1999: 194).

## Notes

1. Unless otherwise stated, all interviews mentioned in the text were carried out by Eva Kolinsky between 2002 and 2004. The interviews and archival research were supported by a grant from the Arts and Humanities Research Council. Additional in-depth interviews were conducted on our behalf by Do Thi Hoang Lan and Professor Karin Weiss.
2. BStU, MfS, ZA, ZAIG, no.20646, 'Information zur politisch-operativen Lage unter den ausländischen Werktätigen in der DDR (Jahreseinschätzung)', September 1988, p.57.
3. BStU, MfS, ZA, HA II, no.22858, 'Information zur politisch-operativen Lage unter den ausländischen Werktätigen in der DDR (Jahreseinschätzung)', 1988, p.163; BStU, MfS, ZA, ZAIG, no.20646, 'Jahreseinschätzung zur politisch-operativen Lage unter den ausländischen Werktätigen in der DDR', 7 September 1989, p.20. Mac Con Uladh (2005a: 66) estimates that 210,000 contract workers were employed in the GDR between 1967 and 1989.
4. BStU, MfS, ZA, HA XX, no.3035, 'Information zum Aufenthalt mocambiquanischer Bürger in der DDR', 19 May 1989, p.94.
5. BStU, MfS, ZA, ZAIG, no.20646, 'Anlage 1: Hinweis zur gegenwärtigen Situation im Zusammenhang mit dem Einsatz ausländischer Werktätiger in der Volkswirtschaft der DDR', [1987], p.85; Gruner-Domić (1996: 215).
6. The cost–benefit details can be found in Gruner-Domić (1996: 226).
7. See BStU, MfS, Außenstelle Halle, BV Halle, AKG, Sachakten, no.2200, 'Bericht', 21 January 1986, pp.6–8.
8. SAPMO-BA, DY 30/2943, Fischer to Löschner, [1987], p.22.
9. It was originally intended that all 17,500 should arrive during 1987 but a lack of suitable accommodation, especially in the Karl-Marx-Stadt and Potsdam Administrative Regions,

delayed the arrival of the remaining 3,342 until the first half of 1988. See: BStU, Außenstelle Chemnitz, AKG, no.2094, 'Information über den Einsatz vietnamesischer Arbeitskräfte in Kombinaten und Betrieben der Leichtindustrie im Bezirk Karl-Marx-Stadt', 3 November 1987, p.10.

10. BStU, MfS, ZA, ZAIG, no.20646, 'Jahreseinschätzung zur politisch-operativen Lage unter den ausländischen Werktätigen in der DDR', 7 September 1989, p.20; ibid., 'Information zur politisch-operativen Lage unter den ausländischen Werktätigen in der DDR (Jahreseinschätzung)', September 1988, p.57; BStU, MfS, ZA, HA IX, no.10020, 'Informations- und Arbeitsmaterial', 24 May 1979, p.41; Müggenburg (1996: 77–78).

11. BStU, MfS, ZA, HA IX, no.10020, 'Informations- und Arbeitsmaterial', 24 May 1979, p.36; also Marburger et al. (1993: 14, 21–22).

12. The point about snowy conditions is made in an interview with H., 4 June 2004. She arrived in East Berlin in December 1987.

13. Interview with H., 31 October 2002.

14. Interview with H., 31 October 2002.

15. Interview conducted by Do Thi Hoang Lan with T., 9 May 2004.

16. Eva Kolinsky's interview with Jens Trombke, formerly the business manager of the Mozambican Association, Leipzig, 2002; see also Scherzer's interview with a former personnel director at Fajas, Suhl, in 1982 (Scherzer 2002).

17. Interview with T., 9 May 2004. He arrived in the GDR in 1981 and worked for six years in Dresden and then in Hoyerswerda. He moved to Berlin after the fall of the Wall.

18. BStU, MfS, Außenstelle Erfurt, Abteilung XVIII, no.203, 'Rückflußinformation zu aktuellen Problemen beim Einsatz ausländischer Arbeitskräfte', 5 May 1989, pp.2–3.

19. This is the opinion of Jens Tromba, as expressed in an interview with Eva Kolinsky, 2002.

20. Interview with H., 4 June 2004.

21. A copy of the agreement is printed in Müggenburg (1996).

22. BStU, MfS, ZA, HA IX, no.10020, 'Informations- und Arbeitsmaterial', 24 May 1979, p.35; Müggenburg (1996: 13).

23. Interview conducted by Karin Weiss with Dr Huong, 16 October 2002.

24. Interview with H., 4 June 2004.

25. LSA, Unterlagen zum Einsatz ausländischer Arbeitskräfte im VEB Waggonbau Ammendorf, no.55,331, 'Einschätzung über das Verhalten und die Lebensweise der 100 moc. Werktätigen im VEB Waggonbau Ammendorf', [1982,], pp.223–24.

26. BStU, MfS, Außenstelle Halle, BV Halle, Abteilung XVIII, Sachakten, no.502, 'Jahresbericht 1988 zum Stand des Einsatzes ausländischer Werktätiger in Kombinaten, Betrieben und Einrichtungen im Bezirk Halle', 21 January 1989, p.38. Only Poland and Angola did not have Regional Commissioners.

27. BStU, MfS, ZA, HA XVIII, no.13130, '5. Durchführungsbestimmung', 1983, pp.97–98.

28. BStU, MfS, ZA, HA II, no.23580, 'Auswertung der Bezirksanalysen zur Ausländerpolitik', 10 January 1977, pp.23–25.

29. BStU, MfS, ZA, HA XVIII, no.5881, 'Jahreseinschätzung zur politisch-operativen Lage unter den ausländischen Werktätigen in der DDR', 30 October 1987, p.9.

30. BStU, MfS, ZA, ZAIG, no.20646, 'Jahreseinschätzung zur politisch-operativen Lage unter den ausländischen Werktätigen in der DDR', 7 September 1989, p.24.

31. Ibid., p.30.

32. Summary of interview with T, 9 May 2004.

33. See the comments of one former Mozambican contract worker in Schmidt (1992: 68–69).

34. LSA, Rat des Bezirkes Halle, Abteilung Amt für Arbeit und Löhne, Aktenführende Stelle: Ausländische Kräfte, no.19,664, 'Mocambique', 25 September 1985, p.409.

35. SAPMO-BA, DY 30/2943, 'Bericht', 11 September 1987, pp.106–8, and 'Information', Anlage [1987], p.78.

36. BStU, MfS, Außenstelle Rostock, BV Rostock, Abteilung II, no.86, 'Operative Information über das Verhältnis vietnamesischer und mocambiquanischer Arbeitskräfte im Bereich der AWU Heringsdorf', 26 May 1989, pp.76–7.
37. LSA, Rat des Bezirkes Halle, Abteilung Amt für Arbeit und Löhne, no.19,667, Letter of the Rat des Kreises Merseburg, 13 October 1988, p.394.
38. See, e.g., BStU, MfS, Außenstelle Erfurt, BdL, no.2029, 'Berichterstattung zum Stand der politisch-operativen Sicherung ausländischer Werktätiger im Bezirk Erfurt', 9 March 1988, p.16.
39. BStU, MfS, Außenstelle Cottbus, BVfS Cottbus, AKG, no.2080, 'Information über vietnamesiche Arbeitskräfte (VAK) in Cottbus', 4 July 1989, p.75.
40. BStU, MfS, Außenstelle Chemnitz, AKG, no.2094, 'Auszug aus der wöchentlichen Lageeinschätzung der KD KMSt/Land vom 7.06.88', p.101.
41. Ibid.
42. Ibid., pp.102–3.
43. BStU, MfS, ZA, ZAIG, no.20646, 'Jahreseinschätzung zur politisch-operativen Lage unter den ausländischen Werktätigen in der DDR', 7 September 1989, p.28.
44. BStU, MfS, Außenstelle Halle, BV Halle, AKG, Sachakten, no.2056, 'Einschätzung über die im Bezirk Halle tätigen ausländischen Werktätigen', 27 September 1988, p.10. At the time the report was compiled, just over 2,000 Vietnamese were employed in the *Bezirk*.
45. BStU, MfS, Außenstelle Dresden, AKG, Pi, no.128/86, 'Information', 20 May 1986, p.8.
46. Ibid.
47. Ibid., p.7.
48. Ibid., p.3. When the complaints were investigated by a special working party set up by the Office for Labour and Wages of the Dresden Regional Council, it was found that the Vietnamese, far from underperforming, had in fact managed to exceed their work norms.
49. BStU, MfS, Außenstelle Gera, KD Schleiz, no.1508, 'Information zum Einsatz und zu Problemen mit vietnamesischen Werktätigen', 8 August 1988, p.287.
50. Ibid., 'Wohngebietsinformation', 16 March 1989, pp.155–56.
51. BStU, MfS, Außenstelle Potsdam, BVfS Potsdam, AKG, no.616, 'Information: Stimmungen/Meinungen unter der Bevölkerung Potsdam zum sogenannten freien Handel', 1 March 1989, p.69.
52. BStU, MfS, Außenstelle Frankfurt (Oder), BVfS Frankfurt (Oder), Abteilung XIX, no.3029, 'Information zu operativ-bedeutsamen Problemen im Zusammenhang mit dem Einsatz ausländischer Werktätiger in der Volkswirtschaft des Bezirkes und zu den zentralen Erkenntissen', 21 March 1989, pp.27–28.
53. For details of the meeting, see: BStU, MfS, ZA, Abteilung X, no.112, 'Vermerk', 30 November 1987, pp.7, 10, 14.
54. See BStU, MfS, ZA, ZAIG, no.20646, 'Jahreseinschätzung zur politisch-operativen Lage unter den ausländischen Werktätigen in der DDR', 7 September 1989, p.27.
55. BStU, MfS, Außenstelle Potsdam, BVfS Potsdam, BdL, no.410210, 'Anlage 2: Ordnung zur Ausfuhr von Waren durch Werktätige aus der SR Vietnam', 1989, p.2.
56. Ibid., 'Operativ-bedeutsame Probleme im Zusammenhang mit dem Einsatz ausländischer Arbeitskräfte im Bereich der Volkswirtschaft des Bezirkes Potsdam', 5 April 1989, p.2.
57. BStU, MfS, Außenstelle Erfurt, BdL, no.2029, 'Berichterstattung zum Stand der politisch-operativen Sicherung ausländischer Werktätiger im Bezirk Erfurt', 9 March 1988, p.9.
58. BStU, MfS, ZA, Abteilung X, no.112, 'Information über die Aus- und Einfuhr von Waren und über Verletzungen zoll- und devisenrechtlicher Bestimmungen der DDR durch Bürger der SRV', 26 September 1988, pp.40–41.
59. Interview with Andreas Czauderna, 8 September 2003.
60. BStU, MfS, ZA, Abteilung X, no.112, 'Information zu Erscheinungen des Schmuggels und der Spekulation durch zeitweise in Betrieben der DDR tätige ausländische Werktätige', February 1988, pp.51–52.

61. Ibid., 'Information über die Aus- und Einfuhr von Waren und über Verletzungen zoll- und devisenrechtlicher Bestimmungen der DDR durch Bürger der SRV', 25 September 1987, pp.109–10.
62. BStU, MfS, Außenstelle Magdeburg, AKG, no.50, 'Befehl 3/81', [1988], p.151.
63. SAPMO-BA, DQ/1879a, 'Vorlage für den Ministerrat', January 1990, p.7.
64. SAPMO-BA, DY 30/2940, 'Information', [1980], p.505.
65. LSA, Rat des Bezirkes Halle, no.19,658, 'Einsatz ausländischer Werktätiger im Rahmen von abgeschlossenen Regierungsabkommen im jeweiligen Territorium', 27 July 1988, pp.1–2; LSA, Rat des Bezirkes Halle, no.19,633, 'Betr. Antrag auf Rückführung', 18 January 1989, pp.1–2.
66. BStU, MfS, Außenstelle Magdeburg, AKG, no.50, 'Lageeinschätzung zu Problemen der Sicherung ausländischer Werktätiger', 28 July 1988, pp.144–45.
67. See the comments of Main Department XVIII in BStU, MfS, ZA, ZAIG, no.20646, 'Rückflußinformation zur Lage unter den ausländischen Werktätigen in der Volkswirtschaft der DDR', 1988, p.75, and ibid., 'Information zur politisch-operativen Lage unter den ausländischen Werktätigen in der DDR (Jahreseinschätzung)', 1988, p.60.
68. Ibid., 'Jahreseinschätzung zur politisch-operativen Lage unter den ausländischen Werktätigen in der DDR', 7 September 1989, p.29.
69. Ibid., 'Bericht ueber die Lage und Reaktionen unter Auslaendern', 8 April 1989, pp.50–51. The difference in earnings was attributed by the Stasi Rostock Regional Administration to the levies by the Mozambican government as both groups of workers were on the same wage scale.
70. Ibid., pp.27–28.
71. LSA, Betriebsakten zum Einsatz mocambiquanischer Werktätiger des Bezirkes, no.19,669, 'Information zu den Vorkommnissen der Gruppe der mocambiquanischen Werktätigen in der Gewächshausanlage Vockerode am 16.6.1988 gegen 17.30 Uhr im Wohnheim', [1988], pp.1–2.
72. BStU, MfS, ZA, ZAIG, no.20646, 'Bericht ueber die Lage und Reaktionen unter Auslaendern', 8 April 1989, p.30.
73. Interview with Dieter Braun, *Evangelisches Missionswerk*, Leipzig, Foreigners' Commissioner, 11 September 2003.
74. Interview in Müller (1996: 63).
75. This is stressed by many East German observers, such as the minders interviewed in Hackert-Lemke and Unterbeck (1999: 99). Eva Kolinsky's interviews with various advisers to foreigners also back this up.
76. See the comments in Broszinsky-Schwabe (1990: 30) and the interview with the East German in charge of a hostel for Mozambicans in Scherzer (2002: 128–29).
77. LSA, Rat des Bezirkes Halle, 4. Abteilung, no.6,387, 'Informationsbericht zur Kontrollberatung am 7.9.1989', 31 August 1989, p.6.
78. BStU, MfS, ZA, ZAIG, no.20646, 'Jahreseinschätzung zur politisch-operativen Lage unter den ausländischen Werktätigen in der DDR', 7 September 1989, p.25.
79. The interview was conducted on 29 October 2002 with Nguyen Tien Duc, a social-service adviser attached to Caritas in Magdeburg.
80. BStU, MfS, ZA, ZAIG, no.20646, 'Jahreseinschätzung zur politisch-operativen Lage unter den ausländischen Werktätigen in der DDR', 7 September 1989, p.31; also Müggenburg (1996: 18). Mac Con Uladh (2005b: 63) states that six marriages took place between East Germans and Mozambicans.
81. BA, DO1/0.9/52087, 'Bericht', 31 October 1985, VPKA Zeulenrode, n.p.
82. Ibid., 'Eingabe', 22 June 1989, n.p. The outcome of the request is not known.
83. BStU, MfS, ZA, Abteilung X, no.339, 'Information', [1988], p.336.
84. Interview with K., 8 September 2003.
85. BStU, MfS, ZA, Abteilung X, no.339, 'Information zur Rückführung vietnamesischer werktätiger Frauen wegen Schwangerschaft', 16 February 1985, p.372.

86. Ibid., 'Information', [1988], p.336.
87. Ibid., 'Information zur Rückführung vietnamesischer werktätiger Frauen wegen Schwangerschaft', 16 February 1985, p.372.
88. BStU, MfS, Außenstelle Erfurt, Abteilung XVIII, no.203, 'Anlage: Operative Probleme und Schlußfolgerungen aus der Beratung AG "Ausländische Werktätigen" beim RdB Bezirk Erfurt am 7.4.1989', 1989, p.8.
89. LSA, Rat des Bezirkes Halle, Amt für Arbeit und Löhne, no.19,662, 'Berichterstattung zur Verwirklichung der Maßnahmen zur sozialistischen Gleichstellung ausländischer Werktätiger in Einsatzbetrieben des Bezirkes Halle', 14 July 1989, p.2.
90. Main Department XVIII drew attention in 1989 to the antipathy of some East Germans towards foreign workers of a 'different skin colour', notably the Cubans and Mozambicans: BStU, MfS, ZA, HA XVIII, no.8880, 'Rückflußinformation zu operativ bedeutsamen Problemen im Zusammenhang mit dem Einsatz ausländischer Werktätiger in verschiedenen Bereichen der Volkswirtschaft der DDR', 7 February 1989, p.10.
91. BStU, MfS, Außenstelle Erfurt, BdL, no.2029, 'Berichterstattung zum Stand der politisch-operativen Sicherung ausländischer Werktätiger im Bezirk Erfurt', 9 March 1988, p.8. Eighteen penal offences were committed against Vietnamese, ten against Cubans and eleven against Mozambicans: ibid., pp.31–32.
92. LSA, RdB Halle, Abteilung Amt für Arbeit und Löhne', no.19,659, 'Aktennotiz zum Vorkommnis am 20.12.88 – tätliche Auseinandersetzung zwischen mocambiquanischen und vietnamesischen Bürgern im Wohnheim des CKB, H.-Beimler-Straße, Bitterfeld', December 1988, pp.1–3.
93. BStU, MfS, Außenstelle Dresden, BV Dresden, AKG, Pi 127/87, 'Information über tätliche Auseinandersetzungen zwischen jugendlichen Bürgern der DDR und mocambiquanischen Werktätigen, die auf Grundlage eines Regierungsabkommens in Betrieben des Bezirkes Dresden tätig sind', 18 September 1987, pp.2–3.
94. BStU, MfS, Außenstelle Frankfurt/Oder, BVfS Cottbus, AKG, no.1356, 'Bericht zum Stand der Untersuchung des Vorkommnisses (Rowdytum gemäß § 215 StGB) vom 8.5.1988 mit Beteiligung mocambiquanischer Werktätiger in der Kreisstadt Spremberg', 12 May 1988, pp.8–9.
95. For the Großenhain incident, see: BStU, MfS, ZA, HA XX, no.3035, 'Abschrift', 13 June 1988, p.71. For the Stollberg incident: ibid., 'Information zur Konzentration von Vorkommnissen unter Beteiligung mocambiquanischer Werktätiger in der DDR', 1988, p.77.
96. BStU, MfS, ZA, ZAIG, no.20646, 'Information zur politisch-operativen Lage unter den ausländischen Werktätigen in der DDR (Jahreseinschätzung)', 19 September 1988, p.64.
97. See, e.g., the observations by the Office for Labour of the Halle Regional Council in 1989: LSA, Aktenführende Stelle: Sekretariat Arbeitsamt Halle, no.20,209, 'Jahresbericht 1989 zum Stand des Einsatzes ausländischer Werktätiger in Kombinaten und Betrieben und Einrichtungen im Bezirk Halle', [1990], p.3.
98. LSA, Betriebsakten zum Einsatz mocambiquanischer Werktätiger des Bezirkes, no.19,669, 'Information über ein besonderes Vorkommnis während der Maifeierlichkeiten im VEB Dampfkesselbau und der Gemeinde Hohenthurm', 3 May 1988, pp.1–2.
99. BStU, MfS, ZA, HA XVIII, no.5881, 'Jahreseinschätzung zur politisch-operativen Lage unter den ausländischen Werktätigen in der DDR', 30 September 1987, pp.5–6. There were 47,700 contract workers, including 18,600 Vietnamese, 13,010 Cubans and 7,800 Mozambicans, in the GDR in June 1987.
100. BStU, MfS, Außenstelle Gera, ZMA, Gera, no.003011, 'Stimmung/Meinung zum derzeitigen Aufenthalt vietnamesischer Bürger in Gera, von Beschäftigten des "konsument"-Warenhaus', 30 October 1987, p.143.
101. BStU, MfS, Außenstelle Chemnitz, AKG, no.2094, 'Auszug aus der wöchentlichen Lageeinschätzung der KD KMSt/Land vom 2.8.88', p.73.
102. Ibid., 'Auszug aus der wöchentlichen Lageeinschätzung der KD Plauen vom 10.8.88', p.8.

103. BStU, MfS, Außenstelle Halle, BV Halle, Abteilung II, Sachakte, no.157, 'Reaktionen der Bevölkerung', 7 June 1989, p.5.
104. Ibid., p.6.
105. Interview with Gabriele Haas-Wittstock, 29 October 2002.
106. This point was made in interviews on 29 October 2002 with Günter Piening and Gabriele Haas-Wittstock, two members of the office of the Foreigners' Commissioners of Sachsen-Anhalt.
107. BStU, MfS, Außenstelle Halle, BV Halle, Abteilung II, Sachakte, no.157, 'Reaktionen der Bevölkerung', 7 June 1989, p.5. There were about 6,400 foreign workers in the Halle Region in 1989.
108. SAPMO-BA, DY 30/2940, 'Information', [1980], pp.505–6.
109. See the letter of the SED Regional Secretary, Siegfried Lorenz, March 1988 in BStU, MfS, Außenstelle Chemnitz, AKG, no.2094, pp.34–35; also ibid., 'Telegramm', 18 March 1987, p.7.
110. BStU, MfS, Außenstelle Chemnitz, AKG, no.2095, 'Auszug aus der wöchentlichen Lageeinschätzung der KD Rochlitz vom 10.8.88', p.7.
111. BStU, MfS, Außenstelle Chemnitz, AKG, no.2094, 'Auszug aus der wöchentlichen Einschätzung der KD KMSt/Land vom 7.6.8', p.90.
112. BStU, MfS, Außenstelle Erfurt, Abteilung XVIII, no.203, 'Rückflußinformation zu aktuellen Problemen beim Einsatz ausländischer Arbeitskräfte', 5 May 1989, p.4.
113. BStU, MfS, ZA, ZAIG, no.20646, 'Jahreseinschätzung zur politisch-operativen Lage unter den ausländischen Werktätigen in der DDR', 7 September 1989, p.25.
114. Ibid., p.26.
115. BStU, MfS, ZA, HA XX, no.3035, 'Information zum Aufenthalt mocambiquanischer Bürger', 19 May 1989, p.95.
116. A ZIJ survey in autumn 1990 carried out among about 1,700 young persons in Leipzig, Dresden and Chemnitz revealed that only 1.2 per cent and 13.0 per cent stated that they were 'very sympathetic' and 'sympathetic' respectively towards Vietnamese as opposed to 18.9 per cent and 10.1 per cent who were 'antipathetic' or 'very antipathetic' respectively: GZ, 'S6004: Jugend und Rechtsextremismus 1990', B70-0074, 34b.
117. Interview with K., 8 September 2003.

*Chapter 5*

# FOOTBALL FANS, HOOLIGANS AND THE STATE

*T*his chapter continues the theme of limitations on possibilities for autonomy and the expression of a sense of self with reference to football fans and hooligans in one of the GDR's most closely monitored sub-systems, top-level sport. Football fandom in the GDR encompassed various combinations of motives and levels of commitment and activity. Among the latter were: membership of registered and unauthorised fan clubs, attendance at matches in the domestic league, reading the sports columns of specialist newspapers such as *Die Neue Fußballwoche*, collecting football ephemera, and watching or listening to East and West German sports programmes on radio and television. While East German fans tended to be football cross-dressers in their attachment to the colours of their favourite teams on either side of the Berlin Wall, the majority had to content themselves with vicarious support for Western clubs, notably Bayern Munich, Schalke 04, Hamburg SV, Hertha Berlin and the even more distant Real Madrid. Some enthusiasts, however, were able to circumvent numerous bureaucratic and political obstacles in order to watch Franz Beckenbauer and the representatives of the 'class enemy' when they competed in Czechoslovakia, Hungary and other neighbouring East European countries. The appeal of the West German game set alarm bells ringing among policy makers and security organs as cross-border links, whether indirectly through the Western media or in person, were regarded as means whereby East German fans could be led into what the authorities decried as 'negative decadent' or 'negative hostile' activities and attitudes. Another concern was the disorderly behaviour of a small number of fans, whether in the GDR or abroad, which, from the late 1970s, became increasingly violent and analogous to football hooliganism in the West. A consistent pattern of nonconformist behaviour in football,

Notes for this section begin on page 149.

which has also been observed by Edelman for the Soviet Union (Edelman 2002) and by Oswald for the Third Reich (Oswald 2008), links up with 'safe' forms of resistance among youth sub-cultures in the last decade of the communist post-totalitarian state which are examined in Chapters 6 and 7.

Not only did nonconformism highlight the failure of the SED to transform its young people according to its notion of the model all-round socialist personality, but football fans' links with fellow spirits across the border also undermined East Germans' identification with the political and social system of the GDR and the SED's ambition, since the early 1970s, to create a separate GDR national identity. Indeed, the generally mediocre performance of East German football teams in international competitions, in contrast to world-class achievements in sports such as swimming and athletics, seriously weakened official claims that success in sport testified to the superiority of the socialist order. Furthermore, football's deep roots in local communities and the ensuing rivalries between clubs – as for example, between Dynamo Berlin and Dynamo Dresden – revealed the survival of strong traditional identities that defied SED efforts to create a unitary state and a harmonious society. With the outcome of football games supposedly affecting worker productivity and mood, and with bragging rights also at stake, many SED, governmental and industrial leaders became directly involved in the battle for footballing supremacy and the upholding of local pride.

While the sub-culture of football undoubtedly possessed a considerable measure of autonomy, regime tolerance was not unbounded. Fans, club officials, players and referees were subjected to close surveillance and arbitrary acts of repression. Given the importance of top-level sport for East-West rivalry during the Cold War, a struggle that was especially intense between the two German states, the Stasi spun an elaborate web of surveillance. From the 1970s onwards, an estimated 3,000 unofficial collaborators were used each year in top-level sport, including many football players, fans and referees, as is discussed in detail later. One of the Stasi's main objectives in setting up such a complex network was to prevent flight to the West, as defection damaged the reputation of the socialist system and deprived the GDR of talent and sports know-how.

## Organisational Restructuring Between Ideology and Performance

An appreciation of the delicate balance in the relationship between the regime and football's multifaceted sub-culture requires a contextualisation of the game's social significance and its organisational structures. Among the key factors in football's emergence in the early days of the Weimar Republic as Germany's most popular sport were its appeal to both the working and middle classes, the increase in leisure time for workers, the construction of large stadiums, the potential for higher earnings and profits for players and business respectively, and, perhaps above all, the close linkage of clubs with strong local and regional identities. East German attendance statistics attest to the continuing popularity of football: an

all-time peak was recorded in the 1951/52 season when over 3.6 million spectators flocked to the 342 matches in the recently established East German *Oberliga*.
Twenty years later, shortly after Honecker came to power, attendances fell to just
over 2 million, albeit for a smaller number of games. The average gate between
the 1970s and the mid 1980s ranged from 10,629 to 13,827, before dropping
below 10,000 for the first time in 1985/86 (Horn and Weise 2004: 419–20).
Popular interest was catered for by East German television and radio as well as
by the daily press and specialist publications such as *Die Neue Fußballwoche* and
*Deutsches Sportecho*.

Although the league structure was modified from time to time, top-level football was clustered around a premier division (*Oberliga*), the second division (*Liga*)
and several regional divisions (*Bezirksligen*). In addition to the league structure,
a competition was held annually for the prestigious cup of the *Freier Deutscher
Gewerkschaftsbund* (FDGB), the East German trade union organisation. Not until 1979 were women able to take part in a supra-regional competition, albeit
in a marginalised space without the status and privileges enjoyed by their male
counterparts (Pfister 2003: 138–42). The men's game was overhauled at least
once per decade in order to reinforce central control, implement socialist tenets,
standardise regulations, raise the quality of the game and eliminate malpractice.
As in other sports, private associations and clubs were banned. The *Deutscher
Turn- und Sportbund der Deutschen Demokratischen Republik* (DTSB), a gymnastics and sports federation, was set up in 1957 as successor to the *Deutscher
Sportausschuß*; it acted as the umbrella organisation for elite and mass sport. The
*Deutscher Fußballverband* (DFV), the German football association, established
in 1958 in place of the *Fachausschuß Fußball*, was the largest of the many sports
associations incorporated into the DTSB.

The nurturing of a socialist football culture was at the top of the agenda in the
immediate postwar years, when private sports clubs were dismantled, the factory
was turned into the fulcrum of sporting activities and football was brought into
line with the production principle. In keeping with the latter feature and the primacy of the collective in socialism, teams received a prefix, the most common one
being BSG (*Betriebssportgemeinschaft*), or 'enterprise sports group', which signified
the linkage with an industrial concern. [1] The trampling on traditional structures
lay behind the first outbreak of serious crowd trouble in May 1949 when the contentious award of a goal to the *Zentral-Betriebssportgemeinschaft Industrie* (Central
Enterprise Sports Group Industry) Leipzig against the champions of the Soviet
Zone, SG Planitz, triggered a pitch invasion by the latter's fans. It was popularly
believed in Planitz that this was yet one more instance of the politically motivated
advancement of the new kind of socialist sport organisation and of the authorities'
plan to turn the club into a similar formation (Teichler 2005: 10–13).

Despite aspirations to create a football culture on socialist foundations, abuses
were legion, partly the result of intrigues by, and rivalries among, high-ranking
SED functionaries and numerous organisations at regional and central level. While
Erich Mielke is the best known of these leaders, Harry Tisch and Egon Krenz, two

of his politburo colleagues, were also involved in a game of political football. Tisch had been head of the SED's Rostock Regional Administration until he became chair of the FDGB in 1975. Eight years later, Krenz was appointed to one of the crucial posts in the party, that of SED Central Committee Secretary for Security, Youth and Sport. Many other political leaders also took a keen interest in football and used their connections and resources to promote their favourite team and boost the prestige of their region or organisation. Internal materials show that the Stasi leadership was eager that the success of top-level footballers and athletes in its sports association should enhance the Ministry of State Security's authority and that popular antipathy should not be provoked by allegations in the media and on the terraces of unsporting behaviour by Dynamo Berlin players and the manipulation of results in the club's favour.[2] With state-owned enterprises and large economic conglomerates known as combines also engaging in, to adopt Stuart Hall's terminology, the 'contested battlefield' (Hall 1981: 233) of sport, central control was weaker in football than seems to have been the case in most other branches of top-level sport. Not only did the main authorities for football – the DTSB, the DFV and the SED Central Committee's Department for Sport – sometimes clash over the development and running of the game, but they also had to work in conjunction with, and on occasions against, the Dynamo Sports Association, the enterprises and other interest groups. In his memoirs, written after German unification, Manfred Ewald, the DTSB president, lamented the mediocrity of his country's football, attributing it to undue interference by central and provincial political and economic functionaries (Ewald 1994: 56–57), an opinion which was shared by the DFV.[3] Among the few notable international successes were Olympic gold for the national team in 1976 and Magdeburg's victory in the European Cup Winners' Cup final against the illustrious AC Milan in 1974. Although East Germany surprisingly defeated the West German team 1–0 in Hamburg at the group stage of the 1974 World Cup, it was the West Germans who went on to win the tournament, thus underlining the superiority of the Western game, much to the chagrin of the GDR's political and sport elites.

Ewald was the mastermind behind the GDR's emergence as a world leader in athletics, swimming, bobsleighing and many other sports. While the sporting prowess of the GDR owed much to the clandestine state drug programme of the state and an intensive talent spotting and training system, it was also linked to the ruthless concentration on sports which reaped a high dividend in terms of medals and world records. Although football was unable to match the success of sports such as athletics, its widespread popularity with East Germans, its social prestige, its significance for local communities and the interventions of top SED functionaries ensured the continuation of generous official support. Thus in 1969, when top-level sport was divided into two tiers, football managed to secure its position in the upper tier – Sport I – which guaranteed state subvention, access to the GDR's comprehensive system of training centres, children's and youth sports schools, and the services of full-time coaches and trainers. This kind of assistance, together with the financial and material backing of sponsors, meant that footballers, despite their relative lack of success in international competition, enjoyed a higher earnings potential than top athletes, much to the annoyance of the latter.

## A Strange World?

Although East German football has been called a 'strange world' (Hesse-Lichtenberger 2002: 277), it was perhaps only the unresolved German national question and the division of Berlin that marked the East German game out from that in most other countries behind the Iron Curtain. In the world of state socialism, where the dominance of a team from the capital was the norm, clubs relocated and changed their names with bewildering frequency in accordance with political and ideological criteria. One of the most notorious incidents concerned a proposal to move BSG Wismut, a team with strong support among local miners employed by its sponsor, the politically and economically important uranium works (Polte 1957: i–viii). With rumours circulating of a general strike by local miners and the players openly opposed to the move, SED and club officials reached a compromise: the team was to continue playing in Aue as the hybrid SC Wismut Karl-Marx-Stadt. Despite the farcical situation, which lasted from 1954 to 1963, the team managed to win the first division title three times during the 1950s, thanks in no small part to their famous striker, Willy Tröger, who had lost his right arm in the final days of the Second World War (Horn and Weise 2004: 346; Leske 2007: 125). The passions aroused in Aue were testimony to the depth of local feeling but also to the kind of disorder and rebelliousness among the miners captured in the unpublished novel *Rummelplatz* by Werner Bräunig (Fenemore 2007: 4).

Not until the early 1970s did popular opposition and the stabilisation of the league structure persuade the SED and the football authorities to call a halt to the relocation of clubs from one part of the country to another. On the other hand, individual players continued to be 'delegated' to leading clubs and were sometimes called up as reservists in the army in order to weaken less privileged opponents. In the absence of an open transfer market and a transparent professionalism, players were induced by club officials and other intermediaries to change affiliation by the bait of an apartment, a car, a well-rewarded sham job and various under-the-counter payments.

The covert pursuit of talented players frequently triggered disputes between the central sports authorities, such as the DTSB, and the clubs and their respective sponsors. Among football's major patrons were large industrial combines like Carl Zeiss Jena, influential regional SED functionaries, the armed forces and Erich Mielke's well-endowed Dynamo Sports Association. Not only were journalists put under pressure to report favourably on Mielke's favourite team, BFC Dynamo, but many players, referees, national coaches, club trainers and officials collaborated clandestinely with the Stasi.[4] When BFC Dynamo won the championship for nine consecutive seasons, from 1979 to 1988, before ever diminishing home support, its supremacy distorted the element of competition in the *Oberliga* and, together with its highly privileged position, reinforced hierarchies of status and turned it into the most unpopular club in the country.[5] Even before the club's first title, it aroused animosity: when it met Lok Leipzig in an away game in 1979, soon after the defection of the BFC Dynamo player Lutz Eigendorf, thousands of Lok fans mocked the Berliners in front of highly embarrassed SED functionaries, chanting: 'Want to bolt to the West, Dynamo is best!' (Berger 2009: 141). There was a tragic outcome: Eigendorf, under close surveillance by four Stasi informers while playing for clubs in the FRG, died in a car crash which Heribert Schwan attributes to a Stasi plot to spike his drink (Schwan 2000: 260-70). While evidence is lacking which unequivocally substantiates the murder thesis, such was the contempt in some circles for so-called 'traitors' that this kind of action cannot be ruled out.

## Regional Rivalry: Saxony and East Berlin

The mocking of Mielke and protests against the arbitrary delegation of players illustrate how the organisational and cultural characteristics of East German football had a bearing on supporters' behaviour and how the environment of the football crowd afforded an opportunity for the repressed to taunt the elite. Passions were inflamed by actual and alleged advantages derived by clubs attached to a powerful sponsor like the Stasi, and, especially in the 1980s, by the blatant favouring of BFC Dynamo by top referees. Success, it was widely believed, was determined in the corridors of economic and political power, rather than on the playing field. Local and regional rivalries were intense in a sport that embodied potent symbols of community identification and a propensity for generating animosity. While the enduring antagonism between Dynamo Dresden and Dynamo Berlin had deep roots in Saxon and Prussian history, it was also fuelled by the preferential treatment accorded to the East German capital as regards the provision of housing and consumer goods. When crowd trouble broke out over the referee's partiality towards BFC at an *Oberliga* match in December 1978, Dresden supporters complained: 'We are cheated everywhere, even on the sports field', and 'referees are bribed'.[6] Their anger was not assuaged by the fact that both clubs belonged to the Dynamo Sports Association, the highly successful umbrella sports organisation of the Ministry of State Security, the Ministry of the Interior and the customs administration. Dresden's fans preferred to distance themselves from the Stasi connection by cultivating their club's credentials as the representative of the less unpopular police. They also took pride in the team's reputation for playing a stylish, attacking game as opposed to the more physical approach of so many other teams in the *Oberliga*, a partial reflection perhaps of Dresden's cultural standing as 'Florence on the Elbe'.

The head of the Stasi, Erich Mielke, who was also chair of the Dynamo Sports Association, was determined that BFC would ultimately prevail over its Dresden comrades. The Saxon club's elegant sweeper, Hans-Jürgen Dörner, remembers Mielke making it clear to the Dresden players at their championship celebrations in 1978 that the time had come for BFC to step into their shoes (Luther and Willmann 2003: 70–71). Ironically, Dresden benefited from the support of Horst Böhm, the head of the Stasi's Dresden Regional Administration. According to Dörner, Böhm and the chief of the Dresden regional police office, Nyffenegger, put local patriotism first in the rivalry with BFC Dynamo (Pleil 2001: 31–32). BFC's success at the expense of Dresden compounded the sense of victimhood among the Saxon club's supporters aroused by an earlier attempt to boost the fortunes of the Berliners. During the playing season, in November 1954, Mielke had ordered the relocation of the Dynamo Dresden players to East Berlin. This broke one of football's unwritten laws, that a team or club should not move, or be moved, from a community in which it was firmly embedded. The Dresden players entered the *Oberliga* as the newly formed SC Dynamo Berlin; the club was renamed BFC Dynamo twelve years later. The depleted Dresden team dropped into a lower division, not returning to the *Oberliga* until 1962.

The antagonism between the fans of the two Dynamo clubs even spread to members of the Stasi's own units in Dresden. When the teams met in 1985, one Stasi officer likened the behaviour of sections of the guards' regiment in the city to that of 'rioting fans'; some guards had hurled abuse at the BFC players, shouting 'Bent champions!' as they left the pitch.[7] Disturbances by spectators were a regular occurrence. Only three years earlier, one Dresden fan had complained to the long-serving head of the SED Central Committee's Department for Sport, Rudi Hellmann, that rioting erupted only when BFC played in Dresden. 'Berlin rowdies', he protested, 'had demolished the stadium and injured a number of children … I am of the opinion that we are all citizens of our republic and that chants of "Prussia" and "Saxony" by BFC supporters do not belong in our stadiums'.[8]

From the other side, one BFC supporter, Heiko, still relishes the sadistic pleasure derived from denigrating and baiting rival fans who hated the Stasi team. He describes his emotions when BFC met its great Dresden rival: 'For example, Dresden: sold out. Thirty thousand Saxons were there, foaming at the mouth: *Stasi-pigs* … And there we were, all three hundred of us, and sang a well-known nursery rhyme to the words of *Ho, ho, hey – Mielke is ok*. That made their blood boil' (Farin and Hauswald 1998: 66). Hostility to BFC within the Dynamo Sports Association was not confined to Dresden. This is apparent from spectator unrest when SG Dynamo Schwerin lost narrowly at home to BFC in 1968. Eager to exact revenge for the heavy defeat in East Berlin earlier in the season, the Schwerin fans and players felt they had been cheated by referee Vetter. Bottles and stones were thrown on to the pitch, the referee was verbally abused and, at the final whistle, had to be accompanied from the field. Although twenty people were arrested, the police, off-duty Stasi officers and Schwerin officials were criticised for their laxity in dealing with the trouble.[9]

## Intra-city Hostility: Union and Dynamo

BFC's success was particularly resented by Union Berlin, its great rival in the East German capital. 'Iron Union', based in a humble but much-loved stadium in the Köpenick district on the outskirts of East Berlin, had experienced several name changes before arriving at that of 1.FC Union Berlin in 1966. It could lay claim to links to various predecessors, starting with SC Union Oberschöneweide in 1910. Although Union surprised itself by winning the coveted FDGB cup in 1968, it never lost its reputation as a yo-yo team. This helped cultivate an image among its fans as the eternal underdog and as a club firmly rooted in working-class traditions, in sharp contrast to the Stasi-sponsored big brother across the city (Farin and Hauswald 1998: 77–78; Luther and Willmann 2000: 103, 136). One Union fan, 'Lopez', reflected:

> Underdog, I always say. In Hamburg I would go to St Pauli because it stands in the shadow of HSV, in Munich to 1860 because Bayern is the Croesus there, in Leipzig I would be a Chemie fan. That has to do with principles. We stood in the shadow of the pigs of BFC, Stasi, police and Mielke and were always the downtrodden team. I don't even find it cool to be the number one. The image of the underdog suits me. (Luther and Willmann 2000: 136)

While the Köpenick club lived in the shadow of BFC and the army team Vorwärts Berlin, or at least until it was despatched unceremoniously to Frankfurt/Oder in 1971 (Leske 2009: 175–85), Union was admitted entry into the small elite designated as 'football clubs' when the national game was restructured in 1965/66. Union's elevation owed much to the intervention of Herbert Warnke, the chair of the FDGB. Moreover, for all their cultivation of the club's underdog image, Union fans were not averse to basking in the glow of their superiority as Berliners over provincial rivals. One fan, 'PID', boasts that they took Cuban oranges and rotten bananas to Karl-Marx-Stadt, aware that these symbols of privilege would annoy the locals. Insult was added to injury when the Berliners showed their disdain for the poor-quality fruit by using it as missiles (Willmann 2007: 40).

Numerous post-unification interviews shed further light on the self-perception of Union fans and their antipathy towards the 'artificially created' BFC as opposed to their own 'genuine' club (Luther and Willmann 2000: 136). BFC was regarded as the supreme representative of the security organs and police, with the advantages of access to players across the GDR, heavy financial subsidies and Mielke's political clout. This situation was criticised by football fans for disturbing what some analysts regard as the delicate balance between the just rewards for skill and endurance on the one hand and the intervention of serendipity on the other (see Giulianotti and Armstrong 1997: 11). How attitudes towards BFC shaped the self-image of Union is apparent from comments by Union fans such as Schwenne, for whom: 'Union wasn't just football, Union was religion. That was a philosophy because it was in opposition to the state' (Farin and Hauswald 1998: 103). In addition to its broad working-class base, Union also enjoyed a tinge of the exotic as it appealed to 'long-haired youths' and punks in the 1980s (Willmann 2007: 77) and also attracted support from Hertha fans across the Berlin Wall. Given the nonconformity of many Union fans and their deep-rooted hostility to BFC, an analogy can be drawn with ordinary people's support for Moscow Spartak, rather than elitist clubs attached to the army or police, as a 'small way of saying "no"' to the Soviet authorities (Edelman 2002: 1442).

Fans' resentment at the authorities' delegation of leading players to BFC, which was by no means confined to supporters of Union and Dynamo Dresden, was compounded by anger at referees' blatant bias in favour of Mielke's team. Several years after German unification, Union's former star goalkeeper, Wolfgang Matthies, remembers, not without bitterness, how his team had played, in effect, against fourteen men of BFC, the eleven players plus the referee and two linesmen, and that whereas Union had been obliged to send its most promising players to BFC, it only received the latter's rejects (Luther and Willmann 2000: 103–4). Animosity was further fuelled when, from 1976 onwards, Union's home games against BFC were transferred by the DFV to the neutral *Stadion der Weltjugend*. It was easier to control Union's unruly fans there than in its tightly enclosed stadium in a forested area of Köpenick (Willmann 2007: 136–37).

A situation similar to that in East Berlin existed in Leipzig, where competition was fierce between Lokomotive Leipzig, or Lok Leipzig, the city's foremost team, and the underdogs at Chemie Leipzig. The latter was regarded by its fans as the 'local' team in contrast to Lok, which had been created in the early 1960s on orders from the central sports authorities and Leipzig's regional SED and DTSB organs and then nurtured as one of the GDR's elite clubs (Fuge 1997: 61, 74–75; 2009: 20–29; Remath and Schneider 1999: 68–69). Chemie had defied the odds when, in 1964, it won the *Oberliga* despite the loss of several talented players as part of a reorganisation of local football to the advantage of its great foe SC (later Lok) Leipzig. A shared self-perception as underdogs promoted an inter-city community of identity between Chemie and Union fans, at least until the Berliners' victory in Leipzig in 1980 condemned Chemie to relegation from the *Oberliga* and triggered two decades of mutual hostility (Fuge 2004: 97).

## 'Bent' Referees

The performance of referees as a cause of ill feeling between fans is a thread running from spectator disorder in the late 1940s through to widespread outrage at referee bias in favour of BFC during its unprecedented run of success in the 1980s. One of the most serious outbursts of disorder occurred at the end of the 1949/50 season when ZSG 'Horch' Zwickau trounced SG Dresden-Friedrichstadt 5–1 before 60,000 fans in Dresden in a game that decided the *Oberliga* title. Zwickau's victory was attributed by rioting fans to the referee's blatant discrimination against the Dresden club. The latter was the thinly disguised successor to Dresden SC 1898, which had won the last German championship, one year before the collapse of the Third Reich. In official eyes, it was a 'politically incorrect bourgeois club' in contrast to Zwickau with its socialist credentials through its links to a state enterprise (Leske 2004: 109–10; Luther 2004: 9–10). Most of the Dresden players, including Helmut Schön, left the GDR for the West soon afterwards. Another notorious incident occurred thirteen years later when the failure of the referee to award a penalty to Motor Wema Plauen in a promotion play-off against Motor Eisenach led to bottles being thrown on to the field and spectators attacking the referee. The violence was provoked by the Plauen fans' conviction that their team, deprived of top-class football for many years, had been cheated by a referee with business connections to the parent enterprise of the Eisenach club.[10] As the largest town on the East–West German border, Plauen was in a politically sensitive location.

Criticism of referees was not confined to the terraces. During the 1985 FDGB cup final between BFC and Dynamo Dresden, Harry Tisch, the chair of the trade union organisation, took exception to Mielke's opinion that Roßner had refereed the game well, countering that such referees were damaging the credibility of the competition.[11] After examining a video recording of the game, a DFV panel deemed Roßner's performance unsatisfactory and banned him from refereeing international and *Oberliga* matches.[12] There was some irony in this decision as East German referees like Rudi Glöckner were highly regarded for their refereeing of international matches; perhaps a question of being 'tops abroad, but flops at home' (Mende 1991: 131). Even SED-controlled daily newspapers such as *Neues Deutschland*, the specialist sport press and the FDJ organ, *Junge Welt*, were, despite Stasi pressure, sometimes openly critical of referees for favouring Mielke's team (Spitzer 2004: 80–83).

The Stasi's main evaluation organ, the *Zentrale Auswertungs- und Informationsgruppe*, or Central Assessment and Information Group (ZAIG), became involved in the tussle. In its review of newspaper reports on BFC matches between the start of the 1968/69 season and the first half of the 1970/71 season, it complained that not only did reporters tend to overlook the misconduct of other teams' supporters, unlike those of BFC, but journalists also showed greater sympathy for Union Berlin.[13] Several years later, in March 1986, when *Junge Welt* found fault with referee Stumpf for awarding a late penalty to BFC in the encounter with Lok Leipzig, Mielke complained to Ewald and Hellmann that such scribbling undermined the reputation of both BFC and the Dynamo Sports Association (*MfS und Leistungssport* 1994: 105).[14]

Stumpf and several other top referees – among them Glöckner, Prokop, Roßner and Supp – were Stasi informers.[15] Had this been public knowledge it would have had an inflammatory effect on visiting dignitaries, trainers and especially opposing fans. A Dynamo Dresden trainer fulminated after the loss of a point in Aue that Stenzel, Supp and others belonged to a 'guild' of referees that discriminated against teams other than Mielke's BFC.[16] This was an indirect reference to BFC officials' presence on key bodies such as the DFV commission responsible for the allocation of matches to referees and their assistants. One football functionary even threatened to strike a leading BFC official in the face after the former, a Lok Leipzig supporter, had criticised the performance of the referee.[17] No written evidence has been unearthed to show that referees were under direct instructions from the Stasi or Mielke to favour BFC but, on the other hand, they were no doubt aware of what was expected of them. They were in effect taking out a special form of occupational insurance, moreover, some would not have wanted to jeopardise the various benefits of officiating at international matches (Leske 2004: 479–81, 530–33; Spitzer 2004: 73–81).

Popular perceptions of the partiality of referees such as Prokop and Stumpf and of BFC's generally poor record in Europe are summed up in a poem entitled *Gemeinsam klapps!!!* ('Together we're ok!!!'). To the annoyance of the Stasi, the scurrilous verses by an unknown author were distributed as a leaflet when BFC met Karl-Marx-Stadt in May 1988. The first few lines, in translation, read:

> BFC leads the way,
> Thanks to Prokop, Stumpf and Habermann.
> And Rossner, Scheurell also ensure,
> That BFC advances to the fore.[18]

## Football Hooliganism as a Societal Issue

Recurrent football violence after 1945 was not a new phenomenon in Germany: attacks on referees and players had been common in the Weimar Republic since the beginning of the 1920s, especially in cities such as Mannheim, Dresden and Leipzig, and subsequently in the Third Reich between about 1934/35 and 1941. The strength of fans' attachment to their club and the intensity of local and regional rivalries, which lay behind most of the incidents, undermined the National Socialist dictatorship's claim to have established a harmonious *Volksgemeinschaft*, or 'national community' (Oswald 2008: 252–56, 270–1, 276–99). In the GDR, although violence erupted in football stadiums during the 1950s and 1960s, it tended to be related to the culture of football rivalry and, for the most part, antagonisms were low-key, ritualistic and verbal. The return of Union Berlin to the top division in the 1970/71 season, however, marked a new departure as the seriousness of incidents in connection with Union's clash with BFC turned embryonic football hooliganism into a social and political issue worthy of the close attention of the Stasi and police (Leske 2004: 432–34). Yet although fan disorder would continue throughout the 1970s, it was not until the 1980s that antisocial behaviour and violence became significantly more widespread and frequent with concomitant spiralling state concern and engagement. Officially recorded offences rose from 960 in 1986/87 to 1,090 in the following season. In the former period, 407 recorded incidents occurred in the stadiums, 282 in the surrounding areas and 250 on the railways.[19] Finally, from about the mid 1980s onwards, the growing infiltration of soccer by skinheads inaugurated a transition towards a more militant and a less casual terrace culture and an increase in the severity of offences.

There is, it should be observed, no universally accepted definition of so hetero-geneous phenomenon as football hooliganism. Not only is the term frequently applied to physical violence and random vandalism as well as lower-order dis-turbances but also to many forms of disorder that are not related directly to the game itself (Spaaij 2007: 411–15, 425–6). Furthermore, a significant element of labelling is involved: the classification of certain types of acts as 'football hooli-ganism' is often dependent on whether they are deemed illegitimate, as has some-times happened in England, by the government, the police and the media. The East German police and Ministry of State Security had no compunction about attaching pejorative labels to violent football supporters and what they regarded as other deviant youth sub-cultures, whether punks, skinheads or heavy-metal fans. They were all subsumed under the category of 'negative decadent forces', which allegedly constituted a key target for Western political and ideological sub-version and a potential springboard for the development of the politically more threatening and autonomous peace, human rights and other so-called 'hostile negative' groups.

However, as the 'negative decadent' label was very broad, Stasi lexicologists sought to differentiate between the small minority of hard-core 'negative deca-dent' fans and a much larger group of supporters involved in minor disturbances. While the distinction is not always clear-cut, it can be illustrated by reference to the Leipzig regional police's breakdown of offences committed by 142 followers of Lok Leipzig and Chemie Leipzig during the 1986/87 season. Over 71 per cent of the acts were committed by offenders aged between 16 and 22 years.[20] Most incidents were low-key: 'undisciplined actions' on public transport and elsewhere, such as drunkenness and urinating in public (60.5 per cent); insulting and provoking spectators, travellers on public transport and the police (14.1 per cent); and throwing fireworks and missiles on to the pitch (9.2 per cent). The most serious offences consisted of damage to train coaches, stadiums and public facilities (7.7 per cent) and physical assaults on other fans, spectators and passers-by (8.5 per cent).

How these categories translate into specific incidents can be ascertained from the voluminous documentation compiled by the Stasi, the police, the SED and the football authorities. Taunts typically levelled at BFC were 'bent champions', 'Jewish pigs', 'Berlin Jews' and 'leaders of Turks'.[21] Chants which the authorities regarded as politically motivated were: 'Every second one a spy',[22] 'The fuzz are work-shy' and 'Stasi out!'[23] A second category, the vandalism which frequently occurred on public transport, at railway stations and in city centres, is described in an official complaint lodged in 1987 by a school group concerning the boorish behaviour of Chemie Leipzig fans during a train journey from Quedlinburg to Leipzig. Bottles were thrown at the pupils, the carriage looked like a cattle truck, fans sprawled on the floor in a drunken stupor, some of the males exposed themselves and many sang Nazi songs.[24]

The Stasi and police tackled football-related disorder with a range of preventive, coercive and other countermeasures. It was not until 1970, however, that the Stasi launched the first major coordinated campaign in football – OV 'Kraketer' – in order to prevent a recurrence of the rioting by Union fans during the derby with BFC in October of that year. In keeping with the 'softer' methods of control characteristic of its 'operational decomposition' strategy, the Stasi aimed to divide and isolate the targets in order to foil 'hostile' and 'negative' actions. Under the direction of Main Department XX of the Stasi Regional Administration of what was then termed Greater-Berlin, Stasi service units were instructed to draw up a list of active Union supporters, to identify their political views and links with the West, and to uncover 'negative' individuals and their leaders. The Union players also came under close surveillance. Reliable unofficial collaborators (IMs) were to penetrate the inner circle of the 'negative' fans and, together with full-time officers, keep watch over every Union game. By using the information acquired through these channels, the key figures were to be apprehended and the problems eradicated as quickly as possible.[25]

As in the state's encounters with many other sub-cultures, this proved to be a Cnut-like aspiration. In December 1971, trouble broke out once more at the BFC encounter with Union at the *Sportforum* in the East Berlin district of Hohenschönhausen. The eight persons arrested were described by the Stasi as of 'unstable and primitive intelligence'.[26] With disorder continuing at Union matches, Mielke urged Krenz to authorise action against what the Stasi boss called 'negative decadent' youths whose behaviour posed a threat to society. An accompanying Stasi information bulletin, which was intended to buttress Mielke's request, noted that twenty-three preliminary criminal proceedings and seventy-four administrative penalty procedures had been instigated during the first half of the 1976/77 season.[27] These measures notwithstanding, the Stasi was obliged to implement other operations, among them OV 'Kontrahent' in 1982 and a series of operational person checks (OPKs), which, according to the ministry's East Berlin Regional Administration, enabled it to identify and infiltrate numerous hard-core and militant groups attached to BFC Dynamo in the mid 1980s.[28]

East Berlin was by no means the only centre of football-related disorder. The kind of antisocial conduct, to which the pejorative label 'hooliganism' is usually attached, is recalled by a fan when his local team, Chemie Leipzig, lost at home to BFC in 1979: 'Hundreds of Leipzigers tried to get to the Berlin supporters. These sought shelter behind the terraces from the stones raining down on them. Giant clouds of dust hung over the events, which continued into the evening. The police attempted to disperse the frenzied mob with packs of dogs' (Remath and Schneider 1999: 71).

The Leipzig regional police force estimated that between 100 and 300 unruly fans had attached themselves to Lok Leipzig and Chemie Leipzig during the 1976/77 season; the bulk of offenders, about 80 per cent, were aged between 15 and 18. A displacement of incidents, it was reported, had occurred from the stadium area to the inner city and the main station. In 1976, nineteen preliminary criminal proceedings had been instituted against fourteen offenders, including five for rowdyism and two for vilification of the state. Forty-six administrative penalty procedures were implemented to deal with minor forms of rowdy behaviour and damage to property.[29] While unpublished internal police and Stasi files are the main sources for these incidents – due to the fact that the GDR press, including specialist sports publications such as *Die Neue Fußballwoche*, tended to play down their significance – reports did appear from time to time in the media. For example, the authorities' growing concern was signalled by the publication in 1983 of a book on deviance among young people. The book described how supporters of Rot-Weiß Erfurt had caused trouble in Aue, Halle and Leipzig in 1979. Three fans were jailed for assault and damage to property (Queißer 1983: 98–99).

## The Escalation of Disorder in the 1980s

The inability of the football authorities, the Stasi and the police to curb disturbances is apparent from the detailed statistics compiled by these bodies from 1978 until the end of the 1989 season. Table 5.1, which is mainly based on data derived from the Stasi's *Zentraler Operativstab*, or Central Operation Staff (ZOS), provides a statistical overview. In its evaluation of the period 1978 to 1981, ZOS highlighted a rise in the number and seriousness of football-related offences, above all at games involving Union Berlin. Of the 472 arrests made between February and December 1980, 245 had occurred in connection with Union. On the other side of the capital, little trouble had occurred at BFC matches due to a heavy police and steward presence.[30] Increasingly, ZOS and other bodies homed in on what they called the hard core among the 'negative decadent' fans, the inveterate football hooligans. Numbers were relatively small, Union having only about 150 to 200 in 1986 (Leske 2004: 455). Aged predominantly between fourteen and twenty-two years, the members of the hard-core groups at Union and elsewhere were primarily responsible for the serious acts of vandalism and assault described elsewhere in this chapter.

Towards the middle of the decade, a significant radicalisation occurred as skinheads added a more explicit racism and lethal militancy to the hooligan scene. This is one reason for MfS Main Department XX's conclusion, in 1988, that while the actual number of incidents showed a slight downward trend, their intensity and seriousness was mounting.[31] It should be mentioned, in parenthesis, that this left an unfortunate legacy: once the controlling hand of the SED and Stasi had been removed with the disintegration of the communist regime, a more powerful wave of violence swept through many of the football grounds of East Germany. This antisocial behaviour has continued to plague the ailing football scene in the former GDR. For example, in October 2007 serious violence broke out between rival fans after the match between Dynamo Dresden's reserve team and Lok Leipzig.[32]

The survey in Table 5.1 of arrests and legal measures can be supplemented with data on the location of incidents and the clubs most affected. Of the 1,099 offences recorded in the *Oberliga* in 1987/88, over 50 per cent were committed by fans of Hallescher Fußballclub Chemie (188), Union Berlin (171), Hansa Rostock (146) and Rot-Weiß Erfurt (126). Meanwhile, Magdeburg (88) and Dynamo Dresden (83) lagged some way behind. Not surprisingly, ZOS concluded that 'a decisive turning point had not been achieved in this area [public order]' despite numerous preventive and security measures.[33] As is apparent from the Leipzig regional police report mentioned above, vandalism and other acts of public disorder were not confined to the grounds of the *Oberliga* clubs. For example, in 1987/88, 42 per cent took place in the stadiums, 35 per cent in the city or town where a game was taking place and 23 per cent on the trains or property of the railway authority.[34] In East Berlin, trouble broke out over the determination of Union and BFC fans to defend their 'home' territory in the capital and to contest the central area, Mitte. BFC was associated with areas such as Prenzlauer Berg, Pankow, Weißensee, Hohenschönhausen and certain cafés and pubs in the vicinity of Alexanderplatz, while Union supporters were encamped in the club's Köpenick bastion (Willmann 2007: 39, 45, 77–78).

**Table 5.1:** Arrests and Proceedings against Offenders at *Oberliga* Matches, 1984–1989.

| Season | Arrests | Preliminary criminal proceedings | Administrative penalty procedures |
|---|---|---|---|
| 1984/85 | 1,027 | 47 | 606 |
| 1985/86 (first half) | 467 | 3% | 40% |
| 1986-87 (first half) | 503 | 35 | n.a |
| 1987/88 | 1,076 | 59 | 929 |
| 1988/89 (first half) | 516 | 42 | 91 |
| 1988/89 (second half) * | 80 | 6 | 49 |

* Includes FDGB cup games

Sources: Leske (2004: 441, 443, 447) and BStU, MfS ZA, HA XX, 221, pp.37, 193, 259, 299, 327.

Table 5.1 does not provide a complete picture as some of the figures were almost certainly massaged by the police and the Stasi before their dispatch to the higher echelons of the SED (Spitzer 2004: 94, 96). Secondly, in what is anyhow a notoriously grey area, internal reports leave no doubt that the figures are an underestimate as many incidents simply went unrecorded and an arrest did not lead automatically to sentencing. Of the 467 persons arrested by the police in the first half of the 1985/86 season, 109 were released after being cautioned.[35] Sometimes, as in the stadiums – which were, in the words of one East German hooligan, 'places of convenience' (Farin and Hauswald 1998: 109) – the police were simply overwhelmed by the scale of their task. One such case occurred at the *Oberliga* match between arch-rivals BFC and Dynamo Dresden in April 1988. With serious overcrowding in the section of the ground occupied by Dresden supporters, and with tension mounting, the police and the Stasi decided not to arrest fans who were destroying seats and shouting abuse at the Berlin team for fear that it would exacerbate an already difficult situation.[36] This was by no means an isolated incident. A supporter of Chemie Leipzig recalls that the police hardly dared intervene when brawls broke out in the *Georg-Schwarz-Sportpark* as they did not wish to have thousands of spectators at their throats (Remath and Schneider 1999: 70). A further example comes from a game between Karl-Marx-Stadt and BFC: a policeman drew his pistol after losing his truncheon while directing fans back to the station; one fan defied him to shoot amid a chorus of abuse (Hahn 2007: 170).

Public transport was another area where the police were overtaxed. Officers accompanying fans to away matches are known to have turned a blind eye to troublemakers on the trains, an indication that unruly behaviour was regarded by some officials as a normal occurrence.[37] Finally, political decisions had a bearing both on the treatment of offenders and the statistical record. This was the case when the SED politburo instructed the security forces to smash the skinhead movement soon after the public furore following attacks by about thirty militant skinheads on visitors at a rock and punk concert at the *Zionskirche* in East Berlin in October 1987. The inebriated skinheads had attended the Union Berlin game against Lok Leipzig earlier in the day.

## Skinhead Penetration of the Hooligan Scene

As is discussed in the Chapters 6 and 7, the 1980s witnessed a growing popularity in Western skinhead music, dress and militancy among young East Germans, including violently oriented football supporters, as an alternative to the dominant political and ideological system and its institutional instruments such as the Free German Youth. The Cold War was being fought on the terrain of culture, and subordination was being increasingly questioned. A qualitative change also became apparent: militant skinheads were more likely to use the occasion of a match to commit pre-meditated violence rather than conducting such acts on an ad hoc basis. East Berlin was the main centre of the skinheads and BFC and Union the two football magnets, both for the capital's skinheads as well as those from the neighbouring administrative regions of Potsdam and Frankfurt/Oder. In the 1987/88 season, fourteen skinheads in Frankfurt/Oder supported the local city team but also, on occasion, BFC, and were responsible for provoking disorder.[38] Not only were the stadiums a 'Mecca' for skinheads (Stock and Mühlberg 1990: 10) but Walter Süß has also likened the cover they gave skinheads to that consciously provided by the Protestant churches for the alternative peace and ecological groups (Süß 1993: 12–13). In addition to the stadiums, typical meeting places included pubs, youth clubs, discos and gyms. A common interest in football, or the opportunity afforded by a sports event for the provocation of disorder, served as a link not only between skinheads across the GDR but also with those in Hungary, the Federal Republic and Czechoslovakia.[39] Trips to football matches in fraternal socialist countries by 'emissaries' in black bomber jackets was a highly unwelcome development for the SED, especially when clashes occurred between visiting East Germans and home fans in those countries (Willmann 2007: 52–53, 84).

The skinheads were able to influence the diffuse extreme-right potential which predated their appearance and found expression in cries like 'Cyanide B for BFC!' and the highly symbolic Hitler salute (Luther and Willmann 2000: 130, 138; Willmann 2007: 23). Two Union supporters, Crille and Uwe Schilling, recall that while radical-right tendencies had always existed, cries of 'Turn on the gas when BFC race through the gas chamber' and 'Germany awake!' were essentially designed to provoke the police and BFC fans rather than articulate a conscious extreme-right political orientation (interview in Luther and Willmann 2000: 128, 130; see also Braun and Teichler 2003: 572–73). Fascist slogans and chants were regarded as particularly challenging forms of provocation as anti-fascism was one of the founding myths of the GDR. Many fans who resorted to extreme-right symbols now insist, perhaps somewhat disingenuously, that they were naive youngsters ignorant of fascist ideology (Willmann 2007: 32, 58, 70, 96, 106).

The arrival of skinheads and the more aggressive behaviour of a growing militant element marked a new trend in football hooliganism. They gave it a more racist edge, were opposed to key aspects of the socialist system, and their violence was often deliberate, with football as the occasion rather than the cause. By the end of December 1985, about thirty to forty skinheads were associated with the two Berlin *Oberliga* clubs, many of them attached to the BFC fan club, *Anale Berlin*.[40] Its following made no secret of their admiration for fascism and engaged in karate to prepare themselves for clashes with opposing fans. In August 1985, fourteen members of the group assaulted passers-by in Dresden and bawled out such fascist songs as 'My father was an SS soldier'.[41] All were arrested, nine receiving prison sentences. Among other *Oberliga* teams with a skinhead element were Lok Leipzig, Hansa Rostock and Energie Cottbus. They were few in number, however, with only two to three skinheads turning up at the Stadium of Friendship in Cottbus.[42] Four skinheads and two sympathisers, all living in Schwerin, attached themselves to Hansa Rostock, helping to form, in April 1988, *Hansa-Fanclub Alf*, named after a character on West German TV. Modelling themselves on the neofascist *Borussen-Front* in Dortmund, they extolled fascism, attacked fans of other clubs, damaged train furnishings and shouted fascist slogans in public.[43]

After several years of relative inactivity, the Stasi and police initiated a series of counter-measures to undermine and ultimately destroy the hard-core skinhead and militant groups. A crackdown was launched against BFC skinheads in August 1987 after the match against Magdeburg and on a more comprehensive scale three months later against skinhead groups across the whole of the GDR (see Chapter 7). The operations shook but did not crush the skinheads.[44] Indeed, the FDGB cup final between BFC and Carl Zeiss Jena at East Berlin's *Stadion der Weltjugend* in June 1988 was the scene of some of the most serious violence ever witnessed at a GDR football game and had been preceded by the first planned gathering of relatively large groups. About 100 to 150 skinheads and other football hooligans gathered in nearby Pankow before proceeding in formation to the match. They chanted fascist songs, clashed violently with other supporters, attacked stewards and damaged stadium property. Shortly before the end of the game, rioting broke out in one of the blocks, fences were destroyed and seats were thrown at stewards.[45] Despite the interrogation of skinhead football hooligans and the many arrests that followed the aforementioned *Zionskirche* incidents in October 1987, the skinheads survived, partly because they were able to go underground temporarily and, as did the *Anale Berlin* group, dress in a less conspicuous manner. Other significant factors were the loose networks formed with Western skinheads and East German youth groups, such as the 'negative' fans at Union and BFC, and the reluctance of Stasi officers to carry out crowd control at BFC matches with the requisite devotion to duty.[46] This may have been prompted by a belief that this kind of work was the responsibility of the more lowly police rather than, as some police officers insisted, the Stasi's failure to clamp down hard on BFC 'rowdies'.[47]

The Stasi viewed the radicalisation of the hooligan scene with increasing alarm. In June 1988, Department XX/2 of the MfS's East Berlin Regional Administration identified, as part of its review of the 1987/88 season, a militant group of skinheads and a number of young fans who attached themselves at matches to the skinheads and, contrary to their usual behaviour, committed penal and a series of minor offences. The main troublemakers were former members of *Anale Berlin* and persistent rowdies who had not been linked to a particular group. These two elements, the Stasi noted, had drawn closer together since the start of the 1987/88 season and had initiated actions with racist, nationalistic and fascist overtones.[48] This development of an embryonic politically motivated hooligan scene was underpinned during 1989 by tighter organisational structures. The skinheads tended increasingly to congregate together in the stadiums rather than, as before, gathering on an ad hoc basis in small groups or as individuals.[49] Finally, the pyramid of 'militant' hooligans was completed by those juvenile supporters who were attracted to skinhead culture, thereby creating what East Berlin's Department XX/2 called a 'reservoir of youthful followers'.[50]

## The State's Counter-offensive

Despite concerted efforts by the football authorities, the SED and the security forces, especially from the end of the 1970s, football-related disorder remained a significant social and political issue. Among a plethora of guidelines and recommendations, similar to those devised in the West to curb antisocial behaviour, were: a more effective use of stewards at matches; restrictions on the sale of alcohol; 'special' football trains; a better liaison between the police, the Stasi and the FDJ; educational measures; and the infiltration of the hard-core element by youthful informers. These were capped by a series of punitive measures, among them the closure of grounds, the use of unmuzzled dogs, exclusion orders, fines, arrests and convictions. The Penal Code gave the police and the Stasi plenty of scope for punishing offenders, above all the articles on rowdiness, public vilification and hindering state or social activity. Article 215 on rowdiness, for example, prescribed punishment of up to five years for anyone who, through disregard for public order or the rules of the socialist community, threatened or caused gross annoyance to people or malicious damage to buildings or equipment.[51]

While all of these measures were implemented during the 1980s, some received greater emphasis as a result of external pressures and events. After the disaster at the Heysel stadium during the 1985 European Cup final between Liverpool and Juventus, in which thirty-nine people were killed and many more injured, the GDR responded to FIFA guidelines with a more rigorous segregation of opposing fans by means of barriers and by the installation of higher perimeter fences. Safety, however, continued to be a matter of great concern for the authorities, particularly as many East German stadiums were urgently in need of modernisation. An outbreak of fire in the wooden stands was an ever-present risk when fans set off fireworks and burnt banners and newspapers. While the Bradford fire disaster in England a fortnight before the Heysel disaster was a painful reminder of this kind of danger, there was a chronic shortage of funds to carry out ground redevelopment on a major scale.

The nurturing of desirable traits by persuasion and example was a favoured method in the prevention of disorder. Appeals were made to fans to behave in a manner deemed appropriate to socialist society, players were urged to play the game fairly, and special sessions were arranged in schools and at the workplace for the discussion of public-order issues. In addition, rowdies were 'named and shamed' in football programmes, the press occasionally carried reports on prison sentences as a warning to others, and parents were informed of their childrens' misdemeanours. However, as this low-key approach enjoyed only limited success,[52] more rigorous forms of control were introduced. Closed-circuit television was used to identify offenders, bans were imposed on miscreants, the sale of tickets was restricted and more stewards were employed on special trains and at the grounds. The stewards' tasks included enforcing the ban on bringing alcohol and missiles into the grounds, and helping to eject unruly fans. All these measures required a high level of cooperation between club officials, the police and the Stasi.[53] Clubs were required to create a special working group for order and safety (*Arbeitsgruppe Ordnung und Sicherheit*) to oversee the various measures at local level and a commission attached to the presidium of the DFV was set up in 1986 as the central policy-steering body. By the end of 1985, most clubs had an established working group, membership consisting of representatives from the clubs and bodies such as the SED, the police, the Stasi and the FDJ.[54]

Stewards were central to the maintenance of public order. Supplied by the clubs, the FDJ and other bodies, the optimistic target was set at 150 to 200 stewards per *Oberliga* club.[55] While body searches could be very thorough, the stewarding system left much to be desired. The turnover among stewards was high and 'negative decadent' fans managed to infiltrate their ranks. Some stewards neglected their duties and, on occasions, became involved in disorderly acts.[56] BFC, which recruited stewards from among its own youthful fans and the central administrative office of the Dynamo Sports Association, did not always appreciate outside assistance. It was reported in 1988 that the stewards provided by the DTSB, most of whom were pensioners, had proved to be a disruptive influence on account of their drunken behaviour.[57]

The myriad unofficial fan clubs which sprang up as part of a mushrooming football fan culture, especially during the 1980s, were another means by which the DFV and other organs hoped to maintain law and order. In 1988, the Stasi estimated that there were 353 fan clubs in the GDR, with an average membership of between five and thirty-five. Dynamo Dresden had the most fan clubs, seventy-four, and a ratio of one registered to four non-registered members.[58] Fan-club names varied widely, reflecting allegiance to a player, a region or a social value. Examples at BFC include 'Bodo Rudwaleit', 'Reiner Ernst', 'The Little Prussians' and 'Black Panther'.[59] The 'Bobby's' were an ironic reflection on the status of BFC as the team of the police and Stasi Dynamo Sports Association (Gläser 2007: 12). In the case of the *Olle-Molle* group at Chemie Halle, a seemingly innocuous name was the cover for the right-extremism of its members (Spitzer 2004: 96). BFC, too, had its militant and radical groups: *Anale Berlin* and *Die Ratten*, the latter attracting, according to one Union fan, hard types among the club's youthful following (Luther and Willmann 2000: 131). The authorities, with their strong abhorrence of independent organisations, were inherently suspicious of all unauthorised fan clubs. There were other reasons, too: such clubs were regarded as focal points for rowdies and 'enemy' forces and conduits for the highly undesirable Western fan culture which had spread rapidly in the FRG during the 1970s, though more hesitantly in the GDR.

As in the West, scarves, club badges, banners, songs and chants all proclaimed an affinity with a team and constituted an East German-style carnival of football as tens of thousands made their way to weekend games (Braun 2004: 440–41; Fuge 2004: 93–98; Leske 2004: 436). Some songs had a political edge. A popular one, based on Uriah Heep's 'Lady in Black', referred to living in the 'Zone' with its mine fields and barbed wire. As Western contacts were limited and no official market existed in the GDR for most football-related items, many banners, scarves, cowls and shirts were home-made (Willmann 2007: 26, 86–87). Some were seized from rival supporters as trophies: one of the fondest memories of Lok Leipzig supporters is the capture of a large BFC banner from visiting Dynamo fans (Franke and Pätzug 2006: 59).

After much procrastination, the authorities decided to mobilise the autonomous fan clubs in the campaign against hooliganism. They were therefore permitted to register as associations in accordance with the 1975 Decree on the Formation of Associations and encouraged to cooperate with the parent football club. While some fan-club members were undoubtedly attracted by the bait of access to players and club discos, others were contemptuous of the bureaucracy involved in, and indeed the very notion of, official registration. Football was their cherished island of autonomy and individual choice.[60] Not surprisingly, progress on the incorporation of fan clubs was uneven: whereas some football clubs, notably Dynamo Dresden and Rot-Weiß Erfurt, were quick off the mark, BFC and Lok Leipzig lagged well behind.[61]

The leading SED and sports functionaries, sensitive to the reputation of the GDR, were determined that antisocial conduct should not occur before TV audiences and the foreign press corps when the national team and East German clubs were involved in international tournaments. Matches between East and West German teams were especially problematic for the SED as many young East Germans openly displayed their allegiance to clubs such as Bayern Munich and Hamburg. Banners unfurled at games involving West German teams in Czechoslovakia and Bulgaria displayed messages such as 'Leipzig greets Germany', 'Stahl Riesa greets Eintracht Frankfurt', and 'Zwickau greets Bayern Munich'.[62] Frequent visits by Hertha fans to Union Berlin matches were viewed by the SED as unwelcome signs of empathy with the clubs across the Wall. One Hertha supporter, Franco, argued that the bond between Union and Hertha supporters was reinforced by their teams' very mediocrity (Luther and Willmann 2000: 93). Crillo, a Union fan, homed in on an even more sensitive issue: he sported on his cap the highly provocative slogan 'Hertha and Union – one nation' (ibid.: 135). When football followers and rock fans clashed at a concert on 7 October 1977 on Alexanderplatz in the centre of East Berlin, Union supporters cried out 'United'. While this was related to the famous English club Manchester United, it could also be interpreted as a link with Hertha (Hahn 2007: 155–56). Likewise, the not infrequent chants in the stadiums of 'Germany, Germany',[63] might have been intended to provoke the police but they also served as a rebuttal of the official SED position under Honecker that the national question had been 'resolved' by the formation of two nations, one socialist and the other capitalist. In general, the record of East German representative teams did little to mobilise support for the Honecker thesis, unlike those of West Germany, whose national team's success in the 1954 World Cup was a crucial factor in the formation of a collective identity in the young Federal Republic.

The Stasi and the police went to great lengths to prevent manifestations of a common German nationhood and links between East and West German fans.

With regard to the latter, the Stasi estimated that approximately 5,000 East Germans attended the thirteen games played by West Germany and the country's clubs in the socialist states of Eastern Europe between March 1979 and March 1981. About 2,000 went to the European Cup game between Bohemians Prague and Bayern Munich in September 1979.[64] In order to forestall East–West German contacts and the violent incidents which threatened to undermine the reputation of the GDR, tight restrictions were imposed on spectator entry to the grounds at international games. In September 1982, when Hamburg played BFC at the *Friedrich-Ludwig-Jahn-Sportpark*, close to the Berlin Wall, several thousand Stasi officers were mobilised to attend the game, ostensibly as spectators. At a quarter-final game in the European Cup between BFC and the holders Nottingham Forest in 1980, most of the tickets were allocated to Stasi officers and family members. In addition, 1,200 MfS officers, several hundred members of the Stasi guard regiment 'F. Dzierzynski' and 800 police were drafted in to control the crowd.[65] In his programme notes, the BFC chairman conveniently overlooked these precautions when calling for a fair sporting atmosphere.[66]

Unofficial collaborators (IMs) were integral to security operations at domestic and international games. OV 'Kraketer', the campaign against the violent fans of Union Berlin, referred to above, was an early example of how the Stasi used IMs to observe and infiltrate the 'negative decadent' football scene. Surveillance, whether in an operational case (OV) or an operational personal check (OPK), was usually comprehensive. As part of one elaborate operation, forty IMs and other kinds of collaborators attached to the Dresden-Stadt District Service Unit and fifty IMs of the local criminal police were deployed at Dynamo Dresden's home game against BFC in March 1987.[67] The radicalisation of the hooligan scene in the mid 1980s gave fresh impetus to the Stasi's search for IMs among the hard-core and other 'negative decadent' fans. Such informers, it was envisaged, would help the ministry and the police to identify the leaders, their links with Western hooligans and skinheads, and any plans to cause disturbances. The key Stasi unit in the capital for controlling the city's hooligan element had an estimated 30 to 50 IMs, of whom 15 to 20 belonged to the hooligan hard core (Willmann 2007: 142).

Recruitment proved difficult as the inveterate hooligans were contemptuous of appeals to socialist convictions, opposed to snitching on their mates and likely to 'betray' any approach by the Stasi. If material incentives were offered, this only served to reinforce their jaundiced view of the Stasi and the police. Given these difficulties, recruiting officers preferred to concentrate on youths not already integrated into a 'negative decadent' football group and who, potentially, had some respect for law and order. 'Atonement' for previous misdemeanours and financial and other material advantages were also used as bait.[68] As the 1980s drew to a close, the use of informers for identifying links between East and West Berlin skinheads grew in importance. OPK 'Echo' homed in on a skinhead fan of BFC Dynamo, Mario Klauss, who exchanged fanzine materials and visited football matches and pubs with West German skinheads. The latter, according to reports by IMS 'Robert', provided Mario and his colleagues, including his brother Heiko, with clothing and advised them on the use of steel bars and other crude implements.[69]

## Confronting the Inexplicable

The intensification and the greater sophistication of the state's operations notwithstanding, football hooliganism managed to survive – even thrive – in a system which, so the regime's sports scientists and ideologues asserted, had removed its basic socio-economic and political preconditions (Braun and Teichler 2003: 580–82). Nor did it fit in with the official notion of young people as 'all-round socialist personalities' integrated into society under the direction of the Thälmann Pioneers, the FDJ and the state schools. These and other state organisations sought, as is also discussed in Chapter 6, to foster a sense of pride in the GDR, dedication to the ideas of socialism, friendship with the Soviet Union, the upholding of law and order, and a high level of knowledge and vocational skills. According to the standard interpretation, which was regurgitated in Stasi internal reports and theses written by officers, football hooliganism was inherent within capitalism, not socialism. Typical of this approach is an analysis compiled in 1981 by the ZOS, according to which the commercialisation of the game impelled profit-hungry clubs in England and West Germany to seek instant success and the players, who were little more than commodities, into an aggressive style of play. Aggression on the field, so ZOS contended, was replicated off it. At a time of growing social misery and unemployment among the working class, young people, in particular, sought in football a violent outlet for their frustrations with everyday life. The violence was exacerbated by the sensationalism of the media and clubs' lack of interest in putting a stop to hooliganism.[70]

But how did the Stasi, the East German football authorities and the SED explain the outbreak of disorder in the GDR analogous to what was popularly regarded as the 'English disease'? As the Stasi failed to uncover any direct steering of the skinheads and hard-core soccer fans by imperialist agencies, and as it insisted that the social conditions for hooliganism were absent in the GDR, it fell back on the convenient catch-all notion of political-ideological subversion, whose main instruments were Western media transmissions, fan culture, the illegal distribution of football literature, and personal contacts between East and West German fans. 'Pliable' individuals and those with a basic negative attitude to social conditions in the GDR who glorified professional football in the West were seen as particularly susceptible. Stasi analysts did not regard football hooliganism simply as an age-related variable – whereby youngsters were more prone to violence than older cohorts – they also sought to identify specific conditions in the family and at work which predisposed East German youths to a kind of behaviour at variance with a socialist personality. The family circumstances which, according to the Stasi, were conducive to 'negative decadent' behaviour included the breakdown of relationships and the failure of parents to control their children's consumption of Western media.[71] There is some irony in this argument as the GDR's liberal divorce legislation was one of the reasons for the country's extremely high divorce rate. After the *Wende*, Bernd Wagner, an officer in the main department of the criminal police and an expert on right-wing extremism and youth violence in the GDR, put forward the related argument that football fans and others who were oriented towards violence came from the margins of society (Wagner 1995: 62).

While further studies are required to test the kind of interpretation advanced by Wagner, preliminary research conducted between October 1987 and November 1989 by two sociologists attached to the Humboldt University does not support the notion of 'abnormality'. Commissioned by the criminal police, on Wagner's initiative (Willmann 2007: 150–51) and with the blessing of the Stasi, the researchers concluded from their study of skinheads, punks and other subcultural groups that the level of qualifications, family status and general circumstances corresponded to a cross-section of society (Kinner and Richter 2000: 273, 279–80). Although they did not focus on football-related violence as such, the overlap between hard-core football fans and skinheads suggests that their results may be of relevance in this area too. Future study of the data on the occupational and social profile of football hooligans, which can be reconstructed from the files compiled by the DVP and the Stasi's Main Departments IX and XX, should shed further light on whether offenders were incorporated into or excluded from mainstream East German society. While the social class of football hooligans, a contentious issue in Western research, can possibly be teased out from the data, some basic methodological problems exist. As the SED was ideologically committed to the notion of itself as the vanguard of the working class, purportedly the most progressive class in society, this had negative repercussions for studies of the GDR's social structure. Not only did official social statistics deliberately obfuscate the growing significance of the intelligentsia and middle-ranked social strata but it was also difficult for social scientists to analyse the representation of working-class youths among the hooligans.

Some of the conditions which officialdom recognised as significant for the genesis of East German football hooliganism can also be found in social scientific and governmental publications in the West. An internal assessment originating in the SED Central Committee of the Department for Sport, with scribbled comments by Egon Krenz, illustrates this point. It stressed the highly charged emotional atmosphere at football matches, heavy drinking, the socialisation of young fans into violence, the release from boredom with everyday life derived from the emotional 'buzz' of risk-taking, a 'primitive urge' to attract attention and enhance the status of the group, opposition to the police, and a desire to demonstrate an alleged superiority and strength. It was also noted that the hard core engaged in hostile actions against socialism and sought to attract recruits.[72] The young male's drive for status, self-esteem, territory and emotional pleasure, which is highlighted in Western research, is captured in the 'kick' derived by one

male BFC fan from the contempt for 'outsiders' and the visceral rivalries so typical of football: 'One travels to show the Saxons or whoever that we are the boss
so-to-speak and that Berliners are the best and the greatest' (Farin and Hauswald
1998: 57). Although these features were, it was conceded, similar to those in the
West, officialdom remained wedded to a crude modelling and cultural diffu-
sion process, or in SED and Stasi jargon, political-ideological subversion by the
imperialist foe and the uncritical emulation of Western norms and behaviour by
morally weak and unstable persons.[73] The SED and Stasi image of the enemy
and the country's so-called 'negative decadent' youth was grounded in the theory
that psychological characteristics are determined by external conditions and influences rather than by internal or cognitive factors intrinsic to socialist society.

The tendency to overlook the specificity of conditions in the GDR was heavily
criticised by Walter Friedrich, the head of the Central Institute for Youth Research in Leipzig (ZIJ). In a confidential memorandum to Egon Krenz in 1987,
he argued that an exaggeration of the responsibility of the class enemy for GDR
youth's growing disenchantment with the socialist system was both simplistic
and a barrier to the urgent need for a long-overdue analysis of conditions in the
GDR. Nor, he argued, should one interpret the verbal abuse of the security forces
at football grounds as a political 'affront' and evidence of planned action.[74] A ZIJ
survey in late 1988 to early 1989 found that 50.5 per cent of those young people
who responded to a question relating to violent football fans found their behaviour explicable compared to 38.7 per cent who did not.[75] This was just part of a
broader problem: numerous other ZIJ research investigations pointed to widespread dissatisfaction with the practice of state socialism, whether the artificiality
of media reports, the rigidity of the FDJ and the SED, the party's failure to seize
the opportunity for change afforded by Gorbachev's reforms in the USSR, or the
lack of consumer goods and fashion items (Saunders 2007: 92–104). In addition,
Friedrich's reference to the authorities' over-reaction to provocation exemplified
the way in which the SED's wide reach and penetration of society politicised
actions not intended as such. Indeed, many football-related troubles stemmed
not just from subjective decisions by referees but also, in part, from the popular
perception that these reflected a politically driven discrimination rather than human fallibility. The SED leaders, as well as the Stasi, were unwilling, however, to
grasp the nettle of self-analysis. It was more convenient to blame external forces
for disorder rather than examine the role played by a number of internal determinants, such as the all-embracing social controls, the friend–foe mentality of state
propaganda, the militarisation of everyday life, and the aggressive masculinity
which underpinned the 'cop culture' of the Stasi and police. The kind of intellectual rigidity which manifested itself in SED, police and Stasi circles not only
led to heavy-handed security measures to curb football-related disturbances but
it also impeded an understanding of the striving for autonomy among football
fans that lay behind the emergence of the sub-cultures of punks, skinheads and
heavy-metal fans.

# Notes

1. As the frequency with which GDR clubs changed names and the use of prefixes such as SG, FC and BSG can cause confusion, the generic name is the one preferred in this chapter. One exception is Berlin Football Club Dynamo where BFC and Dynamo Berlin are used interchangeably.

2. BStU, MfS, ZA, ZAIG, no.4355, 'Referat auf der 3. erweiterten Tagung der Zentralen Leitung der SV Dynamo (Parteiaktivtagung) zur Auswertung des XI. Parteitages der SED', 1986, pp.86–87.

3. SAPMO-BA, DY30/4963, 'Einschätzung zum Leistungsstand und zur Leistungszielerfüllung im DFV der DDR', [1985], p.206.

4. Some eighteen out of seventy-two Dynamo Dresden players in the final twelve years of the GDR were registered as IMs and reported on the internal affairs of the club and the attitudes and actions of their colleagues. See Pleil (2001: 32–53, 116–24, 128–39) and Spitzer (2004: 46). Leske (2007: 34) estimates that about one-third of players in the *Oberliga* were IMs, with an even higher proportion among clubs competing in Europe.

5. See GZ, 'S6096: Jugend und Sport 1987', A46-0211, Table 69.

6. BStU, MfS, ZA, SdM, no.180, 'Bericht über negative Erscheinungen im Zusammenhang mit dem Oberligaspiel Dynamo Dresden gegen Dynamo Berlin am 02.12.1978', [December 1978], pp.8, 9.

7. BStU, MfS, ZA, HA XX, no.2701, 'Information', 22 May 1985, p.13.

8. SAPMO-BA, DY 30/4981, Letter to Hellmann, 30 April 1982, pp.46–47.

9. BStU, MfS, ZA, SdM, no.1431, 'Bericht', 22 May 1968, pp.114–23.

10. See the documentation of June 1963 in SAPMO-BA, DY 12/5335, pp.366, 389, 395–96, 403.

11. BStU, MfS, ZA, HA XX, no.2701, 'Tonbandbericht IMS "Michael Hirsch" vom 3.7.1985', p.15.

12. SAPMO-BA, DY 30/4963, 'Protokoll der Videoauswertung des Endspiels im FDGB-Pokal vom 8. Juni zwischen dem BFC Dynamo und der SG Dynamo Dresden zur Beurteilung der Schiedsrichterleistung', 3 July 1985, pp.195–97.

13. BStU, MfS, ZA, ZAIG, no.4331, 'Erscheinungen der Berichterstattung der Publikationsorgane der DDR über den BFC Dynamo und den 1.FC Union Berlin', 1 February 1971, pp.57–59, 69. Among the papers reviewed were *Neues Deutschland, Die Neue Fußballwoche, Junge Welt* and the SED-controlled regional organs.

15. Stumpf worked as IM 'Peter Richter', Glöckner as IM 'Hans Meyer', Prokop as OibE 'Gustaf', Roßner as IMS 'Schwarz' and Supp as GMS 'Günter'.

16. BStU, MfS, Außenstelle Dresden, BV Dresden, AOPK 3521/86, vol.2, 'Information', 14 March 1986, pp.94–95.

17. BStU, MfS, ZA, AIM 9351/86, vol.1, pt.2, 'Information zur Situation im Fußballverband', July 1985, p.158. The source is the national trainer, Bernd Stange (IMS 'Kurt Wegner').

18. BStU, MfS, ZA, HA XX, no.221, 'Gemeinsam klapps!!!', p.222.

19. Ibid., 'Bericht zum Stand der Sicherheit und Ordnung bei Fußballspielen im Spieljahr 1987/88', 15 July 1988, p.259.

20. StAL, SEDBLLp, no.1681, 'Lage zur öffentlichen Ordnung und Sicherheit bei Fußballspielen der Saison 1986/87', 11 August 1987, pp.16, 18.

21. BStU, MfS, ZA, HA XX, no.221, 'Auswertung des Sicherungseinsatzes zum Fußballoberligaspiel BFC – Dynamo Dresden am 6.4.1988, 17.00 Uhr, im Friedrich-Ludwig-Jahn-Sportpark', 8 April 1988, p.233.

22. Ibid., Information sheet, 11 December 1988, p.295.

23. SAPMO-BA, DY 30/IV 2/2.039/251, 'Information zur Lage auf den Fußballplätzen der DDR und Vorschläge zur besseren Gewährleistung von Ordnung und Sicherheit im Zusammenhang mit Fußballspielen', [1984], p.23.

24. BStU, MfS, ZA, HA XX, no.2700, 'Eingabe wegen Bahnfahrt am 18.10.87 von Quedlinburg über Wegeleben nach Leipzig', 23 October 1987, p.68.

25. The key documents are in BStU, MfS, ZA, HA VIII, no.925, vol.14, pp.6–8, 12–14.
26. BStU, MfS, ZA, HA XX, no.1039, 'Bericht', 27 December 1971, p.8.
27. BStU, MfS, ZA, ZAIG, no.2731, Mielke to Krenz, 10 October 1977, pp.6, 19.
28. BStU, MfS, ZA, HA XX, no.954, 'Auszug aus dem Monatsbericht Juli 1986 der BV Berlin, Abteilung XX, vom 29.7.1986', pp.34–35.
29. StAL, BT/RdBLp, no.24808, 'Information zur Lage auf dem Gebiet der öffentlichen Ordnung und Sicherheit im Zusammenhang mit Fußballspielen in der Stadt Leipzig und auf dem Territorium der Deutschen Reichsbahn', 20 January 1977, n.p.
30. BStU, MfS, Außenstelle Frankfurt (O), BVfS Frankfurt (O), BdL, no.1684, 'Zusammenfassende Darstellung zur Problematik der Ausschreitungen bei Fußballspielen im In- und Ausland, insbesondere für den Zeitraum von 1978 bis 1981', June 1981, pp.12–13, 35.
31. BStU, MfS, ZA, HA XX, no.221, 'Berichterstattung über die Ergebnisse der Erhöhung von Sicherheit und Ordnung bei Fußballspielen', 14 June 1988, p.251.
32. *Der Tagesspiegel*, 30 October 2007, p.16.
33. BStU, MfS, ZA, ZAIG, 3543, 'Bericht zum Stand der Sicherheit und Ordnung bei Fußballspielen im Spieljahr 1987/88', 15 July 1988, p.259.
34. Ibid.
35. Ibid., 'Bericht über den Stand der Realisierung der Aufgabenstellung der Information des ZK der SED "Zur Lage auf den Fußballplätzen und Vorschläge zur Gewährleistung von Ordnung und Sicherheit im Zusammenhang mit Fußballspielen"', 30 December 1985, p.37.
36. See the report in ibid., 'Auswertung des Sicherungseinsatzes zum Fußballoberligaspiel BFC – Dynamo Dresden am 6.4.1988, 17.00 Uhr, im Friedrich-Ludwig-Jahn-Sportpark', 8 April 1988, pp.233–35.
37. Ibid., 'Gesprächsvermerk zu einer Beratung im PdVP Berlin', 20 October 1988, p.281.
38. BStU, MfS, ZA, HA XX/AKG, no.5941, 'Anlage: Berichterstattung zu Entwicklungstendenzen unter negativ-dekadenten Jugendlichen (September 1988)', p.157.
39. BStU, MfS, ZA, HA XX, no.898, 'Einschätzung über die in der DDR existierenden Skinheads bzw. Skinheadgruppen sowie über die Ergebnisse und Wirksamkeit der politisch-operativen Arbeit zur Verhinderung und Unterbindung der von derartigen Jugendlichen ausgehenden Gefährdungen der Sicherheit und Ordnung', 16 December 1987, pp.27–29.
40. BStU, MfS, ZA, HA XX, no.221, 'Bericht über den Stand der Realisierung der Aufgabenstellung der Informationen des ZK der SED "Zur Lage auf den Fußballplätzen und Vorschläge zur Gewährleistung von Ordnung und Sicherheit im Zusammenhang mit Fußballspielen"', 30 December 1985, p.32.
41. BStU, MfS, ZA, HA XX, no.5147, 'Information über Entwicklung von Skinhead's und Fußball-Fan-Clubs des FC Union und des BFC', January 1986, p.250.
42. BStU, MfS, ZA, HA XX, no.221, 'Information über die Situation von Ordnung, Disziplin und Sicherheit im Zusammenhang mit öffentlichkeitswirksamen Sportveranstaltungen im Bezirk Cottbus im Verlaufe des Jahres 1987', 28 December 1987, p.187.
43. BStU, MfS, ZA, ZAIG, no.14287, 'Information über neo-faschistische Aktivitäten einer ehemaligen Gruppierung von jungerwachsenen Rowdys aus dem Bezirk Schwerin', 25 July 1989, pp.163–66.
44. BStU, MfS, ZA, HA XX, no.221, 'Bericht zum negativen Fußballanhang des BFC Dynamo in der Spielsaison 1987/88 und zu den Ergebnissen der politisch-operativen Bearbeitung', 13 June 1988, pp.245–46.
45. Taraschonnek (1989: 14); BStU, MfS, ZA, HA IX, no.1303, 'Informationen', n.d., pp.69–70.
46. BStU, MfS, ZA, HA XX, no.221, 'Bericht über die Erhöhung von Ordnung und Sicherheit bei Fußballspielen', 22 June 1989, p.329.
47. Ibid., 'Gesprächsvermerk zu einer Beratung im PdVP Berlin', 20 October 1988, pp.279–80.
48. Ibid., 'Bericht zum negativen Fußballanhang des BFC Dynamo in der Spielsaison 1987/88 und zu den Ergebnissen der politisch-operativen Bearbeitung', 13 June 1988, p.243.

49. Ibid., 'Berichterstattung über die Ergebnisse der Erhöhung von Ordnung und Sicherheit bei Fußballspielen', 22 June 1989, p.328.

50. Ibid., 'Einschätzung zum jugendlichen Anhang des BFC Dynamo und zur Erhöhung von Sicherheit und Ordnung bei Fußballspielen der 1. Halbserie 1988/89', 29 December 1988, p.306.

51. For a list and discussion of the measures which could be used for combating hooliganism, see the document compiled by ZOS: BStU, MfS, Außenstelle Frankfurt (O), BVfS Frankfurt (O), BdL, no.1684, 'Zusammenfassende Darstellung zur Problematik der Ausschreitungen bei Fußballspielen im In- und Ausland, insbesondere für den Zeitraum von 1978 bis 1981', June 1981, pp.29–38.

52. For example, enterprises and vocational colleges had little interest in helping out: see BStU, MfS, ZA, HA XX, no.2700, 'Beschlußvorlage 10/85 für das Büro des Präsidiums des Deutschen Fußball-Verbandes der DDR. Betr.: Maßnahmen zur Erhöhung von Ordnung und Sicherheit bei Fußballgroßveranstaltungen', 1 March 1985, p.21.

53. Ibid., 'Richtlinie für den Ordnungsdienst bei Fußballveranstaltungen der Oberliga- und Ligamannschaften des DFV der DDR', December 1977, pp.16–17.

54. BStU, MfS, ZA, HA XX, no.221, 'Bericht über den Stand der Realisierung der Aufgabenstellung der Information des ZK der SED "Zur Lage auf den Fußballplätzen und Vorschläge zur Gewährleistung von Ordnung und Sicherheit im Zusammenhang mit Fußballspielen"', 30 December 1985, pp.30, 34–35.

55. BStU, MfS, ZA, ZAIG, no.3543, 'Information über einige aktuelle Erkenntnisse zu Fragen der Gewährleistung von Ordnung und Sicherheit bei Spielen der Fußball-Oberliga der DDR', 2 September 1986, p.3.

56. Ibid., 'Bericht über den Stand der Realisiserung der Aufgabenstellung der Information des ZK der SED "Zur Lage auf den Fußballplätzen und Vorschläge zur Gewährleistung von Ordnung und Sicherheit im Zusammenhang mit Fußballspielen"', 30 December 1985, p.31.

57. Ibid., 'Einschätzung zum jugendlichen Anhang des BFC Dynamo und zur Erhöhung von Sicherheit und Ordnung bei Fußballspielen der 1. Halbserie 1988/89', 29 December 1988, p.307.

58. Ibid., 'Bericht zum Stand der Sicherheit und Ordnung bei Fußballspielen im Spieljahr 1987/88', 15 July 1988, p.261; ibid., 'Protokoll. Erfahrungsaustausch zu Problemen der Ordnung und Sicherheit bei Fußballveranstaltungen am 10.03.1988', 28 April 1988, p.218.

59. Ibid., 'Bericht zum negativen Fußballanhang des BFC Dynamo in der Spielsaison 1987/88 und zu den Ergebnissen der politisch-operativen Bearbeitung', 13 June 1988, pp.243-44. Rudwaleit and Ernst were prominent BFC players.

60. BStU, MfS, ZA, ZAIG, no.3543, 'Information über einige aktuelle Erkenntnisse zu Fragen der Gewährleistung von Ordnung und Sicherheit bei Spielen der Fußball-Oberliga der DDR', 2 September 1986, pp.3–4.

61. BStU, MfS, ZA, HA XX, no.221, 'Bericht über den Stand der Realisierung der Aufgabenstellung der Information des ZK der SED "Zur Lage auf den Fußballplätzen und Vorschläge zur Gewährleistung von Ordnung und Sicherheit im Zusammenhang mit Fußballspielen"', 30 December 1985, pp.32–33.

62. BStU, MfS, Außenstelle Frankfurt (O), BVfS Frankfurt (O), BdL, no.1684, 'Zusammenfassende Darstellung zur Problematik der Ausschreitungen bei Fußballspielen im In- und Ausland, insbesondere für den Zeitraum von 1978 bis 1981', June 1981, p.18.

63. BStU, MfS, ZA, HA XX, no.2700, 'Vorkommnisse/Ausschreitungen im Zusammenhang mit Fußballspielen der Oberliga', 1987, p.72. This document refers to chants by Magdeburg fans while the GDR national hymn was being played before the game between their team and BFC in East Berlin on 8 August 1987.

64. BStU, MfS, Außenstelle Frankfurt (O), BVfS Frankfurt (O), BdL, no.1684, 'Zusammenfassende Darstellung zur Problematik der Ausschreitungen bei Fußballspielen im In- und Ausland, insbesondere für den Zeitraum von 1978 bis 1981', June 1981, pp.15–16.

65. BStU, MfS, ZA, HA XX, no.1823, 'Kartenaufteilung zum Europa-Cupspiel BFC Dynamo gegen Nottingham Forest am 19.3.1980', 17 March 1980, p.55; and ibid., 'Anlage 1', March 1980, p.14.

66. *Programm: Europapokal der Landesmeister Viertelfinale, Rückspiel BFC Dynamo – Nottingham Forest*, 19 March 1980, p.2. One fan, Dall, who attended the game, remembers that about 100 BFC supporters seized scarves, shirts and other items from Forest fans (Willmann 2007: 67).

67. BStU, MfS, Außenstelle Dresden, KD Dresden-Stadt, no.13358A, 'Informationen über die Arbeitsergebnisse der zum Oberligafußballspiel SG Dynamo Dresden – BFC Dynamo am 14.3.87 eingesetzten IM', 27 March 1987, p.71.

68. See Kreklau (1989: 4, 12, 18, 21–24, 29, 31).

69. MDA, HA XX/2, 'Einleitungsbericht zur OPK "Echo"', 22 March 1989, p.29; ibid., '[IM] Bericht', 21 January 1989, pp.8–9. An interview with the brothers, Mario and Heiko, can be found in Farin and Hauswald (1998). There is a letter of complaint – *Beschwerde* – from the brothers' father, Manfred, dated 22 February 1989, in which he takes issue with their detention on four occasions by the police: MDA, Letter from Manfred Krause to the PdVP Berlin, 22 February 1989, pp.27–28.

70. BStU, MfS, Außenstelle Frankfurt (O), BVfS Frankfurt (O), BdL, no.1684, 'Zusammenfassende Darstellung zur Problematik der Ausschreitungen bei Fußballspielen im In- und Ausland, insbesondere für den Zeitraum von 1978 bis 1981', June 1981, pp.6–10.

71. Ibid., pp.10–11; BStU, MfS, ZA, HA IX, no.1039, 'Bericht', 23 June 1970, p.16.

72. SAPMO-BA, DY 30/IV 2/2.039/251, 'Zur Information zur Lage auf den Fußballplätzen und den Schlußfolgerungen', [1984], p.31.

73. BStU, MfS, Außenstelle Frankfurt (O), BVfS Frankfurt (O), BdL, no.1684, 'Zusammenfassende Darstellung zur Problematik der Ausschreitungen bei Fußballspielen im In- und Ausland, insbesondere für den Zeitraum von 1978 bis 1981', June 1981, pp.10–14.

74. SAPMO-BA, DY 30/IV 2/2.039/248, Appendix to a letter to Krenz, 28 July 1987, pp.59, 67.

75. This question was part of the ZIJ investigation into historical awareness carried out among 2,095 young pupils, apprentices, workers, white-collar employees and students across the whole of the GDR. See GZ, 'S6001: Geschichtsbewußtsein 1988', A73-0403, 2b.

# Chapter 6

# SUB-CULTURES: PUNKS, GOTHS AND HEAVY METALLERS

## The State and Youth Sub-cultures

$S$ED officials and publicists were fond of lauding young people's commitment to the GDR and a socialist system that provided them with ample educational, employment and leisure opportunities. This kind of stance has survived the end of the GDR, Wolfgang Schmidt, a former high-ranking Stasi officer, insisting, twelve years after reunification, that 'no state in German history has ever done so much for its youth' (cited in Anon.: 2004: 127). While the combined appeal of egalitarian socialist ideology and authoritarian paternalism undoubtedly helped promote a measure of identification with the GDR, the SED, realising that loyalty was often conditional, eventually, if reluctantly, settled for high levels of passivity and resignation among the younger generation towards the state socialist system. SED tolerance did not, however, extend readily to certain inchoate forms of youthful divergence from official cultural preferences, such as the *Halbstarke* ('rebels without a cause') of the 1950s and the punks of the 1980s. Moreover, party and state functionaries looked with a mixture of alarm and hostility at young people's engagement with what they regarded as 'hostile' political activities in autonomous peace, human rights and ecological groups sheltered by the evangelical churches. The linkage between the churches and young people in these groups was in part a self-fulfilling prophecy, a consequence of the state's fear of a political youth culture and of its own alienation of dissident and nonconformist youth after it sought, in 1965, to slam the door shut on the growing autonomy and diversity of styles in culture.

---

While this and the next chapter concentrate on the relatively small punk and skinhead scenes in the 1980s, their situation was not dissimilar to that of earlier youth sub-cultures and their fraught relationship with the state authorities. The discussion is also linked to questions of self-determination and the creation of a space for self-development for young people raised in the previous chapter on football fans and hooligan behaviour. Among the main threads running through the forty years of relations between the state and East German youth were the strong pull of Western popular culture for young East Germans, their search for self-expression in a post-totalitarian system, and the SED's fears of political and cultural subversion by the forces of imperialism. The general challenge posed by youth sub-cultures to the social and cultural steering mechanisms of the regime was sharpened, as Mark Fenemore has pointed out, by the emergence of the new postwar generation for whom the 'right to work' became less important than the 'right to party' (Fenemore 2007: 158). Given these conflicting interests, official youth policy zigzagged between coercion and a grudging toleration of noncon-formism. Any significant shift by the SED towards liberalisation and cultural autonomy in the fluid area between the public and the private, as in the years 1963 to 1965, was eagerly seized upon by East German youth (Ohse 2003: 81, 365–67; Fenemore 2007: xi–xii). The consequent pressures from below for more autonomy so alarmed the authorities that they returned to the seductively decep-tive comfort of a policy of constraint, material incentives and prescription in the vain hope of turning East German youth into uniform socialist personalities.

## Officialdom's Hostility to Western Youth Sub-cultures

The ruling elite and many SED functionaries regarded with utmost hostility and suspicion the spread eastwards and the reception of new international youth sub-cultures from the U.S.A. and Western Europe. Their negativity manifested itself in two attacks on rock'n'roll at a time when the border with West Berlin was still open. In 1958, the SED party leader, Walter Ulbricht, denounced it as an 'expression of impetuosity' characteristic of the 'anarchy of capitalism', while fel-low politburo member and Defence Minister Willi Stoph warned that it was 'a means of seduction to make the youth ripe for war' (quoted in Poiger 2000: 193). It was even feared that African-American musical rhythms could lead to racial degeneration and that the physical movements of rock stars might encourage effeminacy among young men (Ohse 2003: 58). Anxieties were compounded by the upsurge in the popularity of 'beat' music and, inspired by the Beatles and the Rolling Stones, by the proliferation of amateur groups and bands such as the But-lers (or the Klaus Renft Combo) and the Five Stones (Fenemore 2007: 168–73). The distaste for a seemingly rebellious youth was not confined to palaeolithic functionaries but also reflected what McDougall has called 'something of an anti-beat "cultural consensus" … between the older generation and the communist regime' (McDougall 2004: 187–88; see also Fenemore 2007: 172, 198). Combined with uninhibited dancing, long hair and new styles in clothing, especially jeans, rock'n'roll 'symbolised', according to Fenemore, 'an attitude of rebelliousness that challenged existing conventions and values' (Fenemore 2007: 140). Not all functionaries fell into the category of dinosaurs, however, thus reflecting the confusion in official circles towards an appropriate response to a fundamentally Western-inspired modernity in culture. Among the critical minority was Gerd Eisler, head of East German radio, who contended, in 1955, that 'the blowing of the jazz trumpet' – 'still less the playing of the electric guitar!' – 'does not signify the downfall of socialism' (quoted in McDougall 2004: 177).

The engrained mistrust of youth in state and party circles is reflected in a service instruction issued by Erich Mielke, head of the Stasi, in 1966, one year after the SED's termination of the short-lived liberal course in culture. According to this key strategic document, which would remain in force for the next two decades, young people's 'lack of experience of life, ignorance of the capitalist system, desire for adventure, impressionability, [and] excessive self-confidence' made some susceptible to the machinations of the imperialist enemy, thereby undermining a belief in the future of socialist society Decadent ideas were supposedly spread through the illegal distribution in the GDR of Western literature and records, personal contacts, and the reception of West German TV and radio programmes. The Stasi painted a pessimistic picture of the impact of the enemy's 'focused' activities on sections of East German youth: flight from the GDR, arson in factories, disturbances of the peace and the oddly phrased 'alcohol abuse at so-called parties' (cited in Süß1993: 55-58; also Ohse 2003: 127-29). It was, therefore, the self-appointed task of party, school, Stasi and police to extend surveillance and infiltration in order to protect the younger generation from the plague of subversion and the cultural contamination that was attributed in public statements to steering, directly or indirectly, from West Germany. Top-secret Stasi reports show, however, that ministry officers were fully aware that no 'enemy' centre existed for the central coordination of operations to subvert East German youth and establish 'negative' groups.[1]

Among groups defined as 'negative' by state and party authorities were 'gangs' of Elvis Presley fans in the late 1950s that supposedly committed rape and other crimes (Poiger 2000: 197–99). These fans and the many other undesirable expressions of American and West European youth culture were seen not only as a threat to the political stability of the state but also as contrary to the norms of socialist behaviour and consciousness. One attempt to codify appropriate norms was the unveiling by Ulbricht at the SED Fifth Party Congress in 1958 of the ten commandments of the new socialist morality. For the most part platitudinous, the commandments exhorted citizens of the GDR to act in the spirit of mutual support, strengthen socialist labour discipline, and live a clean and healthy life (Dennis 2000a: 87). Where exhortation was found wanting, punitive measures were implemented to protect socialist society from alleged risks to its moral and political well-being. These included the arrest of adolescent rock fans and the use of stewards (*Ordnungsgruppen*) from the official youth organisation to enforce good behaviour at dances in the late 1950s (Poiger 2000: 197–98).

It was not possible, however, for the SED and state organs to suppress by force or administrative fiat the widespread enthusiasm for Western rock'n'roll and 'beat' groups such as the Beatles and Rolling Stones. Many East German youngsters, as Alan McDougall has observed, considered their taste in music – as well as in dress, dancing and hair style – to be a personal rather than a political matter (McDougall 2004: 130). More flexible methods were required. In 1963, as part of its search for a general accord with the disaffected East German population after the building of the Berlin Wall – a policy which also comprised economic reform and cultural liberalisation – the politburo issued the communiqué *Der Jugend Vertrauen und Verantwortung* ('Trust in and responsibility for the young'). The communiqué, which had the backing of Ulbricht and reform-oriented functionaries such as Kurt Turba in the party's youth sections, urged that 'Whatever beat (*Takt*) people choose is up to them; the main thing is that they remain tactful (*taktvoll*)' (ibid.: 178). The FDJ tried, with mixed results, to promote a livelier self-image, more 'beat' groups were permitted to perform in public, and amateur bands mushroomed. Beatles records were released in the GDR, albeit on the state's Amiga record label. The popular radio station DT–64, which became a permanent feature after the FDJ festival, *Deutschlandtreffen* ('Germany meeting') in East Berlin in May 1964, enjoyed some success in catering for young East Germans' avid interest in Western pop music. The programme was, however, only transmitted on weekday evenings.

## Honecker Changes Tune

In late summer 1965, the liberal direction in cultural policy fell victim to the opposition of its many conservative critics and sceptics. In October, the security forces used violence to suppress a 'beat' demonstration in Leipzig and a change of approach by Ulbricht was signalled by his denunciation of the 'monotony of yeah, yeah, yeah' at the infamous SED Central Committee plenum two months later. But the party could not, it soon transpired, control the airwaves nor prevent the emergence of new youth sub-cultures. Ironically, Erich Honecker, a former chair of the FDJ and one of the reactionary opponents of the cultural thaw, would endorse a significant relaxation of restrictions on 'beat' music shortly after he became SED leader in 1971. As part of a well-orchestrated campaign to boost his political image and establish a general rapprochement with the population, he declared, in December 1971, that as long as socialism remained the premise, there would be no taboos in literature and art. This prompted the release of a backlog of critical literary works by authors such as Ulrich Plenzdorf and Stefan Heym. Plenzdorf's novel, *The New Sufferings of Young W.*, a realistic depiction of youthful sub-culture and an individual's striving for self-identity, proved highly popular in both East and West Germany. Rock music, too, was a beneficiary of the thaw, although the SED was clearly intent on control through the 'domestication' of the rock scene. The World Youth Festival in 1973 was a musical highpoint of the new course: rock musicians performed everywhere in a relaxed atmosphere and records from the U.S.A. appeared on East German labels.

There was another side to the coin, however: in line with what Ohse calls a policy of 'repressive tolerance', over 23,000 disciplinary talks were conducted with potential 'rowdies' and 2,293 short-term prison sentences imposed during the run-up to the festival (Ohse 2003: 341, 351–52, 372; Kaiser 2004: 271). Subsequently, in 1975, the banning of the highly popular and increasingly system-critical group Klaus Renft Combo was an indication of the limits of SED tolerance and the problems inherent in a more open cultural policy. In a further twist, the ban was followed by the exodus westwards of many rock musicians (Rauhut 2005: 71; Siegfried 2005: 59–61). The regime's difficulties in incorporating critical members of the cultural intelligentsia were exposed by its expatriation of Wolf Biermann in 1976; this was the clearest expression of the shift – although by no means a complete reversal – in policy direction.

The year 1976 also witnessed violent clashes between police and East German youths at the thousandth anniversary of the founding of the Thuringian town of Altenburg attended by over two thousand young people, including, in official parlance, 'deadbeats' (*Gammler*). Popular East German bands such as Karat and Babylon performed at open-air concerts. The police used force to curb violent and drunken behaviour and provocative political slogans; over one hundred people were arrested and six imprisoned (Rauhut 2005: 72–73). The SED Central Committee Secretariat and the Ministry of State Security and Ministry of the Interior subsequently framed a strategy to control events involving young people. Mielke instructed his departments to draw up lists of youth 'groupings' and prominent individuals and to deploy unofficial collaborators (IMs) to combat their influence. Schools, state institutions and event organisers were required to report to the Ministry of the Interior any signs of 'concentrations of young people with previous convictions who were likely to re-offend' (Michael 2005: 74).

## New Sub-cultures: Punk, Goths and Heavy Metal

Neither Mielke's officers nor FDJ functionaries could, however, prevent youthful divergence from socialist respectability. By the early 1980s, older fashions and musical trends were giving way to new ones such as punk, heavy metal and hip-hop. Furthermore, as the 1980s progressed, a small number of young people actively engaged in the alternative political culture comprising 'unofficial' peace, ecological, gay and human rights groups. In the middle of the decade, the Stasi's Main Department XX reckoned that about 400 groups of various kinds and a broad spectrum of young people were of 'operative interest' on account of their 'negative decadent' and 'hostile negative' traits. The long list included heavy-metal fans, skinheads, fascists, members of football fan clubs, punks, 'rowdy-criminal' types, gays, peace and human rights activists, and would-be émigrés. The imperialist 'enemy', it was contended, aspired to manipulate these individuals in pursuit of its nefarious goals: the erosion of youth's willingness to do military service; undermining the communist upbringing of young people; encouraging immorality and decadence; and weakening economic performance.[2]

While the SED and the security forces were far more concerned about the political challenge posed by the emigration movement and human rights and peace activists – in Stasi jargon, 'hostile negatives' – they looked with disdain and suspicion at 'decadent' punks, skinheads, heavy metallers, goths and new romantics. Dedicated to original hard rock, heavy-metal performers and fans wore leather clothing, chains and studs. Turnover among groups and fans was rapid and new forms such as 'black metal' soon appeared. The aggressive physicality of their music, according to the Stasi, encouraged disorderly conduct by youngsters.[3] Pale-faced goths, dressed in black, sought alternatives to the predictability of everyday life. Although they contravened what one Stasi report called 'social norms' by desecrating graves,[4] they were not regarded as politically significant and aroused less antipathy among the police and security forces than heavy metallers and punks. However, what particularly alarmed the SED and Stasi was a possible coalescence between the 'negative decadent' and the 'hostile negative' strands and the potential of such a development for 'enemy' interference in the internal affairs of the GDR.[5]

Like their predecessors, the so-called 'decadent' sub-cultures of the late 1970s and 1980s did not, at first, constitute an organised and clearly articulated political reaction to problems in state socialism; they were essentially multifaceted forms of self-expression and youth disgruntlement, and a protest against conformity, consumerism and restrictions on individuality in a state which appeared increasingly anachronistic to the younger generation. Towards the end of the 1980s, however, some East German punks became involved in environmental issues and in an 'unofficial' peace movement that was evolving into a rudimentary political opposition. In a parallel but separate development, some of the more militant skinheads and neo-fascists forged loose links with extreme-right groups in the Federal Republic and, as discussed in the next chapter, concocted a rudimentary ideology based on a fervent German ethno-nationalism with the goal of a united Germany within the 1937 borders of the Third Reich.

## Punk GDR-style

The new fringe youth sub-cultures, whether poppers and punks or goths and skinheads, first appeared in the GDR as the 1970s drew to a close. They lagged slightly behind those in the West, which provided much of the initial impetus for new fashions in dress, music, dance and hair styles, even though it was difficult from behind the Berlin Wall to obtain a full picture of the scene in London or Manchester (Stock and Mühlberg 1990: 166). As one fifteen-year-old East German female punk stated in a 1982 interview: 'Well, I came across it [punk] when I saw a few from over there [FRG], how they dressed, and I liked that' (quoted in

Furian and Becker 2000: 11; see also Stock 2000: 60). This was a highly disturbing development for the East German authorities, who had been quick to disparage punks as pseudo-revolutionaries and musical illiterates when they emerged in West Germany in 1977/78 (Breyvogel 2005: 80–81).

A few punks became visible in East Berlin, Leipzig, Weimar, Gotha and several other cities in 1979 and 1980. They congregated in the capital's discos, pubs, the Treptow Park of Culture and the Plänterwald drinking halls, threw themselves into dancing the pogo, and sometimes clashed violently with other groups. Distance between audience and bands was discouraged at gigs (Friedrich and Schneider 2005: 117; Galenza 2005: 100–1; Horschig 2005: 17–19, 39–40). 'You gathered', according to Kaiser, a member of the East Berlin band, *Planlos*, 'and made music and had a party. It wasn't about stars. It didn't really matter who was on stage' (quoted in Boehlke and Gericke 2007: 54). Among the earliest punk bands were *Schleim-Keim*, *Planlos*, *Wutanfall* and *Rosa Extra*, the latter the name of an East German sanitary towel (Anon. 2005: 43). Inspired by the Sex Pistols, the Clash and other bands in the U.K. and West Germany, they performed without official permission in attics, studios, pubs and backyards (Furian and Becker 2000: 11).

Despite many similarities, the punk scene in the GDR was not a carbon copy of that in the West, and exhibited many of its own characteristics: not only did Eastern punks reject the perceived aridity of the music of the Puhdys and other established East German rock groups as well as the nonconformist cultural icons of an earlier generation such as Wolf Biermann, but they also sought an alternative to the dreary routine of state socialism, whether at school or work (Stock 2000: 60; Stadtmuseum Dresden 2007: 15). In contrast to punk in the West, which drew heavily on the unemployed, the East German scene attracted young people who saw no future in capitalism or state socialism and resisted the pressure to conform exerted by the FDJ, school, the Sport and Technology Society and other agents of the state (Büscher and Wensierski 1984: 28–29; Wagner 1995: 45; Michael 2005: 72–73; Stock 2000: 60–61). Their distinctive style of dress and provocative lyrics signified their insubordination, a point stressed by interviewees both before and after the collapse of the GDR. Henryk Gericke, a member of a punk band, recalled 'the shock it meant to sport an anti-haircut, chains and torn-apart clothes for the first time' (Gericke 2007: 15). Karsten Pauer had been determined that he would not be demeaned by having to save for several years in order to buy a car, a television or a 'crap washing machine and that his life would not be programmed by teachers, employees and parents' (Furian and Becker 2000: 111). The Erfurt punk band *Schleim-Keim* took up this theme, protesting fiercely against the state's mania for regulating performance: 'Norm, norm, norm, you were born to be a norm; norm, norm, norm, you have died for a norm; blessed be the norm'.[6]

Punks formed a conspicuous, albeit minority element among East German youth sub-cultures. In 1981, the Stasi identified 1,000 punks and a broader group of about 10,000 sympathisers (Michael 2005: 74). Three years later, punk was already losing momentum as the first generation of punk had been de facto dissolved by Stasi and police persecution (Galenza and Havemeister 2007: 83). Numbers had dropped to about 900, of whom 400 were located in East Berlin, 95 in Leipzig and 60 each in Magdeburg and Cottbus.[7] After a brief revival, the active scene fell to 655, including some 200 punks and 80 sympathisers in East Berlin and 105 punks in the Potsdam Region.[8] Such figures are necessarily imprecise as the boundaries between punks, skins, heavy metallers and others were fluid and turnover rapid. For example, many skins were originally punks and some punk bands used elements of ska music (Horschig 2005: 21). The task of the security forces in classifying punks was hindered by the proliferation of sub-genres – 'filthy punks' (*Schmuddelpunks*), Nazi punks, fashion punks and 'black eagles' – a process that was spurred on by punk reactions to state repression and changes in fashion. *Schmuddelpunks* rejected standards of cleanliness and 'black eagles' were football fans who wore a black scarf to denote their anarchist inclinations. They attended BFC Dynamo matches and from about 1982/83 drifted into the violent strand associated with the more extreme right-wing-oriented skinheads (ibid.: 22). Although most punks did not engage as a rule in premeditated violence, drunkenness often led to aggression boiling over at gigs and other events. A Stasi report described an outbreak of disorder at a performance by two punk bands, *Klick und Aus* and *Pfff...*, at a clubhouse in Coswig in 1985:

> Among those present on the first day were numerous punks, who demonstrated their role as social outsiders by their extreme appearance and behaviour. Inspired by the aggressive music of the *Klick und Aus* and *Pfff...* groups, they turned the hall of the clubhouse into an unacceptable state. Tables and seats were partly destroyed or damaged. Broken glass, cigarette stumps and other rubbish were heaped up on the floor. (quoted in Michael 2005: 89)

Punks often responded in kind to attacks by skinheads. The most notorious clash between skins and punks, at East Berlin's *Zionskirche* in 1987, is described in Chapter 7. Despite subsequent police surveillance and other countermeasures, violence did not abate: in June 1988, about thirty punks and skinheads from the East Berlin, Gera, Karl-Marx-Stadt and Neubrandenburg Administrative Regions (*Bezirke*) came to blows on the beach at Zinnowitz on the Baltic coast and demolished wicker beach chairs in front of about 300 holidaymakers.[9]

There is no doubt that punks did things likely to whiten a Stasi officer's hair. Safety pins through noses and cheeks, lips coloured black, hair cut short and dyed in bright yellow and green, straps and old chains, torn and 'trashy' clothes – all offended the Ministry of State Security's strict sartorial code and its law-and-order mentality. Gericke likens the impact of the first punks on the East German authorities and citizens to 'the landing of aliens' whose 'colourful appearance among the anaemic colours of the East, their reckless aggressive ways and energy driven music' challenged an overtaxed system (Gericke 2007: 23). A Mohican hairstyle was sufficient for punks to be hauled in and their hair cut off by police officers; style had been politicised by the state (Stock and Mühlberg 1990: 165;

Furian and Becker 2000: 63). The role of punks as provocateurs and outsiders is fondly recalled by a former East German punk, Mario Schulz ('Colonel'): 'The start was that I liked the music. I did not quite understand the English texts, but this ostentatious existence as an outsider, this capacity to shock, that pleased me. I was already – someone else would probably express it differently – an awkward sod' (quoted in Furian and Becker 2000: 85). Commenting on the politicisation of elements of punk in the mid 1980s ranging from left- to fascist-punks, he asserted: 'That was all the same to me. We would have stuck a picture of Adolf Hitler or Lenin on our jackets, but only to shock people, not because we were communists or fascists. We were punks, we were outsiders, we wanted to shock' (ibid.: 85).

To the chagrin of the SED, punks looked askance at regular employment and withdrew from the FDJ and the trade union organisation, the FDGB, thereby infringing not only the socialist work ethic and the officially enshrined duty to work but also undermining the use of the workplace as an instrument of state and party control. Bernd Lade, a member of the punk band *Planlos*, objected fiercely to conditions in factories which reduced workers to 'small arseholes' and having to dance to the tune of the foremen and managers (ibid.: 33). Thomas Bautzer, a former punk, explains how he became a punk out of frustration with life and work. It made him feel sick that he had to get up at 4.30 every morning, go to work in the docks, spend every day with the same stupid fools, shitty bourgeois and repulsive old men (ibid.: 88). The disparagement of conventional jobs in state firms was picked up in investigations conducted in 1986 and 1987 by Loni Niederländer of the sociology department of the Humboldt University in East Berlin and by Gunhild Korfes of the Academy of Sciences.[10] While they found that skinheads usually performed their work in a disciplined manner, punks frequently changed their workplace and job, missed shifts, drank alcohol at work and sought jobs with private firms.[11]

Not only did punks' attitude to work fail to conform to the state's notion of the all-round socialist personality but so too did their view of family life in socialist society. About 80 per cent of the punks in Niederländer's study lived either alone or in small groups and possessed little or no furniture. Their rooms were filthy and they spent most of their time drinking. Unlike skinheads, punks did not enjoy a good relationship with their parents, in part a reflection on the punks' rejection of the family as a basic social and legal entity.[12] Most punks were single or in a nominal marriage and their general attitude was summed up by a fifteen-year-old punk: 'As for marriage. We don't go in for such a thing. Anyway – marriage and such like I find absolute crap. And likewise bringing children into the world' (quoted in Furian and Becker 2000: 14). Despite a higher incidence of divorce among the parents of punks than those of skinheads, Niederländer found no striking differences as regards other social characteristics. Furthermore, none of the young punks came from 'asocial' families, 85 per cent of their fathers possessed a vocational qualification and about 20 per cent had completed a course of study at an institution of higher education.[13]

While the anti-dance of the pogo and the primitive unmelodic lines of music to the accompaniment of screamed vocals and cacophonous drumming fell foul of the musical tastes of Mielke, the minister and his officers were more agitated by the lyrics of songs with 'hostile-negative, rabble-rousing remarks against the socialist state'.[14] The Dresden band *Letzte Diagnose* homed in on one particularly sensitive area with the provocative cry of 'Observed, denounced, controlled. What did he do?'[15] Another Dresden band, *Paranoia*, attacked the state's armaments' drive, encouraged soldiers to get rid of their tanks and weapons, and denounced the mines and fences around the [Soviet] 'Zone', a disparaging comment on the GDR's aspirations for legitimacy as a separate German state.[16] *Rosa Extra*, meanwhile, criticised the Soviet Union for ruining Germany, and the Leipzig band *L'Attentat* railed against the city's ugly houses, dilapidated buildings, foul-smelling pubs and the 'dead sea of people' (Michael 2005: 88)

## Negative Perceptions of Punk

As discussed in Chapter 5, political-ideological subversion by the imperialist enemy was regarded by SED and state bodies as the major determinant of the existence of punks and other troublesome youth sub-cultures. With regard to punks, the Stasi's brains' trust, the Central Assessment and Information Group, informed top SED leaders such as Egon Krenz and Werner Krolikowski that Western political-ideological subversion fostered a negative attitude towards the political and social order of the GDR, as exemplified by punks' identification with 'bourgeois' concepts of freedom and 'pseudo-pacifist' ideas.[17] That a small number of young people were susceptible to the siren songs of the West was attributed by the authorities to a number of factors conducive to maladjustment, such as broken family relationships, a person's failure to realise their potential at school and vocational college, poor discipline, and shirking at work.[18]

Seeking to identify what it regarded as the source of the problem, the Stasi tracked with its usual diligence the myriad links with, and influence of, the 'operational area', above all the reception of electronic media and personal contacts with Western punks in restaurants, clubs, parks and private apartments. For example, top-secret investigations conducted by the Stasi offices in the Potsdam, Dresden and Leipzig Administrative Regions (*Bezirke*) in 1985 uncovered contacts between West German punks and East German punk bands such as *Paranoia*, *Schleim-Keim* and *L'Attentat*.[19] Records, cassettes, letters and fanzines were also exchanged.[20] Much to the annoyance of the state authorities, reports on punks in the GDR appeared in West German books (e.g., Büscher and Wensierski 1984) and magazines, such as *Der Spiegel* and *Tip*.[21] East German punks also developed loose networks with punks in Czechoslovakia, Hungary, Bulgaria, Poland and Romania, and even corresponded with others in England, Australia and Finland (Stadtmuseum Dresden 2007: 21, 33). Despite the frequency of communications across the inter-German border, the Stasi came to the unremarkable conclusion in July 1989 that: 'no indications could be established of enemy centres, organisations, institutions and forces which have directly inspired and organised hostile-negative actions by young people and young adults against existing societal relations in the GDR'.[22] In other words, while Western influence on punk and other sub-cultures is undeniable, the security mentality of the SED and the Stasi and their lack of self-criticism caused them to fall back on the convenient scapegoat of political-ideological subversion. As the 1980s drew to a close, the gathering dissatisfaction with this politically obsolete paradigm emerges from a report by the Leipzig-based *Zentralinstitut für Jugendforschung* (ZIJ) on the youth scene and problem groups in the GDR. The research team warned against interpreting the 'difference of the scene' as an 'abnormal and antisocial occurrence' and urged that ways be found to reduce conflicts to a minimum rather than, as was normally the case, aggravating them.[23]

## Attacks on Punks

With the exception of the final three to four years of SED rule, the police and the Stasi sought to weaken and crush the punk scene by undercover means as well as by an array of overt measures ranging from criminalisation to forced deportation to the West. Although punks enjoyed greater individual space in the FRG than in the GDR, West Germany was not, it should be stressed, a haven of tolerance. Punks also suffered severe discrimination there. In 1982, fierce clashes occurred between police and punks in Hanover after it was revealed that the police were keeping records on punks, whom they likened to criminals (Breyvogel 2005: 93–94). It was, however, characteristic of the GDR that it pursued the nonconformist punks and 'threatening' youth sub-cultures more harshly, more comprehensively and over a longer period than was the case in West Germany (Kaiser 2004: 267–68).

The first major campaign, launched by the criminal police in early 1981, involved house searches and raids, disciplinary talks, arrests, interrogations and lengthy prison sentences. Schools, pub landlords and enterprises were encouraged to exert pressure. Detention by the police could entail, as one young East Berlin punk, Apollo, recalled, having to stand for three to four hours, being hit and called 'rubbish and a piece of dirt' (Stock and Mühlberg 1990: 176). Among those harshly penalised were Sid and Major. Both were banned from East Berlin, obliged to report to the police and forbidden to change their place of work. Sid was imprisoned on five occasions for infringing these restrictions and Major, an East Berliner, was forced to live in a Sorb village, where she was regarded as an outsider and criminal (Horschig 2005: 23–24; Michael 2005: 74). What happened when the police raided an apartment in East Berlin, which was used by punks as a meeting place, is described by a former punk:

The police stormed in, they locked us all in a room, then chose one and took him into the kitchen where he was beaten up by several 'pigs'. They grabbed the next one and dragged him into the kitchen. By the time it was over they had beaten up and taken away everybody, including the girls. During the journey to the police station they were beaten on the back seats of the numerous police vans that had turned up and then for half the night in the police station they were threatened and beaten. I came home late that day and found the flat in a catastrophic state. The whole kitchen, cupboards, curtains, cooker, walls, and even the ceilings, were spattered with blood … The people who had been beaten up were between 15 and 18 years of age. Taking legal proceedings against the police would have been a mockery. (Horschig 2005: 24–25)

In 1981, the main responsibility for combating punks was assigned to the Stasi which, together with the police, continued the policy of repression. Restrictions were imposed on freedom of movement, concerts were banned, force was used to prevent punks from attending gigs, and some were conscripted before their official call-up date (Horschig 2005: 26, 30, 38–39; Michael 2005: 80). But not only did repression fail to destroy the appeal of punk, its very harshness also aroused a deep antipathy to the state and drove some into political opposition. As one punk, Hotte, stated, arbitrary imprisonment and the 'terror' of the 'cops' turned his dislike of the system into an intense hatred (quoted in Stock 2000: 63). The limits of repression are apparent from a report sent by Main Department XX of the Stasi's East Berlin Regional Administration to Günter Schabowski and Erhard Krack. It was admitted that 'administrative measures of repression' by the police and Stasi, rather than eliminating the concentrations of 'negative decadent' young people, had only served to accelerate their retreat from the public into the private sphere.[24] Krack was Lord Mayor (*Oberbürgermeister*) of the East German capital and Schabowski a politburo member and First Secretary of the SED's East Berlin Regional Executive.

The campaign against punks was intensified in 1984. The Stasi, police and other state institutions were authorised to keep a detailed record of the situation among 'negative decadent' young people; two years later, this brief was extended to include unregistered punk bands (Horschig 2005: 26; Michael 2005: 77). Among other measures were the use of the law to curb unlicensed performances, such as those on church premises, and attempts to improve coordination between Stasi and police units in the offensive against punks.[25] Advice was given to schools and youth organisations on how to differentiate punks from new romantics and other groups, a task which often defeated Stasi officers (Michael 2005: 77). The Stasi also shifted towards a policy of banning punk groups deemed to be hostile to the GDR's social and political order. The East German Penal Code contained many clauses with sufficient elasticity to achieve this goal by criminalising petty offences, nonconformism and unlicensed groups. For example, six bands were closed down in 1983, including the East Berlin band *Namenlos*. Its members were arrested in August of that year and sentenced to imprisonment of between one and one-and-a-half years on a charge of disparaging the state (ibid.: 78). Contacts with the Western media were also severely punished. One East Berlin punk, Karsten Pauer, was arrested in September 1982 after giving interviews to the West German magazines *Tip* and *Der Spiegel*. Interrogated by the Stasi, he was sentenced to seventeen months' imprisonment on trumped-up charges. In addition, as one of his friends had scrawled obscene graffiti on a street wall, Pauer had also come under suspicion of warped sexual behaviour and engaging in sexual orgies (see Furian and Becker 2000: 115).

Klaus Michael's excellent study of East German punks has shown that they were more likely to be severely punished according to the GDR's highly politicised Penal Code than were members of the political opposition and the peace, ecological and other small autonomous groups. The disparity can be attributed in part to the lower level of interest shown by the Western media in the punks' plight and to negative attitudes among many East Germans, not excluding some Church officials and congregation members. Popular antipathy to punks was sometimes expressed in extreme form, such as remarks that they should be gassed or put in a labour camp. Relations between punks and the peace and ecological groups which found shelter in the churches also ran far from smoothly, and although protests against the state occasionally formed the basis of joint actions – like the laying of wreaths at former National Socialist concentration camps – punks, unlike sections of the alternative political culture, disdained any form of dialogue with the state (Michael 2005: 78–79; see also Niederländer 1990: 18; Horschig 2005: 19, 28–30; Gericke 2007: 25).

By the mid to late 1980s, confronted by state repression and an escalation of attacks by extremist skinheads, some punks became involved in the Church from Below, a grassroots reform movement which had emerged in 1987 out of the alternative political culture. Punks also drew increasingly on the social and welfare work of the evangelical churches with their commitment to marginal groups. About a third of punks in the capital, according to Stasi sources, were integrated into the open youth work of the congregations of the Galilee Church and the Church of the Saviour.[26] This form of church engagement also provided opportunities for young people to express their own feelings and to criticise official state ideology and practices, in other words, 'to give people a degree of responsibility' (Shanghai 1997: 17–18). Some church premises, as at the *Elisabethkirche* in East Berlin, were used by punks when founding an anti-fascist group, and punks became more active in unofficial ecological and peace groups (Wagner 1995: 46), thus reinforcing Stasi suspicions that 'hostile clerical forces' were encouraging punks in 'hostile negative' actions and in 'decadent' alternative life styles.[27] Outside the capital, for example, in Potsdam and Dresden, punks formed anti-Nazi leagues in reaction to growing right-wing extremism and the militant skinhead scene of the late 1980s.[28]

## The Deployment of Informers

As part of its multi-pronged attack on the punk scene, the Ministry of State Security resorted to the usual battery of 'decomposition' measures, notably operational cases (OVs) and operational person controls (OPKs), to discredit individuals and to splinter, disorientate and ultimately dissolve a group. OV 'Namenlos', whose main aim was the liquidation of the eponymous punk band formed in 1983, was terminated with the imprisonment of Michael Horschig and two other band members in the following year. Soon after his release, Horschig resumed his activities in the punk band *Namenlos – Kein Talent*, becoming a target of IMs and OPK 'Schwarz' in 1987 for his involvement in a variety of political opposition activities (Preuß 1999: 55–61). Eager to obtain insider information, the Stasi recruited punks as IMs to report on members of the scene as well as on youth in other 'negative decadent' groups and evangelical church circles in general. Punks were aware that they were under observation: a member of the Dresden band *Paranoia* believes that this reflected the sickness of a system so fearful of its own youth that it criminalised punks and others (Stadtmuseum Dresden 2007: 15). The Stasi often dangled the bait of a lighter sentence, concert tickets and records from the West in return for collaboration, as happened to Michael Rosche, who served as IM 'Klaus Müller' from March 1985 until his flight to West Germany in September 1989. His offence had been to steal a moped from a drunken friend (Shanghai 1997: 25–30). Controllers experienced many difficulties in running punks as they were often unreliable and failed to supply information on a regular basis. IM 'Koslow', used by the Mühlhausen District Service Unit as an informer against 'negative decadent' circles, informed his wife of his Stasi links and left her to compile reports which he then signed.[29]

Although the Stasi had difficulty in enlisting punks as informers on account of what MfS officers called their 'feeling of belonging together', it was able to catch two of the Leipzig punk scene's big fish – Frank 'Zappa' Zappe and Iman Abdul-Majid.[30] The latter, the son of an Iraqi resident in Leipzig and a key figure in the city's punk bands *Wutanfall* and *L'Attentat*, was recruited in 1982 as an informer by the criminal police before, four years later, transferring to the Stasi as IM 'Dominique'. In doing so, he hoped to expedite his application to leave the GDR. Although not a punk himself, Sören Naumann, the manager of the Dresden punk bands *Dresdner Musikbrigade* and *Fabrik*, was deployed as an IM in Stasi operations in the city's alternative cultural scene. Analogous to the internal structure of some of the tiny human rights groups, one punk band in Jena consisted mainly of IMs. It took advantage of the good offices of Ulrich Kasparick, the minister responsible for youth work (*Jugendpfarrer*), in allowing it to use church rooms in order to undermine his work on behalf of the peace and human rights groups in the city. The band's loud noise, drunkenness and damage to property led to so many complaints from the public that an exhausted Kasparick gave up his post.

Since the end of SED rule, few punks have been prepared to talk about their collaboration with the Stasi. One exception is Shanghai, the lead performer of a punk band.[31] Recruited in June 1987 as IMS 'Steffen Herbst', he provided his controller with detailed written and oral reports over the next two years. According to his account, contact was first made in June 1986 when two Stasi officers in civilian dress forced their way into his apartment on the day his grandmother died. Taken with his girlfriend to the local police station for questioning, he was accused of being a 'terrorist'. The motive for his collaboration, so he states, was to help reduce violence and ensure law and order at punk events. Although denying any knowledge of his allotted role in subverting and breaking up the band, he nevertheless provided details about its gigs. In a plea typical of many former IMs, he has also justified his collaboration on the grounds that it guaranteed the survival of the band and that it was possible to have meaningful communication with the Stasi. The uniformed police, on the other hand, did not, he asserts, have the intelligence to understand him and, together with SED 'big shots', constituted the main enemy.

## An Uncertain Future

Several punk bands were able to reform after being banned, springing up like 'mushrooms from the soil' (Furian and Becker 2000: 22), and some of their music found its way to the West on cassettes and records. By the mid 1980s, punk was making greater use of church premises for concerts, diversifying but, in several cases, losing some of its original subversive impulses (Michael 2005: 83–87; Gericke and Havemeister 2007: 87, 89). One former member of the punk band *Namenlos*, Jana Schloßer, recalls that when she came out of prison in 1984 things had already changed: 'The Stasi had pretty well managed to smash punk' (quoted in Furian and Becker 2000: 106). While her remarks apply primarily to the impact of repression on the first wave of punk, internal divisions over the direction of the punk 'movement' were also responsible for its decline and shifts in emphasis. With regard to the latter, some groups were tempted by new, albeit limited, opportunities for officially tolerated but relatively harmless punk music on DT–64, gigs in FDJ clubs and making a few records on the Amiga label. In contrast, others resisted temptation and adhered to the writer Bert Papenfuß's insistence on maintaining their artistic autonomy and aggressive lyrics (Michael 2005: 90; Reagan 2005: 58; Galenza and Havemeister 2007: 95, 97). In summary, while some punks had survived persecution and internal conflicts, by the late 1980s skinheads had emerged as the focal point of 'negative decadence' and of the Stasi's attentions The future seemingly belonged to them, not to the punks.

## Notes

1. The absence of a central steering agency is also recognised by a former top Stasi officer, Wolfgang Schmidt, in Anon. (2004: 129).
2. BStU, MfS, ZA, HA XX/AGK/II, no.97, 'Einschätzung ausgewählter Probleme der politisch-operativen Lageentwicklung unter jugendlichen Personenkreisen im Jahre 1985/86', 20 October 1986, pp.2, 10–14.

3. BStU, MfS, Außenstelle Halle, BV Halle, Sachakten, no.774, 'Information über aktuelle Erscheinungsformen gesellschaftswidrigen Auftretens und Verhaltens negativ-dekadenter Jugendlicher sowie Ergebnisse und Wirksamkeit der politisch-operativen Arbeit zu ihrer Unterbindung und Zurückdrängung', 13 April 1989, pp.21–22.

4. BStU, MfS, ZA, HA XX/AKG, no.80, 'Einschätzung aktueller Erscheinungsformen gesell-schaftswidrigen Auftretens und Verhaltens negativ-dekadenter Jugendlicher sowie Ergebnisse und Wirksamkeit der politisch-operativen Arbeit zu ihrer Unterbindung und Zurückdrän-gung', 23 March 1989, p.19.

5. BStU, MfS, ZA, HA XX /AKG, no.5940, 'Berichterstattung über Entwicklungstendenzen unter negativ-dekadenten Jugendlichen sowie die Wirksamkeit politisch-operativer Maßnah-men zur Zurückdrängung – Zeitraum 1.1.1988 bis 20.5.1988', 30 May 1988, pp.28–29.

6. BStU, MfS, ZA, ZAIG, no.3366, 'Information zu aktuellen Erscheinungsformen gesell-schaftswidrigen Auftretens und Verhaltens negativ-dekadenter Jugendlicher, sogenannter Punker in der DDR', 1986, p.30.

7. BStU, MfS, ZA, HA XXII, no.17399/6, 'Information über beachtenswerte Erscheinungen unter negativ-dekadenten Jugendlichen in der DDR', 11 May 1984, p.23.

8. BStU, MfS, ZA, HA XX/AKG, no.80, 'Einschätzung aktueller Erscheinungsformen gesell-schaftswidrigen Auftretens und Verhaltens negativ-dckadcnter Jugendlicher sowie Ergebnisse und Wirksamkeit der politisch-operativen Arbeit zu ihrer Unterbindung und Zurückdrän-gung', 23 March 1989, p.13.

9. Ibid., p.17.

10. On the background to the report, see BStU, MfS, Außenstelle Halle, BV Halle, AKG, no.2357, 'Information: Problemhintegründe für die Lebensweise junger Bürger, die zu Punk- und Skin-Head-Gruppen gehören', [1987], p.1. The investigation, carried out between May 1986 and January 1987, drew on interviews with technical college students, case studies of indi-vidual factory workers and files of municipal courts of justice. See also Chapter 7.

11. BStU, MfS, ZA, HA XXII, no.18438, 'Information: Problemhintergründe für die Lebens-weise junger Bürger, die zu Punk- und Skin-Head-Gruppen gehören', [1987], p.56.

12. Ibid., 57–58.

13. Ibid., p.58. These observations are derived only from court records and refer to those commit-ting an offence.

14. BStU, MfS, ZA, ZAIG, no.3366, 'Information zu aktuellen Erscheinungsformen gesell-schaftswidrigen Auftretens und Verhaltens negativ-dekadenter Jugendlicher, sogenannter Punker in der DDR', 1986, p.10.

15. Ibid., p.30.

16. Both extracts are reproduced in ibid., p.29.

17. BStU, MfS, ZA, HA XXII, no. 17399/6, 'Information über beachtenswerte Erscheinungen unter negativ-dekadenten Jugendlichen in der DDR', 17 May 1984, p.5.

18. Ibid.

19. Ibid., Information zu aktuellen Erscheinungsformen gesellschaftswidrigen Auftretens und Verhaltens negativ-dekadenter Jugendlicher, sogennanter Punker', 1986, p.15.

20. Ibid., pp.15, 19.

21. Ibid., 'Information über beachtenswerte Erscheinungen unter negativ-dekadenten Jugendli-chen in der DDR', 17 May 1984, p.3; see also Süß (1993: 61) and Niederländer (1990: 18).

22. BStU, MfS, Außenstelle Halle, BV Halle, Abteilung XX, Sachakten, no.774, 'Einschätzung zur politisch-operativen Lage unter negativ-dekadenten Jugendlichen/Jugenderwachsenen', 3 July 1989, p.30. Department XX of the Halle Regional Administration was referring here to punks, goths and heavy-metal fans.

23. MDA, 'Jugendszene – Jugendeinrichtungen – Problemgruppen', [1989], p.2. This is part of a lengthy summary of four ZIJ investigations: 'FDJ-Aufgebot DDR40', 'Jugendklubs', 'Geschichtsbewußsein' and 'Jugendradio II'.

24. BStU, MfS, ZA, HA XX, no.898, 'Information über beachtenswerte Erscheinungen und Entwicklungen unter negativ beeinflußten Jugendlichen und Jungerwachsenen in der Hauptstadt der DDR, Berlin', 16 March 1987, p.107.

25. BStU, MfS, ZA, ZKG, no.2331, 'Hinweise zur politisch-operativen Bearbeitung von Erscheinungsformen gesellschaftswidrigen Auftretens und Verhaltens negativ-dekadenter Jugendlicher, besonders sogenannter Punker, innerhalb der DDR', July 1986, pp.2–5. This is a circular from Mittig to heads of service units.

26. BStU, MfS, ZA, HA XX, no.898, 'Information über beachtenswerte Erscheinungen und Entwicklungen unter negativ beeinflußten Jugendlichen und Jugenderwachsenen in der Hauptstadt der DDR, Berlin', 16 March 1987, p.102. On the incorporation of punks into the open youth work of the churches, see BStU, MfS, ZA, ZAIG, no.3366, 'Information zu aktuellen Erscheinungsformen gesellschaftswidrigen Auftretens und Verhaltens negativ-dekadenter Jugendlicher, sogennanter Punker in der DDR', 1986, p.9.

27. Ibid., pp.9–10.

28. BStU, MfS, ZA, HA XX/AKG, no.80, 'Einschätzung aktueller Erscheinungsformen gesellschaftswidrigen Auftretens und Verhaltens negativ-dekadenter Jugendlicher sowie Ergebnisse und Wirksamkeit der politisch-operativen Arbeit zu ihrer Unterbindung und Zurückdrängung', 23 March 1989, pp.17–18.

29. It is not clear against which type of 'negative decadent' group the IM was deployed. See Urbach (1983: 32).

30. For the details in the remainder of this paragraph, see Michael (2005: 80–81, 83).

31. The text of his interview appeared in a brochure published by the Sachsen-Anhalt Regional Branch of the BStU; see Shanghai (1997: 34–35, 39, 41–42, 46–47).

*Chapter 7*

# SKINHEADS AND RIGHT-WING EXTREMISM IN AN ANTI-FASCIST STATE

## Skinhead Sub-culture

Skinheads first appeared in working-class areas of London, Manchester and other British cities in the late 1960s. Usually associated with aggressive and chauvinistic behaviour, some became supporters of the National Front and racist 'oi-skin' bands stirred up hatred against black and Asian immigrants. It was not until the beginning of the 1980s, however, that Western skinhead music, fashion accessories and militancy began to appeal to young East Germans, notably in East Berlin and nearby Potsdam. The early skinheads, who tended to be former heavy metallers, football hooligans or punks, endeavoured to follow the fashion set by their British and West German contemporaries; that is, tight-fitting jeans, braces, a black, green or orange bomber jacket, a shaven head and highly polished Doc Marten boots. As many of the highly prized accessories were difficult to acquire other than through personal contacts in the West, some skinheads had to content themselves with more conventional sporting attire.[1]

The first comprehensive set of statistics, compiled by the Ministry of State Security in December 1987, estimated that the GDR had 800 skinheads aged 16 to 25 and thirty-eight skinhead groups. The Administrative Region (*Bezirk*) of East Berlin, with some 350 skinheads, 200 sympathisers and eleven groups, occupied first place, followed by that of Potsdam with 120 skinheads and five groups.[2] Skins frequented pubs, football grounds, discos and youth clubs, many indulging in drunken and aggressive behaviour. Links were sought outside the GDR, with some meetings taking place in neighbouring Hungary and Czechoslovakia with local and West German skinheads.[3] The GDR skinhead sub-culture was heterogeneous: not all skinheads were right-wing extremists; oi-skins tended to be apolitical, more interested in alcohol, music and football; SHARP-skins denoted 'Skinheads Against Racial Prejudice'; red-skins constituted an anti-racist group; and fashion skins (*Modeskins*) did not adhere to an extreme-right tendency (Farin 1997: 54–56; Madloch 2000: 73).

Bernd Wagner, a former high-ranking official in the GDR criminal police and an authority on right extremism in post-unification Germany, has identified the following periods in the development of East German skinhead subculture (Wagner 1995: 62–63). Skins began to split off and develop a clearer identity separate from punks around 1982/83, coinciding with an increase in numbers and violence. Then from about 1985/86, the skinhead scene assumed a more political character and conflicts with the authorities became more frequent. This signified the emergence of a counter-culture with a systematic hostility to the dominant culture. Physical violence, often spontaneous, was also sometimes driven by what Wagner calls an increasingly ideologically based friend–foe image. Among the main targets of attacks by skinheads, usually carried out in groups, were foreigners, especially those with a dark skin, gays, goths, punks, disabled persons, and younger members of the army and police with contacts with the youth scene; even 'ordinary' people were not spared (Niederländer 1990: 17).

Clashes with what skinheads denigrated as smelly, dirty, lazy and pacifist punks were often fierce contests over hegemonic control of alternative sub-cultures, which culminated in the brutal attacks on punks at an evening concert in East Berlin's *Zionskirche* in October 1987. These incidents were characteristic of the 'militaristic code and macho aggressiveness' of the violent skins, as expressed in the phrase 'Where words don't help, the fist will' (Hockenos 1993: 74–75). By the late 1980s, the skinheads had undoubtedly gained the upper hand over the punks and other groups. The goths proved relatively easy targets as they could expect little sympathy from the police and the public. Gays, often the victims of robbery, especially by young skinheads, were reluctant to seek redress from the authorities for fear of prejudice and intimidation.

## Right-wing Extremist Incidents

Extremist views and incidents were not confined to the GDR's final decade. Minor incidents such as the daubing of swastika graffiti on school and factory walls and the desecration of Jewish cemeteries in Potsdam, Dresden, East Berlin and elsewhere had flared up from time to time from the 1950s onwards. Teenage schoolchildren and even pupils at the elite children's and youth sport schools were involved in right-wing extremist activities, 600 in the first five months of 1978. Extremist-oriented groups of four to six members were founded in the early 1960s in the Leipzig, Gera, Magdeburg and Karl-Marx-Stadt Administrative Regions (Eisenfeld 2002: 227–28; Engelbrecht 2008: 61). Nor were the army and the state security forces immune: about 730 extreme-right incidents were recorded in the National People's Army between 1965 and 1980 (Madloch 2000: 69–70; Eisenfeld 2002: 224–25). Dismissal and deportation also awaited serious offenders, with the West German government sometimes stepping in (Schmidt 1993: 61–62), such as when, in 1968, it bought the twenty-year-old Arnulf Winfried Priem out of his GDR prison. Priem would become one of Germany's most infamous militant extremists. Frank Hübner, imprisoned in the notorious Bautzen prison in 1984 on a charge of 'illegal contacts', was also bought out, fourteen months after his incarceration. He would become chair of the neo-Nazi *Deutsche Alternative* in 1991.

## Skinhead Groups

The 1980s witnessed, according to the criminal police, an escalation of right-wing extremist violence by about 500 per cent between 1983 and 1987, as well as the evolution of a rudimentary organisational structure (Ross 2000: 89). Relatively tightly organised and small militant groups such as the Lichtenberg Front, founded in 1986, coexisted with a much larger number of informal groups and cliques. Meeting at football grounds, pubs and youth clubs, group members committed sporadic acts of violence, chanted provocative slogans and cultivated their fondness for skinhead music and clothing. One such group, the small fan club of the football team Lok Leipzig, *Härte 10*, attracted the attention of the police. Its seven members glorified fascism and sought to imitate the West German paramilitary *Wehrsportgruppe Hoffmann*.[4]

At the end of December 1987, the Stasi's East Berlin Regional Administration singled out eleven skinhead groups as 'operationally significant', ranging in size from a very loosely organised group of eight in Hellersdorf to the seventeen members of the *Sandow* group in Lichtenberg. The *Ostkreuzler* group in the central district of Mitte was regarded as an exception in that some of its ten or so members rejected the glorification of fascist ideas. Among the skinheads' most popular meeting places were the *Sputnik* café in the Greifswalderstraße and the *Café Nord* on Schönhauser Allee, both in the Prenzlauer Berg district, and the *Mokka-Milch Eisbar* on Karl-Marx-Allee, not far from Alexanderplatz in the centre of East Berlin.[5] By the spring of 1988, the Stasi had uncovered eighteen skinhead 'groupings' with about 180 members in the capital, most of them with a stable hard-core membership of four to eight.[6] The most significant group, the Lichtenberg Front, took its name from a working class district in East Berlin and was described by Ingo Hasselbach as a *Kameradschaft* or 'clandestine brotherhood'. Later, in 1988, Hasselbach and André Riechert founded the 30 January Movement, which, according to the former, was the first neo-Nazi party in the GDR. Hasselbach's father, the head of GDR state radio, had moved from West Germany in 1964 after serving a four-year prison sentence relating to his activities on behalf of the KPD. The 30 January Movement was dissolved by the MfS in March 1989 (Hasselbach 1996: 3; Ross 2000: 77–78).

Feelings of solidarity among skinheads were reinforced by their distinctive attire, hairstyle and music as well as by regular binges. A sense of self-worth and identity was also underpinned by acts of violence which were usually committed in a group where the pressure to conform, both in behavioural and ideological terms, was intense (Gruhn 1989: 35–48). One skinhead informer – IMS 'Diana Wolf' – reported at a meeting with her Stasi controller in September 1986 that she became a skinhead in Hennigsdorf after her release from Bautzen prison in April because: 'Being a skin[head] means respect and recognition for me but also power and strength. I am respected in the group and I have a good feeling ... Previously no one took the slightest notice of me, but now that I've got a bald head and the clothes they all look at me' (Bartl 1989: 78). This kind of sentiment also emerges from a report drawn up by the criminal police of the Cottbus Regional Administration. Eight young people, between 14 and 22 years of age, who had committed acts of rowdyism, had become skinheads because, according to the compilers of the report, 'They consciously wished to be different from most other young people in order to obtain recognition'.[7]

Pumped up by alcohol, skins chanted their battle cry 'Oi! Oi! Oi!' and fascist-type slogans such as 'Heil Hitler!' and 'Germany Awake!' Such slogans did not, however, necessarily signify a commitment to right extremism but rather might denote a desire for kicks, an act of provocation and a self-distancing from socialist society.[8] This was certainly the view of 'Michael', who had become a skinhead in 1985 after a period in which going to football matches and discos had filled a gap in his life after he had left the FDJ youth organisation and his apprenticeship. At that time, his identity as a skinhead was not linked to a conscious political opposition to the GDR. As he told his interviewer in 1990, while everything in the GDR was 'crap', being a skinhead was trendy and different (Korfes 1992: 52).[9]

This pattern of non-conformity is one reason why the Stasi originally classified skinheads as a 'negative decadent force' rather than 'hostile negatives' with the traits of a political opposition. Until well into the 1980s, the MfS regarded the skinheads as 'under control' and a less serious threat than punks, as is apparent from the circular sent in July 1986 by Rudi Mittig, the Stasi's' second-highest ranking officer, to the leaders of service units..[10] The criminal police concurred, dismissing, in its evaluation of youth crime between 1984 and 1986, skinhead glorification of fascism and neo-Nazi ideas as little more than isolated incidents.[11]

## Violence at the *Zionskirche*, October 1987

The escalation of violence in 1987 not only prompted an urgent reappraisal of this judgement but it also corroborated the view of the information office of the East Berlin *Zionskirche* that the police had been seriously mistaken in trivialising the skinhead threat.[12] A favourite meeting place for punks, the church and its associated environmental library were a regular target of the police and Stasi. In September, a brutal attack by skinheads on a Mozambican in Dresden (Madloch

2000: 74) was the prelude to the most serious outbreak of skinhead violence in the GDR on the evening of 17 October 1987. About 30 inebriated skinheads attacked visitors at the end of a concert in the *Zionskirche* organised by the Church from Below and Silvio Meier, an active participant in the open youth work of the evangelical churches. The main attractions were the West Berlin punk band Elements of Crime, which had already performed a few months earlier in East Berlin, and the capital's own group, *Die Firma*. An estimated 500 to 1,000 fans turned up to listen to them.[13]

Earlier in the day, about eighty skinheads, including several from West Berlin, had met up at the nearby *Sputnik* café to celebrate the birthday of one of the GDR's most militant extremists, Ronny Busse, a self-appointed assault-unit leader (*Sturmbannführer*) (ibid.). The Western skinheads, collected by their GDR comrades at the Friedrichstrasse border crossing, were kept under surveillance by the Stasi. Among their number was André Riechert, whose father was a Stasi officer with responsibility for combating right-wing extremism. The younger Riechert had been involved in the Lichtenberg Front. After a day's hard drinking, about thirty of the group left the café at 9.30 PM in order to exact revenge on the punks for alleged insults on the previous day at the *Haus der Jungen Talente*. Shortly before the end of the concert, the skinheads stormed the church, screaming 'Sieg Heil!' 'Jewish pigs!' 'Stasi bastards!' and 'Skinhead power!' The skinheads smashed furniture and beat up members of the audience with bottles and bicycle chains before, outnumbered, they were repelled by punks. They then proceeded to create mayhem around the corner on Schönhauser Allee (Siedler 1991: 61; Madloch 2000: 74). Although the police had known about the concert and, as a precaution, had stationed a few vans in the vicinity of the church, they did not react until emergency calls by members of the public at about 10.30 PM alerted local police stations to the gravity of the situation. As the violence had abated before the arrival of patrol cars, it was not deemed necessary for the police to take further action.[14] The tardiness of the police remains a puzzle: while they may have been uncertain as to how to cope, it is also reasonable to assume that they were unsympathetic to the plight of the punks and the church organisers.[15]

The violence at the *Zionskirche* was not an isolated occurrence. A few days later, about twenty skinheads clashed with bouncers at a dance at a hotel in the Tierpark area of East Berlin.[16] Elsewhere, others injured two experienced policemen and a voluntary police helper, damaged furniture and attacked three persons after a disco for skinheads at a restaurant in Velten. Even after they had been dispersed by one of the policemen firing shots into the air, they returned and caused over 3,000 GDR Marks worth of damage. The skinheads came primarily from a group of about eighty in Velten and Oranienburg.[17] The two towns belonged to the District (*Kreis*) of Oranienburg, which, besides the Potsdam and Königs Wusterhausen districts, formed the main skinhead centres in the Potsdam Administrative Region.[18] The Sachsenhausen concentration camp, then one of the GDR's National Memorials, was situated a short distance from Oranienburg town centre.

## The State Strikes Back

While the Stasi had taken a keener interest in skinheads since 1986, the scale of the brutality of the *Zionskirche* incidents and widespread public criticism so alarmed the SED leaders that they authorised the security forces to implement an elaborate programme of counter-measures in which 'gentle' violence was no longer deemed adequate (Fenemore 2007: 230). The files of the Stasi, the criminal police, the Ministry of the Interior and the SED all testify to the thoroughness of investigations as well as to the authorities' determination to eradicate the skinhead and extremist problem. The SED envisaged a 'broad societal front' against groups of young people attracted to fascism, violence and 'decadence'. This was to encompass a concerted propagation of the socialist way of life by enterprises, schools, the FDJ, youth clubs, pubs, restaurants and parents. In addition, the daily organ of the FDJ, *Junge Welt*, and the electronic media were required to denounce fascism, violence and terror 'more convincingly' than hitherto; a more significant punitive and educational role was allocated to the organs of justice; the general public were to be reassured of the determination of the government to tackle the problems; and efforts were intensified to counter the anticipated adverse comments in the Western press.[19] The DVP, the people's police, was entrusted with drawing up reports on all incidents before submitting them to the MfS, especially Main Departments VII, IX and XX, the three units co-responsible for the overall campaign. The Stasi strategy was detailed in a letter sent on 11 November 1987 by Major-General Paul Kienberg, the head of Main Department XX, to all regional administrations: the compilation of comprehensive records on all known skinheads; the identification of ring leaders, militant skins and football hooligans; the initiation of preliminary criminal proceedings; the deportation of the most notorious skinheads to West Germany; and tightening restrictions on entry into the GDR for Western skinheads and neo-Nazis.[20]

One of the main planks of the campaign was the trial of offenders before an invited audience and the publication of proceedings in the media as a demonstration of the state's resolve to deal with troublemakers and as a warning to other miscreants. However, since it was regarded as politically advisable in a self-styled anti-fascist state to play down right-wing extremism, offenders were to be indicted for 'excessive hooliganism'. Reports, which targeted a young audience through *Junge Welt* and special radio programmes for East German youth, were to stress the state's refusal to tolerate violence and neo-fascism.[21] This policy would continue into 1989: in March of that year, the SED's East Berlin Regional Executive, with Günter Schabowski at its head, advocated further measures to criminalise and publicly discredit the 'skinhead scene' (Madloch 2000: 79).

The initial move against the *Zionskirche* offenders had already backfired: when the East Berlin district court sentenced the first four to between one and two years' imprisonment in December 1987, public protests, especially against the relative mildness of Busse's sentence, led to the imposition of an additional eighteen months' to four years' imprisonment.[22] One citizen's letter of complaint to Honecker at the end of the year urged that the neo-fascist threat be openly addressed by the media and schools, and all skinhead offenders be arrested.[23] With the relevant political and judicial authorities apparently having failed to reach agreement on the appropriate length of sentence, the subsequent increase in sentence was agreed between Egon Krenz and Günter Wendland, the State Prosecutor. Permission to publish details of the heavier sentences in a press release was secured from Honecker.[24] A subsequent trial of a further eight perpetrators in January 1988 ended in sentences of between fifteen months and three years. Although the two trials were the first official ones openly conducted against right-wing extremists in the GDR, the court verdicts steered clear of such terminology, referring instead to 'excessive hooliganism' and 'public insult' (Ross 2000: 137). Wendland specifically ruled out any reference in the charges to fascist and anti-semitic slogans to ensure that the trial did not furnish the 'enemy' with support for accusations that young people in the GDR were attracted to fascist ideology.[25]

The official crackdown was bolstered by the politburo's decision on 2 February 1988 to combat anti-socialism among the country's youth (Kelch 1989: 13). The SED, not the Stasi, it should be stressed, was the initiator of policy. This is apparent from a meeting in Dresden in August 1988 between Wolfgang Herger, the head of the SED Central Committee Department for Security, and representatives of the State Prosecutor, the police, the Stasi and the party. The DVP and the Stasi received instructions as to how to proceed against skinheads, punks and other 'negative decadent' groups and how to coordinate matters with the local SED authorities.[26] How the security forces should prevent or suppress 'rowdiness' among young people was detailed in a letter from Colonel-General Mittig on the same day as the politburo resolution.[27] Action soon followed, with more skinheads arrested for offences such as the desecration of Jewish cemeteries, assaults on African contract workers in Dresden and Halle, and painting graffiti on the walls of the former Sachsenhausen concentration camp. In total, between late November 1987 and July 1988, forty-nine skinheads were sentenced in nine separate trials.[28]

These mini show trials were flanked by assessments in various public forums and the media as part of the general offensive against extremism. Typical of the media campaign was the lengthy article in the *Neue Berliner Illustrierte* magazine concerning five teenagers who, between January and March 1988, had desecrated 222 gravestones in the Jewish cemetery on East Berlin's Schönhauser Allee, not far from the local police station. The damage occurred at a sensitive time in the SED's negotiations with the Conference on Jewish Material Claims and the reorientation of relations with the GDR's Jewish Communities and Israel (see Chapter 2). The offenders were sentenced to between two-and-a-half and six-and-a-half years' imprisonment. Following the regime's standard interpretation, the origin of their 'distorted' ideology with fascist-like elements was attributed to West German TV and radio programmes. Their family life had been so disrupted, so the article alleged, that they had no one with whom they enjoyed a close emotional bond.[29] While the report did acknowledge, albeit cautiously, the existence of fascist-type elements, it was yet a further example of the SED's reluctance to countenance an open debate on right-wing extremism, preferring instead to depict such incidents primarily as serious rowdy actions committed by antisocial elements.

## Unofficial Informers

Unofficial informers were allotted a key role in combating skinhead militancy and neo-fascism. In December 1987, the Stasi's East Berlin Regional Administration employed seventeen IMs in operations against skinheads; 60 per cent of these had been recruited in 1986 and 1987.[30] By March 1989, the number had increased to twenty in East Berlin and 100 in the whole of the GDR.[31] In the second most significant centre of skinhead activity, the Potsdam area, ten IMs were engaged against seventy-five skinheads and 122 sympathisers in April 1988.[32] Elsewhere, the Cottbus Regional Administration had twenty-three IMs involved in the surveillance of 'negative decadent' young people in operational cases (OVs) and operational person controls (OPKs), of which ten were primarily involved in campaigns against skinheads, punks and heavy-metal fans.[33] The basic functions of the IMs were to uncover right-wing extremists and their meeting places, to restrict violent actions, and to identify the groups' clandestine organisational structures and goals. Links between neo-Nazis in the FRG and the GDR were also assiduously investigated by the Stasi. For example, Main Department XXII/1 used IMB 'Seemann' from 1987 to late 1989 to seek out, as part of OV 'Skorpion', the views and intentions in West Berlin of Arnulf Winfried Priem, Andreas Pohl and their comrades in the *Nationalistische Front* and other neo-Nazi groups.[34]

Dissertations written by Stasi officers as part of their training at the Juridical College in Potsdam provide invaluable insight into the MfS's thinking on the use of agents attached to 'negative decadent forces' like the skinheads. While most IMs were recruited from among what the MfS called 'negative decadent' groups, it did not wish to draw on those with firm neo-fascist views. Experience had shown that it was operationally advantageous if candidates were already members of a skinhead group and that the youths, preferably aged 17 to 25 years, could be enticed by playing on their sense of adventure, expectations of material gain and the MfS's intervention on their behalf in the courts of law or at work. Commitment to the socialist cause was not expected to be a significant motive, a factor normally regarded as highly desirable by recruiters. An appeal to what skinheads regarded as typical German virtues such as a sense of duty, steadfastness and loyalty was seen as a more effective means of persuasion (Wejwoda and Goers 1980: 17–36; Taraschonnek 1989: 18–32). Although some 'negative decadents' were enlisted as IMs while serving a prison sentence, the Stasi had reservations about this form of recruitment as many terminated their link soon after their release and the removal of the pressure to conform.[35] There was another problem: one IM, Jens-Uwe Vogt, the leader of a hard-core group of skinheads and the *Anale Berlin* football hooligans in East Berlin, turned and used his Stasi experience to the advantage of his own group. Vogt, a former punk, was involved in the *Zionskirche* affray.[36]

In order to overcome scruples about informing on their comrades and to encourage them to continue with their work, controlling officers were expected to arrange regular meetings with skinhead IMs in special apartments. As the MfS regarded these IMs as unpredictable and often lacking in self-confidence, a controller was to praise good work and to focus on establishing a close and stable relationship cemented by trust in, and respect for, the authority of the officer. Disturbing this relationship by a change of controller was deemed undesirable as it might reinforce skinheads' deep-rooted suspicions of the Stasi and the police and heighten fears over the threat of reprisals by group members should their collaboration be discovered. In addition to the usual risk of IMs breaking their cover, the Stasi was also concerned about their involvement in violent actions, which often arose spontaneously. The IMs, it was recognised, might be unable to stand aside as it would arouse suspicion and put them at great personal risk. On the other hand, they were expected to avoid incitement and to keep their own involvement in violence to a minimum. Furthermore, they could not be guaranteed blanket immunity from prosecution for certain types of acts, particularly if other members of the group were imprisoned (Taraschonnek 1989: 47–54).

The expansion of the IM network and other counter-measures led initially to a decline in violent offences and drove the militants underground. Lasting success proved elusive, however. New structures soon evolved and militants deliberately placed followers in official state organisations such as the Society for Sport and Technology (GST). Skinheads were also encouraged to serve as volunteers in the armed forces and the riot police in order to gain experience in parachute jumping, undersea diving and various forms of martial arts (Siegler 1991: 72; Madloch 2000: 75). Contacts were fostered between skinheads across regional boundaries, the anonymity of East Berlin making it a favourite gathering point for skinheads from Potsdam and Frankfurt/Oder.[37] While an early call-up was a form of discipline favoured by the SED and security forces, it backfired when skinheads committed acts of disorder in the army (Wiedemann 1985: 14). Permanent or temporary losses due to military service, imprisonment or emigration were partly filled by the recruitment of young teenagers or 'baby skins', who were eager to prove themselves to the 'hard core' by their bravura and acts of aggression.[38] The overall failure to crush the skinheads can be illustrated in numerical terms: Stasi estimates in March 1989 of 1,126 skinheads and sympathisers, including 431 in the Administrative Regions of East Berlin, 263 in Potsdam and 93 in Cottbus, indicated that little had changed since the end of 1987.[39]

## Fascos

The most significant development in organisational and ideological terms was the emergence of the 'fascos', a term first coined in 1986, and regarded by Konrad Weiss, the East German film director, as a more dangerous group than the skinheads.[40] The fascos grew out of the more extreme skinheads who sought to escape the attention of the security forces after the *Zionskirche* incident and established themselves in East Berlin, Potsdam, Cottbus, Guben and several other towns. Operating in small, highly disciplined clandestine units of between six and twelve individuals, they imposed strict membership criteria and met several times per week to discuss aims and beliefs. As their name suggests, they were committed to National Socialist ideology, with Hitler's *Mein Kampf* as one of their main texts. For some, like Ingo Hasselbach, prison constituted 'an ideal environment for acquiring the rudiments of Nazism' from old National Socialists such as Henri Schmidt, the former Gestapo chief of Dresden. Schmidt, who had been responsible for the deportation of thousands of Jews from the city, regarded Jews as 'an inferior, poisonous race', which had ruined the German economy (Hasselbach 1996: 60–62). Hasselbach had been incarcerated in 1987 on a charge of 'rowdy behaviour', crying out 'The Wall must fall' in front of Soviet troops and Stasi officers (ibid.: 46). As the Stasi was aware, prisoners were not entirely cut off as some maintained regular communication with skinheads on the outside and prepared for reintegration into their former group after their release.[41]

More ideologically driven than the skinheads, the fascos were the progenitors of a crude right-wing extremism underpinned by a sharp distinction between friend and foe and a glorification of violence. In the final two years of the GDR, the small right-wing extremist minority emerged from youth and alternative sub-cultures and assumed the characteristics of a societal movement (Wagner 2002: 16). By the time of the *Zionskirche* incidents, a loose hybrid of xenophobia, nationalism and anti-communism had taken shape. Far from a homogeneous ideology, considerable differences existed on issues such as the security offered by the GDR's social system and the policies of the Third Reich. While basic aspects of the Third Reich and National Socialist ideology were praised, some skinheads opposed Germany's launching of the Second World War[42] and mass murder.[43] However, the basic tenets and goals of a right-wing extremist ideology were discernible: the restoration of Germany within its 1937 borders; a united Germany based on ethno-nationalism; a pronounced antipathy towards foreignness; the establishment of Germany as a world power; the rejection of both the East and West German political systems; a hostility towards liberal democracy; and a militant anti-communism. Other key elements and demands were: the revival of concentration camps for leftists, homosexuals, 'asocials' and subversive elements in general; the punishment of sexual relations with 'non-Aryans'; and the destruction of the 'unworthy life' of the physically and mentally 'handicapped' (Taraschonnek 1989: 17–18; Wagner 1995: 66; Madloch 2000: 76; Ross 2000: 114–15, 122; Saunders 2003: 51). One self-styled neo-Nazi expressed the latter sentiment under interrogation:

> In my opinion, people, for example, those with physical disabilities, have no right to live because, in nature, sick animals also have to die or are eaten by other animals. Such people are a burden on society … What we like about fascism were, for example, the concentration camps. In my opinion, the Jews did not have the right to live in Germany. Communists

and socialists were against the social system at that time and thus had to be gassed or shot like the Jews. What I like best about this system was, above all, German order and that they have done so much for their young people. (Taraschonnek 1989: 64)

## Germanness

With the quickening of the authorities' interest in fascos and skinheads, studies were conducted in the later 1980s by sociologists, the Stasi and the criminal police which, along with records of interrogations and personal recollections, provide an insight into the pivotal role played by 'Germanness' (*Deutschtum*) in skinhead and right-wing extremist thinking. Germanness was associated with strength, productive and disciplined work, and cleanliness (Niederländer 1990: 17). In East Berlin, Germanness sometimes evolved into a form of Prussianism which discriminated not only against foreigners but Saxons and Mecklenburgers too.[44] This kind of attitude was resented: in Cottbus, one skinhead accused all Berliners of belittling others out of a false sense of superiority.[45] Among the skinheads' main grievances, which emerge from Stasi and police files, were the poor work ethic, absenteeism and wastage endemic in the state socialist economy. This is illustrated in a statement by one skinhead under cross-examination:

> I go to work regularly and am of the opinion that I am industrious and do good work. That is the thing which marks out a genuine skin. I belong to a group where every member acts just like that. On the whole, we are industrious and cannot stand shirking at work and sponging. On the other hand, I have an aversion, like my group members, to foreigners and people of a different nationality.[46]

Despite the insistence on hard work as a cardinal feature of Germanness, not all skinheads were dedicated workers. A Stasi report of November 1987 asserted that many remained in their job in order to avoid possible prosecution for asocial behaviour.[47] The criminal police in the Cottbus Administrative Region found that of eight skinheads aged 14 to 22 who, in 1988, were accused of penal offences, especially rowdyism, two did not go to work and five frequently missed shifts and performed poorly in their jobs or studies.[48]

These caveats aside, skinheads were critical of those who failed to measure up to their notion of Germanness. Attitudes towards allegedly dirty and lazy punks are encapsulated by the insistence of one skinhead that as order, not anarchy, should prevail in a state, punks 'can live in the dustbin' (Kinner and Richter 2000: 281). Foreigners, too, were associated with indolence, filth and disorder, as well as depriving East Germans of housing and consumer goods (ibid.: 281, 285). Growing antipathy towards foreign contract workers in the late 1980s sometimes escalated into brutal attacks, as in 1988 against a Mozambican who was thrown from a moving train by five youths and workers (Ross 2000: 93). Foreigners were also accused of bringing AIDS into the GDR and of treating East German women as prostitutes (Kinner and Richter 2000: 285). An apprentice at the lignite works in Jänschwalde told his questioners: 'What's more, negroes rape our German girls and women and the Poles buy up everything in the shops'.[49] Another skinhead sought to enlighten the Cottbus police with the information that:

> There is an entire housing complex with negroes and a house full of Poles in Hoyerswerda. If they weren't there everyone in Hoyerswerda would have a flat, which is not the case at the moment. I am for violence against foreigners. Someone has got to chuck them out. We skinheads felt called upon to do it.[50]

Homosexuals and Jews were regarded as unworthy of being labelled 'German'. One skinhead under police questioning stated that during the Third Reich communists and socialists should have been gassed or shot like the Jews. This was not, however, a representative view among the skinheads.[51] Typical forms of antisemitism included the desecration of Jewish graves and cries of 'Jewish pigs!' as well as bomb threats and hate mail sent to the Jewish synagogue in the Prenzlauer Berg district of East Berlin (Ross 2000: 222). Antipathy towards homosexuals was widespread among eight Cottbus skinheads interrogated by the police. 'Non-German', 'cannot stand such people', 'an affront to the honour of a German', and 'make little attempt to practise normal sexuality and have female mannerisms' are just some of their statements.[52]

## The Failure to Crush Skinheads and Fascos

The Stasi, the state body with overall responsibility for smashing the militant skinhead and fasco phenomenon, was keen to blame others for the failure to suppress extremism.[53] The East Berlin Regional Administration deplored a sharp fall in the willingness of the East German public to provide information to help combat skinhead violence after the initial burst of cooperation between December 1987 and March 1988.[54] Teachers in schools and technical colleges, as well as fellow pupils, public transport users and visitors to discos, were also criticised for their passive response to skinhead actions.[55] Some pub and restaurant landlords and staff were also inactive, either underestimating manifestations of neo-fascism or afraid of violent retribution by skinheads.[56] The Stasi did not spare the FDJ, the DVP and other societal partners. The police were criticised for being ill-prepared to deal with skinhead violence, especially as at the *Zionskirche* in October 1987.[57] And while conscious of the inherent difficulties in working with skinheads, the Stasi was dissatisfied with FDJ local organs for their erratic policy towards controlling skinheads and for their inadequate efforts at involving them in the youth organisation's activities.[58] What the Stasi failed to mention, however, was the rapid decline in the influence of the FDJ during the 1980s.

As in other areas of responsibility, the Stasi lamented deficiencies in the administration of its own operations, including delays in transferring information from interrogations of 'negative decadent' youths by Main Department IX to

Main Department XX.[59] In December 1987, the latter acknowledged that it was difficult to assess the value of the seventeen IMs used by the East Berlin Regional Administration against skinheads.[60] Almost two years later, and despite an improvement in cooperation with the DVP, the head of Main Department XX was still complaining about related problems: the fear, as well as indifference, of many citizens towards skinhead activities; the FDJ basic organisations' neglect of focused and preventive work with skinheads; a failure to recruit adequate numbers of 'hard-core' skinheads as IMs; and delays in operations against 'negative decadent' skinhead and neo-fascist groups. The list was extended to the need for a speedier flow of information between the DVP and MfS district units and for a greater effort in uncovering the growing contacts of former East German skinheads based in the FRG with those remaining in the GDR.[61]

## Seeking an Explanation

With skinhead violence and right-wing extremism gathering momentum, the SED, the Stasi, the DVP and other organisations were obliged to seek a better understanding of the skinhead phenomenon and the younger generation's involvement in 'politically negative' groups.[62] The evangelical churches, members of the cultural intelligentsia – such as Konrad Weiss and the critical writer Stefan Heym – and the Leipzig Central Institute for Youth Research (ZIJ) were also concerned about these issues. In a review of research investigations covering over 3,000 young people in the youth scene and 'problem' groups during the 1980s, ZIJ researchers warned against an exaggeration of external steering and urged that greater attention be given to internal social conditions.[63] This kind of approach, which deviated from that favoured by the SED, also underpinned sociological investigations carried out by Loni Niederländer of Berlin's Humboldt University with the assistance of Gunhild Korfes of the Academy of Social Sciences. Their comparative study of punks and skinheads, conducted in 1986 and early 1987 (see Chapters 5 and 6), was soon followed by one undertaken by Niederländer on behalf of the criminology section of her university, whose director, Professor Stelzer, was a Stasi Officer on Special Assignment (OibE). The report was commissioned with the knowledge of the MfS by Lieutenant-General Nedwig, the head of the main department of the criminal police. Due to commence in May 1988, the completion date of the project was set for December 1989.[64]

The second investigation was based primarily on the records of 596 skinheads and 'politically negative' young people caught up in criminal proceedings and on 1,238 transcripts of the questioning of the accused and witnesses between October 1987 and November 1989.[65] Given the nature of the empirical data, the findings cannot be regarded as strictly representative but they do provide significant indicators as to the social profile of the skinheads and other militants. Based on a sample in which all social strata and classes were included, the key finding was that qualifications, family status and general circumstances corresponded to a cross-section of society (Niederländer 1990: 16–17; Siegler 1991: 73; Kinner and Richter 2000: 273–74). Two exceptions were age and gender, with young males forming a clear majority.[66] The educational and occupational profile of the sample shows a preponderance of the main social stratum in the GDR – that is, skilled workers (see Table 7.1). The social status of parents exhibits a similar pattern: intelligentsia, 24 per cent; craft workers, 14 per cent; skilled workers, 47 per cent; and unskilled workers, 15 per cent (Niederländer 1990: 16; Kinner and Richter 2000: 279).

**Table 7.1:** Social Profile of Individuals with Neo-fascist Orientation, 1989

| Social Status | Region 1 | Region 2 | Other Regions | Average |
|---|---|---|---|---|
| School pupils | 5 | 4 | 9 | 4 |
| Apprentices | 24 | 29 | 22 | 24 |
| Semi-skilled workers | 3 | 8 | 5 | 4 |
| Skilled workers | 53 | 45 | 44 | 50 |
| Technical college students | 2 | 3 | 3 | 2 |
| Without a profession | 13 | 11 | 17 | 14 |
| | 100% | 100% | 100% | 100% |

*Source:* Kinner and Richter (2000: 279). The results are based on a sample of 596 persons.

The Niederländer surveys, as well as criminal police materials and ZIJ findings, largely support the contention that skinheads and members of right-wing extremist groups were not socially marginalised, did not have a deprived family background and were not losers in East German-style socialist modernisation (Ross 2000: 104, 106; Engelbrecht 2008: 102–4). They also underscore the thesis of Konrad Weiss that the skinheads were 'our children' raised in the country's own kindergartens and schools.[67] Indeed, two of the GDR's leading right-wing extremists came from the ranks of the GDR 'establishment', including officers in the armed forces: Ingo Hasselbach's father was the head of GDR state radio, and André Riechert's a major in the Stasi. Well represented in organisations such as the FDJ and the GST, skinheads served willingly in the army and were normally well regarded at work. Nor were they seen as outsiders by some of their peers. A ZIJ survey in 1988 revealed that while 64 per cent of young people in the sample rejected skinheads, 4 per cent were sympathisers and 30 per cent perceived skinheads as victims of 'certain circumstances in society' (Brück 1992: 39, 41). Some skinhead complaints, as detailed in the Niederländer report, were also typical of the GDR more generally: the lack of freedom to travel, the inconvertibility of the GDR Mark, consumer supply problems, wastage in the economy and, as the 1980s progressed, a socio-economic antipathy to foreign workers (Kinner and Richter 2000: 282). This indicates that skinheads expressed a dissatisfaction which was becoming increasingly open and widespread.

## The Import Thesis

Whereas the East German authorities struggled to account for the existence of non-conformist sub-cultures in society, they had an even greater problem in explaining why right-wing extremism had gained a foothold in a state which, through extensive de-nazification in the immediate postwar years and the establishment of a new socialist order, claimed to have removed the preconditions for fascism and militarism. After all, skinhead violence and neo-fascist tendencies were, like football-related hooligan behaviour, supposed to be inherent in the exploitative imperialist system with its impoverished working class and, in the case of Western skinheads, xenophobic and violent individuals mostly recruited from the lower social strata.[68] The issue became even more politically sensitive with the spread of an East German form of right-wing extremism at the very time – the late 1980s – that the SED was seeking to refurbish its anti-fascist image by courting Jewish organisations at home and abroad. Hence the party's ideologues and security and armed services clung doggedly to the scapegoat thesis; that is, manifestations of right-wing extremism were primarily the product of the imperialist foe's attempted political-ideological subversion of the socialist system.[69] Thus when right-wing extremist ideas, but also constructive criticism, surfaced in a politically pivotal body like the NVA, they were suppressed and condemned as the product of the class enemy's subversion strategy (Wiedemann 1985: 11–12; Wenzke 2005: 251–54). A floundering FDJ leadership, too, clutched at the straw man of political-ideological subversion as its influence on East German youth evaporated in the course of the 1980s. An FDJ Central Council report, discussed by the SED politburo on 2 February 1988, asserted that enemy ideological subversion in the form of personal links and TV and radio programmes transmitted by the West German broadcasters ARD, ZDF and RIAS sought to foster indifference and hostility to socialism among East German youth.[70] Their impact on East German youth could be seen, according to the FDJ leadership, in 'asocial, decadent and rowdy behaviour' generally, but especially in the activities of skinheads, punks, heavy metallers, goths, football hooligans, and peace and human rights groups.[71]

The MfS, a trenchant advocate of the 'import' thesis, was mobilised to uncover links between former East German citizens and their East German skinhead 'comrades', to track meetings in other state socialist countries, and to seize skinhead-related records, books, videos and magazines imported from the West.[72] Allergic to any form of East–West communication, the Stasi was especially keen to forestall contacts between East German right-wing extremists and West German neo-Nazis and militants, including groups like the *Nationalistische Front* and the *Wiking-Jugend*. The sum of its efforts by the beginning of 1988 amounted to little more than uncovering relatively loose contacts and the supply of various types of equipment and information.[73] Indeed, Stasi officers conceded in confidential internal documents that no direct steering was conducted by organisations in the West and that West German neo-Nazi groups enjoyed little success in infiltrating the GDR (Dalski and Jerie 1986: 8, 31, 25–33; Ross 2000: 24–25, 76, 101). The whole notion of external steering was dismissed contemptuously by an East German skinhead when interviewed by ARD: 'and that it's all supposed to be directed from the West, like it wouldn't have come into our heads if Westerners hadn't drawn our attention to it – no it's definitely not directed from the West' (quoted in Ross 2000: 82).

In order to rescue vestiges of the 'import' thesis, the SED and its agencies fell back on a pathology of 'negative decadence', according to which certain individuals were predisposed to Western political-ideological subversion as a result of chequered family, educational and occupational biographies. The sources of maladjustment of the socially 'deformed' youth were variously identified as 'remnants' from Germany's imperialist past, the negative influence of peers, broken homes, deficiencies in the upbringing of children, poor neighbourhood facilities, and the inadequacies of work collectives and the FDJ.[74] With regard to the skinhead problem, a trainee officer at the Juridical College in Potsdam, Torsten Gruhn, homed in on the passivity of schools and parents, the lack of decisive action by the police, a fear of skinheads prevalent among members of the public, and the insensitivity of the FDJ to the needs of young people. Often unable to find interesting leisure activities, youngsters found an outlet in the music, distinctive outfit and heavy drinking of skinheads, and, unlike in the FDJ, derived a boost to their self-esteem in these milieux (Gruhn 1989: 29–31, 38, 52–53; see also Weimann 1989: 15). While this kind of analysis did not mark a radical shift, it did at least have the merit of broadening the perspective to incorporate a critique of the functioning of official agents of socialisation and social provision (see Saunders 2007: 71). It did not, however, approach the level of self-criticism to be found elsewhere, as in the 1987 Niederländer and Korfes report, which insisted that social relations within the GDR itself were the essential springboard for an analysis of the skinhead problem as external ideological influence needed 'fertile ground'.[75] Moreover, to combat the helplessness engendered by the official 'import' thesis, they urged a recognition that, 'Internal and external conditions act together and complement each other'.[76]

## Patterns of Prejudice

While the Stasi and the FDJ were happy to shift much of the responsibility for the emergence of right-wing extremist views and embryonic structures, as well as the growing disenchantment of East German youth, on to the shoulders of family and schools, they were unwilling to recognise that they, too, were part of the problem. The rise of the extreme right had its various roots in the authoritarian structures and mentalities of East German state socialism; the growing militari-sation of life; the significance attached to virile and aggressive masculinity; the unresolved national question; the fragility of the anti-fascist paradigm; and the frequently harsh personal reality behind the rhetoric of socialist brotherhood and friendship between peoples. These problems were compounded by the gathering crisis of the communist system in the Soviet Union, Poland and other East Euro-pean countries, the inflexibility of an ageing SED leadership, and the precipitous decline during the 1980s in young people's identification with the GDR and sup-port for core aspects of its social and political system (Dennis 2000a: 269–70).

The SED regime's failure to nurture a 'culture of contact' with foreigners, whether Westerners, members of the community of socialist states or con-tract workers and students from Asian and African countries, was fundamen-tal to a growing animosity during the 1980s towards foreigners among sections of the population as well as to the ethno-nationalism of skinheads and right-wing extremists. This xenophobia was selective, as certain groups like Poles and non-white foreigners from Africa attracted higher levels of hostility than West Europeans and Americans (Poutrus, Behrends and Kuck 2000: 19–21; Saunders 2003: 51–52). It should be stressed, however, that this is not a pattern which can be applied across the population as a whole since several surveys also picked up widespread sympathy among young people for members of fraternal countries, albeit on a declining curve as the 1980s progressed (Friedrich 2002: 37–38). In 1988, a ZIJ survey of young people drew attention to 'insufficient tolerance', 'antipathy, distancing and conflictual behaviour' towards 'Soviet citizens (Rus-sians), Poles, Africans (blacks), as well as Vietnamese and Asians' (Ross 2000: 165; see also Saunders 2007: 80). Such attitudes, partly determined by a sense of superiority, were picked up in another ZIJ investigation in the same year: 12 per cent of a sample of 325 pupils and 15 per cent of 444 apprentices agreed with the statement that 'The Germans were always the greatest in history' (Schu-barth and Schmidt 1992: 20; Bugiel 2002: 110). With limited opportunities to acquaint themselves with other nationalities and cultures and to develop a mutual tolerance and understanding, East Germans would be ill-prepared for the multiple transformation shocks to their identity, socio-economic status and value system after German unification in 1990. The dramatic changes helped fuel an escalation in xenophobia, with a survey of about 2,800 young East Germans in December 1990 registering a high level of antipathy towards black Africans (44 per cent), Poles (32 per cent), Vietnamese (52 per cent), Turks (54 per cent) and gypsies (56 per cent).[77]

The SED's tortuous approach to German nationhood and East German state identity created a vacuum for the kind of ethno-nationalism advocated by skin-heads and fascos, one which also had popular appeal beyond this tiny minority. A corollary of the contradictions in the SED stance on nationality was an infla-tion of the role of the anti-fascist myth as a core element of state legitimacy and identity. The myth, while functioning as an ideological glue for the political elites, especially Honecker and other party veterans, underwent a decline in popular support during the 1980s as its many ambiguities came under closer scrutiny (Madloch 2000: 101, 103–4). Among the myth's flaws were the virtual exclusion of the suffering of Gypsies, homosexuals and Jehovah's Witnesses during the Third Reich, the downplaying of Jewish victimhood, and the ambivalence in the portrayal of German attitudes to the National Socialist regime's Jewish policy. The SED's stubborn adherence to the 1935 Comintern's outmoded and economistic definition of fascism as 'the open terroristic dictatorship of the most reactionary, most chauvinistic and most imperialistic elements of finance capital' blocked critical analysis of the multifaceted nature of National Socialist racism and of the GDR's neo-fascist minority. This was also true of the SED's eagerness to present the GDR and its citizens as virtual victors of history while highlighting the neo-fascist potential of capitalist West Germany. In March 1989, with SED hegemony crumbling, Konrad Weiss used the pages of *Kontext*, an underground publication, to attack this line of argument claiming that East Germans were only too ready to suppress the disturbing memories of the terrible National Socialist past. Much to the annoyance of the authorities, Weiss went on to embed his argument in a wide-ranging critique of the lack of a democratic tradition in the GDR, as exemplified by the cult of the party leadership, the imposition of party discipline, the pressure to conform and the use of force for the resolution of conflicts.[78]

The East German writer Stephan Hermlin, himself a Jew, whose writings had helped further the anti-fascist myth, added an authoritative voice to the debate. In August 1988, in a radio interview about neo-Nazism on the West German radio station *Deutschlandfunk*, Hermlin contended that while the GDR seriously intended to eradicate anti-semitism, the anti-fascist education of young people had been neglected in the last two to three years in school, higher education and the media.[79] Hermlin's criticism was backed up by ZIJ findings which revealed that most young people had little interest in the historical roots of the GDR, had a poor understanding of fascism, and were recipients of a history that was taught in a tendentious, highly selective and dull manner (Nothnagle 1999: 22–26, 36–38, 139–41, Engelbrecht 2008: 86–89). One major ZIJ investigation into historical consciousness among about 2,000 young people in 1988 found that 12 per cent of pupils and 15 per cent of apprentices believed that 'fascism had its good side', and 4 and 11 per cent respectively that 'Hitler only wanted the best for the German people' (Schubarth and Schmidt 1992: 20; Bugiel 2002: 99). Not until after German unification, however, could these results be made public and the ZIJ's researchers voice their criticism of how the National Socialist past had been taught in schools. In their view, the assertion that millions of (East) Germans were suddenly transformed after the collapse of the Third Reich into active builders of socialism subsequently led to confusion and naivety in dealing with the right-wing extremist phenomena in the GDR (Schubarth and Schmidt 1992: 14–17, 20). When a further study was undertaken of about 2,800 pupils, apprentices and young workers in Saxony in December 1990, 9 per cent of the pupils, 17 per cent of apprentices and 2 per cent of A-level students agreed with the statement that 'The Jews are Germany's misfortune' (Schubarth 1992: 87).

While all these results point to a considerable authoritarian potential, as well as of racist and nationalistic views, among young people who had been raised in the GDR, over 75 per cent in the 1988 survey rejected the view that 'fascism also had its good side'. Moreover, in October 1989, 54 per cent of pupils between the ages of 14 and 15 years believed that the anti-fascist goals of the GDR had been realised (Schubarth and Schmidt 1992: 20, 25). This kind of finding is a pertinent reminder of the positive elements of an anti-fascist education and of the democratic potential among young East Germans.

While the SED, Stasi, DVP and FDJ were mainly responsible for the campaign against right-wing extremism and militant skinheads, and the army stamped down hard on incidents, not only did the authorities' hostility to the alien and 'exotic other' feed prejudices but their own authoritarian structures and mentalities also provided a normative underpinning for the very extremists they sought to destroy. How the overlap between official values and those of the skinheads was manipulated by the Stasi emerges from the thesis of Rainer Taraschonnek, a trainee officer attached to Department XX of the Stasi's East Berlin Regional Administration. In recruiting skinheads as IMs, he recommended that 'typical German virtues' upheld by skinheads be utilised, notably punctuality, loyalty, steadfastness and a sense of duty. These were, of course, also characteristics which underpinned the self-image of the MfS. Another recommendation, based on the experience of an officer in the Stasi Prenzlauer Berg District office, was that advantage be taken of a prospective candidate's militant behaviour and his 'Prussian-German obedience'. It was even suggested that a recruiter should emphasise his own status as a 'German officer' (Taraschonnek 1989: 31).

As Walter Süß has pointed out, while the approach developed by West German scholars such as Wilhelm Heitmeyer, which seeks to locate right-wing extremism in the problems and risks associated with modernisation and individualisation, may not be salient for the less developed GDR, the Bielefeld sociologist's emphasis on an unscrupulous willingness to use force and the ideology of inequality as constituent elements of right-wing extremism has some explanatory value.[80] Intolerance, repression, intimidation and force were part and parcel of the socialisation of young people in the GDR as exemplified by the role in society of the NVA and the GST, the use of military toys and the pervasive friend–foe dichotomy. [1] Since 1978, practical and theoretical pre-military training was a compulsory part of the school curriculum for pupils aged 14 to 16. This was reinforced by the broader activities of the GST, with a membership of about 679,820 in 1988, as the mass organisation responsible for pre-military training and preparing young people for the armed forces (Heider 1998: 177–90). Like the NVA, its martial elements appealed to the militant skinheads and fascos, who regarded service in the armed forces as a duty. As one skinhead said of the NVA: 'I was able to strengthen my physical fitness properly because sport is one of the most important activities during military service'.[82] The harsh discipline of the East German military regime also served to reinforce the authoritarianism and aggressive masculinity which were central to skinhead culture (Fenemore 2007: 184–87). It should be noted, however, that many young East Germans became more sceptical towards military service as they grew older and became less reticent about criticising militarisation as the 1980s progressed, even though only a small minority actively protested (Saunders 2007: 59–63, 66–68). [3]

## More Than a Postscript

Whereas the SED and Stasi had generally managed to keep the lid on right-wing extremism, the chaotic months between the fall of the Berlin Wall and German unification afforded many new opportunities for the creation of links between right-wing extremists in East and West Germany and the proliferation in the GDR of small extremist parties and social movements (Madloch 2000: 88–89). Violence, too, escalated. Among the most notorious incidents were the attacks on foreigners in the Saxon town of Hoyerswerda in 1991 and against asylum seekers in Rostock-Lichtenhagen in the following year. And whereas at the beginning of the 1990s little difference existed between East and West with regard to the regional pattern of extreme-right violence, by 2005 the incidence of such offences per head of population was much higher in the former. Of the *New Länder*, Saxony-Anhalt and Brandenburg had the highest ratings with 4.29 and 3.78 incidents per 100,000 inhabitants respectively (Bundesministerium des Innern 2005: 40). These two *Länder* also had the highest incidence of right-wing extremist attacks on Germans with a dark skin and foreigners (Bergdorf 2009: 115).

After the Wall fell, militant skinheads and neo-Nazis were able to travel unhindered to the West and acquire bomber jackets, Doc Martens and other characteristic forms of attire. The Monday evening demonstrations in Leipzig, which had been instrumental in the felling of the SED in late 1989, underwent significant changes, with the extreme right becoming bolder and more visible on the streets, especially from about mid December, as increasing numbers of extremists came across from the West. All right-wing extremist West German organisations had been active since the autumn in seeking to extend their influence in the GDR, among them the NPD (German National Democratic Party) and *Republikaner*, who attempted to put down organisational roots, the *Nationale Alternative* with its close links to the GDR's extremist skinhead scene, and the *Deutsche Volksunion* (DVU), which focused on mobilising supporters rather than creating organisational structures (Madloch 2000: 91–92; Bugiel 2002: 122–30; Wagner 2002: 24–25; Engelbrecht 2008: 121). However, the political influence of all four parties remained low in the face of the overwhelming popularity of the broad-based conservative Alliance for Germany constructed by West German chancellor Helmut Kohl from the Christian Democratic Union, Democratic Awakening and the German Social Union. Two other forms of right-wing extremism received decisive impulses from the West: first, the small militant organisations such as the *Deutsche Alternative*, the *Freiheitliche Deutsche Arbeiterpartei*, the *Nationale Offensive*, the *Nationalistische Front*, the *Nationale Liste* and the *Wiking-*

*Jugend* (Wagner 2002: 22); and, second, the diffuse militant sub-cultural scene which was influenced in part by, and entwined with, the burgeoning skinhead scene and its other East German forbears.

Care must be taken, however, not to exaggerate elements of continuity, notably the legacy of political socialisation and restrictive collective educational practices within the authoritarian structures of the GDR, as an explanation for rising xenophobic violence, the desecration of Jewish graves and other elements of right extremism in the five *New Länder* of eastern Germany. Family, peers and the Western media, for example, offered alternative models and values to the official organs of socialisation, and account must also be taken of disenchantment with the political system of the unified Germany, the search for a clear national identity, and the classic reaction of the more vulnerable social strata to abrupt socio-economic dislocation in a society undergoing rapid modernisation after 1990 (Bugiel 2002: 333–46; Friedrich 2002: 21–30, 64; Engelbrecht 2008: 129–41, 164–65).

# Notes

1. See the Stasi report in Süß, (1993: 89).
2. BStU, MfS, ZA, HAXXII, no.17625, 'Einschätzung über die in der DDR existierenden Skinheads bzw. Skinheadgruppen sowie über die Ergebnisse und Wirksamkeit der politisch-operativen Arbeit zur Verhinderung und Unterbindung der von derartigen Jugendlichen ausgehenden Gefährdungen der Sicherheit und Ordnung', 21 December 1987, pp.139–40. The Stasi acknowledged that the figures were not complete as some MfS regional administrations had not submitted full returns.
3. Ibid., pp.141, 144–45.
4. BStU, MfS, ZA, HA XX/AKG/II, no.97, 'Einschätzung ausgewählter Probleme der politisch-operativen Lageentwicklung unter jugendlichen Personenkreisen im Jahre 1985/86', 20 October 1986, p.15.
5. BStU, MfS, ZA, HA XXII, no.17625, 'Einschätzung über die im Territorium existierenden Skinheads bzw. Skinheadgruppen sowie über die Ergebnisse und Wirksamkeit der von derartigen Jugendlichen ausgehenden Gefährdungen der Sicherheit und Ordnung', 1 December 1987, pp.120–21, 125–26. The report indicates that seventeen Stasi IMs and twenty-four unofficial informers of the criminal police were involved in operations against skinhead groups.
6. BStU, MfS, ZA, HA XX/AKG, no.5936, 'Berichterstattung zur Einschätzung der Lage bezüglich der Bekämpfung des mit neofaschistischer Gesinnung verbundenen öffentlichen kriminellen und rowdyhaften Verhaltens Jugendlicher und deren Zusammenschlüsse', 29 March 1988, p.53.
7. BStU, MfS, ZA, HA IX, no.1278, 'Auswertungsbericht/Information zu einer Gruppierung von Skinheads in Cottbus', 6 May 1988, p.2.
8. See Bartl (1989: 106–7); he draws here on the work of Wolfgang Brück, a member of Leipzig's ZIJ.
9. 'Michael' was imprisoned after the *Zionskirche* incidents in 1987 and joined the NPD after his release in February 1990.

10. The circular is in Süß (1993: 69).

11. BStU, MfS, ZA, HA IX, no.772, 'Information über die Wirksamkeit der Vorbeugung und Bekämpfung der Jugendkriminalität sowie kriminell gefährdeter und krimineller Gruppierungen Jugendlicher und Jugenderwachsener in den Jahren 1984 bis 1986', 13 March 1987, p.89.

12. BStU, MfS, ZA, HA XX, no.898, 'Abschrift des vom Informationsbüro der Zionskirche herausgegebenen Materials zur Berliner Skinheadszene', May 1988, p.3.

13. Rauhut (1996: 179–80). Rauhut states that two members of Elements of Crime were Stasi informers over many years. Mario would be stabbed to death in 1992 by right-wing extremists.

14. BStU, MfS, ZA, HA IX, no.1588, 'Urteil: In Namen des Volkes', 1987, pp.29–49; BStU, MfS, ZA, HA XXII, no.17625, 'Stellungnahme zur Information vom 3.11.1987 über ein Gespräch mit KLATT, Alexander', 9 November 1987, pp.89–90. See also Hockenos (1993: 79–80) and Waibel (1996: 56–57).

15. On the first point, see the IM report in BStU, MfS, HA XXII, no.17625, 'Information entgegengenommen durch Hauptmann Kreutel am 22. Oktober 1987', 23 October 1987, p.41.

16. Ibid., 'Operativ-Information Nr. 267/435/87', 6 November 1987, p.86.

17. SAPMO-BA DY30/885, 'Bericht über tätliche Angriffe auf Angehörige der Volkspolizei durch Mitglieder einer "Skinhead"-Gruppierung am 01.11.1987 in Velten, Kreis Oranienburg', 16 November 1987, pp.10–12. This report was compiled by the SED's Central Commmittee Department for Security.

18. BStU, MfS, ZA, HA XX/AKG, no.5941, 'Berichterstattung über im Bezirk Potsdam existierende Jugendliche, die sich mit neofaschistischer Gesinnung öffentlich kriminell und rowdyhaft verhalten', 10 May 1988, p.90.

19. SAPMO-BA DY30/885, 'Bericht über tätliche Angriffe auf Angehörige der Volkspolizei durch Mitglieder einer "Skinhead"-Gruppierung am 01.11.1987 in Velten, Kreis Oranienburg', 16 November 1987, pp.14–17.

20. Süß (1993: 74–77).

21. BStU, MfS, ZA, HA IX, no.1588, 'Vorschlag zur Durchführung einer gerichtlichen Hauptverhandlung vor geladener Öffentlichkeit', November 1987, pp.152–55; BStU, MfS, ZA, HA XXII, no,17625, 'Einschätzung über die in der DDR existierenden Skinheads bzw. Skinheadgruppen sowie über die Ergebnisse und Wirksamkeit der politisch-operativen Arbeit zur Verhinderung und Unterbindung der von derartigen Jugendlichen ausgehenden Gefährdungen der Sicherheit und Ordnung', 21 December 1987, pp.150–51; also Ross (2000: 133–34).

22. BStU, MfS, ZA, HA IX, no.1588, 'Generalstaatsanwaltschaft der DDR: "Zum Verlauf des Verfahrens gegen Busse und andere"', 14 December 1987, p.12.

23. BStU, MfS, ZA, HA XX, no.898, Letter to Honecker, 30 December 1987, p.417. The Council of Ministers, the Volkskammer and other organs of state also received a copy.

24. BStU, MfS, ZA, HA IX, no.9875, Wendland to Krenz, 4 December 1987, pp.3, 5–6.

25. BStU, MfS, ZA, HA IX, no.1588, 'Generalstaatsanwaltschaft der DDR: "Zum Verlauf des Verfahrens gegen Busse und andere"', 14 December 1987, p.12.

26. BStU, MfS, ZA, HA XX/AKG, no.5940, 'Information über die Lage unter negativ-dekadenten Jugendlichen im Bezirk Dresden', 23 September 1988, pp.114, 116.

27. Süß (1993: 87).

28. Repression by court sentencing continued until the end of SED rule. Some 289 criminal proceedings linked to right-wing extremism were carried out between January and December 1989; see Madloch (2000: 81).

29. Neue Berliner Illustrierte, no.29, 1988, pp.28–29. A Stasi report put the number of graves at 251: BStU, MfS, ZA, HA XX/AKG, no.80, 'Einschätzung aktueller Erscheinungsformen gesellschaftswidrigen Auftretens und Verhaltens negativ-dekadenter Jugendlicher sowie Ergebnisse und Wirksamkeit der politisch-operativen Arbeit zu ihrer Unterbindung und Zurückdrängung', 23 March 1989, pp.16–17.

30. BStU, MfS, ZA, HA XXII, no.17625, 'Einschätzung über die in der DDR existierenden Skinheads und Skinheadgruppen sowie über die Wirksamkeit der politisch-operativen Arbeit zur

Verhinderung und Unterbindung der von derartigen Jugendlichen ausgehenden Gefährdungen der Sicherheit und Ordnung', 21 December 1987, p.147.

31. BStU, MfS, ZA, HA XX/AKG, no.80, 'Einschätzung aktueller Erscheinungsformen gesellschaftswidrigen Auftretens und Verhaltens negativ-dekadenter Jugendlicher sowie Ergebnisse und Wirksamkeit der politisch-operativen Arbeit zu ihrer Unterbindung und Zurückdrängung', 23 March 1989, p.24. This is not the exact number as three Stasi regional administrations failed to submit figures. The IMs engaged in spying on other 'negative decadent' groups were punks (103, with 25 in Potsdam), heavy-metal fans (89) and goths (36). While a fourth unit, the Dresden Regional Administration, did not submit figures for heavy metallers and goths, it did so for punks.

32. BStU, MfS, ZA, HA XX/AKG, no.5941, 'Berichterstattung über im Bezirk Potsdam existierende Jugendliche, die sich mit neofaschistischer Gesinnung öffentlich kriminell und rowdyhaft verhalten', 7 April 1988, pp.83, 86.

33. BStU, MfS, ZA, HA XX/AKG, no.5940, 'Berichterstattung über Entwicklungstendenzen unter negativ-dekadenten Jugendlichen sowie die Wirkamkeit politisch-operativen Maßnahmen zur Zurückdrängung – Zeitraum 1.1.1988 bis 20.5.1988', 30 May 1988, p.32. The Rostock Region used nine IMSs against skinheads, including three informers active in cross-regional surveillance. Six 'negative decadent' groups – skinheads, punks, heavy-metal fans – with about sixty-five members were active in the Rostock Administrative Region: BStU, MfS, ZA, HA XX/AKG, no.5941, 'Berichterstattung zur weiteren Zurückdrängung und Verhinderung von Gefährdungen der Sicherheit und Ordnung, die von kriminell/rowdyhaften Jugendlichen/Jugenderwachsenen ausgehen', 30 March 1988, p.7.

34. BStU, MfS, ZA, IMB 'Seemann' – Reg.-Nr. XV/3726/80 – II, passim.

35. Behnke (1979: 21). The reference here is to young 'negative decadent' IMs in the so-called political underground, not to skinheads and punks.

36. Rüddenklau (1992: 135). The information about Vogt as a punk and his involvement in the *Zionskirche* incidents is taken from: BStU, MfS, ZA, HA XXII, no.17625, 'Stellungnahme zur Information vom 3.11.1987 über ein Gespräch mit KLATT, Alexander', 9 November 1987, p.93.

37. BStU, MfS, ZA, HA XX/AKG, no.80, 'Einschätzung aktueller Erscheinungsformen gesellschaftswidrigen Auftretens und Verhaltens negativ-dekadenter Jugendlicher sowie Ergebnisse und Wirksamkeit der politisch-operativen Arbeit zu ihrer Unterbindung und Zurückdrängung', 23 March 1989, p.15.

38. BStU, MfS, ZA, HA XX/AKG, no.5941, 'Berichterstattung über Jugendliche, die sich mit neofaschistischer Gesinnung öffentlich kriminell und rowdyhaft verhalten', 8 June 1988, p.99.

39. BStU, MfS, ZA, HA XX/AKG, no.80, 'Einschätzung aktueller Erscheinungsformen gesellschaftswidrigen Auftretens und Verhaltens negativ-dekadenter Jugendlicher sowie Ergebnisse und Wirksamkeit der politisch-operativen Arbeit zu ihrer Unterbindung und Zurückdrängung', 23 March 1989, pp.13–14. The figures for Potsdam and Cottbus include sympathisers. The report estimates that there were about 3,510 'negative decadent' young people, including 1,151 heavy-metal fans and 603 goths. The main department of the criminal police estimated that, without including sympathisers, about 15,000 persons could be regarded as forming a violent-oriented right-wing extremist potential between 1989 and 1990 (see Bugiel 2002: 148).

40. Weiss, 'Die neue alte Gefahr. Junge Faschisten in der DDR', *Kontext*, March 1989. *Kontext* was an East German samizdat publication, and Weiss's article was written in November 1988. It can be found at: http://.bln.de.k.weiss/tx_gefahr.htm.

41. BStU, MfS, ZA, HA XX/AKG, no.80, 'Einschätzung aktueller Erscheinungsformen gesellschaftswidrigen Auftretens und Verhaltens negativ-dekadenter Jugendlicher sowie Ergebnisse und Wirksamkeit der politisch-operativen Arbeit zu ihrer Unterbindung und Zurückdrängung', 23 March 1989, p.14.

42. BStU, MfS, ZA, HA IX, no.1278, 'Auswertungsbericht/Information zu einer Gruppierung von Skinheads in Cottbus', 6 May 1988, p.2.

43. Opposition to the National Socialist policy of mass murder was expressed by twenty skinheads from Frankfurt/Oder and Strausberg who were targeted in Stasi preliminary court proceedings

(EVs) in 1989: BStU, MfS, ZA, HA XX/AKG, no.5941, 'Information über herausgearbeitete Motivationen bei Ermittlungsverfahren', 18 July 1989, pp.172–73

44. BStU, MfS, ZA, HA XXII, no.17625, 'Einschätzung über die in der DDR existierenden Skinheads bzw. Skinheadgruppen sowie über die Ergebnisse und Wirksamkeit der politisch-operativen Arbeit zur Sicherheit und Unterbindung der von derartigen Jugendlichen ausgehenden Gefährdungen der Sicherheit und Ordnung', 21 December 1987, p.141.

45. BStU, MfS, ZA, HA IX, no.1278, 'Befragungsprotokoll', 30 March 1988, p.111.

46. 'Studie über Erkenntnisse der Kriminalpolizei zu neofaschistischen Aktivitäten in der DDR', in Kinner and Richter (2000: 280–81).

47. BStU, MfS, ZA, HA XXII, no.17625, 'Referat zur Skinhead-Problematik', 23 November 1987, p.17. On the other hand, the Main Department refuted this, depicting the skins as hardworking in line with their 'so-called Germanness': ibid., 'Einschätzung über die in der DDR existierenden Skinheads bzw. Skinheadgruppen sowie über die Ergebnisse und Wirksamkeit der politisch-operativen Arbeit zur Verhinderung und Unterbindung der von derartigen Jugendlichen ausgehenden Gefährdungen der Sicherheit und Ordnung', 21 December 1987, p.142.

48. BStU, MfS, ZA, HA IX, no.1278, 'Auswertungsbericht/Information zu einer Gruppierung von Skinheads in Cottbus', 6 May 1988, p.2. The report was compiled by two officers of the Cottbus Region criminal police.

49. Ibid., 'Befragungsprotokoll', 3 March 1988, p.106.

50. Ibid., 'Befragungsprotokoll', 7 April 1988, p.118.

51. Ibid., 'Auswertungsbericht/Information zu einer Gruppierung von Skinheads in Cottbus', 6 May 1988, p.4.

52. See the documents in ibid., March-April 1988, pp.106, 118, 138, 149.

53. Süß (1993: 29–30).

54. BStU, MfS, ZA, HA XX/AKG, no.5936, 'Berichterstattung zur Einschätzung der Lage bezüglich der Bekämpfung des mit neofaschistischer Gesinnung verbundenen öffentlichen kriminellen und rowdyhaften Verhaltens Jugendlicher und deren Zusammenschlüsse', 30 June 1988, p.85.

55. BStU, MfS, ZA, HA XXII, no.18438, 'Information: Problemhintergründe für die Lebensweise junger Bürger, die zu Punk- und Skin-Head-Gruppen gehören', [1987], pp.59–61. This is part of the Niederländer and Korfes report.

56. BStU, MfS, ZA, HA XXII, no.17625, 'Einschätzung über die in der DDR existierenden Skinheads bzw. Skinheadgruppen sowie über die Ergebnisse und Wirksamkeit der politisch-operativen Arbeit zur Verhinderung und Unterbindung der von derartigen Jugendlichen ausgehenden Gefährdungen der Sicherheit und Ordnung', 21 December 1987, p.148.

57. BStU, MfS, ZA, HA XXII, no.18438, 'Information: Problemhintergründe für die Lebensweise junger Bürger, die zu Punk- und Skin-Head-Gruppen gehören', [1987], p.61.

58. BStU, MfS, ZA, HA XX/AKG, no.80, 'Einschätzung aktueller Erscheinungsformen gesellschaftswidrigen Auftretens und Verhaltens negativ-dekadenter Jugendlicher sowie die Ergebnisse und Wirksamkeit der politisch-operativen Arbeit zu ihrer Unterbindung und Zurückdrängung', 23 March 1989, pp.22–23.

59. Ibid., p.29.

60. BStU, MfS, ZA, HA XXII, no.17625, 'Einschätzung über die in der DDR existierenden Skinheads bzw. Skinheadgruppen sowie über die Ergebnisse und Wirksamkeit der politisch-operativen Arbeit zur Verhinderung und Unterbindung der von derartigen Jugendlichen ausgehenden Gefährdungen der Sicherheit und Ordnung', 21 December 1987, pp.146–47.

61. BStU, MfS, Außenstelle Halle, BV Halle, Sachakten, no.774, 'Information über aktuelle Erscheinungsformen gesellschaftswidrigen Auftretens und Verhaltens negativ-dekadenter Jugendlicher sowie Ergebnisse und Wirksamkeit der politisch-operativen Arbeit zu ihrer Unterbindung und Zurückdrängung', 13 April 1989, pp.24–28.

62. BStU, MfS, ZA, HA XXII, no.18438, 'Forschungsauftrag', 29 April 1988, p.52.

63. MDA, 'Jugendszene – Jugendrichtungen – Problemgruppen', [1989], pp.5a, 23. The report drew on four ZIJ investigations.

64. BStU, MfS, ZA, HA XXII, no.18438, 'Forschungsauftrag' 18 April 1988, p.52. See also Süß (1993: 33–36).
65. Kinner and Richter (2000: 273–74); some 500 transcripts of other persons questioned were also used.
66. Only 3 per cent were 26 years or older and females accounted for about 20 per cent (Niederländer 1990: 16; Kinner and Richter 2000: 279–80). However, exceptionally, some groups had a higher proportion of older members. The age of members of the militant fascist SS-Division Walter Krüger in Wolgast ranged between sixteen and 36 years; the group included teachers and other 'respected' citizens (see Ross 2000: 100). The group was founded in July 1988 as the *SS-Geheimorganisation Wolgast*, changing its name in January 1989 (BStU, MfS, ZA, HA IX, no.2372, pp.8–11, 33–35).
67. Weiss's 'our children' thesis first appeared in *Die Kirche*, June 1988. This was the weekly newspaper of the Evangelical Church of Berlin-Brandenburg (see Siegler 1991: 152–53).
68. BStU, MfS, ZA, HA XXII, no.17625, 'Referat zur Skin-Problematik', 23 November 1987, pp.6–7.
69. BStU, MfS, ZA, HA XX/AKG/II, no.97, 'Einschätzung ausgewählter Probleme der politisch-operativen Lageentwicklung unter jugendlichen Personenkreisen im Jahre 1985/86', 20 October 1986, pp.5–8.
70. The reference to TV and radio programmes can be found in ibid., p.19. The popularity of West German radio and TV programmes among apprentices, pupils and young workers did, of course, constitute a significant counter to the indoctrination strategies of the SED.
71. Süß (1993: 79–86).
72. BStU, MfS, ZA, HA XX/AKG, no.80, 'Einschätzung aktueller Erscheinungsformen gesellschaftswidrigen Auftretens und Verhaltens negativ-dekadenter Jugendlicher sowie Ergebnisse und Wirksamkeit der politisch-operativen Arbeit zu ihrer Unterbindung und Zurückdrängung', 23 March 1989, pp.10–13.
73. Süß (1993: 25).
74. BStU, MfS, ZA, HA IX, no.10712, 'Thesen zur Beratung am 16. Februar 1989', 10 February 1989, p.19.
75. BStU, MfS, ZA, HA XXII, no.18438, 'Diskussionsgrundlage – Ursachen und Ursachenbekämpfung', 24 February 1988, p.80.
76. Ibid., 'Information: Problemhintergründe für die Lebensweise junger Bürger, die zu Punk- und Skin-Head-Gruppen gehören', [1987], pp.61, 62.
77. Friedrich and Schubarth (1991: 1056). The percentages derive from adding together the categories 'antipathy' and 'great antipathy'.
78. Weiss's comments appeared in *Kontext*, 8 March 1988, pp.9–10. The critique of the FDJ is to be found in SAPMO-BA DY 24/14101, 'Zum Beitrag von Konrad Weiss: "Die neue alte Gefahr. Junge Faschisten in der DDR"', [n.d.], pp.1–6.
79. SAPMO-BA DY30/839, Staatliches Komitee für Rundfunk – Redaktion Monitor. 5. Beitrag, Moderator Hans-Joachim Wiese, DLF, 3 August 1988, pp.138–140.
80. Süß (1993: 5–7, 40–42).
81. Ibid: 7, 41; see also Engelbrecht (2008: 91–94).
82. BStU, MfS, ZA, HA IX, no.1278, 'Befragungsprotokoll', 27 April 1988, p.101.
83. We return to the development of anti-semitism and racism in the 1980s in Chapter 8.

*Chapter 8*

# CONCLUSION: MINORITIES, PRESENT AND PAST

## Minority Groups in the New Social and Political Landscape

*I*n this chapter we reflect on the minorities' varied interactions with the party-state for an appreciation of the East German political system and in particular the potential, however limited, for agency in society. We also review the radically different environment in which minorities found themselves after the sudden collapse of SED hegemony in 1989. While the new Berlin Republic established by the incorporation of the GDR into the Federal Republic in October 1990 introduced a series of civil rights, greater individual autonomy and a curtailment of comprehensive and intrusive state repression, it was far from a paradise for the contract workers and several other minorities discussed in this book. The socio-economic situation in the five eastern *Länder* bore little resemblance to the flourishing landscape promised by West German chancellor Helmut Kohl in the run-up to the crucial *Volkskammer* election in March 1990. The conditions surrounding economic, monetary and social union in the treaty between the FRG and the GDR in May 1990 and the sudden exposure to market forces led to the rapid disintegration of the East German economy and the closure of many firms. Unemployment soared to over one million by mid 1991.

Under these circumstances, most foreign contract workers, essentially economic migrants, had little option but to return home. Until the promulgation of new legislation in 1993 and 1997, the remaining former contract workers, mainly Vietnamese, were caught up in a nightmare of uncertainty over jobs, residency and civil rights. They also experienced a backlash of xenophobic violence in towns such as Rostock and Hoyerswerda. In September 1991, a week-long siege by extreme right-wing youths of an apartment block for asylum seekers in Hoyerswerda caused serious injury to several residents. Some neighbours were sympathetic to the acts, many others were passive bystanders. Eleven months later, right-wing youths and west German neo-Nazis staged an orgy of intimidation against more than 200 gypsy asylum seekers and about 120 Vietnamese and their children at a hostel in the Lichtenberg district of Rostock. The police were unable – or perhaps unwilling – to prevent them storming and setting fire to the hostel.

The outburst of violence in Rostock, Hoyerswerda, Cottbus, Leipzig, Wismar, Quedlinburg and elsewhere in eastern Germany constituted the behavioural expression of an amalgam of social vulnerability, ideological uncertainties, an unavoidable reshaping of national and personal identities, and prejudice against foreigners. Cries of 'Foreigners out!' and 'Jobs for Germans!' in these towns articulated the widespread antipathy picked up in opinion polls. An investigation conducted in Saxony-Anhalt and Saxony in March- and April 1992 among 4,300 young people aged 14 to 25 found that 54 per cent of the Saxons were negatively disposed to foreigners (Schubarth 1992: 87). While the physical and verbal attacks attracted a degree of popular sympathy, the exclusive nationalism of the radical right-wing political parties was supported by only a small minority of easterners and numerous public demonstrations against the Rostock pogrom and other hostile acts signalled a commitment by many ordinary east Germans, politicians, churches and grassroots organisations to a peaceful and more tolerant society.

Jehovah's Witnesses were in a more fortunate position than the former contract workers: free of state-directed persecution, their organisation was officially recognised as early as March 1990 by the Modrow government, and sixteen years later, after much controversy, by the Berlin *Land* government as a corporation in public law. Like the Witnesses, the East German Jewish Communities experienced immediate benefits from the end of SED rule: in April 1990, after the accession to power of a CDU-led coalition government under Lothar de Mazière, the East German parliament asked for forgiveness for the persecution suffered since 1945 by East Germany's Jews. Yet the reconfiguration of the Jewish Communities into state associations, and especially the merger of the capital's Community with its western counterpart in January 1991, was an uneasy process due to the disparity in size and influence, personal rivalries, eastern resistance to abrupt change, and differences over political biographies. Several officials in east Berlin, like the chair Peter Kirchner, felt that their interests were overridden by the larger and wealthier organisation. Further, many east German Jews, whether or not members of Communities, were obliged to reassess their national, Jewish and social identities in the unfamiliar and sometimes alien environment of the new all-German state.

Two significant developments provided a boost to Jewish life in the *New Länder*: the contribution to the regeneration of Judaism outside communal confines by organisations such as the Jewish Cultural Union, which had emerged from 'We for Ourselves' (*Wir für uns*), and, secondly, an increase in the number of eastern congregations as a result of the immigration into Germany of Jews from the former Soviet Union. The Russian Jews, who had endured prejudice and discrimination in their own country, enjoyed the status of *Kontingentflüchtling* (a refugee as a member of a contingent) under legislation regulating the admission of migrants and within the context of humanitarian aid. However, a plethora of adjustment problems accompanied the influx: though highly educated, many had inadequate German, poor employment prospects and little knowledge of Jewish traditions or faith. The process of integration for Russian Jews was further impeded by the perceptible increase since 1992 of racism and anti-semitic abuse, especially by young east Germans, as well as by violence and overt intimidation initiated by neo-Nazis and militant skinheads. In the first half of the 1990s, Jewish cemeteries were desecrated in Dresden, Guben and east Berlin, and, in September 1992, the Jewish barrack at the former National Socialist concentration camp of Buchenwald was the target of an arson attack. Anti-semitism was highly correlated with xenophobia, although hostility was more widespread against the primary targets, foreigners (Kurthen 1997: 59–61, 79–82).

Other sites of violence and xenophobia were football stadiums and adjacent areas, whether in Leipzig, Berlin or Dresden. Clashes between police and hooligans on the occasion of a game on 3 November 1990 between Sachsen Leipzig and FC Berlin (formerly Chemie Leipzig and BFC Dynamo respectively) ended in the tragic death of the eighteen-year-old Mike Polley, accidentally shot by police, and in serious injury to several policemen and fans. A few months later, in March 1991, the European Cup encounter between Dynamo Dresden and Partisan Belgrade was abandoned on account of crowd trouble. Serious outbreaks of public disorder, on a scale not seen in the GDR, continued into the new millennium: in May 2006, rampaging fans led to the abandonment of the local derby between Union Berlin and Dynamo Berlin, and in February of the following year, local hooligans brutally attacked police at the end of Lok Leipzig's home cup match against Erzgebirge Aue's reserve team. A partial explanation for the initial upsurge in violence and aversion to foreigners not only at football grounds but elsewhere should be sought in the security vacuum after the collapse of the *ancien regime* when long-established state and party controls had been removed and in the greater space afforded for the expression of xenophobic prejudices and behaviour by skinhead militants and other violently oriented groups.

## Popular Perceptions of the GDR Past and *Ostalgie*

Earlier manifestations of aversion to foreigners and racism have been discussed in previous chapters revolving around socio-economic chauvinism in a shortage society against foreign contract workers, the fragile socio-political legitimacy and fractured state identity of the GDR, the SED and Stasi's entrenched friend–foe image, and the suppression of liberal values. The unmastered past in the sense of a prescribed anti-fascism that underplayed the victimhood of Jews, Jehovah's Witnesses, homosexuals and other minorities reinforced a lack of tolerance of 'outsiders'. How these general determinants played out during East German times varied according to age, gender, economic status, political position, locality and time period. Similarly, after 1989, political and socio-demographic factors exerted a strong influence over east German reactions to the dramatic collapse of state socialism, escalating unemployment and entry into the challenging world of the capitalist FRG. Once the overwhelming majority in the GDR, its former citizens now formed a demographic minority in the new united Germany. One of their most common reactions was a form of nostalgia or *Ostalgie* for the loss of the social networks associated with employment by state firms and other fundamental features of the former centralised economic system (Dennis 2000b: 89). The nostalgia for the social security and general social paternalism associated with the East German administrative command system was prevalent not only among east Germans, especially older cohorts, but also among Vietnamese who had lost their contracted jobs and in many cases had had to resort to illicit street trading.

East German nostalgia was underpinned by resentment at perceived west German stripping of the assets of their country; on the other hand, west Germans tended to see this as whingeing by easterners unable or unwilling to cope with the pressures of transformation and ungrateful for the vast financial transfers from west to east. So sharp were the differences in perception and mutual antipathy that the weekly magazine *Der Spiegel* evoked, in late 1992, the notion of a 'Wall in the head'. Positive memories of selected features of the GDR and shared experiences (including negative ones) as east Germans, together with a sense of discrimination and the disparity of treatment since unification, persuaded some to wish for the return of the GDR. According to a survey conducted in 1999 by the Social Science Research Centre Berlin-Brandenburg, 9 per cent of east Germans were in favour of such a development (Winkler 1999: 53).[1] However, not only was this a minority view but east–west value convergence was apparent with regard to political pluralism, the territorial integrity of the new nation-state and consumerism. And not all in the GDR garden had blossomed: while mostly resentful of attempts to equate the GDR with the Third Reich and to depict the country as little more than a totalitarian coercive system with the Stasi at the epicentre, public opinion surveys identified east Germans' negative perceptions of intrinsic characteristics of the GDR, such as restrictions on travel, doping in elite sport, the shortage of supplies, spying on colleagues, the SED monopoly of power and being held under tutelage.[2] It is these and other restrictions on human and civil rights which was a central feature of the experiences of minorities in the GDR.

## Differing Experiences

Despite frequent professions of commitment to religious freedom, to the provision of opportunities for youth to develop their talents creatively and to the GDR's solidarity with peoples seeking freedom from colonialism, Honecker's state retained many of the restrictions and oppressive features associated with the Stalinist period. A hierarchy of victimhood is discernible, too. Jews and Jehovah's Witnesses suffered severe persecution in the 1950s and neither subsequently received due compensation from the SED for their ordeals under the National Socialist regime. After the failure to crush the Jewish and Witness organisations, the latter endured more systematic persecution by the East German state than the numerically smaller and less active Jewish congregations. Although the goths, football fans, punks, heavy metallers and skinheads of the 1980s were oppressed in a more sporadic manner than the Witnesses, they too were infiltrated by informers, fined and sometimes imprisoned. Official attitudes towards the skinheads were ambivalent and policies fluctuated: after initial toleration and an underestimation of the threat posed by the militant element, the SED and Stasi attempted to smash the embryonic movement after the *Zionskirche* incident in October 1987. Foreign workers, whether from Mozambique, Poland, Cuba or Vietnam, came into a different category of treatment and perception for while they were not regarded as politically hostile or 'negative decadents', they were discouraged from mixing freely with the local population and were deported for minor infringements of their contracts. Stasi informers and their own group leaders kept them under regular surveillance. In light of the experiences of these ethnic, peace and religious groups as well as youthful sub-cultural minorities, it is difficult to agree with Panikos Panayi's conclusion in his wide-ranging survey of ethnic minorities in Germany, at least as regards the GDR, that the two German states had been transformed over four decades into 'relatively tolerant republics' (Panayi 2000: 234).

But why were the SED and its agents of control so hostile to many minority groups and, despite the unofficial Church-state concordat of 1978, to the Protestant churches too? While an anathema to difference and the rejection of pluralism can be traced back to authoritarian and militaristic traditions and the allergy to modernity embedded in the prewar KPD, this negativity was reinforced by the mutual hostility and suspicion associated with the ideological, cultural, economic and political contest between the Soviet and American superpowers and their respective allies after 1945. As was discussed in Chapters 2 and 3, the 1950s in particular were a time of intense persecution of the Protestant churches, the Jehovah's Witnesses and Jewish groups as part of the SED campaign against religion. The campaign typified ,the paranoia against purported enemies at a time when the Cold War was at freezing point. Although the religious organisations managed to survive the threat to their existence, they were still regarded as actual or potential agents of the West and, in the case of the Jewish Communities, of Zionism too. Even during periodic thaws in the Cold War, they were never free of the suspicion of pursuing political-ideological subversion on behalf of the forces of imperialism, especially those of West Germany and the U.S.A. Furthermore, the very presence of religious communities challenged the organisational monopoly of the SED, offered an alternative faith to Marxism-Leninism and in short threatened the authority and power of the SED regime.

As for what in the eyes of authority were 'deviant' or 'negative decadent' youth sub-cultures – such as punks, football hooligans and skinheads – they allegedly constituted a threat to the social, political and moral health of society, a contamination that, supposedly emanating from the West, was fostered internally by an unstable family and peer environment. The skinheads were reclassified in the late 1980s as 'hostile negatives' – that is, as representing a higher level of threat and enmity to the socialist order. The accentuated friend–foe image, which found expression in the classification of so many minority groups as 'negatives', functioned as a form of regime consolidation and ideological cohesion for SED functionaries and Stasi personnel. A loyal and ideologically uncritical security service was regarded as vital for a state situated on the precarious geographical and political border between two rival systems, and one which suffered throughout its history from a legitimacy gap as the more vulnerable of the two German republics. While the Stasi and police remained largely loyal to the SED until the fall of the Wall, monism stifled the kind of critical attitude that might have helped narrow the GDR's chronic legitimacy deficit and obviate the dementedly precautionary security principle.

Cold War dichotomies do not, however, adequately explain the negative aspects of the regime's treatment of, and attitudes towards, Mozambican, Cuban and Vietnamese workers from countries that had engaged in armed struggle against South Africa and the U.S.A., the enemies of world socialism. While emphasising in public statements the community of interest between the GDR and liberated states, the discouragement of close private contacts with East Germans reflected officialdom's fears of the exotic 'other', an intrinsic suspicion of foreignness, and a sensitivity to popular socio-economic chauvinism among the local East German population, especially in the industrial conurbations with high concentrations of foreign workers. In this respect, it is appropriate to refer to East Germans as 'insiders' and foreigners as 'outsiders' in a shortage economy and in a society where inter-cultural contacts were both limited and prescribed. Vietnamese and Polish workers in particular were seen by sections of the indigenous population as a threat to the heavily state-subsidised but, in the 1980s, declining East German levels of prosperity. While notions of cultural superiority vis-à-vis foreign groups – such as Poles, Vietnamese, Russians and Mozambicans – can be located in East German popular culture, many East Germans harboured feelings of inferiority vis-à-vis their West German sibling and also resented being called upon 'to learn to be victorious' from the generally unloved big brother in the Soviet Union. Intermittent popular xenophobia against Poles points to an overlapping of attitudes between the state and some East Germans in the interstices of society. The regime did not hesitate to tap anti-Polish sentiment when, in the early 1980s, it sought to insulate the GDR from the threat posed by the Solidarity movement to communist rule in Poland. There are also various indications of a confluence between popular and state antipathy towards Judaism and the East German Jewish community. However, while prejudice and oppression were widespread in the 1950s, less so later, there can be no equation of the GDR with the Third Reich and its genocidal racism and the elimination of those that Nazi social theorists deemed to be 'life unworthy of life'..

## The Limits to Dictatorship

Despite the numerous restrictions imposed on minorities, the SED and its many willing helpers – whether police, Stasi officers, informers or party activists – enjoyed only limited success in realising their goals. The term 'limited success' covers the failure to stamp out the Jehovah's Witnesses in the 1950s and 1960s and to subvert and destroy the militant skinhead, punk and football hooligan subcultures of the 1980s. Even the closely observed foreign workers managed to form their own loosely-structured ethnic networks and to pursue limited informal and entrepreneurial contacts with East Germans. If the small Jewish congregations and the umbrella State Association of Jewish Communities were often outwardly compliant, then this was partly because of the devastation wrought by the Holocaust, the losses due to flight during the anti-semitic campaigns of the 1950s, and the inexorable process of senescence. Communal weaknesses notwithstanding, many Jewish leaders and Community members voiced their opposition to the regime's anti-Zionism and from the end of the 1970s numerous attempts were made, both within and outside the Communities, to reactivate and foster Jewish identity and traditions.

How to explain the limited reach of the SED and its numerous associates? First, the higher echelons of the regime were frequently at odds over policy and its implementation. This is illustrated by the fierce internal party opposition to Ulbricht in the 1950s and his eventual overthrow in 1971, by internal disagreements over the liberalisation of cultural policy, by criticism of Honecker's commitment to an economically distorting subvention of social policy, and by serious reservations about his rapprochement with West Germany. Some of these divisions were the result of personal rivalries and of differences over the adjustment of Marxist-Leninist ideology to political and economic change, others concerned territorial disputes and contests over status, resources and influence between large central and regional bureaucracies in a series of shifting alignments and interactions.

Second, the multiplicity of tasks performed by SED and state organs often stretched material and staffing resources to their limits. This is reflected in the inability to provide adequate accommodation for the sharp increase in the number of Vietnamese and Mozambican workers in the late 1980s, especially in areas with a housing shortage. Also, time and time again, the Stasi and police complained about the burden of their work. While this was a typical institutional lament, the two organisations were undoubtedly carrying out jobs for which they were either ill-equipped (such as combating inefficiencies in the state-run economy) and for which, and this is particularly relevant for the Stasi district service units, they simply lacked the requisite resources. This meant, in the 1980s, a concentration on those areas that enjoyed a higher priority, such as the ultimately unsuccessful stemming of the emigration movement, rather than on foreign workers, football fans and Jehovah's Witnesses.

Third, changes in the international environment help account for fluctuations in policies and levels of coercion in a state that was highly penetrated by external forces, whether Soviet or West German, especially in the economic, cultural and security spheres. This kind of development is apparent in the SED's shift to a philo-semitic policy in the late 1980s when Honecker was wooing the U.S.A. to help boost foreign trade and the GDR's external legitimacy. The GDR's sensitivity and vulnerability to external perceptions and influences also helps account for the greater emphasis on the 'softer' forms of repression typical of the era of détente. Further, the GDR's growing dependence on West German economic assistance and financial transfers gave the SED pause for thought in the way it treated so-called 'hostile decadents' and 'hostile negatives', not wishing to damage the reputation of the GDR by creating martyrs of well-known individuals and groups, especially those attached to the alternative peace movement.

Finally, even when the security forces were authorised to take more open and vigorous measures – as, for example, when the skinheads became a major target on account of their links to militant right-wing extremism – the state could not smash them as it encountered a powerful sub-cultural solidarity. This was also true of football hooligans and, to a lesser extent, punks despite their enfeeblement by internal divisions and by rivalries for cultural hegemony within the alternative scene. While the state might imprison individuals, it could not so easily suppress ideas and beliefs, especially those that were transmitted and sustained by the Western mass media and personal contacts over the German–German border. Despite an elaborate apparatus of censorship and security, and despite the Party leadership's hopes for a homogenisation of culture, individual and collective identities could no more be extinguished in the GDR than had been the youth sub-cultures of the Third Reich. In the view of Detlev Peukert, the survival of the Edelweiß Pirates and the swing movement demonstrated that, 'National Socialism, even after years in power, still did not have a complete grip on German society: indeed that parts of society increasingly slipped from its grasp, the more it perfected its formal armoury of methods of organisation and repression' (Peukert 1987: 175). This assessment is valid, too, for the 20,000 or so East German Jehovah's Witnesses whose fervent religious faith enabled them to survive persecution, both as an organisation and as individuals, and to continue to perform their vital mission work.

Returning to the issues raised in Chapter 1 concerning typologies of rule and authority as social practice, it has been argued throughout this book that while the GDR was a form of dictatorship to which the label 'totalitarian' is not inappropriate in the 1950s and early 1960s, it is better designated 'post-totalitarian' from the mid-to-late 1960s onwards with a greater emphasis on 'operational decomposition' and on the implementation of an informal social contract with the population. In addition to acknowledging the application of less brutal forms of authority, post-totalitarianism also recognises an asymmetry in the balance of power and the co-optation of legions of citizens as members of political parties and mass organisations and as informers in the Stasi apparatus of surveillance. Even members of minority groups were enmeshed in the clandestine structures of the state, notably as IMs or as regular confidants of state and party organisations.

But despite the undoubtedly extensive and intrusive modes of ideological and political control, society in the East German dictatorship was far from moribund and undifferentiated and was capable of influencing the operation of the levers of power and the framing of official policy. 'Subjects' could not simply be ruled or dictated to by fiat or coerced into loyalty. Punks, skinheads, gays, Jehovah's Witnesses, Jews by faith and origin, foreign workers, Sorbs and members of the unofficial peace movement were able to exert their own sense of worth and self-determination in myriad ways. Our conclusion is that the history of minorities in the GDR, and that of the country in general, cannot be explained from a simplistic top-down perspective; even the well-established communist dictatorships of the twentieth-century did not command the arsenal of controls so effectively as to dictate and command from above, much as they might wish to do so, and nor were the organs of party and state so cohesive as is often depicted. The shape of the system, in which a multiplicity of state organs and a diversity of social groups and actors were embedded and interacted among and between each other, has been a matter of lively debate and skilful historiographical draughtsmanship. Whether it can be encapsulated as a 'honeycomb full of cross-cutting little cells' (Fulbrook 2005: 292) or a Rubik's cube, rather than a hierarchical pyramid, any configuration should embrace the intersecting and shifting layers of complicity, accommodation, retreat, cooperation, idealism and human agency typical of the experiences and actions of the wide range of minorities explored in this book.

## Notes

1. About 1,500 east German adults were questioned. Support for the return of the GDR was above average among unemployed respondents.
2. The research was conducted in 1997 by the Social Science Research Centre Berlin-Brandenburg: see Winkler (1997: 49).

# REFERENCES

## Articles and Books

Agethen, M. (2002) 'Gedenkstätten und antifaschistische Erinnerungskultur in der DDR', in Agethen, M., Jesse, E., and Neubert, E. (eds), *Der missbrauchte Antifaschismus: DDR-Staatsdoktrin und Lebenslüge der deutschen Linken*, Freiburg, Basel and Vienna: Herder, pp.128–44.

Ahbe, T. (2005) 'Der Osten aus der Sicht des Westens: Die Bilder von den Ostdeutschen und ihre Konstrukteure', in Bahrmann, H., and Links, C. (eds), *Am Ziel vorbei: Die deutsche Einheit – eine Zwischenbilanz*, Berlin: Ch. Links Verlag, pp.268–81.

Almond, G.A., and Roselle, L. (1993) 'Model Fitting in Communism Studies', in Fleron, F.J., and Hoffmann, E.P. (eds), *Post-communist Studies and Political Science: Methodology and Empirical Theory in Sovietology*, San Francisco and Oxford: Boulder, pp.27–75.

Anon. (2004) 'Was hat das mit unserer sauberen Gesellschaft zu tun? Der Geheimdienst dirigierte die Putzkolonne', in Rauhut, M., and Kochan, T. (eds), *Bye bye, Lübben City: Bluesfreaks, Tramps and Hippies in der DDR*, Berlin: Schwarzkopf and Schwarzkopf, pp.126–33.

———— (2005) 'Provokation, Paranoia und Parties', in Galenza, R., and Havemeister, H. (eds), *Wir wollen immer artig sein ... Punk, New Wave, HipHop, Independent-Szene in der DDR 1980–1990*, 2nd edn., Berlin: Schwarzkopf and Schwarzkopf Verlag, pp.41–50.

Arendt, H. (1951) *The Origins of Totalitarianism*, New York, Harcourt, Brace.

Association of Jewish Communities (1988) *Beware Lest the Nightmare Recur: Remembrance of the Nazi Pogrom in the Night of 9 November 1938*, Dresden: Verlag Zeit im Bild.

Axen, H. (1996) *Ich war Diener der Partei. Autobiographische Gespräche mit Harald Neubert*, Berlin: Edition Ost.

Bajohr, F. (2008) 'Vom antijüdischen Konsens zum schlechten Gewissen: Die deutsche Gesellschaft und die Judenverfolgung 1933–1945', in Bajohr, F., and Pohl, D., *Massenmord und schlechtes Gewissen: Die deutsche Bevölkerung, die NS-Führung und der Holocaust*, Frankfurt am Main: Fischer Taschenbuch Verlag, pp.15–79.

Barker, P. (2000) *Slavs in Germany: The Sorbian Minority and the German State since 1945*, Lampeter: Edward Mellen Press.

Bauerkämper, A. (2005) *Die Sozialgeschichte der DDR*, Munich: R. Oldenbourg Verlag.

Behrends, J.C., Lindenberger, T., and Poutrus, P. (eds) (2003) *Fremd und Fremd-Sein in der DDR: Zu historischen Ursachen der Fremdenfeindlichkeit in Ostdeutschland*, Berlin: Metropol.

Bergdorf, H. (2009) 'Fruchtbare Felder: Rechtsextremismus in Ostdeutschland', *Deutschland Archiv* 42(1): 115–20.

Berger, J. (2009) *Meine zwei Halbzeiten: Ein Leben in Ost und West*, Reinbek: Rowohlt.

Besier, G. (2003) 'Vorurteile, Verfolgungen und Verbote: Zur sozialen Diskriminierung der Zeugen Jehovas am Beispiel der "Christlichen Verantwortung"', in Besier, G., and Vollnhals, C. (eds), *Repression und Selbstbehauptung: Die Zeugen Jehovas der NS- und der SED-Diktatur*, Berlin: Duncker and Humblot, pp.135–58.

Bessel, R., and Jessen, R. (eds) (1996) *Die Grenzen der Diktatur: Staat und Gesellschaft in der DDR*, Göttingen: Vandenhoeck and Ruprecht.

Beyme, K. von (1998) 'The Concept of Totalitarianism: A Reassessment after the End of Communist Rule', in Siegel, A. (ed.), *The Totalitarian Paradigm after the End of Communism: Towards a Theoretical Reassessment*, Amsterdam: Rodopi, pp.38–54.

Bodemann, Y.M. (1996) 'Reconstructions of History: From Jewish Memory to Nationalized Commemoration of Kristallnacht in Germany', in Bodemann, Y.M. (ed.), *Jews, Germans, Memory: Reconstructions of Jewish Life in Germany*, Ann Arbor: University of Michigan Press, pp.179–223.

Boehlke, M., and Gericke, H. (eds) (2007) *Punk in der DDR: Too Much Future*, Berlin: Verbrecher Verlag.

Borneman, J., and Peck, J.M. (1995) *Sojourners: The Return of German Jews and the Question of Identity*, Lincoln: University of Nebraska Press.

Borries, F. von, and Fischer, J.-U. (2008) *Sozialistische Cowboys: Der wilde Westen Ostdeutschlands*, Frankfurt am Main: Suhrkamp Verlag.

Braun, J. (2004) 'Sportfreunde oder Staatsfeinde? Fußballfans im Visier der Staatsmacht', *Deutschland Archiv* 37(3): 440–47.

Braun, J., and Teichler, H. J. (2003) 'Fußballfans im Visier der Staatsmacht', in Teichler, H.J. (ed.), *Sport in der DDR: Eigensinn, Konflikte, Trends*, Cologne: SPORT und BUCH, pp.561–86.

Brehmer, H. (1991) 'Anti-Semitismus im Geheimdienst', *Zwie-Gespräch* 3: 25–28.

Breslauer, G.W. (1978) 'On the Adaptability of Soviet Welfare-state Authoritarianism', in Ryavec, K.W. (ed.), *Soviet Society and the Communist Party*, Amherst: University of Massachusetts Press, pp.3–25.

Breuer, W. (ed.) (1990) *Ausländerfeindlichkeit in der ehemaligen DDR: Studie zu Ursachen, Umfang und Auswirkungen von Ausländerfeindlichkeit im Gebiet der ehemaligen DDR und zu den Möglichkeiten ihrer Überwindung*, Cologne: Institut für Sozialforschung und Gesellschaftspolitik.

Breyvogel, W. (2005) 'Bunte Vielfalt und Anarchie: Jugendkultur und Rockmusik der 1980er Jahre', in Stiftung Haus der Geschichte der Bundesrepublik Deutschland (ed.), *Rock! Jugend und Musik in Deutschland*, Berlin: Ch. Links Verlag, pp.86–95.

Broder, H.M. (1993) *Erbarmen mit den Deutschen*, Hamburg: Hoffmann and Campe.

Broszinsky-Schwabe, E. (1990) 'Die DDR-Bürger im Umgang mit "Fremden": Versuch einer Bilanz der Voraussetzungen für ein Leben in einer multikulturellen Welt', in Kleff, S., Broszinsky-Schwabe, E., Albert, M-T., Marburger, H., and Karsten,

M-E., *BRD-DDR: Alte und neue Rassismen im Zuge der deutsch-deutschen Einigung*, Frankfurt am Main: Verlag für Interkulterelle Kommunikation, pp.18–44.

Brown, A. (1983) 'Pluralism, Power and the Soviet Political System: A Comparative Perspective', in Solomon, S.G. (ed.), *Pluralism in the Soviet Union: Essays in Honour of Gordon Skilling*, London: Macmillan, pp.61–107.

Brück, W. (1992) 'Skinheads als Vorboten der Systemkrise: Die Entwicklung des Skinhead-Phänomens bis zum Untergang der DDR', in Heinemann, K.-H., and Schubarth, W. (eds), *Der antifaschistische Staat entläßt seine Kinder: Jugend und Rechtsextremismus in Ostdeutschland*, Cologne: PapyRossa Verlag, pp.37–46.

Bugiel, B. (2002) *Rechtsextremismus in der DDR und in den neuen Bundesländern von 1982–1998*, Münster: LIT Verlag.

Bundesministerium des Innern (ed.) (2005) *Verfassungsschutzbericht 2005*, Cologne: Druckhaus Locher.

Büscher, W., and Wensierski, P. (1984) *Null Bock auf DDR: Aussteigerjugend im anderen Deutschland*, Reinbek: Spiegel-Verlag.

Dahrendorf, R. (1967) *Society and Democracy in Germany*, New York: Doubleday.

Dennis, M. (1988) *German Democratic Republic: Politics, Economics and Society*, London: Pinter.

——— (1993) *Social and Economic Modernization in Eastern Germany from Honecker to Kohl*, London: Pinter.

——— (2000a) *The Rise and Fall of the German Democratic Republic, 1945–1990*, Harlow: Pearson/Longman.

——— (2000b) 'Perceptions of GDR Society and its Transformation: East German Identity Ten Years after Unity', in Flockton, C., Kolinsky, E., and Pritchard, R. (eds), *The New Germany in the East: Policy Agendas and Social Developments since Unification*, London: Frank Cass, pp.87–105.

——— (2004) 'Constructing East Germany: Interpretations of GDR History since Unification', in Dennis, M., and Kolinsky, E. (eds), *United and Divided: Germany since 1990*, Oxford: Berghahn, pp.17–35.

Dennis, M., with LaPorte, N. (2003) *The Stasi: Myth and Reality*, Harlow: Pearson/Longman.

Deutscher Bundestag (ed.) (1995) *Materialien der Enquete-Kommission 'Aufarbeitung von Geschichte und Folgen der SED-Diktatur in Deutschland'*, 9 vols., Baden-Baden: Nomos Verlag, and Frankfurt am Main: Suhrkamp Verlag.

Diedrich, T., and Ehlert, H. (1998) '"Moderne Diktatur" – "Erziehungsdiktatur" – "Fürsorgediktatur" oder was sonst? Das Herrschaftssystem der DDR und der Versuch seiner Definition: Ein Tagungsbericht', *Potsdamer Bulletin für Zeithistorische Studien* 12: 17–25.

Dirksen, A. (2006) 'Children of Jehovah's Witnesses under Two Dictatorships', *Religion, State and Society* 34(2): 191–210.

Dirksen, H.-H. (2000) '"Zeugen Jehovas müssen verschwinden": Der vergebliche Kampf der Staatssicherheit', in Yonan, G. (ed.), *Im Visier der Stasi: Jehovas Zeugen in der DDR*, Niedersteinbach: Edition Corona, pp.15–23.

——— (2001a) *'Keine Gnade den Feinden unserer Republik': Die Verfolgung der Zeugen Jehovas in der SBZ/DDR 1945–1990*, Berlin: Duncker and Humblot.

——— (2001b) 'Jehovah's Witnesses in the German Democratic Republic', in Hesse, H. (ed.), *Persecution and Resistance of Jehovah's Witnesses During the Nazi Regime*, Bremen: Edition Temmen, pp.210–28.

Dirksen, H.-H., and Dirksen, A. (2001) 'Kinder der Zeugen Jehovas: Staatliche Ausgrenzung und soziale Repression', in Vollnhals, C., and Weber, J. (eds), *Der Schein der Normalität: Alltag und Herrschaft in der SED-Diktatur*, Munich: Olzog Verlag, pp.218–86.

Döring, H.-J. (1999) '*Es geht um unsere Existenz*': Die Politik der DDR gegenüber der Dritten Welt am Beispiel Mosambik und Äthiopien, Berlin: Ch. Links Verlag.

Dornberg, J. (1969) *The Other Germany: Europe's Emerging Nation behind the Berlin Wall*, New York: Doubleday.

Eckert, R. (2008) 'Schuld und Zeitgeschichte: Zwölf Thesen zur Auseinandersetzung mit den deutschen Diktaturen', *Deutschland Archiv* 41(1): 114–21.

Eckhardt, U., and Nachama, A. (eds) (2003) *Jüdische Berliner: Leben nach der Schoa*, Berlin: Jaron Verlag and Stiftung 'Neue Synagoge Berlin – Centrum Judaicum'.

Edelman, R. (2002) 'A Small Way of Saying "No": Moscow Working Men, Spartak Soccer, and the Communist Party, 1900–1945', *American Historical Review* 107(5): 1441–74.

Eichler, K. (2001) *Die Zeugen Jehovas in Gera: Eine Dokumentation*, Wissenschaftliche Hausarbeit, Friedrich-Schiller-Universität Jena.

Eisenfeld, B. (2002) 'Rechtsextremismus in der DDR: Ursachen und Folgen', in Agethen, M., Jesse, E., and Neubert, E. (eds), *Der missbrauchte Antifaschismus: DDR-Staatsdoktrin und Lebenslüge der deutschen Linken*, Freiburg, Basel and Vienna: Herder, pp.221–36.

Elsner, E.-M., and Elsner, L. (1992) *Ausländer und Ausländerpolitik in der DDR*, hefte zur ddr-geschichte, 2, Berlin: "Helle Panke" and Gesellschaftswissenschaftliches Forum.

Elsner, E.-M., and Elsner, L. (1994) *Zwischen Nationalismus und Internationalismus: Über Ausländer und Ausländerpolitik in der DDR 1949–1990*, Rostock: Norddeutscher Hochschulschriften Verlag.

Engelbrecht, J. (2008) *Rechtsextremismus bei ostdeutschen Jugendlichen vor und nach der Wende*, Frankfurt am Main, Berlin and Bern: Peter Lang.

Engelmann, R. (1995) 'Zum Wert der MfS-Akten', in Deutscher Bundestag (ed.), *Materialien der Enquete-Kommission 'Aufarbeitung von Geschichte und Folgen der SED-Diktatur in Deutschland'*, vol.8, Baden-Baden: Nomos Verlag, and Frankfurt am Main: Suhrkamp Verlag, pp.243–96.

Engler, W. (1999) *Die Ostdeutschen: Kunde von einem verlorenen Land*, Berlin: Aufbau-Verlag.

Eschwege, H. (1984) *Selbstbehauptung und Widerstand. Deutsche Juden im Kampf um Existenz und Menschenwürde, 1933–1945*, Hamburg: Christians.

——— (1991) *Fremd unter meinesgleichen: Erinnerungen eines Dresdner Juden*, Berlin: Ch. Links Verlag.

——— (ed.) (1966) *Kennzeichen J. Bilder, Dokumente, Berichte zur Geschichte der Verbrechen des Hitlerfachismus an den deutschen Juden 1933–1945*, East Berlin: VEB Deutscher Verlag der Wissenschaften.

Ewald, M. (1994) *Ich war der Sport*, Berlin: Elefanten Press.

Farin, K. (1997) 'Urban Rebels: Die Geschichte der Skinheadbewegung', in Farin, K. (ed.), *Die Skins: Mythos und Realität*, Berlin: Ch. Links Verlag, pp.9–68.

Farin, K., and Hauswald, H. (1998) *Die dritte Halbzeit: Hooligans in Berlin-Ost*, Bad Tölz: Verlag Thomas Tilsner.

Fehér, F., Heller, A., and Márkus, M. (1983) *Dictatorship over Needs. An Analysis of Soviet Societies*, Oxford and New York: Basil Blackwell.

Feige, M. (1999) *Vietnamesische Studenten und Arbeiter in der DDR und ihre Beobachtung durch das MfS*, Magdeburg: Landesbeauftragte für die Unterlagen des Staatssicherheitsdienstes der ehemaligen DDR in Sachsen-Anhalt, Sachbeiträge (10).

Fenemore, M. (2007) *Sex, Thugs and Rock 'n' Roll: Teenage Rebels in Cold-war East Germany*, Oxford: Berghahn Books.

FES (1991) *Zur Situation der ehemaligen vietnamesischen Gastarbeiter: Eine Studie über die aus der einstigen DDR vorzeitig zurückgekehrten Arbeitnehmer/Innen in der SR Vietnam*, Bonn: Friedrich-Ebert-Stiftung, Forschungsinstitut.

Fox, T.C. (1999) *Stated Memory: East Germany and the Holocaust*, Rochester, NY, and Woodbridge: Camden House.

Franke, T., and Pätzug, V. (2006) *Von Athen nach Althen: Die Fanszene von Lok Leipzig zwischen Europacup und Kreisklasse*, Dresden: SDV Verlag.

Fricke, K.W. (1979) *Politik und Justiz in der DDR: Zur Geschichte der politischen Verfolgung 1945–1968: Berichte und Dokumentation*, Cologne: Verlag Wissenschaft und Politik.

——— (1984) *Die DDR-Staatssicherheit: Entwicklung, Strukturen, Aktionsfelder*, Cologne: Verlag Wissenschaft und Politik.

Friedrich, A.J., and Schneider, R. (2005) 'Leipzig von unten: Punk- und Independent-Szene, Aktionen, Zeitschriften und Bands', in Galenza, R., and Havemeister, H. (eds), *Wir wollen immer artig sein … Punk, New Wave, HipHop, Independent-Szene in der DDR 1980–1990*, 2nd edn., Berlin: Schwarzkopf and Schwarzkopf, pp.102–45.

Friedrich, C.J. (1969) 'The Evolving Theory and Practice of Totalitarian Regimes', in Friedrich, C.J., Curtis, M., and Barber, B.R., *Totalitarianism in Perspective: Three Views*, London: Pall Mall Press, pp.123–64.

Friedrich, C.J., and Brzezinski, Z.K. (1965) *Totalitarian Dictatorship and Autocracy*, 2nd edn., New York: Praeger.

Friedrich, W. (1990) 'Mentalitätswandel der Jugend in der DDR', *Aus Politik und Zeitgeschichte*, 13 April, 16/17: 25–37.

——— (2002) *Rechtsextremismus: Ein Ergebnis der DDR-Sozialisation?* Leipzig: Rosa-Luxemburg-Stiftung Sachsen.

Friedrich, W., and Schubarth, W. (1991) 'Ausländerfeindlichkeit und Rechtsextremismus bei der ostdeutschen Jugend', *Deutschland Archiv* 24(10): 1052–65.

Fuchs, J. (1994) *Unter Nutzung der Angst: Die 'leise' Form des Terrors – Zersetzungsmaßnahmen des MfS*, BF informiert, no.2, Berlin: BStU.

Fuge, J. (1997) *Ein Jahrhundert Leipziger Fußball: Die Jahre 1945 bis 1989*, Leipzig: Connewitzer Verlagsbuchhandlung.

——— (2004) 'Von Fußball-Anhängern und Schlachtenbummlern', in Willmann, F. (ed.), *Fußball-Land DDR: Anstoß, Abpfiff, Aus*, Berlin: Eulenspiegel Verlag, pp.93–100.

——— (2009) *Der Rest von Leipzig: BSG Chemie Leipzig*, Kassel: AGON Sportverlag.

Fulbrook, M. (2004) 'Ein ganz "normales Leben"? Neue Forschungen zur Sozialgeschichte der DDR', in Timmermann, H. (ed.), *Das war die DDR: DDR-Forschung im Fadenkreuz von Herrschaft, Außenbeziehungen, Kultur und Souveränität*, Münster: LIT Verlag, pp.115–34.

———— (2005) *The People's State: East German Society from Hitler to Honecker*, New Haven, CT: Yale University Press.

Furian, G., and Becker, N. (2000) *'Auch im Osten trägt man Westen': Punks in der DDR – und was aus ihnen geworden ist*, Berlin: Verlag Thomas Tilsner.

Galenza, R. (2005) 'Zwischen "Plan" und "Planlos": Punk in Deutschland', in Stiftung Haus der Geschichte der Bundesrepublik Deutschland (ed.), *Rock! Jugend und Musik in Deutschland*, Berlin: Ch. Links Verlag, pp.96–103.

Galenza, R., and Havemeister, H. (2007) 'Entweder Oder im Niemandsland', in Boehke, M., and Gericke, H. (eds), *Punk in der DDR: Too Much Future*, Berlin: Verbrecher Verlag, pp.81–101.

Garbe, D. (1994) *Zwischen Widerstand und Martyrium: Die Zeugen Jehovas im Dritten Reich*, Munich: R. Oldenbourg Verlag.

Gay, R. (2002) *Safe Among the Germans: Liberated Jews After World War II*, New Haven, CT: Yale University Press.

Gebhard, M. (ed.) (1971) *Die Zeugen Jehovas: Eine Dokumentation über die Wachtturmgesellschaft*, Schwerte/Ruhr: Verlag Hubert Freistühler.

Geller, J.H. (2005) *Jews in Post-Holocaust Germany, 1945–1953*, Cambridge: Cambridge University Press.

Gericke, H., (2005) 'Schatten voraus! Punk, im Jahr zwölf nach Punk', in Galenza, R., and Havemeister, H. (eds), *Wir wollen immer artig sein … Punk, New Wave, HipHop, Independent-Szene in der DDR 1980–1990*, 2nd edn., Berlin: Schwarzkopf and Schwarzkopf, pp.94–100.

Gericke, H., and Havemeister, H. (2007) 'Too Much Future' in Boehlke, M., and Gericke, H. (eds.), *Punk in der DDR: Too Much Future*, Berlin: Verbrecher Verlag, pp. 7–38.

Gieseke, J. (2001) *Mielke-Konzern: Die Geschichte der Stasi 1945–1990*, Stuttgart and Munich: Deutsche-Verlags-Anstalt.

———— (2003a) 'Volkspolizei und Staatssicherheit: Zum inneren Sicherheitsapparat der DDR', in Lange, H.-J. (ed.), *Die Polizei der Gesellschaft: Zur Soziologie der Inneren Sicherheit*, Opladen: Leske and Budrich, pp.93–120.

———— (2003b) 'Die Einheit von Wirtschafts-, Sozial- und Sicherheitspolitik: Militarisierung und Überwachung als Problem einer DDR-Sozialgeschichte der Ära Honecker', *Zeitschrift für Geschichtswissesnschaft* 51(11): 996–1021.

Giullianotti, R., and Armstrong, G. (1997) 'Introduction: Reclaiming the Game – An Introduction to the Anthropology of Football', in Armstrong, G., and Giulianotti, R. (eds.), *Entering the Field. New Perspectives on World Football*, Oxford and New York: Berg, pp.264–97.

Gläser, A. (2007) 'Es fährt ein Zug nach Nirgendwo', in Willmann, F. (ed.), *Stadionpartisanen: Fans und Hooligans in der DDR*, Berlin: Verlag Neues Leben, pp.11–18.

Granata, C. (2009) 'The Cold War Politics of Cultural Minorities: Jews and Sorbs in the German Democratic Republic, 1976–1989', *German History* 27(1): 60–83.

Grimmer, R., and Irmler, W. (2002) 'Hauptaufgaben und Methoden der Abwehr', in Grimmer, R., Irmler, W., Opitz, W., and Schwanitz, W. (eds), *Die Sicherheit: Zur Abwehrarbeit des MfS*, vol.1, Berlin: Edition Ost, pp.239–331.

Groehler, O. (1993) '"Juden erkennen wir nicht an"', *Konkret*, March, 3: 50–54.

———— (1995) 'Antifaschismus und jüdische Problematik in der SBZ und der frühen DDR', in Groehler, O., and Keßler, M., *Die SED-Politik, der Antifaschismus und die Juden in der SBZ und der frühen DDR*, Berlin: Gesellschaftswissenschaftliches Forum, pp.5–31.

Grundmann, S., Müller-Hartmann, I., and Schmidt, I. (1991) 'Ausländer in Ostdeutschland', *BISS Public* 1(3): 6–75.

Gruner-Domić, S. (1996) 'Zur Geschichte der Arbeitskräfteemigration in die DDR: Die bilateralen Verträge zur Beschäftigung ausländischer Arbeiter (1961–1989)', *Internationale wissenschaftliche Korrespondenz zur Geschichte der deutschen Arbeiterbewegung* 32(2): 204–30.

Hacke, G. (2000) 'Zwischen Duldung und Illegalität', in Yonan, G. (ed.), *Im Visier der Stasi: Jehovas Zeugen in der DDR*, Niedersteinbach: Edition Corona, pp.264–97.

—— (2003) 'Die Perzeption der Zeugen Jehovas unter der nationalsozialistischen und der kommunistischen Diktatur', in Besier, G., and Vollnhals, C. (eds), *Repression und Selbstbehauptung: Die Zeugen Jehovas unter der NS- und der SED-Diktatur*, Berlin: Duncker and Humblot, pp.309–28.

Hackert-Lemke, H., and Unterbeck, H. (1999) '"…das war in der DDR so festgelegt…": Betreuerinnen erinnern sich an ausländische Vertragsarbeiter', in Adler, H. et al. (eds), *Zwischen Räumen: Studien zur sozialen Taxonomie des Fremden*, Berlin: Berliner Blätter, pp.87–104.

Hahn, A. (2007) 'Ausbruch aus der Langweile', in Willmann, F. (ed.), *Stadionpartisanen: Fußballfans und Hooligans in der DDR*, Berlin: Neues Leben, pp.155–74.

Hall, S. (1981) 'Notes on Deconstructing "the Popular"', in Samuel, R. (ed.), *People's History and Socialist Theory*, London: Routledge and Kegan Paul, pp.227–40.

Harsch, D. (2007) *Revenge of the Domestic: Women, the Family, and Communism in the German Democratic Republic*, Princeton, NJ: Princeton University Press.

Hartewig, K. (2000) *Zurückgekehrt: die Geschichte der jüdischen Kommunisten in der DDR*, Cologne, Weimar and Vienna: Böhlau Verlag.

Hasselbach, I. (1996) *Führer-Ex: Memoirs of a Former Neo-Nazi*, London: Chatto and Windus.

Havel, V. (1989) *Living in Truth*, trans. A.G. Brain, London: Faber and Faber.

Hecht, J. (2001) 'Archivalische Quellen des Staatssicherheitsdienstes zur Gesellschaftsgeschichte der DDR', in Timmermann, H. (ed.), *Die DDR in Deutschland: Ein Rückblick auf 50 Jahre*, Berlin: Duncker and Humblot, pp.405–24.

Heider, P. (1998) 'Die Gesellschaft für Sport und Technik (1952–1990)', in Diedrich, T., Ehlert, H., and Wentzke, R. (eds), *Im Dienst der Partei: Handbuch der bewaffneten Organe der DDR*, Berlin: Ch. Links Verlag, pp.169–99.

Hensel, J. (2004) *After the Wall: Confessions from an East German Childhood and the Life that Came Next*, trans. J. Chase, New York: Public Affairs.

Herf, J. (1997) *Divided Memory: The Nazi Past in the Two Germanys*, Cambridge, MA: Harvard University Press.

Hertle, H.-H., and Sälter, G. (2006) 'Die Todesopfer an Mauer und Grenze: Probleme einer Bilanz des DDR-Grenzregimes', *Deutschland Archiv* 40(4): 667–76.

Hesse-Lichtenberger, U. (2002) *Tor! The Story of German Football*, London: WSC Books.

Hirch, W. (2000) 'Erarbeitung einer "Dokumentation" über Jehovas Zeugen als MfS-Auftragswerk', in Yonan, G. (ed.), *Im Visier der Stasi: Jehovas Zeugen in der DDR*, Niedersteinbach: Edition Corona, pp.53–66.

—— (2001) 'Die wissenschaftliche Darstellung der "Zersetzung" in Abschlussarbeiten der Juristischen Hochschule Potsdam', in Hirch, W. (ed.),

*Zersetzung einer Religionsgemeinschaft: Die geheimdienstliche Bearbeitung der Zeugen Jehovas in der DDR und Polen*, Niedersteinbach: Edition Corona, pp.18–65.

—— (2003a) 'Die Politik des Ministeriums für Staatssicherheit gegenüber den Zeugen Jehovas', in Besier, G., and Vollnhals, C. (eds), *Repression und Selbstbehauptung: Die Zeugen Jehovas unter der NS- und der SED-Diktatur*, Berlin: Duncker and Humblot, pp.115–33.

—— (2003b) *Die Glaubensgemeinschaft der Zeugen Jehovas während der SED-Diktatur: Unter besonderer Berücksichtigung ihrer Observierung und Unterdrückung durch das Ministerium für Staatssicherheit*, Frankfurt am Main: Peter Lang.

Hockenos, P. (1993) *Free to Hate: The Rise of the Far Right in Post-communist Eastern Europe*, London: Routledge.

Horn, M., and Weise, G. (eds) (2004) *Das große Lexikon des DDR-Fußballs*, Berlin: Schwarzkopf and Schwarzkopf.

Horschig, M. (2005) 'In der DDR hat es nie Punks gewesen', in Galenza, R., and Havemeister, H. (eds), *Wir wollen immer artig sein … Punks, New Wave, HipHop, Independent-Szene in der DDR 1980–1990*, 2nd edn., Berlin: Schwarzkopf and Schwarzkopf, pp.17–40.

Hough, J.F. (1977) *The Soviet Union and Social Science Theory*, Cambridge, MA: Harvard University Press.

Hübner, P., and Tenfelde, K. (eds) (1999) *Arbeiter in der SBZ/DDR*, Essen: Klartext Verlag.

Huong, N.V. (1999) 'Die Politik der DDR gegenüber Vietnam und den Vertragsarbeitern aus Vietnam sowie die Situation der Vietnamesen in Deutschland heute', in Deutscher Bundestag (ed.), *Materialien der Enquete-Kommission "Überwindung der Folgen der SED-Diktatur im Prozess der deutschen Einheit"*, vol.7(2), Baden-Baden: Nomos Verlag, and Frankfurt am Main: Suhrkamp Verlag, pp.1301–63.

Hürtgen, R. (2001) 'Der Vertrauensmann des FDGB in den siebziger und achtziger Jahren: Funktionsloser Funktionär der Gewerkschaften?' in Hürtgen, R., and Reichel, T. (eds), *Der Schein der Stabilität: DDR-Betriebsalltag in der Ära Honecker*, Berlin: Metropol Verlag, pp.143–58.

Hüttmann, J. (2007) '"De-De-Errologie" im Kreuzfeuer der Kritik: Die Kontroversen um die "alte" bundesdeutsche DDR-Forschung vor und nach 1989', *Deutschland Archiv* 40(4): 671–81.

Illichmann, J. (1997) *Die DDR und die Juden: die deutschlandpolitische Instrumentalisierung von Juden und Judentum durch die Partei- und Staatsführung der SBZ/DDR von 1945 bis 1990*, Frankfurt am Main, Berlin and Bern: Peter Lang.

Jahn, M. (2001) 'Einleitung', in Hirch, W. (ed.), *Zersetzung einer Religionsgemeinschaft: Die geheimdienstliche Bearbeitung der Zeugen Jehovas in der DDR und Polen*, Niedersteinbach: Edition Corona, pp.6–17.

Jarausch, K.H. (1997) 'The German Democratic Republic as History in United Germany: Reflections on Public Debate and Academic Controversy', *German Politics and Society* 15(2): 33–48.

Kaiser, P. (2004) 'Heckenscheren gegen Feindfriseuren. Das Vokabular der Macht: Asozialität, Dekadenz und Untergrund', in Rauhut, M., and Kochan, T. (eds), *Bye bye, Lübben City: Bluesfreaks, Tramps und Hippies in der DDR*, Berlin: Schwarzkopf and Schwarzkopf, pp.267–82.

Kapferer, N. (2000) 'Nostalgia in Germany's New Federal States as a Political and Cultural Phenomenon of the Transformation Process', in Williams, H., Wright, C., and Kapferer, N. (eds), *Political Thought and German Unification: The New German Ideology?* Basingstoke: Macmillan, pp.28–49.

Käppner, J. (1999) *Erstarrte Geschichte: Faschismus und Holocaust im Spiegel der Geschichtswissenschaft und Geschichtspropaganda der DDR*, Hamburg: Ergebnisse Verlag.

Kaufman, J. (1997) *A Hole in the Heart of the World: Being Jewish in Eastern Europe*. London: Viking Penguin.

Kerz-Rühling, I., and Plänkers, T. (2004) *Verräter oder Verführte: Eine psychoanalytische Untersuchung Inoffizieller Mitarbeiter der Stasi*, Berlin: Ch. Links Verlag.

Kessler, M. (1995) *Die SED und die Juden: zwischen Repression und Toleranz. Politische Entwicklungen bis 1976*, Berlin: Akademie Verlag.

Kinner, K., and Richter, R. (eds) (2000) *Rechtextremismus und Antifaschismus*, Berlin: Karl Dietz Verlag.

Klemperer, V. (2004) *The Diaries of Victor Klemperer 1945–59: The Lesser Evil*, trans. M. Chalmers, London: Phoenix.

Knabe, H. (2000) 'Strafen ohne Strafrecht: Zum Wandel repressiver Strategien in der Ära Honecker', in Timmermann, H. (ed.), *Die DDR: Recht und Justiz als politisches Instrument*, Berlin: Duncker and Humblot, pp.91–109.

Kocka, J. (1994) 'Eine durchherrschte Gesellschaft', in Kaeble, H., Kocka, J., and Zwahr, H. (eds.) *Sozialgeschichte der DDR*, Stuttgart: Klett-Cotta, pp. 547–53.

Kocka, J. (1999) 'The GDR: A Special Kind of Modern Dictatorship', in Jarausch, K.H. (ed.), *Dictatorship as Experience: Towards a Socio-cultural History of the GDR*, Oxford: Berghahn Books, pp.371–92.

—— (2003) 'Bilanz und Perspektiven der DDR-Forschung: Hermann Weber zum 75. Geburtstag', *Deutschland Archiv* 36(5): 764–69.

Kolinsky, E. (1999) 'Multiculturism in the Making? Non-Germans and Civil Society in the New Länder', in Flockton, C., and Kolinsky, E. (eds), *Recasting East Germany: Social Transformation after the GDR*, London: Frank Cass, pp.192–214.

—— (2000) 'Unexpected Newcomers: Asylum Seekers and Other Non-Germans in the *New Länder*', in Flockton, C., Kolinsky, E., and Pritchard, R. (eds), *The New Germany in the East: Policy Agendas and Social Developments since Unification*, London: Frank Cass, pp.148–64.

—— (2005a) '"Paradies Ostdeutschland": Migrationserfahrungen ehemaliger Vertragsarbeiter und Vertragsarbeiterinnen aus Vietnam', in Weiss. K., and Dennis, M. (eds), *Erfolg in der Nische? Die Vietnamesen in der DDR und in Ostdeutschland*, Münster: LIT Verlag, pp.97–117.

—— (2005b) 'Meanings of Migration in East Germany and the West German Model', in Dennis, M., and Kolinsky, E. (eds), *United and Divided: Germany since 1990*, Oxford: Berghahn, pp.145–75.

Kölner Kunstverein (ed.) (2005) *Project Migration*, Cologne: DuMont Literatur- und Kunstverlag.

Korfes, G. (1992) '"Seitdem habe ich einen dermaßen Haß": Rechtsextremistische Jugendliche vor und nach der "Wende" – exemplarische Biographien', in Heinemann, K.-H., and Schubarth, W. (eds), *Der antifaschistische Staat entläßt seine Kinder: Jugend und Rechtsextremismus in Ostdeutschland*, Cologne: PapyRossa Verlag, pp.47–63.

Kornai, J. (1992) *The Socialist System: The Political Economy of Communism*, Oxford: Clarendon Press.

Kowalczuk, I.-S., and Wolle, S. (2001) *Roter Stern über Deutschland: Sowjetische Truppen in der DDR 1945 bis 1994*, Berlin: Ch. Links Verlag.

Krüger-Potratz, M. (1991) *Anderssein gab es nicht: Ausländer und Minderheiten in der DDR*, Münster and New York: Waxmann.

Kundera, M. (1983) *The Book of Laughter and Forgetting*, trans. M.H. Heim, Harmondsworth: Penguin.

Kurthen, H. (1997) 'Antisemitism and Xenophobia in United Germany: How the Burden of the Past Affects the Present', in Kurthen, H., Bergmann, W., and Erb, R. (eds), *Antisemitism and Xenophobia in Germany after Unification*, Oxford: Oxford University Press, pp.39–87.

Lange, M.G. (1961) *Politische Soziologie: Eine Einführung*, Berlin and Frankfurt am Main: Verlag Franz Vahlen.

Laqueur, W. (1994) *The Dream That Failed*, Oxford: Oxford University Press.

Ledeneva, A. (1998) *Russia's Economy of Favours: Blat, Networking and Informal Favours*, Cambridge: Cambridge University Press.

Leske, H. (2004) *Erich Mielke, die Stasi und das runde Leder: Der Einfluß der SED und des Ministeriums für Staatssicherheit auf den Fußballsport in der DDR*, Göttingen: Verlag Die Werkstatt.

——— (2007) *Enzyklopädie des DDR-Fußballs*, Göttingen: Verlag Die Werkstatt.

——— (2009) *Vorwärts: Armeefußball im DDR-Sozialismus. Aufstieg und Fall des ASK/ FC Vorwärts Leipzig/Berlin/Frankfurt*, Göttingen: Verlag Die Werkstatt.

Lindenberger, T. (1996) 'Alltagsgeschichte und ihr möglicher Beitrag zu einer Geschichte der DDR', in Bessel, R., and Jessen, R. (eds), *Die Grenzen der Diktatur: Staat und Gesellschaft in der DDR*, Göttingen: Vandenhoeck and Ruprecht, pp.298–325.

——— (1998) 'Die Deutsche Volkspolizei (1945–1990)', in Diedrich, T., Ehlert, H., and Wenzke, R. (eds), *Im Dienst der Partei: Handbuch der bewaffneten Organe der DDR*, Berlin: Ch. Links Verlag, pp.97–152.

——— (1999a) 'Die Diktatur der Grenzen: Zur Einleitung', in Lindenberger, T. (ed.), *Herrschaft und Eigen-Sinn in der DDR: Studien zur Gesellschaftsgeschichte der DDR*, Cologne, Weimar and Vienna: Böhlau Verlag, pp.13–44.

——— (1999b) 'Creating State Socialist Governance: The Case of the Deutsche Volkspolizei', in Jarausch, K.H. (ed.), *Dictatorship as Experience: Towards a Socio-cultural History of the GDR*, Oxford: Berghahn Books, pp.125–141.

——— (2007) 'SED-Herrschaft als soziale Praxis – Herrschaft und "Eigen-Sinn": Problemstellung und Begriffe', in Gieseke, J. (ed.), *Staatssicherheit und Gesellschaft. Studien zum Herrschaftsalltag in der DDR*, Göttingen: Vandenhoeck and Ruprecht, pp.23–47.

Linz, J.J. (2000) *Totalitarian and Authoritarian Regimes*, Boulder, CO: Lynne Riemer.

Linz, J.J., and Stepan, A. (1996) *Problems of Democratic Transition and Consolidation: Southern Europe, South America and Post-communist Europe*, Baltimore, MD: Johns Hopkins University Press.

Löwenthal, R. (1970) 'Development vs. Utopia in Communist Policy', in Johnson, C. (ed.), *Change in Communist Systems*, Stanford, CA: Stanford University Press, pp.33–116.

Lüdtke, A. (1995) 'Introduction: What is the History of Everyday Life and Who Are its Practitioners?' in Lüdtke, A., *The History of Everyday Life: Reconstructing Historical Experiences and Ways of Life*, Princeton, NJ: Princeton University Press, pp.3–40.

—— (1998) 'Die DDR als Geschichte: Zur Geschichtsschreibung über die DDR', *Aus Politik und Zeitgeschichte*, 28 August, 6: 1–16.

Ludz, P.C. (1970) *The German Democratic Republic from the Sixties to the Seventies*, New York: AMS Press.

Luther, J. (2004) 'So rollte den Ball im Osten', in Willmann, F. (ed.), *Fußball-Land DDR: Anstoß, Abpfiff, Aus*, Berlin: Eulenspiegel Verlag, pp.9–21.

Luther, J., and Willmann, F. (2000) *Und niemals vergessen: Eisern Union!* Berlin: BasisDruck.

—— (2003) *BFC: Der Meisterclub*, Berlin: Das Neue Berlin.

Mac Con Uladh, D. (2005a) 'Guests of the Socialist Nation? Foreign Students and Workers in the GDR, 1949–1990', Ph.D. dissertation, University College London.

—— (2005b) 'Die Alltagserfahrungen ausländischer Vertragsarbeiter in der DDR: Vietnamesen, Kubaner, Mozambikaner, Ungarn und andere', in Weiss, K., and Dennis, M. (eds), *Erfolg in der Nische? Die Vietnamesen in der DDR und in Ostdeutschland*, Münster: LIT Verlag, pp.51–68.

McDougall, A. (2004) *Youth Politics in East Germany: The Free German Youth Movement 1946–1968*, Oxford: Clarendon Press.

McNeill, T. (1998) 'Soviet Studies and the Collapse of the USSR: In Defence of Realism', in Cox, M. (ed.), *Rethinking the Soviet Collapse: Sovietology, the Death of Communism and the New Russia*, London: Cassell, pp.51–72.

Madarász, J.Z. (2003) *Conflict and Compromise in East Germany, 1971–1989*, Basingstoke: Palgrave Macmillan.

—— (2006) *Working in East Germany. Normality in a Socialist Dictatorship 1961–79*, Basingstoke: Palgrave Macmillan.

Madloch. N. (2000) 'Rechtsextremismistische Tendenzen und Entwicklungen in der DDR, speziell in Sachsen, bis Oktober 1990', in Kinner, K., and Richter, R. (eds), *Rechtsextremismus und Antifaschismus: Historische und aktuelle Dimensionen*, Berlin: Karl Dietz Verlag, pp.63–145.

Marburger, H., Helbig, G., Kienast, E., and Zorn, G. (1993) 'Situation der Vertragsarbeitnehmer der ehemaligen DDR vor und nach der Wende', in Marburger, H. (ed.), *'Und wir haben unseren Beitrag zur Volkswirtschaft geleistet': Eine aktuelle Bestandsaufnahme der Situation der Vertragsarbeiter der ehemaligen DDR vor und nach der Wende*, Frankfurt am Main: Verlag für Interkulturelle Kommunikation, pp.4–75.

Maser, P. (1989) *Glauben im Sozialismus: Kirchen und Religionsgemeinschaften in der DDR*, Berlin: Verlag Gebr. Holzapfel.

—— (2003) 'Helmut Eschwege: Ein Historiker in der DDR', *Horch und Guck*, 12(4): 21–23.

Mehrländer, U., Ascheberg, C., and Uelzhöffer, J. (1996) *Repräsentativuntersuchung '95: Situation der ausländischen Arbeitnehemer und ihrer Familienangehörigen in der Bundesrepublik Deutschland*, Bonn: Bundesministerium für Arbeit und Sozialordnung.

Meier, H. (1994) 'Identifikation mit der DDR durch ihre Bürger', in Keller, D., Modrow, H., and Wolf, H. (eds), *Ansichten zur Geschichte der DDR*, vol.4, Eggersdorf: Verlag Matthias Kirchner, pp.269–88.

Meining, S. (2002) *Kommunistische Judenpolitik: Die DDR, die Juden und Israel,* Münster: LIT Verlag.

Mende, J. (1991) 'Schwarze Männer mit weißen Westen?' in Friedemann, H. (ed.), *Sparwasser und Mauerblümchen: Die Geschichte des Fußballs in der DDR 1949–1991,* Essen: Klartext Verlag, pp.129–33.

Meng, M. (2005) 'East Germany's Jewish Question: The Return and Preservation of Jewish Sites in East Berlin and Potsdam, 1945–1989', *Central European History* 38(4): 606–36.

Mertens, L. (1997) *Davidstern unter Hammer und Zirkel: die Jüdischen Gemeinden in der SBZ/DDR und ihre Behandlung durch Partei und Staat 1945–1990,* Hildesheim: Georg Olms Verlag.

Meuschel, S. (1992) *Legitimation und Parteiherrschaft in der DDR,* Frankfurt am Main: Suhrkamp Verlag.

_____(2000a) 'Theories of Totalitarianism and Modern Dictatorships: A Tentative Approach', *Thesis Eleven* 61: 87–98.

——— (2000b) 'The Other German Dictatorship: Totalitarianism and Modernization in the German Democratic Republic', *Thesis Eleven* 63: 53–62.

*MfS und Leistungssport* (1994) BStU, Reihe A: Dokumente, 1, Berlin: BStU.

Michael, K. (2005) 'Macht aus diesem Staat Gurkensalat: Punk und die Exerzietien der Macht', in Galenza, R., and Havemeister, H. (eds), *Wir wollen immer artig sein … Punk, New Wave, HipHop, Independent-Szene in der DDR 1980–1990,* 2nd edn., Berlin: Schwarzkopf and Schwarzkopf, pp.72–93.

Monteath, P. (2004) 'The German Democratic Republic and the Jews', *German History* 22(3): 448–68.

Mueller, K. (1998) 'East European Studies, Neo-totalitarianism and Social Science Theory', in Siegel, A. (ed.), *The Totalitarian Paradigm after the End of Communism,* Amsterdam: Rodopi, pp.55–90.

Müggenburg, A. (1996) *Die ausländischen Vertragsarbeitnehmer in der ehemaligen DDR: Darstellung und Dokumentation,* Berlin: Bonner-Universitätsbuchdruckerei.

Müller, B. (1996) *Ausländer im Osten Deutschlands: Eine Rostocker Studie,* Cologne: ISP.

Müller, C.T. (2005) '"O" Sowjetmensch!" Beziehungen von sowjetischen Streitkräften und DDR-Gesellschaft zwischen Ritual und Alltag', in Müller, C.T., and Poutrus, P. (eds), *Ankunft – Alltag – Ausreise: Migration und interkulturelle Begegnung in der DDR-Gesellschaft,* Cologne, Weimar and Vienna: Böhlau Verlag, pp.17–134.

Müller, W. (2003) 'Auch nach 1990: Zweierlei Geschichtsschreibung?' *Jahrbuch für Historische Kommunismusforschung 2003,* Berlin: Aufbau-Verlag, pp.242–67.

Müller-Enbergs, H., with Muhle, H. (2008) *Inoffizielle Mitarbeiter des Ministeriums für Staatssicherheit. Teil 3: Statistiken,* Berlin: Ch. Links Verlag.

Naimark, N.M. (1979) 'Is It True What They're Saying about East Germany?' *Orbis* 23(3): 549–77.

Niederländer, L. (1990) 'Zu den Ursachen rechtsradikaler Tendenzen in der DDR', *Neue Justiz* 44(1): 16–18.

Nimtz, W. et al (1975) *Geschichte. Lehrbuch für Klasse 9,* 6th edn, Berlin: Volk und Wissen Volkseigener Verlag.

Nothnagle, A.L. (1999) *Building the East German Myth: Historical Mythology and Youth Propaganda in the German Democratic Republic, 1945–1989,* Ann Arbor: University of Michigan Press.

Offenberg, U. (1998) *'Seid vorsichtig gegen die Machthaber': die jüdischen Gemeinden in der SBZ/DDR 1945–1990*, Berlin: Aufbau Verlag.

Ohse, M.-D. (2003) *Jugend nach dem Mauerbau*, Berlin: Ch. Links Verlag.

Ostmeyer, I. (2002) *Zwischen Schuld und Sühne: Evangelische Kirche und Juden in SBZ und DDR 1945–1990*, Berlin: Institut Kirche und Judentum.

Ostow, R. (1989) *Jews in Contemporary East Germany: The Children of Moses in The Land of Marx*, Basingstoke: Macmillan.

——— (1996) *Juden aus der DDR und die deutsche Wiedervereinigung: Elf Gespräche*, Berlin: Wichern Verlag.

Oswald, R. (2008) *"Fußball-Volksgemeinschaft": Ideologie, Politik und Fanatismus im deutschen Fußball 1919-1964*, Frankfurt am Main: Campus Verlag.

Panayi, P. (2000) *Ethnic Minorities in Nineteenth and Twentieth Century Germany: Jews, Gypsies, Poles, Turks and Others*, Harlow: Longman.

Peukert, D. (1987) *Inside Nazi Germany: Conformity, Opposition and Racism in Everyday Life*, trans. R. Deveson, London: Penguin.

Pfister, G. (2003) 'The Challenge of Women's Football in East and West Germany: A Comparative Study', *Soccer and Society*, 4 (2–3): 128–48.

Plato, A. von (1998) 'Zur Geschichte des sowjetischen Speziallagersystems in Deutschland: Einführung', in von Plato, A. (ed.), *Sowjetische Speziallager in Deutschland 1945 bis 1950: Studien und Berichte*, Berlin: Akademie Verlag, pp.10–75.

Pleil, I. (2001) *Mielke, Macht und Meisterschaft: Die 'Bearbeitung' der Sportgemeinschaft Dynamo Dresden durch das MfS 1978–1989*, Berlin: Ch. Links Verlag.

Poiger, U.G. (2000) *Jazz, Rock and Rebels: Cold War Politics and American Culture in a Divided Germany*, Berkeley: University of California Press.

Pollack, D. (1999) 'Modernization and Modernization Blockages in GDR Society', in Jarausch, K.H. (ed.), *Dictatorship as Experience: Towards a Socio-cultural History of the GDR*, Oxford: Berghahn Books, pp.27–45.

Polte, W. (1957) *Toor! Spieler des SC Wismut Karl-Marx-Stadt erzählen*, East Berlin: Sportverlag.

Poutrus, P. G., Behrends, J. C., and Kuck, D. 'Historische Ursachen der Fremdenfeindlichkeit in den neuen Bundesländern', *Aus Politik und Zeitgeschichte*, 39: 15–21.

Preuß, T. (1999) 'Stasi, Spaß und E-Gitarren: Die Geschichte der Berliner Punkband Namenlos', in Galenza, R., and Havemeister, H. (eds), *Wir wollen immer artig sein … Punk, New Wave, HipHop, Independent-Szene in der DDR 1980–1990*, 2nd edn., Berlin: Schwarzkopf and Schwarzkopf, pp.51–61.

Queißer, W. (1983) *Jugendstreiche oder Rowdytum?* East Berlin: Verlag Neues Leben.

Raendchen, O. (2000) 'Fremde in Deutschland: Vietnamesen in der DDR', in Hinz, H.-M. (ed.), *Zuwanderungen – Auswanderungen: Integration und Disintegration nach 1945*, Wolfratshausen: Edition Minerva Hermann Farnung, pp.78–101.

Rauhut, M. (1996) *Schalmei und Lederjacke:. Udo Lindenberg, BAP, Underground: Rock und Politik in den achtziger Jahren*, Berlin: Schwarzkopf and Schwarzkopf.

——— (2005) '"Am Fenster": Rockmusik und Jugendkultur in der DDR', in Stiftung Haus der Geschichte der Bundesrepublik Deutschland (ed.), *Rock! Jugend und Musik in Deutschland*, Berlin: Ch. Links Verlag, pp.70–78.

Reagan, R. (2005) 'Im Tal der Ahnungslosen: Untergrund in Dresden', in Galenza, R., and Havemeister, H. (eds), *Wir wollen immer artig sein … Punk, New*

*Wave, HipHop, Independent-Szene in der DDR 1980–1990*, 2nd edn., Berlin: Schwarzkopf and Schwarzkopf, pp.146–59.

Rebiger, B. (2005) *Jewish Berlin: Culture, Religion, Daily Life Yesterday and Today*, Berlin: Jaron Verlag.

Remath, C., and Schneider, R. (eds) (1999) *Haare auf Krawall: Jugendsubkultur in Leipzig 1980 bis 1991*, Leipzig: Connewitzer Verlagsbuchhandlung.

Richert, E. (1961) *Die Sowjetzone in der Phase der Koexistenzpolitik*, Hannover: Niedersächsische Landeszentrale für Politische Bildung.

—— (1968) 'Möglichkeiten und Grenzen der DDR-Forschung', *Deutschland Archiv* 1(2): 144–48.

Riedel, A. (1994) *Erfahrungen algerischer Arbeitsmigranten in der DDR ... 'hatten ooch Chancen, ehrlich!'* Opladen: Leske and Budrich.

Röhr, R. (2001) *Hoffnung, Hilfe, Heuchelei: Geschichte des Einsatzes polnischer Arbeitskräfte in Betrieben des DDR-Grenzbezirks Frankfurt/Oder 1966–1991*, Berlin: Berliner Debatte Wissenschaftsverlag.

Rose, G. (1971) *"Industriegesellschaft" und Konvergenztheorie. Genesis, Strukturen, Funktionen*, East Berlin: Deutscher Verlag der Wissenschaften.

Ross, C. (2002) *The East German Dictatorship: Problems and Perspectives in the Interpretation of the GDR*, London: Arnold.

Ross, C., and Grix, J. (2002) 'Approaches to the German Democratic Republic', in Grix, J. (ed.), *Approaches to the Study of Contemporary Germany: Research Methodologies in German Studies*, Birmingham: University of Birmingham Press, pp.47–77.

Ross, G. (2000) *The Swastika in Socialism. Right-wing Extremism in the GDR*, Hamburg: Verlag Dr Kovač.

Rüchel, U. (2001) *'... auf deutsch sozialistisch zu denken ...': Mozambikaner in der Schule der Freundschaft*, Magdeburg: Landesbeauftragte für die Unterlagen des Staatssicherheitsdienstes der ehemaligen DDR in Sachsen-Anhalt.

Rüddenklau, W. (1992) *Störenfried: DDR-opposition 1986–1989*, Berlin: BasisDruck.

Rupnik, J. (1988) *The Other Europe*, London: Weidenfeld and Nicolson.

Sabrow, M. (2008) 'Die DDR in der Geschichte des 20. Jahrhunderts', *Deutschland Archiv* 41(1): 121–30.

Sartori, G. (1987) *The Theory of Democracy Revisited*, Chatham, NJ: Chatham House Publishers.

—— (1993) 'Totalitarianism, Model Mania and Learning from Error', *Journal of Theoretical Politics* 5(1): 5–22.

Saunders, A. (2003) 'Ostdeutschland: Heimat einer xenophoben Tradition?' *Berliner Debatte Initial* 14(2): 50–59.

—— (2007) *Honecker's Children: Youth and Patriotism in East(ern) Germany, 1979–2002*, Manchester: Manchester University Press.

Scherzer, L. (2002) *Die Fremden*, Berlin: Aufbau-Verlag.

Schmeidel, J.C. (2008) *Stasi: Shield and Sword of the Party*, London: Routledge.

Schmidt, I. (1992) 'Ausländer in der DDR – Ihre Erfahrungen vor und nach der "Wende"', in Heinemann, K.-H., and Schubarth, W. (eds.), *Der antifaschistische Staat entläßt seine Kinder: Jugend und Rechtsextremismus in Ostdeutschland*, Cologne: PapyRossa Verlag, pp. 64–76.

Schmidt, M. (1993) *The New Reich: Violent Extremism in Unified Germany and Beyond*, trans. D. Horch, London: Hutchinson.

Schmidt, R. (2003a) 'Religiöse Selbstbehauptung und alltägliches Verhalten: Anmerkungen über den Umgang der Zeugen Jehovas mit staatlicher Repression – Fallbeispiele aus Leipzig und der Oberlausitz', in Besier, G., and Vollnhals, C. (eds), *Repression und Selbstbehauptung: Die Zeugen Jehovas unter der NS- und der SED-Diktatur*, Berlin: Duncker and Humblot, pp.181–99.

————— (2003b) *Religiöse Selbstbehauptung und staatliche Repression: Eine Untersuchung über das religiös-vermittelte, alltägliche und konspirative Handeln der Zeugen Jehovas unter den Bedingungen von Verbot und Verfolgung in der SBZ/DDR 1945–1990. Fallstudien und Beispiele aus der Stadt Leipzig und der Region Zittau/Oberlausitz*, Berlin: Logos Verlag.

Schmidt, W. (1989) 'Jüdisches Erbe deutscher Geschichte im Erbe- und Traditionsverständnis der DDR', *Zeitschrift für Geschichtswissenschaft* 37(8): 692–714.

Schroeder, K. (1993) *Der SED-Staat: Partei, Staat und Gesellschaft 1949–1990*, Munich: Carl Hanser Verlag.

Schröder, R. (1993) *Deutschland schwierig Vaterland: Für eine neue politische Kultur*, Freiburg, Basel and Vienna: Herder.

Schubarth, W. (1992) 'Rechtsextremismus: eine subjective Verarbeitungsform des Umbruchs?' in Heinemann, K.-H., and Schubarth, W. (eds), *Der antifaschistische Staat entläßt seine Kinder: Jugend und Rechtsextremismus in Ostdeutschland*, Cologne: PapyRossa Verlag, pp.78–99.

Schubarth, W., and Schmidt, T. (1992) '"Sieger der Geschichte": Verordneter Antifaschismus und die Folgen', in Heinemann, K.-H., and Schubarth, W. (eds), *Der antifaschistische Staat entläßt seine Kinder: Jugend und Rechtsextremismus in Ostdeutschland*, Cologne: PapyRossa Verlag, pp.12–28.

Schürer, G. (1994) 'Die Wirtschafts- und Sozialpolitik der DDR', in Keller, D., Modrow, H., and Wolf, H. (eds), *Ansichten zur Geschichte der DDR*, vol.3, Eggersdorf: Verlag Matthias Kirchner, pp.131–71.

Schwan, H. (2000) *Tod dem Verräter. Der lange Arm der Stasi und der Fall Lutz Eigendorf*, Munich: Droemer Knaur.

Schweigler, G.L. (1975) *National Consciousness in Divided Germany*, London: Sage.

Seliger, E. (1975) 'Despite Persecution by the Clergy, Nazis and Communists', *The Watchtower*, July 15, pp.423–26.

Setz, W. (ed.) (2006) *Homosexualität in der DDR: Materialien und Meinungen*, Hamburg: Männerschwarm Verlag.

Shanghai (1997) *Der Punk im Schrank: Ein Report über die Einflußnahme des MfS auf die Punkrockszene in Sachsen-Anhalt*, Magdeburg: Landesbeauftragte für die Unterlagen des Staatssicherheitsdienstes der ehemaligen DDR Sachsen-Anhalt.

Shlapentokh, V. (1999) 'The Soviet Union: A Normal Totalitarian Society', *Journal of Communist and Transition Politics* 15(4): 1–16.

Siegler, B. (1991) *Auferstanden aus Ruinen: Rechtsextremismus in der DDR*, Berlin: Edition Tiamat.

Siegfried, D. (2005) 'Unsere Woodstocks: Jugendkultur, Rockmusik und gesellschaftlicher Wandel um 1968', in Stiftung Haus der Geschichte der Bundesrepublik Deutschland (ed.), *Rock! Jugend und Musik in Deutschland*, Berlin: Ch. Links Verlag, pp.52–61.

Sillge, U. (1991) *Un-Sichtbare Frauen: Lesben und ihre Emanzipation in der DDR*, Berlin: LinksDruck Verlag.

Skilling, H.G. (1970) 'Group Conflict and Political Change', in Johnson, C. (ed.), *Change in Communist Systems*, Stanford, CA: Stanford University Press, pp.215–34.

Spaaij, R. (2007) 'Football Hooliganism as a Transnational Phenomenon: Past and Present Analysis: A Critique – More Specificity and Less Generality', *The International Journal of the History of Sport*, 24 (4): 411–31.

Spitzer, G. (2004) *Fußball und Triathlon: Sportentwicklung in der DDR*, Aachen: Meyer and Meyer Verlag.

Stach, A. (1994) 'Ausländer in der DDR: Ein Rückblick', in Stach, A., and Hussain, S. (eds), *Ausländer in der DDR: Ein Rückblick*, Berlin: Die Ausländerbeauftragte des Senats Berlin, pp.4–25.

Stadtmuseum Dresden (ed.) (2007) *Renitenz im Elbflorenz: Punk in Dresden 1980–89*, Dresden: Stadtmuseum Dresden.

Statistisches Amt der DDR (ed.) (1990) *Statistisches Jahrbuch der Deutschen Demokratischen Republik '90*, Berlin: Rudolf Haufe Verlag.

Stern, F. (1996) 'The Return to the Disowned Home: German Jews and the Other Germany', *New German Critique* 67: 57–72.

Stock, M. (2000) 'Jugendkulturen, Politik und Wissenschaft in der DDR', in Furian, G., and Becker, N. (eds), *'Auch im Osten trägt man Westen': Punks in der DDR – und was aus ihnen geworden ist*, Berlin: Verlag Thomas Tilsner, pp.56–63.

Stock, M., and Mühlberg, P. (1990) *Die Szene vom Innen: Skinheads, Grufties, Heavy Metals, Punks*, Berlin: Links Verlag.

Suckut, S. (ed.) (1996) *Das Wörterbuch der Staatssicherheit: Definitionen zur 'politisch-operativen Arbeit'*, Berlin: Ch. Links Verlag.

Süß, W. (1993) *Zu Wahrnehmung und Interpretation des Rechtsextremismus in der DDR durch das MfS*, BStU, Reihe B: Analysen und Berichte, no. 1, Berlin: BStU.

Teichler, H. J. (2005) 'Tumulte in Planitz', *Horch und Guck*, 14(51): 10–13.

Thomas, R. (2009) 'DDR-Forschung in Multiperspektive', *Deutschland Archiv* 42(1): 147–50.

Thompson, M.R. (1998) 'Neither Totalitarianism nor Authoritarianism: Post-totalitarianism in Eastern Europe', in Siegel, A. (ed.), *The Totalitarian Paradigm after the End of Communism: Towards a Theoretical Reassessment*, Amsterdam: Rodopi, pp.303–28.

—— (2002) 'Totalitarian and Post-totalitarian Regimes in Transition and Non-transitions from Communism', *Totalitarian Movements and Political Religions* 3(1): 79–106.

Timm, A. (1997a) *Hammer, Zirkel, Davidstern: Das gestörte Verhältnis zu Zionismus und Staat Israel*, Bonn: Bouvier.

—— (1997b) *Jewish Claims against East Germany: Moral Obligations and Pragmatic Policy*, Budapest: Central European University.

Voigt, D., and Mertens, L. (eds) (1992) *Minderheiten in und Übersiedler aus der DDR*, Berlin: Duncker and Humblot.

Vollnhals, C. (1996) 'Die kirchenpolitische Abteilung des Ministeriums für Staatssicherheit', in Vollnhals, C. (ed.), *Die Kirchenpolitik von SED und Staatssicherheit. Eine Zwischenbilanz*, Berlin: Ch. Links Verlag, pp.79–119.

—— (2002) 'Denunziation und Strafverfolgung im Auftrag der "Partei": Das Ministerium für Staatssicherheit', in Vollnhals, C., and Weber, J. (eds), *Der Schein der Normalität*, Munich: Olzog Verlag, pp.113–56.

Wagner, B. (1995) *Jugend – Gewalt – Szenen: Zu kriminologischen und historischen Aspekten in Ostdeutschland. Die achtziger und neunziger Jahre*, Berlin: Dip.

———— (2002) 'Kulturelle Subversion von rechts in Ost- und Westdeutschland: Zu rechtsextremen Entwicklungen und Strategien', in Grumke, T., and Wagner, B. (eds), *Handbuch Rechstradikalismus: Personen – Organisationen – Netzwerke vom Neonazismus bis in die Mitte der Gesellschaft*, Opladen: Leske and Budrich, pp.13–28.

Waibel, H. (1996) *Rechtsextremismus in der DDR bis 1989*, Cologne: PapyRossa Verlag.

WBTS (1982) *You Can Live Forever In Paradise on Earth*, New York: Watchtower Bible and Tract Society of New York and International Bible Students Association.

Weber, H. (2007) 'Die Stalinisierung der KPD: Alte und neue Einschätzungen', *Jahrbuch für Historische Kommunismusforschung*, Berlin: Aufbau-Verlag, pp.221–44.

Weiss, K. (2005) 'Nach der Wende: Vietnamesische Vertragsarbeiter und Vertragsarbeiterinnen in Ostdeutschland heute', in Weiss, K., and Dennis, M. (eds), *Erfolg in der Nische? Die Vietnamesen in der DDR und in Ostdeutschland*, Münster: LIT Verlag, pp.77–96.

Weiss, K., and Dennis, M. (eds), *Erfolg in der Nische? Die Vietnamesen in der DDR und in Ostdeutschland*, Münster: LIT Verlag.

Weitz, E.D. (1997) *Creating German Communism: From Popular Protest to Socialist State*, Princeton, NJ: Princeton University Press.

Wenzke, R. (2005) 'Zwischen "Prager Frühling" 1968 und Herbst 1989: Protestverhalten, Verweigerungsmuster und politische Verfolgung in der NVA der siebziger und achtziger Jahre', in Wenzke, R. (ed.), *Staatsfeinde in Uniform? Widerstandiges Verhalten und politische Verfolgung in der NVA*, Berlin: Ch. Links Verlag, pp.199–428.

Westphal, G. (2001) 'The Persecution of Jehovah's Witnesses in Weimar, 1945–1990', in Hesse, H. (ed.), *Persecution and Resistance of Jehovah's Witnesses During the Nazi Regime, 1933-1945*, Bremen: Edition Temmen, pp.229–50.

Willmann, F. (ed.) (2007) *Stadionpartisanen: Fußballfans und Hooligans in der DDR*, Berlin: Verlag Neues Leben.

Winkler, G. (ed.) (1997) *Sozialreport 1997: Daten und Fakten zur sozialen Lage in den neuen Bundesländern*, Berlin: Verlag am Turm.

———— (ed.) (1999) *Sozialreport 1999: Daten und Fakten zur sozialen Lage in den neuen Bundesländern*, Berlin: Verlag am Turm.

Wippermann, W. (2009) *Dämonisierung durch Vergleich: DDR und Drittes Reich*, Berlin: Rotbuch Verlag.

Wolffsohn, M. (1995) *Die Deutschland-Akte: Juden und Deutsche in Ost und West. Tatsachen und Legenden*, Munich: Edition Ferenczy.

———— (1998) *Meine Juden – Eure Juden*, Munich and Zürich: Piper.

Wrobel, J. (2006a) 'Jehovah's Witnesses in National Socialist Concentration Camps, 1933–45', *Religion, State and Society* 34(2): 89–125.

———— (2006b) 'Jehovah's Witnesses in Germany: Prisoners during the Communist Era', *Religion, State and Society* 34(2): 169–90.

Wroblewsky, V. von (2001) *Eine unheimliche Liebe: Juden in der DDR*, Berlin and Vienna: Philo Verlagsgesellschaft.

Ziemer, K. (2006) 'Totalitarian and Authoritarian Systems: Factors in Their Decline and Hurdles in the Development of Democratic Orders', in Borejsza, J.W., and Ziemer,

K. (eds), *Totalitarian and Authoritarian Regimes in Europe: Legacies and Lessons from the Twentieth Century*, Oxford: Berghahn Books, pp.158–73.

## Juridical College (JHS) Theses

Baenz, E. (1976) 'Die Gestaltung der Auftragserteilung und Instruierung an inoffizielle Mitarbeiter, die zur Durchführung von Maßnahmen der Zersetzung in der Vorgangsvorbereitung gegen staatsfeindliche Gruppen der verbotenen WTG (Zeugen Jehova) zum Einsatz gelangen', BStU, MfS, ZA, JHS, no.23501.

Bartl, J. (1989) 'Untersuchungen zum Stand der Erfüllung der politisch-operativen Aufgabenstellung zur vorbeugenden Verhinderung und Bekämpfung von Skinheads im Verantwortungsbereich der Kreisdienststelle Oranienburg', BStU, MfS, ZA, JHS, no.21598.

Bartnik, J. (1977) 'Die Beachtung der Feindhandlungen, Struktur und menschenfeindlichen Lehren der Zeugen Jehovas bei der Auswahl und Gewinnung geeigneter inoffizieller Mitarbeiter zur Bearbeitung der staatsfeindlichen Tätigkeit der verbotenen Organisation Zeugen Jehovas', BStU, MfS, ZA, JHS, no.001/889/76.

Behnke, L. (1979) 'Die Notwendigkeit der Zusammenarbeit mit IM aus dem Kreis der negativ-dekadenten Jugendlichen und die dabei gewonnen Erkentnisse und Erfahrungen', BStU, MfS, ZA, JHS, no.001/1051/79.

Bergner, H. (1976) 'Die Erarbeitung geeigneter Anknüpfungspunkte für die Ausarbeitung und Anwendung von Zersetzungsmaßnahmen bei Gruppen mit antisozialistischer Zielsetzung (Am Beispiel der in der DDR illegal tätigen Organisation "Zeugen Jehova")', BStU, MfS, ZA, JHS, no.23504.

Dalski, J., and Jerie, D. (1986), 'Darstellung operativ-bedeutsamer Erscheinungen und Handlungen neonazistischer Potentiale des Operationsgebietes, deren Auswirkungen auf die DDR, und daraus resultierende Schlußfolgerungen', BStU, MfS, ZA, JHS, no.20411.

Gruhn, T. (1989) 'Ursachen und Bedingungen für das Entstehen operativ bedeutsamer Personenzusammenschlüsse jugendlicher und jugendwachsener DDR-Bürger – bezogen auf Skinheadgruppierungen im Bezirk Potsdam sowie der von ihnen sozial-negativen operativ bedeutsamen Handlungen – und sich darausgehenden Konsequenzen für das politisch-operative Arbeit der BV Potsdam', BStU, MfS, ZA, JHS, no.21463.

Kelch, P. (1989) 'Zu einigen Erfahrungen bei der wirksamen Einbeziehung gesellschaftlicher Kräfte in die Zurückdrängung neofaschistisch-rowdyhafter Handlungen Jugendlicher', BStU, MfS, ZA, JHS, no.21433.

Kleinow, H.-J., and Wenzlawski, G. (1977) 'Aufgaben der Kreisdienststellen zur Aufdeckung der subversiven Tätigkeiten der Funktionäre der WTG mit dem Ziel ihrer Einschränkung und der Entwicklung von Ausgangsmaterialien für die operative Vorgangsbearbeitung', BStU, MfS, ZA, JHS, no.001.320/77.

Kownatzki, G. (1979) 'Die Zersetzung der verbotenen Organisation "Zeugen Jehova" im Kreisgebiet durch Zurückdrängung und Einschränkung des Einflusses der Funktionäre der Organisation auf die Mitglieder der WTG. Schlußfolgerungen für die systematische und zielgerichtete Zersetzung der Organisation "Zeugen Jehova"', BStU, MfS, ZA, JHS, no.001.615/79.

Kreklau, D. (1989) 'Die Gewinnung jugendlicher und jungerwachsener IM aus dem negativ-dekadenten Fußballanhang und die kontinuierliche Zusammenarbeit mit ihnen', BStU, MfS, ZA, JHS, no.21466.

Prescher, J. (1980) 'Die erfolgreiche Anwendung politisch-operativen Maßnahmen des MfS bei der Zerschlagung von Kurierverbindungen des Ostbüros der Organisation "Zeugen Jehova" (Wiesbaden/BRD) in die DDR zur Unterbindung ihres Einflusses auf die "Zeugen Jehova" in der DDR', BStU, MfS, ZA, JHS, no.001.843/79.

Riedel, J. (1980) 'Die Verallgemeinerung von Erfahrungen aus der operativen Bearbeitung von Funktionären der verbotenen Organisation "Zeugen Jehovas" in OV, insbesondere der Durchführung von Maßnahmen der Zersetzung, Verunsicherung und Differenzierung', BStU, MfS, ZA, JHS, no.135/80.

Roß, T. (1988) 'Analysierung operativ bedeutsamer Aktivitäten neo-nazistischer Organisationen, Gruppen und Kräfte des Operationsgebietes, BRD/WB in den Jahren 1986 und 1987 sowie ihre politisch-operative Einschätzung zur Präzisierung von Schwerpunkten der operativen Bearbeitung dieser Feindpotentiale durch die Abteilung XXII/I', BStU, MfS, ZA, JHS, no.21169.

Taraschonnek, R. (1989) 'Erfordernisse der Erziehung und Befähigung von inoffiziellen Mitarbeitern (IM) zur operativen Bearbeitung von rechtsextremistischen Erscheinungen unter Jugendlichen in der Hauptstadt', BStU, MfS, ZA, JHS, no.001-334/80.

Urbach, D. (1983) 'Anforderungen an die Ehrlichkeit und Zuverlässigkeit bei der inoffiziellen Zusammenarbeit mit negativ-dekadenten Jugendlichen', BStU, MfS, ZA. JHS, no.20718.

Weimann, U. (1989) 'Möglichkeiten der Qualifizierung der IM-Arbeit zur Verhinderung feindlich-negativer Erscheinungen unter Jugendlichen im Verantwortungsbereich der KD-Hellstedt', BStU, MfS, ZA, JHS, no.21546.

Wejwoda, R., and Goers, W. (1980) 'Besonderheiten bei der Gestaltung der inoffiziellen Zusammenarbeit mit jugendlichen Personenkreisen mit negativen und dekadenten Verhaltensweisen', BStU, MfS, ZA, JHS, no.001.689/70.

Wenzlawski, G., and Kleinow, H.-J. (1975) 'Erkenntnisse und Erfahrungen zur Durchführung wirksamer operativer Maßnahmen gegen die Tätigkeit der in der DDR verbotenen Organisation "Zeugen Jehova" (Wachtturmgesellschaft) zur Bekämpfung ihrer staatsfeindlichen Tätigkeit', BStU, MfS, ZA, JHS, no.001.901/75.

Wiedemann, H. (1985) 'Rechtliche Möglichkeiten und Voraussetzungen einer effektiven Vorbeugung und Bekämpfung von politisch-operativ bedeutsamen Störungen sozialistischer Beziehungen in der NVA und den Grenztruppen der DDR, Ursachen und Bedingungen für derartige Straftaten', BStU, MfS, ZA, HA IX, no.473 (JHS 701/85).

Wollenburg, H.-J. (1978) 'Der zielgerichtete Einsatz inoffizieller Mitarbeiter zur Entwicklung einer wirksamen Oppositionsbewegung im Rahmen der Zersetzung der auf dem Gebiet der DDR illegal tätigen Wachtturmgesellschaft', BStU, MfS, ZA, JHS, no.001.615/79.

# INDEX